W9-AUU-044

COLORADO

COUNTRY

COLORADO RIVER

Grand
Junction

A Map
of the
COLORADO
PLATEAU

Cortez
FOUR
CORNERS
Durango

RIVER

NAVAJO
RESERVOIR

CHACO

NEW
MEXICO

Gallup
ZUNI

3 9077 05027 7915

979.13 W686f
Wilkinson, Charles F., 1941-
Fire on the plateau

HISTORY & TRAVEL MAR 2 5 2003

CENTRAL LIBRARY OF ROCHESTER
AND MONROE COUNTY
115 SOUTH AVE
ROCHESTER NY 14604-1896

A SHEARWATER BOOK

# FIRE ON THE PLATEAU

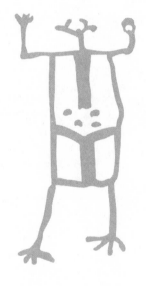

For Ann

# CHARLES WILKINSON

# FIRE
## ON THE
# PLATEAU

## Conflict and Endurance in
## the American Southwest

### Illustrations by Diane Sylvain

ISLAND PRESS / Shearwater Books

*Washington, D.C.  ·  Covelo, California*

*A Shearwater Book*
*published by Island Press*

Copyright © 1999 Charles F. Wilkinson

All rights reserved under International and Pan American Copyright
Conventions. No part of this book may be reproduced in any form or by
any means without permission in writing from the publisher: Island Press,
Suite 300, 1718 Connecticut Avenue NW, Washington, D.C. 20009

Shearwater Books is a trademark of The Center for Resource Economics.

The author is grateful for permission to use "Grand Canyon National
Park" by Michael Kabotie (Lomawywesa) from *Migration Tears:
Poems About Transitions,* pp. 40–41 (Los Angeles: American Indian
Studies Center, University of California-Los Angeles, 1987).

Portions of this book were printed in different form in
*Heart of the Land* (Pantheon, 1994); *Arrested Rivers* (University Press
of Colorado, 1994); and the 1996 Brigham Young University Law Review.

*Library of Congress Cataloging-in-Publication Data*
Wilkinson, Charles F., 1941–
Fire on the Plateau  :  conflict and endurance
in the American Southwest / Charles Wilkinson.
p.    cm.
Includes bibliographical references.
ISBN 1-55963-647-5 (cloth)
1. Indians of North America—Colorado Plateau—History.
2. Indians of North America—Colorado Plateau—Government relations.
3. Indians, Treatment of—Colorado Plateau.
4. Colorado Plateau—History.   5. Colorado Plateau—
Description and travel.   I. Title.
E78.C617W55   1999
979.1'300497—dc21            99-18908
CIP

Printed on recycled, acid-free paper

Manufactured in the United States of America

10   9   8   7   6   5   4   3   2   1

# C o n t e n t s

# THE COLORADO
# PLATEAU

Geologists, beginning with John Wesley Powell, recognize the Colorado Plateau as a physiographic province—the Plateau Province—isolated from adjacent regions. Just a few dozen million years ago, the Plateau was a flat plain, a former ocean floor with rivers flowing across it. Then gigantic forces caused the region to rise. But the rivers held resolutely to their courses, cutting into the ground as the landmass rose around them. This left slashes of canyon cuts all across the Plateau. The Grand Canyon is the most spectacular, but scores upon scores of others are fabulous in their own right. Wind and water have worked on the soft rocks in other ways, crafting all manner of monuments, pillars, arches, natural bridges, spires,

# Introduction

minarets, cliffs, and crags ablaze in every hue of earth color, but with the red—all variations of red, always the red—the most memorable to our eyes.

The Plateau is barriered in nearly every direction. The southern border is the Mogollon Rim, a cliff for most of its 200-mile run, a thousand feet high or more in places; below the rim, down in the Salt River Valley, are Phoenix and its suburbs. To the southwest and southeast, modest mountain ranges separate the Plateau from lower-lying Las Vegas and Albuquerque. On the west, the province is bounded by the high and jagged Wasatch Range and beyond the Wasatch lies Salt Lake City. The crest of the Uinta Range, nearly in Wyoming, marks the northern boundary, and the lower beginnings of the Colorado Rockies define its eastern side. The Plateau Province therefore includes about half of Utah, northern Arizona, the northwest corner of New Mexico, and a long strip in westernmost Colorado, some 80 million acres in all. By way of comparison, the entire state of Arizona holds 73 million acres.

Throughout almost all of its reach, this land is arid, a desert. Except for the mountain spines above 10,000 feet, it receives 10 inches of precipitation a year or less, the traditional measuring stick for defining a desert. (Scientists now also require a high rate of evaporation for classification as a desert, and the Plateau's bright sun, heat, and winds qualify it within this framework too.) A small part is "hot" desert, mostly in deep canyon bottoms in the southwestern area of the Plateau; the hot desert receives the lowest amount of precipitation, sometimes as little as 3 inches a year. The bulk of the Plateau's landmass is 5,000 feet or higher. Apart from the upper alpine reaches, this is "cold" desert—more than half of the precipitation comes in the form of snow. Deliciously temperate springs and autumns precede and follow the chill winters of the high desert. Summers, mid-May through mid-September, are blast-furnace torrid.

Remote, rugged, and dry, at once forlorn and glorious, this is a separate place: a place with its own distinctive landscape, history, and future.

Many of my travels, first as a law student and young Arizona lawyer, then as a staff attorney with the Native American Rights Fund, later when teaching and writing about the laws, land, and people of the West, have

# Introduction

taken me to the Colorado Plateau. Some have come as part of the joy of writing this book, for I have made a point of getting out on the Plateau about once a month. Other trips have been with family, friends, or students. Still other visits have been as a lawyer working for the Navajo and Hopi on tangled issues involving ideas and events that go back decades, centuries, more. Inevitably, working with Indians is working with time.

For it is this other sense, our sense of time, that becomes so fully engaged on the Colorado Plateau. All the recently made dams, reservoirs, coal mines, coal-fired power plants, transmission lines, oil and gas rigs, uranium mines, mills, and dumps, all the motels, condominiums, and espresso shops, prove how quickly our kind can move, how little time we need to reach big results. Yet time's longer and more profound side still pervades the Colorado Plateau. Deep time is laid bare everywhere: in all the stripped-off rocks of this brittle, elevated land that holds some of the finest displays of exposed geology anywhere on earth. The ancient cultures have left us their handiwork and their ideas. Indian people on the reservations, having heard the old stories over and over, possess a precise consciousness that stretches far back and blends into the remembered earth. The quiet of the deep canyons and the long still vistas, encompassing so much sacred ground, slow us down, take us far back, and hold us there. The Colorado Plateau is a place where we can discover great distances, both of terrain and time.

This book recounts my journey through the Colorado Plateau, a journey through place and time and self. The journey was unstructured. It depended on requests for assistance from Indian tribes and community groups, on family and teaching schedules, on the beckonings of my personal interests, and on flashes of suspicion that caused me to drop everything and track down a lead. I did a great deal of formal research—in the literature, library collections, and government documents—but the travels mattered more. Fascinating and valuable though the reading has been, my best learning took place at arduous late-night meetings, listening to the deliberations of earnest Indian people; at the base of a power plant with 700-foot stacks, trying to imagine how the coal somehow produced elec-

# Introduction

tricity for cities hundreds of miles away; in a blue-ribbon trout stream below a 400-foot dam, casting a fly and wondering about the societies submerged by the reservoir; in a twisty back canyon, where the Ancestral Pueblo people once resided, moving down a faint trail with a backpack and a boy; and beneath a great natural arch in a conversation of reconciliation with the father who forced me west in the first place.

During my explorations of more than three decades, I found a land that sears into my heart and soul, a place that has taught me and changed me. I also discovered a land of conflict and endurance, a land that has given birth to one of the great chapters in American history.

The methods of conquering the tribes were many and diverse: war, land sales, bad resource deals, cultural assimilation, and the treachery of their friends. As for the land, the most notable conquest took place from about 1955 through 1975. I have come to call it the Big Buildup. The cities surrounding the Plateau—Denver, Albuquerque, El Paso, Phoenix, Tucson, Las Vegas, Salt Lake City, San Diego, Los Angeles—had exhausted their own local resources. Civic leaders organized a concerted campaign for the rapid, wholesale development of the energy and water of the Colorado Plateau.

Indisputably the Big Buildup achieved the objectives that its architects intended. It made the modern Southwest. It transformed it from a backwater region of 8 million people at the end of World War II into a powerhouse of 32 million today. It was one of the most prodigious peacetime exercises of industrial might in the history of the world.

The consequences of this conquest—for the land, rivers, air, and human health—were many, and they are with us still. So, too, are the consequences for the tribes. Among other things, the linchpin for the Big Buildup was Black Mesa, sacred ground for the Hopi and Navajo, who leased their coal and water at prices far below market value.

Standing near the center of the Big Buildup was an eminent Salt Lake City lawyer named John Boyden, who represented both the Ute and Hopi tribes. For years, charges had swirled that during the decisive times of the 1960s Boyden, in violation of his high ethical and legal obligations to his

# Introduction

tribal clients, also worked in the dark for Peabody Coal Company and other development interests that wanted Indian land, minerals, and water. At first, as I began to look into these episodes, I doubted that Boyden had acted wrongly or, if he had, that it could be proved. The evidence was thin. But gradually, by the plain luck that sometimes accompanies perseverance, I uncovered the truth about Boyden's dealings. His story is the story of the conquest of Black Mesa and the two tribes—and, in turn, the story of the conquest of the Colorado Plateau. There are ways in which Boyden's story is the story of us all.

Yet, for all the many conquests, the homefires of endurance burn still. This is a big land, and its rough, dry landscape gives it the shield of remoteness. The wild desert country, as I learned, can still heal us. The Indian people, against all odds, have held on. They own a third of the Colorado Plateau. Their cultures—battered all over, to be sure—remain strong.

The tribal endurance raises questions that burn in the coals of every piñon fire and twine through all the back canyons of the tribal homelands. Why, for all the effort, all the money, all the military might and threat of it, for all the industrial efforts, for all the apparent helplessness of the tribes, for all the *inevitability* of the final result, has the forced assimilation never finally taken? Why is the Colorado Plateau still Indian country? Why do the Navajo tell the Coyote stories to this day and fight—successfully—to send their children to their own Indian schools? Why, after the warfare in the sagebrush bowl on upper Milk Creek between two military forces, one native, one from the newer nation, and after all the consequences of that battle, do the Ute hold nearly 2 million acres? Why do the Hopi still perform Home Dance, with all its pageantry, dedication, and commitment of weeks of time just to prepare for this one ceremony? Why do the tribes still govern themselves and their land by the old values and priorities?

One might surmise that this is simply because no one yet wants the tribes' lands and minds badly enough. Perhaps. But in learning the story of the Colorado Plateau, one finds another reason: the tribes possess a tenacity—a tenacity stronger than all the technology and guile levied against it, a tenacity that will not, will not ever, let go.

# Introduction

If that tenacity is the secret, then the secret inside it is the core value that creates the tenacity: a reverence—think that word through—for the land, for a particular place. Romanticism? The story of the Colorado Plateau makes it plain that, in this age when we careen toward an uncertain destination, a true and lasting commitment to place may be as valuable to us as any serum.

# Part One

# BEDROCK

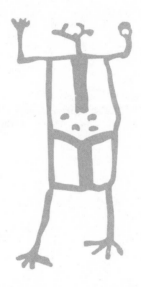

# ROUTE 66

I remember the first time I saw the Colorado Plateau. It was in December 1963 during my beginning year in law school. Still new to the arid West, I was heading home from Stanford, the passenger of an anthropology graduate student who had responded to my notice on a campus bulletin board: "Christmas Vacation—need ride back East." We had decided to take the southerly Route 66 because of winter storms on the more direct highways farther north combined with the dubious condition of her beaten-up Ford.

Not that I had ever heard of the Colorado Plateau or even thought much about the Southwest. I did know about the road I was traveling, old Route 66, storied in song and pop culture, America's Main Street, escape valve for Oklahomans fleeing the Dust Bowl, great national connector between Chicago and Los Angeles. I chuckled at the kitsch along the road in Arizona and New Mexico. Hokey billboards and highway signs sported outsized cowboys and Indians. At the "men only" establishments, neon cowgirls beckoned travelers with animated come-hither gestures. Wigwam Village in Holbrook, Arizona, was one of the many pseudo trading posts. Nor were the local proprietors limited to a Real West theme, as evidenced by tacky stopover spots like the bright pink Andy Womack's Flamingo Motel in Flagstaff. The main route between east and west had its own flair, all right.

Still, everything whizzed by and I was glad that it did. This place was just mileage that had to be logged in order to get home. Sure, the San Francisco Peaks north of Flagstaff looked sublime. That view struck me as the real West: mountains. But all the rest, the redrock formations and the broad open range country, were sterile, gritty. Nor did I find anything compelling in the people. When we came into Gallup, New Mexico, my driver pointed out the Navajos standing around on the sidewalks. I had never seen an Indian in person before. To make conversation, I asked her how she could tell they were Navajos. Her description of their distinctive facial characteristics—the high cheekbones and oriental features—interested me no more than the sagebrush and rock landscape.

Today, my senses race when I am in that country. The buttes and mesas coax my eyes toward them, and the redrock walls make concentration lines on my forehead as the colors change with the new angles and intensities of a day's light. Sagebrush, so common in the Southwest, has a scent uncommon in the extreme: I'll tear off a handful and stuff it in my shirt pocket for a hike or, if I'm driving, lodge it on the dashboard so that the car will fill up with magic. The sparse piñon-juniper rangeland is an old friend by now and it makes me laugh, too, because I am on its side: this "worthless" shrub-forest, scorned by ranchers and silviculturists, has won out. Today the sweet nuts of the piñon draw $16.99 a pound at your local market.

My emotions ride with the people as well. Although I never could have imagined such a thing in 1963, a decade after my first trip though Gallup on Route 66 I stood before a federal judge in a high-ceilinged Albuquerque courtroom trying to help rectify discrimination against Navajo children in the Gallup schools. I put my whole body into my presentation to the judge—not just because the children had been wronged by the denial of their civil rights but also, in a larger sense, because by then I had come to respect the worth and distinctiveness of Navajo culture, so that the legal wrong seemed doubly crass and raw.

What is it that causes a place to occupy a cherished spot on the best wall of a person's mind? A place, such as a sparse high-desert landscape, where a person's taste will have to be acquired? A place where the cultures are different and hard for outsiders to comprehend? This is a complicated matter. But it is one that tells us a great deal about our humanity, as the force of place is created by peoples and history as well as terrain, by the ordinary as well as the elegant and the dramatic, by the emotional and spiritual as well as the quantifiable, by the incremental passage of time that eventually breeds intimacy, by all of the things that allow a person to acquire a profound understanding of the story of a place. In my case, while my superficial visit on Route 66 in 1963 conveys my initial impression of the place, the true origins of my fascination with the Colorado Plateau are not to be found there. But I know where they are found, and that has to do with Paul Roca.

**M**y next contact with the Southwest took place a year and a half after my Route 66 trip. By then I was working as a summer law clerk for the Lewis & Roca firm, at forty lawyers the largest in Phoenix. One of the other clerks was Mariana Roca, daughter of Paul, a senior partner. Mariana and I, thrown together in the first professional venture for both of us, became fast friends. Since she was living at home and regularly invited me over for dinner, I quickly got to know Paul—and his passion for the Southwest.

Paul, in his early fifties, was a rumpled sort. Of medium height and build, he wore his pants low at the waist and they brushed the floor at the heels of his cowboy boots. He had a way of standing, locking his knees, that made his legs look saggy, concave. The informality of Phoenix suited him well: except for court appearances, lawyers went without jackets year-round and dispensed with neckties during the hot season.

One of the Southwest's most respected lawyers, Paul wrote much of Arizona's Insurance Code and became an expert in the laws affecting blood banks. When asked if his clients objected to his hefty fees, he would answer dryly: "My clients take pride in having the most expensive attorney between Houston and Los Angeles." An impatient practitioner, Paul wanted things to happen right now. His tirades were legend, although he always directed them to the world-at-large rather than people in the office. I am convinced that Paul, who had his theatrical side, staged most, perhaps all, of his tantrums—either to remind people of the importance of the job at hand or just to punctuate slow days with a little excitement.

Paul was anything but impatient when it came to the history of the Southwest. If he had your attention, he would take as long as you wanted, answer as many questions as you asked, tell as many stories as you could absorb. I was a willing captive and Paul became a mentor–uncle–best friend that summer. We spent all kinds of time together—some of it with him telling his stories and me listening, some of it arguing about law, politics, and grammar over beer or Paul's explosive *toros bravos* (two shots tequila, one shot Kahlua), playing poker, and getting out into the country around Phoenix or the family's summer place up north near Prescott.

Despite my devotion to Paul, when I left Phoenix in August I never expected to return. I had no determination to stay in the West and assumed I would go into practice in New York City or maybe San Francisco. Phoenix, just a backwater town then, was only a summer lark. I couldn't help defining Phoenix by my mother's initial reaction to it: when I told her I was going to clerk there with a good firm, she responded, so help me, "Phoenix? Phoenix *where?*"

Yet, once back at law school, I began to miss the firm and Paul. A couple of professors mentioned that working at Lewis & Roca would be an outstanding professional opportunity. When Paul called and made an offer, I jumped at it. After another two and a half years in Arizona with Paul, there would no longer be any doubt that I would live my life in the West.

Paul loved the Southwest with every bone in his body. Born to a Hispanic family in Tucson, he was fascinated by Sonora, the Mexican state south of Arizona. He scoured old journals and church documents and set out on jeep trips into the Sonoran backcountry to photograph dozens of Catholic missions, some in reasonably good shape, some in ruin, some overwhelmed by sand dunes and barely visible to the naked eye. Many had been lost to memory until Paul's rediscoveries. He wrote a fine account of his explorations, *Paths of the Padres through Sonora.* Later, just before his death in 1979, he wrote a similar book on Chihuahua, the neighboring state to the east.

The history of Arizona was intimate and personal for Paul. He had once worked as a legislative assistant for Carl Hayden, who served in Congress, first as a representative, then as a senator, from statehood in 1912 until the 1970s. The association with Hayden, who had seen and shaped so much history, made statehood a recent happening for Paul—including the long series of events leading up to it, beginning with the Treaty of Guadalupe Hidalgo of 1848 when the United States took the Southwest from Mexico. Paul loved to tell stories about Arizona and the Southwest, anywhere, anytime, waving his arms, pacing, heeling the floor with his cowboy boots, his enthusiasm building upon a beer or two, reaching the highest spirit of all after a round of *toros bravos.*

I managed to get Paul to tell me a very substantial percentage of his stories. Before knowing him, I had no sense of the West. Then, through his stories, Paul gave me the West. I had to unwrap the gift myself, but I received it from Paul.

I was born in Ann Arbor, just before Pearl Harbor. My father went overseas with the Army Medical Corps, and my mother and I moved to Saginaw, where her sister lived. After the war, our family moved east. I went to

# BEDROCK

grade school in Bronxville, New York, and high school in Westport, Connecticut, suburbs of New York City.

I had two sides to my youth. In one way, it was indelibly bright: I got outdoors whenever I could, fishing New England streams and the Atlantic Coast and playing every sport I could find, especially baseball. Yet, although my mother was wonderful, my home was dark with my father's rages. By every account, he was a brilliant doctor and researcher and a nurturing teacher. But he drank too much, took too many pills on his own prescriptions, and was a good deal rougher on me than he should have been, subjecting me to relentless criticism and ridicule and administering some good, stiff beatings that inflicted no permanent damage but left me sore of body and spirit.

When it came time to go to college, I went as far away from my father as I could conceive: to Ohio, to Denison University. Four years later, my understanding of geography somewhat expanded by then, I packed up to go to law school in California. Although I had no idea of such a thing at the time, I was going west out of the same blend of stubbornness, hope, and romanticism that had propelled millions before me.

At first the West, even California, didn't take for me. The primary color was brown, the terrain was rocky and sere, the trout streams skimpy. My trip across Route 66 symbolized my obliviousness: my eyes just couldn't see what was there.

Paul's stories began to change that. I learned about the people of Arizona—Geronimo, Marcos de Niza, the Babbitts, the Goldwater family. He told me in detail the saga of the Mormons—the assassination of Joseph Smith in Nauvoo, Illinois, the Mormon Trail to Utah, and the church's creation of an empire in the Intermountain West. Paul expounded on the labor strikes in the copper mines, the personalities of the two Phoenix newspapers, Arizona governors, the land frauds, and the ghost towns. He never complained about wrongs to the Hispanics, but I think he still thought of the Southwest as it was before the 1848 treaty, when it was all Mexico, and before that Spain. He especially admired the California missions, such stable and productive outposts at the northern reaches of the Spanish Empire in the New World. Paul, always a stickler for accuracy,

8

fumed about how Albuquerque should properly have an "r" after the first "u" and succeeded in having a bill introduced in the New Mexico legislature to set the record straight. The legislature has yet to act.

One day we got up before dawn and went out to hunt doves west of Phoenix. I have never done much hunting and had no luck that day. Paul shot a bagful, and the little birds were delicious in white wine and sour cream at dinner that evening. But it was the morning, rather than the statistics of hunting or the taste of the cuisine, that has most stayed with me. For it was then that I first began to take some interest in the desert.

From the time Paul picked me up in the dark in his veteran Jeep, the adventure had an easy, languid pace to it. I hunted casually, spending as much time trying to understand the land as scouting for doves. Nothing was sterile to my eyes that day. Instead, in the cool, early morning air I saw many shades of green, mostly pale, in a broad, thin forest of stately saguaro, wispy ocotillo, and spread-winged palo verde. I found a two-foot chunk of ironwood and was taken aback at its weight. Paul had given me some information about the species, explaining that Indians used the peanut-flavored seeds in the spring and that ironwood, with its density and rich texture, made a good medium for sculpting. I came upon my first rattler and, from a distance, inspected his taut, brown presence as he lay uncoiled and still until a lone cloud took away his sunny spot and he slid off into a pile of rocks.

I finished up my hunting, such as it was, before Paul did and sat down on a log in the shade of a mesquite tree, content to watch him hunt. Soon he came over, put down his shotgun, and sat down beside me. We began talking, and I made some mistake about Arizona geography. That may have been the time I placed the Grand Canyon south of Tucson, down near the Mexican border.

Paul—grand master of the well-placed sigh—sighed, took a long stick, leaned forward, and slowly drew a map of Arizona in the sand. The state, he explained, had three main land regions. He drew a line, trending southeast, that cut the state about in half. The southwestern part was in the Basin and Range Province. This embraced the Sonoran Desert and included Phoenix and Tucson. Then he drew a second line, parallel to the first, creating a narrow strip. This was a transition zone that took in several mountain ranges, including the White Mountains in eastern Arizona.

"This third region—most of the northern half of the state, the area above the Mogollon Rim—is the Colorado Plateau. It goes way up into Utah and over into Colorado and New Mexico. Like this. In many ways it's the most interesting part of Arizona." He explained that there were deep, remote canyons and dramatic rock formations. He said that much of the area was Indian land and that the Mormons had accumulated tremendous power, both in Arizona and up into Utah.

"The Colorado Plateau," Paul continued slowly, "is still mostly in the nineteenth century. You should put it on your list."

This was the first I had ever heard of the Colorado Plateau. But what Paul said and the way he said it—the careful, solemn, almost reverential way he talked about the land and how the Plateau was still in the nineteenth century—made a real imprint on me. That night, back in my apartment, my list of places to go in the West, a list comprised mostly of suggestions from Paul, grew by one.

In December 1968, I took a job with a large law firm in San Francisco. I made the change, I think, because Phoenix—still epitomized by my mother's words—seemed so far off the main track. Although Paul had lit the coals, I still did not feel passion toward the Southwest. My destiny, I thought, lay elsewhere.

My two and a half years in the Bay Area marked a time of new intensity for me. Spurred on by Paul's stories, I went on a frenzied reading spree about the West. Howell's Bookstore was near my office, and lunchtime visits yielded piles of western books. I focused on the rich and extensive literature of California: the missions that Paul found so compelling, the Gold Rush, the Indian tribes, the mountain men, the Progressive Era, and the writing of Steinbeck, London, Muir, and many others. Enthusiasm, not enlightenment, directed my course. I read, cover to cover, all seven inter-

minable, turgid volumes of Bancroft's history of California. When I told Paul of this during a long-distance call, he curtly replied, after one of his patented sighs, "*Charles,* Bancroft is not for *reading,* it's for *research*—and it's not all that good for that."

I also tried to explore the state. I did a number of backpacking trips and spent good amounts of time on the coast and in the Gold Country. Whenever I could, I angled assignments in rural areas: a hearing on a corporate matter in the Gold Country town of Jackson, a deposition in Weaverville, near the Trinity Alps, an airplane accident trial in Eureka, on the North Coast.

For all the intellectual ferment of my crash course in California and the West, I realized almost immediately that I had made a mistake professionally in moving to San Francisco. Lewis & Roca had an expansive, exciting practice that included labor law, voting rights cases, major criminal trials, and other important public issues. The firm also did a huge amount of pro bono work that included civil rights law, my greatest interest. Among many other commitments, Lewis & Roca had donated literally thousands of hours of attorneys' time to *Miranda v. Arizona,* the 1966 Supreme Court case that announced the "Miranda warnings" required for police questioning. Lawyers at Lewis & Roca were not only allowed, but expected, to take on public service cases, and I handled a steady caseload representing indigent black and Hispanic juvenile offenders.

In San Francisco, the practice was far more commercial, much less satisfying. The firm was doing essentially no pro bono work when I came. And although I was able to get permission to handle a few free cases for indigents, it was a continuing struggle to secure the firm's grudging consent. The work for the firm's regular clients was intellectually challenging and intricate—somewhat, I thought to myself, like an architect crafting tiny, precise model buildings with an X-Acto knife. But the "buildings" I made—briefs for banks and insurance companies—never once stirred my soul.

By the early 1970s, the practice of law was changing. Public interest firms sprang up to protect civil rights, the environment, consumers, and farmworkers. Public defenders' offices and the federal Legal Services Program were providing attorneys to poor people. Buoyed by the new opportunities, I began to look around.

On a blue-sky spring day in 1971, I drove over the Bay Bridge to meet with a small, young nonprofit firm in Berkeley. When I had asked how to get there, they directed me toward the neighborhood, then told me that their office was the one above the bagel factory. There I met David Getches, John Echohawk, Bruce Greene, and Joe Brecher. They plainly loved their work for Indian tribes and were going to expand to fifteen lawyers and move to Boulder, Colorado. They told me they had just filed a NEPA case. Not knowing of the National Environmental Policy Act, then just a year old, I almost, but just barely didn't, ask the bright question that was actually in my mind. The question was: "Isn't the Nepa Tribe located along the Colorado River?"

If I had asked that question, I don't believe I would have been offered a position with the Native American Rights Fund.

David Getches, the director, called back a week later and asked me to join the firm. As a non-Indian with no background in Indian law, a person with my credentials could never get a job at NARF today. Fortunately for me, back then modern Indian law was just getting started and NARF had to take what was available.

**P**erhaps I should have felt apprehension over the decision to go to NARF. The organization was brand new, and because of that, risky. The little I knew about Indians came from books. Still, Getches and the other lawyers were substantial people. The Ford Foundation was putting a major grant and its prestige behind the effort, the first national law firm serving Indian people.

And I knew I had to try this because of what I believed in. Even as a little boy, I felt a kinship with dispossessed people. My favorite team was the Brooklyn Dodgers, with Jackie Robinson, Roy Campanella, Don Newcombe, and others in the first wave of black players. I stood up for them against the barbs and taunts of the patrician New York Yankee fans, whose team was both whiter and more successful. My father, too, molded my views. For all he tormented me, he was an enlightened southerner who hated segregation.

One morning in May 1954, I laid the New York *Herald Tribune* out on the living room floor, my chosen site for reading the paper. Normally the front page was worth just a sideways glance on the way to the real meat, the sports section and the Dodgers. But that day banner headlines announced the Supreme Court's decision in *Brown v. Board of Education.* I let out a "yippee," pounded the floor, and, in the kind of split second that only a twelve-year-old can manufacture, hollered out my determination to become a lawyer. Although the years since have blurred the clarity, I was certain that I wanted to be part of a profession that could accomplish such a high objective as getting rid of segregation.

So the Dodgers, my father, and an impetuous reaction to a newspaper headline led me to law school and to pro bono work for minority people in Phoenix and San Francisco. Going with NARF, I was sure, would be the logical next step.

If anything, NARF turned out to be far more than I dared hope—it was blessed, miraculous, electric good fortune. It opened up so much: the chance to know Indian people, to get out to reservations all across the West, to become involved in pressing public issues—to help make buildings I did believe in. And for all my dreams, and they were legion, I could never have imagined that over the next quarter of a century I would be drawn ever more to the Colorado Plateau. Never could I have imagined that this distant outpost would steadily build in my mind, that the land would come to inflame my passions, and that the people I met and the ideas I learned there would fundamentally shape the way I understand the world.

But all of that was in the future, unknown to me when, just after Labor Day in 1971, I struck out from the Bay Area for Boulder, Colorado, traveling an arc that would take me back to Arizona and to the Plateau that Paul had diagrammed in the desert sand.

C h a p t e r 2

# MEXICAN HAT

**B**y the fall of 1971, the Native American Rights Fund had been operating in Colorado for several months. The expansion was going ahead on schedule: NARF soon would have fourteen attorneys and a support staff twice that large. The solid, stuccoed, three-story building, a former fraternity house, had been converted into law offices over the summer. Hardly conventional but efficient and comfortable, a fine place to work, the offices evidenced the organization's seriousness of purpose: rather than just rent space, NARF had taken an option to purchase and in 1973 would buy the building, unheard of for public-interest legal firms.

NARF's ambitious priorities included the return of tribal lands, the

enforcement of treaty rights to water, land, hunting, and fishing, the asser-
tion of tribal jurisdiction over all persons, Indian and non-Indian, on the
reservations, and a campaign to end discrimination against Indians in the
schools. This made for challenging work. Since NARF chose its litigation
according to its national significance to Indians, the cases raised serious
social and economic questions eliciting both public sympathy and strident
opposition from powerful interests. When I arrived, my desk had six or
seven files on it. Three of them involved discrimination against Navajo
children in Arizona, New Mexico, and Utah public school districts. Within
a year, these Indian education cases would introduce me to deep-seated
social concerns on the Colorado Plateau.

The other cases, too, helped give me a grounding in Indian law, history,
and society. The prime example was the file labeled "Menominee Termination." This Wisconsin tribe had been "terminated" in 1954. Termination,
the most extreme version of the assimilationist policies that Congress had
pushed since the nineteenth century, dominated Indian affairs during the
1950s and into the 1960s. The rubric was to make Indians "equal." The reality, however, meant breaking treaties and ending long-standing federal
commitments to Indians. Thus termination called for selling off tribal
lands, cutting off federal education and health programs for individual
Indians, ending special economic programs for tribes, and putting the former reservations under state jurisdiction. Sink or swim. Of the roughly
five hundred tribes in the country, Congress had terminated three large
tribes (including the Menominee), six middle-sized ones, and about forty
small Indian groups in California.

Termination had been a disaster for the Menominee. When the federal
health clinic pulled out, not a single doctor or dentist remained in the
county. Menominee children suffered discrimination in the public schools.
Adults tasted racism in state courts; before termination, all cases had gone
to tribal or federal courts. The tribe had been able to stave off an outright
sale of Menominee land—250,000 acres of deep woods fed by the Wolf
River and its tributaries—by having it transferred to a state corporation

with tribal shareholders. By the late 1960s, however, the debt-ridden corporation had begun selling land, 9,500 acres in all, to pay state property taxes, never before applicable to the tribe. This loss of forestland, dotted with lakes, prime hunting territory, sacred ground, stung the Menominee. Termination was tearing their homeland apart.

Menominee taught me about the essence of federal Indian law. Since Congress had dismantled the tribe and our job was to reconstitute it, the work required me to parse out and understand the intricacies of tribal sovereignty and federal power over Indians—the two foundations of my new field. My reading took me back to old opinions of Chief Justice John Marshall, still valid, making it clear that Indian tribes are sovereigns: governments. The words on paper became real for me on a frigid winter evening in 1971 when I sat through a long meeting in a jam-packed Grange Hall in Keshena, Wisconsin, and listened to plea after plea from fiery, dark-skinned orators. This is *our* sovereignty, *our* land. The state has no business here. This is Menominee country. When I saw the fires of tribalism burning that hot, especially in a tribe that the federal government had terminated, finally cast aside, I knew this was a cause worth fighting for.

For the Menominee, who had built their movement into a statewide issue and attracted national political support, relief came quickly. By 1973, Congress had passed the Menominee Restoration Act, putting the land back into reservation status, recognizing tribal sovereignty over that land, and reactivating federal programs for the Menominee. Although I drafted the words for the statute, I was just putting down the dreams of Menominee people expressed that night in Keshena and at many other gatherings.

**M**y new career had both depth and scope. The law was captivating, a mix of old and new, a chance to immerse myself in nineteenth-century treaties and some of John Marshall's greatest opinions and to see them applied more than a century later. And as I became exposed to many Indian people, I gained some understanding of Indian culture—which, after all, was ultimately what tribal leaders had charged NARF to protect through Indian law. I saw, as had many before me, how the Indian experience has such profound complexity, both vibrancy and tragedy, at once lightness and weight. Through experiences small and large, I began to find new facets in our humanity. And I started to view people and land and places differently.

I had no idea, for example, that it would be so much plain fun to be around Indians. The old stereotype of Indians as taciturn and humorless is all wrong. Indian societies are easygoing, lighthearted, with much more laughter and joking around than in Anglo cultures.

Teasing is a big part of Indian humor. One evening I was supposed to attend a Menominee meeting at a house on the main street of Keshena, a settlement of a few hundred. I showed up half an hour late, to the considerable delight of Shirley Daly: "Charles got lost in Keshena! How can *anyone* get lost in Keshena?" This had many future permutations, one of which was: "How are the Menominee supposed to make any progress when they've got a lawyer who gets lost in Keshena?" The hallways of NARF offered no respite. I had a pair of cowboy boots that were kind of stubby, lacking the classic, long-toed look. "Hey, folks, here comes Charles. He's still got those teeny-tiny, sawed-off boots! Hey, Charles, why don't you take a good long lunch today and go downtown and buy some *real* ones?"

If humor is one thread of a culture, another is food and the ways it is acquired. One day at Menominee, Ada Deer took me over to her aunt and uncle's for supper. We had bear and deer meat, wild rice, and cranberries from a nearby bog. The dinner table was the product of traditional hunting and gathering: hardly a morsel came from the grocery store. Another time, I went out fishing with Warren "Pootch" Kakwich on the Red River, a tributary of the Wolf. We caught a mess of brook trout. Back at Pootch's house, we cleaned the fish and he took several of them out to the garage. He opened two freezers, both chock full. "That's deer and that's bear. There's some squirrels and rabbits. Those birds are grouse and partridges. These trout go over here with the others. These freezers will take us through the whole winter."

One of my trips at NARF was down to Oklahoma, once called the Indian Territory, once on the way to statehood as an Indian state before the land rushes that took the oil as well as most of the land. Yvonne Knight and I went there on a case to reinstate three Pawnee boys who had been suspended from school for wearing their hair in traditional braids. Yvonne was a member of the Ponca Tribe of Oklahoma.

We spent two arduous days with Pawnee people who would be witnesses at the hearing on Monday. Since the local school required that the young boys cut their braids, we wanted to bring in evidence of assimilationist policies and how they had been discredited. The Pawnees stood solidly behind the boys and, since many people wanted to testify, we took written statements from anyone who wanted to participate. The most agonizing came from elderly Pawnee men, born near the turn of the century, who were students in Bureau of Indian Affairs' boarding schools in the 1910s and 1920s. The young boys all had their braids cut off and their traditional buckskin clothes thrown away. All Native American religious practices were prohibited. Teachers washed their mouths out with yellow lye soap whenever they spoke Pawnee. One boy had his earrings torn from his ears.

We took Saturday and Sunday off, spending most of our time visiting with Yvonne's family, since the Pawnee and Ponca are neighboring tribes. I met her grandmother, who used to braid Yvonne's hair before she went off to school in the morning. On Saturday evening, Yvonne invited me to my first Indian ceremony, the Gray Horse Dances. "They are very traditional," she explained.

The dancing was done on bare ground under an open-air pavilion, a broad roof supported by wooden posts. The smells of fresh, green growth filled the spring evening air. I loved the warrior dances, all color and motion. Then the women came out. At first, their slow and easy pace seemed like a letdown.

"Watch them closely," Yvonne whispered. "It takes a long time to learn how to make the fringe on the shawl move exactly like tall grass in a spring breeze. Look at that lady up in front. Isn't she mesmerizing?"

Yes, she was. Over a lifetime, the woman had learned to express the subtlety and precision and grace of a dance done in many previous lifetimes.

**W**ith all of us in our twenties or early thirties, and with a common mission and challenging work, NARF created close personal relationships. This led to many insights into Indian country, especially from the Indian attorneys. Yvonne and I worked together on several cases. Yvonne, as gifted a lawyer as I have ever known, just out of law school, was at once my junior and my senior. Some of my best lessons came out of heated discussions interspersed by Yvonne's affectionate but vehement warnings: "Look, white man, you just slow down and listen for a minute." Tom Fredericks, Mandan from North Dakota, was another talented young lawyer in a time when Native American attorneys could still be counted in the dozens. Tom's family ran cattle on the Fort Berthold Reservation in North Dakota and he grew up both an Indian and a cowboy, rising before dawn and laboring all day long. From the beginning, I could see his no-quit attitude and good judgment.

Browning Pipestem, an Otoe who worked at NARF for a year before going back home to practice in Oklahoma, left a lasting impression on me. One night we had a long discussion about Indian identity. Browning, like his father, is an orator and an imposing man. (He was once a pulling guard at the University of Oklahoma.) I work at a stand-up, slant-top desk, and we were both standing, leaning against the desk on our elbows.

"When I was little, I had this white friend." Browning paused and looked right at me. Pauses were an integral part of a conversation for him.

"One afternoon," Browning finally continued, "the white kid said, 'Come 'ere.' He had a pad of Brillo." Another long pause.

"That kid started rubbing that Brillo on top of my wrist. He rubbed and rubbed, rubbed and rubbed. Then he rubbed some more. Real hard."

Browning just looked at me, now with perspiration on his face.

"Finally," Browning said, "I asked that kid what he was doing. He said, 'Look, I'm your friend. Maybe if I keep using this stuff, we can rub that Indian color off you.'"

"Charles, I'm telling you, it took me a long time to get over that. To realize that I didn't want to rub any of that off."

Through Browning, Yvonne, Tom, the Pawnee men with their long and moving stories, the Menominee, and many other Indian people, I came to realize the extent of the brute force and cunning that have been leveled against the Indian way—and also the tenacity with which Indian people have responded. Essentially the work of NARF, on behalf of the tribes, was to use the law to allow Indian tribes to govern themselves, to make the cultural decisions in their own ways, and to keep their reservations—their homelands—intact.

I spent as much time with John Echohawk as with anyone at NARF. John grew up on the Colorado Plateau, in Farmington, New Mexico. His father, a Pawnee, was a government engineer assigned to the Farmington area. John, who acquired every one of his father's Indian genes, must have modeled for the Indian head nickel. Some might question my chronology, but the proof lies in John's face. John, however, has a flip side. His normal visage, like the nickel, might be stolid and imposing but, upon a remark that tickles him, he can flash an 18-inch grin. The contrast between the grin and the stolidity is a thing to behold.

Like me, John loves to fish and we made excursions to Colorado's good trout water, the Saint Vrain near Boulder, the South Platte an hour southwest of Denver, the streams of wide-open South Park, the headwaters of the Cache La Poudre in Rocky Mountain National Park. These were times to fish, but also to explore Colorado, to talk, times to be young, times to wonder at the heavy responsibilities we had so joyfully assumed.

The Navajo education cases were moving toward trial and I had planned to go down to the reservation to meet with the other lawyers and the parents. A week or so before my first trip down to Navajo, John and I got up early and drove over to the Roaring Fork, the bigwater, freestone river near Aspen on the Western Slope. On the way back, five or six satisfying rainbows in our creels, John talked about Navajo and Hopi. He had grown up near Navajo and at NARF was representing Hopi elders desperately trying to stop the coal leasing on Black Mesa.

"You know," John reflected as he drove through the darkness, "it is really something working for these traditional Hopi people. Farmington is right next to the New Mexico part of the Navajo Reservation, and I had the same respect for the traditional Navajo when I was little. The tribes in the Southwest are so distinctive. It's sure interesting to learn about them."

He told me that I should read up on Navajo history and culture to prepare for my education cases. This was something I had already begun to appreciate—that, beyond knowing about Indian issues generally, you also had to learn about the specific tribes. Every tribe is different. John's advice, though, was a good reminder. I had to do much more learning about Navajo.

"When you're down at Navajo," John continued, "try not to work all the time. Be sure to get out and see the land. There are some beautiful spots." Then came that wide-open grin. "And see if you can't manage to fish the San Juan River below Navajo Dam. There are some monster rainbows in there."

The Navajo Nation, located in Arizona, New Mexico, and Utah, has long held a special place in Indian affairs. The tribe has far and away the highest number of members: 200,000 living in Indian country, no less than one-fifth of all reservation Indians. Navajoland encompasses 17 million acres, an area larger than West Virginia and nine other states. Almost one-third of all Indian land outside of Alaska is Navajo territory.

DNA Legal Services, the largest Indian legal services program, has its headquarters in Window Rock, the capital of the Navajo Nation. NARF was the national "Backup Center" for Indian legal services programs on the reservations, and DNA had referred the Navajo school matters to us as cocounsel. Because of the expanse of the Navajo Reservation, not all the issues could be addressed at once. The DNA lawyers had already brought two suits against the school districts in the Gallup and Kirtland areas. Although DNA recommended a third suit, in San Juan County, Utah, a complaint had not yet been filed. It was a measure of the lack of experience

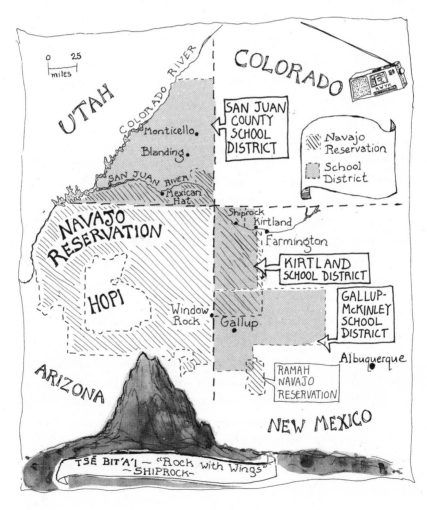

and stature of Indian lawyers in those days that these cases were assigned to me, NARF's "senior trial attorney," with no background in Indian law and a grand total of five years of practice, much of it carrying partners' briefcases at my two private firms.

The lawsuits in the Gallup and Kirtland areas arose because Navajo parents had repeatedly complained to DNA attorneys about the treatment of their children in the state-run schools. The schools attended by Navajo children were overcrowded and run-down. Not only did Anglo teachers and administrators suspend and expel Navajo children at high rates, but they were disrespectful of Navajo traditions. The school district made no efforts to bring Navajo culture and language into the classrooms. The DNA lawyers explained that trying to correct these conditions would mean lengthy lawsuits. The Navajo parents might have to give depositions—perhaps testify in federal court in Albuquerque. Were they sure they wanted to take all of this on? The parents were adamant. This had gone on too long. It was time to do something about it.

*Natonabah v. Board of Education of the Gallup-McKinley County School District* was the first case scheduled to go to trial. This New Mexico school district educated nearly eight thousand Navajo students living on the eastern side of the reservation. The complaint charged racial discrimination on the basis that the facilities in the predominantly Navajo schools were markedly inferior to those in schools where most of the students were non-Indians. The suit also alleged misuse of federal funds targeted for Indian children. *Natonabah* would require us to dissect the school district's complicated finances over the past several years. It was by far the biggest case I'd ever undertaken. We had sued the State of New Mexico, and the state attorney general had brought Jeff Bingaman, a good lawyer who would later become United States senator, into the case as special counsel. The United States had intervened on behalf of the Navajo plaintiffs. In all, a dozen lawyers were working on the litigation.

I will never forget how intimidated I felt when I climbed on the plane to Albuquerque for final preparation with my several cocounsel before the trial began a week later. It was a hectic, stressful week as all the lawyers scrambled to digest the hundreds of school district, state, and federal documents relating to the case. Several last-minute depositions were taken, some on the reservation, some in Santa Fe, the state capital. The lawyers on our side held meetings whenever we could, strategizing and struggling to get on top of the sprawling case.

After dinner on the evening before the trial, I went back to my room to prepare the opening statement—our roadmap for the judge—in which I would summarize the evidence we would present and explain why the court should take the extraordinary step of ordering sweeping reform of a state school district. I was exhausted: not only had I had little sleep that week, but I had somehow managed to lose my glasses. My eyesight is terrible, and my backup pair of glasses, with a prescription long out of date, left me looking at the world through a blur. Still, this was pleasurable work. My task was to rise above the details in the stacks of documents and tell the story of the case and of the Navajo children: how the sorry school conditions amounted (in the words of one Supreme Court opinion) to "built-in headwinds," how they denied the children (as one study of Indian education put it) "an even chance."

I lost track of time and finally finished up about two or three in the morning. I straightened up all of my papers, then got in the motel shower and turned the spray on my face. With my opening statement finally completed, in the quietude I began crying, then sobbing in jerks and fits. It was out of joy. I found myself saying out loud: "This is what you chose to do. This is where you chose to be. You didn't know it would be exactly like this, but this is why you became a lawyer. Get some sleep and be ready."

Comforted by the shower and anchored by my moment of realization, I got into bed and slept briefly but well. A few hours later, I was up and getting dressed. I met the other lawyers working on our side in the motel lobby at 6:30 A.M. for the first day of trial.

We walked out into the warming day toward our car. We passed the swimming pool. Many Navajo people—eight, twelve, fifteen, I can't be sure—were kneeling around the pool, the men wrapped in blankets, the women dressed in their thick velvet.

# BEDROCK

"What are they doing?" I asked Alan Stay, a DNA attorney who lived on the reservation.

"They are praying for us," he answered. "They need water for these prayers and this is the only water around."

The trial in front of Judge Howard Bratton went well. The evidence inexorably showed how the school district had favored the schools in and around Gallup as compared with the schools on the reservation. Our statistician, Paul Smith of Harvard, prepared a large chart that tied our case together and demonstrated it vividly. Vertically he listed the district's elementary and secondary schools: the thirteen predominantly Navajo schools on top, the twelve mostly non-Indian schools on the bottom. Horizontally the chart listed all manner of educational categories: student/teacher ratio, teachers' salaries, number of teacher's aides, square footage per student in buildings and playgrounds, number of library books per student, expenditures per student for school lunches, maintenance, athletics, and so forth. Whenever a school was more than 10 percent deficient in a particular category, Paul would place a black dot across from the school in the box corresponding to that category. So if Ramah Elementary School, a mostly Indian school, had teachers' salaries more than 10 percent below the district-wide average, it would get a black dot.

Paul put more than a hundred black dots on the chart. And nearly all of them were on the top half of the chart opposite the mostly Indian schools. The impact was devastating—one courtroom observer said it looked like someone had fired a shotgun at the top half of the chart—showing an undeniable pattern of allocating fewer district resources to the mostly Indian schools. Paul testified that it seemed to make no difference what categories were chosen: he had done numerous computations in addition to the ones set out on the chart, and they all came out the same way—to the disadvantage of the Indian children. There was much more to the trial, but the black dots on that chart set the context for the whole case.

Seven months later, in February 1973, I received a call from Phil Horton of the Justice Department in Washington. He had no way of knowing that my shaking left hand was bouncing the phone against my ear as he told me

26

that he had just received the judge's ruling in the mail—our copy hadn't arrived yet—and said, "It looks like your clients have won on all counts."

The second lawsuit, *Denetclarence v. Board of Education,* was against the Kirtland School District in northwestern New Mexico that served Navajos in the Shiprock area. This suit never went to trial, however, as we were able to reach a settlement in a matter of months. It helped that the *Natonabah* ruling had set a precedent. As fundamentally, Indian children in Shiprock fared better than in Gallup. Recent local elections had sent a heartening sign that reservation Indians had survived the termination era and were ready to take control of their affairs: Navajos in the Shiprock area had waged a get-out-the-vote campaign and now held a majority on this school board. The settlement in *Denetclarence* called for a Navajo bilingual program and dealt with several minor infractions.

The Shiprock case brought with it personal dimensions that the Gallup litigation had not. In the first case, I got out to the reservation several times but spent most of my time in office meetings. On my visits to the Shiprock area, I began to develop more of a sense for the land. Although I never found the opportunity to pursue John Echohawk's suggestion on fishing the nearby San Juan River, I did take two or three long hikes in the sagebrush terrain, always in view of the Shiprock formation itself—the neck of a long-dormant volcano, rising up a full 1,800 feet from the desert floor, one of the Plateau's most stirring landmarks. "Shiprock," an Anglo name, is in one sense accurate, as the monument's graceful reach does evoke a ship's sails. It goes without saying, though, that the term is imported, since sailing ships have hardly been the transportation of choice on the Colorado Plateau. The original Navajo name, *Tsé Bit'a'i,* does even more justice to the upsweeping and inspiring formation. It means "rock with wings."

Many other images would join it, but the Rock with Wings became the first natural structure on the Colorado Plateau to take a permanent place in my consciousness.

# BEDROCK

The third Navajo school case, far more than the others, drew me squarely into the densest thickets of places, people, and events on the Colorado Plateau. The case involved the schools of San Juan County, Utah. The school district encompasses the entire county and is believed to be geographically the second-largest school district in the lower 48 states, extending north from the Four Corners almost to Moab, more than one hundred miles. The western border is the Colorado River and Lake Powell, trending southwest all the way down to the Arizona line, nearly to Page. The expansive area, mostly open range country intersected by canyons, draws, mesas, and ridges, with the Abajo Mountains near the center, is lightly populated— 9,600 people lived in the county in 1974. Monticello and Blanding, the two largest towns, with 2,000 and 3,000 residents, respectively, were both founded at the turn of the century by Mormon pioneers. North of the San Juan River, San Juan County remains 90 percent Mormon.

The southern quarter of the county, below the San Juan River, lies within the Navajo Reservation. When I began my work on this case, about half of the county's population was Navajo. (It is a higher portion now, as the Navajo population continues to grow.) In the northern part of the county, there were five elementary schools and a junior high. A K–4 school was located in Bluff, where students were split about equally between Anglos and Navajos. Only two elementary schools were on the reservation, in Mexican Hat and Montezuma Creek. My files told me that the reservation's schools were badly overcrowded and substandard compared to county schools up north—substandard, apparently, to just about any schools in the country.

Bad enough. But the most severe problem was the busing. Since both of the county's high schools were up north, in Monticello and Blanding, the Navajo children had to endure bus rides of several hours a day just to go to school. One route was over 150 miles roundtrip.

I had never been to the Utah part of the reservation, so I set aside several days to go down there to get a better understanding of the situation.

# Mexican Hat

On the way, I swung south into Arizona to stop off in Window Rock and meet with my colleagues at the DNA headquarters office.

DNA is an abbreviation for Dinebeiina Nahiilna Be Agaditahe, meaning in Navajo "the organization that brings well-being to the people," and this was an institution that lived up to its name. The DNA office was a patched-together structure built by the employees themselves in the 1960s when the firm started up as part of the War on Poverty. Even early in the morning, when I arrived, the waiting room was nearly filled with Navajo people. Two bilingual paralegals circulated around, patiently getting the facts about pickup truck repossessions, personal injuries, wage garnishments, divorces, disputes over grazing areas, traffic tickets, complaints against the BIA and the tribe for mishandling benefits, and the myriad other grievances, small and large, for which the Navajo people had never before had any recourse. The interview sheets were then turned over to staff lawyers (mostly Anglo) or to Navajo advocates—nonlawyers who could appear in Navajo Tribal Court and otherwise assist their clients. The waiting room was a busy scene, but not noisy, for the interviews were conducted in whispers and murmurs.

That morning I met with Peterson Zah, executive director of DNA, and Rick Collins, director of litigation. Pete Zah had grown up in the traditional way at Low Mountain, attended Arizona State University, then returned to the reservation. Pete, in blue jeans, still in his early thirties but with a trace of gray in his black hair, conveyed a quiet competence and compassion. Years later Zah—such a contrast to Peter MacDonald, who as tribal chairman took bribes and ended up in tribal jail and federal prison—became president of the Navajo Nation, honest, progressive, always on top of the challenging issues in that demanding office. Rick, tall and slender with a full blond beard, a non-Indian from Harvard Law School, stayed with DNA for four years and then worked at NARF before going into teaching and becoming a distinguished professor of Indian and constitutional law.

In our meeting, which lasted a couple of hours, we talked mostly about constitutional problems we faced in the San Juan County school case. The Navajo parents, resolute in their determination to end the busing, wanted two high schools constructed on the reservation, one near Monument Valley and another at Montezuma Creek. But these new schools would be located far from the communities in the northern part of the county, and the students would be virtually all Navajo. In turn, the Blanding and Monticello schools would lose almost all of their Indian students. Although the whole point of building the new schools would be to improve the education of the Indian children, might the courts find that this arrangement would create a segregated school district in violation of *Brown v. Board of Education?*

Another concern was how the new schools would be funded. The county might have to hold a bond election to pay for construction. We didn't expect many votes from northern San Juan County. And, despite the turnout for the recent school board elections at Shiprock, Navajo people were just learning about voting. Did a judge have the power to order a school board to issue bonds for construction if the electorate voted down a bond issue?

We finished and I stood up to go. It had been a good meeting. We had satisfied ourselves that the extreme distances between the communities in San Juan County and the burdens of the current long-range busing would—constitutionally as well as educationally—justify creating a school system with essentially single-race schools. The funding, however, presented serious obstacles and we agreed to keep a focus on the issue.

As Pete was walking me toward the door, he stopped and said, "Look. Let's really try to settle this case. Those school administrators will perform a lot better if they're carrying out their own agreed-upon plan than if they're hit over the head with a federal court injunction. If we do need to pass a bond issue, I think we'll get some additional votes up north if we settle this case peaceably and don't go through a long, drawn-out court battle. Maybe the Mormon Church will even give the bonds its blessing."

"And don't forget the kids. We've been talking about a lot of legal issues, and that's fine, but don't forget about those kids. I've spent some time up there and that busing is just not right. Let's all of us put everything we have into this."

# Mexican Hat

"One last thing, Charles. Work closely with Eric." Pete was referring to Eric Swenson, just out of law school, the head of the DNA office in Mexican Hat. I had already talked to Eric on the phone several times, but had not yet met him. "He's so damn mad about this busing that he can hardly speak. Eric's a good lawyer, but he'll need to work hard to keep his emotions down."

We shook hands. I remembered (Navajo culture was still new to me and I sometimes forgot) to grip Pete's hand lightly and look down to show respect. The vise-grip, in-your-eye, pump-up-and-down approach is not for this nation.

On the four-hour drive from Window Rock to Mexican Hat, I tuned to KWYK, a station in Farmington that one of the Navajo advocates at DNA had told me about. My fascination with radio began when I was eight or nine, listening to the Brooklyn Dodgers' games, lying in my bed or sitting on the edge of it, absorbed by my crackly little RCA radio as it brought into my bedroom the green grass of Ebbets Field and the enthusiasm of the faithful fans—and the heroes themselves in their clean white flannel uniforms. If anything, as the years pass I grow even more devoted to radio, more immediate than the newspapers, more spontaneous than television. My intellect may reach for a book. But my emotions side with radio, underdog to literature and the fancier media, yet fun, frank, and authentic, the best purveyor of local color.

The KWYK announcer, a Navajo, was the trailblazer in Navajo-language programming. The program was a big hit on the reservation—which the merchants in Farmington realized because their Navajo business boomed when their ad copy was written up in Navajo. Other towns bordering the reservation followed suit and put on their own Navajo-language shows several hours each day. So I made my way across vast Navajoland at midday, tuned to an announcer I could not understand (except for occasional insertions of words like "Chevrolet," "President Nixon," and "Trading Post"), reveling in the mixed format of traditional Navajo squaw dance songs and country music. No doubt about it: new winds of tribal pride blew in Indian country.

# BEDROCK

I reflected on Pete's comment about Eric Swenson during the drive to Mexican Hat. I'd already discovered what Pete meant about Eric's anger: his outrage burned up the line. "You can't believe what these people are going through. Those bastards up in Monticello just won't give the Navajos the time of day. There's only one thing that's going to help these kids and that's a hammer of an injunction from Salt Lake City." He had also politely scolded me: "I know you've got those other cases to finish up, but we need you down here. The parents are really fed up with this busing. It's the number-one topic at every chapter meeting."

Mexican Hat is near the center of some of the most exciting country I've ever known—Cedar Mesa rises just across the San Juan River, and Monument Valley is a few miles to the south. But as I drove up to the DNA double-wide in August 1974, Mexican Hat seemed like the end of the earth. Beyond the end of the earth: a person had to drive forever to get there, from any direction. I remembered that Eric's telephone hookup was some kind of radio contraption. He sounded like he was at the bottom of a rain barrel—underwater. This was the only phone in Mexican Hat, a 24-party line, kind of hard on the confidentiality of attorney–client privilege and lawyers' strategy discussions about hammers of injunctions from Salt Lake City.

If the DNA office in Window Rock was spartan, the one in Mexican Hat was primitive. This wasn't even a new double-wide. Most of the doors and windows were poorly fitted and so, in a place that specialized in sand and wind, a steady red flow trickled in. I could just imagine my smashingly dressed secretary in San Francisco gliding into my office on the thirty-fourth floor of the Bank of America Building: "You might be careful with your calls this morning, Mr. Wilkinson. It sounds like there are at least eight people listening in. And would you like me to scrape that layer of sand off your desk?"

If anyone was up to the task of practicing law under these circumstances, it was Eric. Hair down to his shoulders, informal, energetic, he was six foot four and sturdy. (He had been a defensive lineman in college just a few years ago.) He hated injustice and saw it every morning when Navajo people began to filter into his office. Often his overworked secretary had to act as an interpreter during intake.

Eric had his blessings, though, in this end-of-the-world law office. He had struck gold with his advocate, Herb Yazzie, who had a brilliant legal mind. (Later Herb went to law school and by the 1990s had become attorney general of the Navajo Nation in Pete Zah's second administration.) Moreover, the Navajo people at the northern end of the reservation energized Eric—he was devoted to their cause and they gave him their respect for his courage and dedication. This support had its tangible sides: since Eric and DNA touched such deep chords with the Navajo people, there were plenty of volunteers—especially for the school case.

It was late afternoon when I arrived, but Eric, Herb, and I met for a few hours to go over the case. DNA had several people working on it and a great deal had been done. Eric and Herb had obtained a stack of records from the school district. Jack Hennessy, a DNA paralegal, had written a long memorandum analyzing discrimination in the district schools. Volunteers had obtained affidavits from Navajo people, students, parents, and elders. The two area chapters (the local units of Navajo government, 110 in all) had been briefed at meetings and were solidly behind the case. During our meeting, a group of parents came in and plaintively discussed their concerns for their children, all in high school. Herb did the translating.

One woman said that the high school in Blanding had no sign of Navajo culture—neither displays of art or blankets nor the use of Navajo history or culture in classes. Navajo students were suspended and expelled at high rates. "Our children just don't feel welcome there." Another woman added: "Even if the schools did honor our culture, those children would still be exhausted from the bus rides. My daughter is on that bus two hours in the morning and another two hours coming home. It's very cruel."

Afterward the three of us went out for dinner and beer. The reservation is dry by tribal law, but there was a good bar at the San Juan Inn just across the river. Eric and Herb emphasized that this was the perfect night to go out for dinner. The delivery truck with the hoagies comes through just once a week and tonight the sandwiches would be fresh. New colleagues, quickly becoming friends, we talked for hours in a rambling way about the different things that had converged to bring us together—law, the Navajo people, education, the big distances of southern Utah, and the Mormon Church.

# DE∫ERET

The influence of the Mormon Church suffused society in San Juan County. In every discussion I had about the school case, the subject of the Mormons came up in some fashion. Many Navajo people felt insulted and deeply resentful about the church's attitudes toward Indians. Others objected to relentless Mormon proselytizing and to programs specifically targeting Navajo children—often designed to remove them from their Navajo families and place them in Mormon homes. In a different spirit, some people expressed their admiration for the Mormons' civic commitment and love of family. The church also exerted sweeping political power. Virtually every public official in San Juan County and across southern Utah was Mormon. Mormons controlled state government. Mormons ran the schools, the county commission, the courts, the police, the welfare agencies, everything. Officially the church was apolitical, but many an election and legislative initiative has turned on a signal from a Mormon official.

I realized early on that if I was to understand the school case, I had to understand the reasons for the church's grip on southern Utah. Paul Roca had helped set the context by telling me the great saga of the church's founding years, culminating in the ordeal and heroism of the 1840s, when the Mormons were forcibly driven from Illinois and tens of thousands emigrated west on the Mormon Trail to the Valley of the Great Salt Lake, where the pioneers founded Salt Lake City. Church leaders, however, were not content to rest there. Brigham Young wanted the city to be the hub of an empire, not an isolated outpost. Mormon leaders recruited and organized expeditions to establish Mormon communities in unsettled areas throughout the Southwest and beyond.

In the entire, extraordinary Mormon colonization program that Brigham Young conceived, the settlement of the interior Colorado Plateau—the San Juan country, the Four Corners area—was the most dramatic and heroic venture of all. In the late 1870s, there were still no non-Indian settlements in the core of the Colorado Plateau. The Navajo occupied a large area. The Hopi lived on Black Mesa. Western Colorado belonged to the Ute under the Treaty of 1868. Inside the edges of a few thin communities rimming the interior Plateau—Rosa on the upper San Juan River, Animas City (now Durango), Green River, Wyoming, on the upper Green River, and the small Mormon towns of Moenkopi, Kanab, and Escalante—an area covering a good 25,000 square miles held a non-Indian population of a few hundred, living in scattered family farms and ranches, missionary homes, mining shacks, and government Indian Office housing.

Then, in 1880, after a harrowing journey through country unexplored by non-Indians, the Hole-in-the-Rock Expedition managed to establish a base in San Juan County. From the Mormons' side this effort, and the other communities it spawned, turned the interior Colorado Plateau into Mormon country. In their eyes, Mormons had conquered the land, brought in the Lord, and kept the peace with the Indians. Their determination to hold this, their homeland, and to run it the way they saw fit, was forged in the story of this grueling and courageous nineteenth-century expedition that burns today in church lore and in the minds of Mormon people across southern Utah.

**E**lizabeth Morris Decker and 230 other Mormon pioneers pulled their train of wagons, a thousand head of cattle, and four hundred horses into Forty-Mile Spring on November 15, 1879. This stopover marked a trying time for the members of the Hole-in-the-Rock Expedition, as it would soon become known. Their mission was to settle southeastern Utah, but they had reached the end of the line, the point at which the trail running southeast down the Escalante River drainage turned from a faint track into nothing. The realization set in that they had almost no information about this country. Hardly anyone, except Indians, did. The Escalante, after all, was the last river in the continental United States to be put on the maps, just a decade earlier, by John Wesley Powell. On the horizon to the east lay the Henry Mountains, the last range to be mapped, also by Powell.

The settlers' plight had grown steadily worse. Seventy-five miles back, on the other side of the little village of Escalante, the explorers had driven their stock through ponderosa pine forests with rich bunchgrasses on the shady forest floors. The expedition gradually descended into piñon-juniper country with some grass but mostly the less desirable sagebrush. They had left the piñon-juniper stands 20 miles ago.

Now, by Forty-Mile Spring, they found themselves in sandy, scrubby desert country with nothing but saltbush for the animals. Over the past 15 miles, the terrain had been repeatedly criss-crossed by side canyons, gulches, and washes. It had become ever more agonizing work to maneuver eighty wagons—each with a full team of horses and jam-packed with food for their long journey, beans and seed wheat for planting at their destination, work implements, and the belongings of whole families—down into rocky gashes, then angle the bulky vehicles back up the other side. The Deckers' family cavalcade was typical: in addition to their eleven cows, Lizzie, as she was called, and Cornelius, her husband of four years, had six horses hitched to their main wagon and trailed another wagon behind.

The weather, too, had been harsh. Two feet of just-fallen snow covered what little vegetation might have been available for their cattle and horses. To be sure, Forty-Mile Spring was tucked down in a shallow wash, and two large rock monuments gave some cover, so the expedition had a measure of shelter from the wind. Still, it was bitter cold.

Lizzie Decker had the comfort of being surrounded by ample relations during the three weeks that the pioneers made camp at Forty-Mile Spring. The Decker clan included five separate families, all from Parowan, Utah. She had Cornelius and her two boys, William and Eugene. Her sister, Emma, the wife of Cornelius' brother, Nathaniel Decker, also was in the assemblage. Solace came, too, from the church services held every Sunday and Thursday. Lizzie Decker, who had been in the church choir since she was a little girl, had a fine voice and loved to sing the hymns.

# Deseret

One might imagine that this procession would have taken some relief from the spectacular surroundings. The Straight Cliffs, the vertical edge of Kaiparowits Plateau, growing higher as the pioneers moved southeast, defined the route of the Hole-in-the-Rock Expedition on the west. In addition to the Henry Mountains, rounded Navajo Mountain and long Waterpocket Fold made up other parts of the horizon. An abundance of natural arches and bridges graced the lower Escalante. The country is so compelling that today the Colorado Plateau has the largest concentration of substantial national parks and monuments of any place in the world.

Sentiments about arches and glorious vistas, however, were not for the Hole-in-the-Rock pioneers. In researching the history of the expedition, I noticed that the journals and letters, including Lizzie Decker's, barely mentioned the landscape. At first this surprised me. Even from the scant information available, I could tell that Lizzie Decker was a high-spirited person—a person likely to be drawn to beauty.

When I went to the Hole-in-the-Rock trail, especially at Forty-Mile Spring, I tried to place myself in Lizzie Decker's position. Soon it came to me that, in a small and much less demanding way, I once had an experience similar in some respects to hers during my own first crossing of the Colorado Plateau on old Route 66 across the Plateau's southern edge. It was bitter cold that December, too. If I had kept a journal, it never would have occurred to me, except perhaps for San Francisco Peaks, to mention the physical surroundings. This dry, stark land is an acquired taste. I didn't acquire it on my much easier Route 66 trip and I am quite sure that I never would have acquired it in December 1879 with danger and privation all around and small children in tow.

To the members of the Hole-in-the-Rock Expedition, this was hard country. It was not a country they had personally chosen, for church officials had selected the families for the mission and set their destination. The travelers did, however, make good use of one imposing bit of scenery. They discovered, less than 2 miles from Forty-Mile Spring, a natural amphitheater, with a massive overhang making a "ceiling" nearly 75 feet high. To the

Deckers this structure, which the pioneers named Dance Hall Rock, fit perfectly into family tradition, for their courtship had begun when Cornelius squired the dainty, curly-haired Lizzie to church dances. Almost every evening the gaiety swirled all around in their splendid hall as Lizzie and Cornelius, and dozens of other couples, danced out their enthusiastic reels, accompanied by three fiddles that the practical but celebratory Mormons had managed to pack in their chock-full wagons.

Yet a depressed air, a foreboding, set in deeper as each day at Forty-Mile Spring went by. Virtually no one had any information on what lay beyond. When reports from the scouts began to trickle in, there was no good news to be found. The land up ahead would be much rougher on the wagons and the animals. The drop down into Glen Canyon, carved out by the Colorado River 15 miles to the south, was precipitous and dangerous. The country beyond the Colorado seemed far more perilous and difficult to travel than the rigorous terrain that lay on this side.

**L**izzie Decker and her colleagues had been sent on this mission in fulfillment of Brigham Young's grand scheme to make Utah—and the Southwest, the whole West, if he could—Mormon country. Acting for his Lord and his church, Brigham Young was both a product of, and a force behind, one of the most tumultuous, tortured, and moving series of events in American history. Every last adult member of the Hole-in-the-Rock Expedition knew these events like the backs of their hands. Mormon history was as much a part of their arduous journey as their wagons and horses and the clothing, family albums, and fiddles they had so carefully packed.

Joseph Smith founded the Church of Jesus Christ of Latter Day Saints in 1830. Although this was a Christian religion that looked to the Bible, the primacy of the *Book of Mormon,* which Smith had translated from gold plates given to him by the Angel Moroni, made Mormonism "a new religious tradition." From the outset Mormonism was a dynamo, rapidly enlisting dedicated adherents. By the mid-1840s, due in part to vigorous missionary work in Great Britain, Scandinavia, and other foreign countries, worldwide LDS Church membership reached fifty thousand.

Yet the Mormons were hounded by locals. Violence and anger pushed the Saints ever west, from New York to Ohio to Missouri to Illinois. There they founded Nauvoo, which quickly became the largest city in the state, but the hostility was everywhere, every moment. Events hit a heinous and bloody nadir in 1844 when a mob shot and killed Joseph Smith.

Today it is hard to comprehend the virulence—the thuggery—that so relentlessly drove the Mormons westward. Part of it was the perceived extremism of LDS doctrine. Joseph Smith had in mind a theocracy: his vision was to construct a separate Mormon homeland, a Zion, a New Jerusalem, a world capital where "God himself be the sole proprietor." The highest church officials (the First Presidency—the president and his two counselors—and the Council of Twelve) were "prophets, seers, and revelators" who spoke directly with God. The Millennium and Second Coming were close at hand. Most radical of all, from the perspective of nearby pioneer communities, was the observance of polygamy, practiced since sometime in the 1830s, announced by Smith to church leaders in 1843 after a revelation, and finally publicly acknowledged in 1852. Joseph Smith had forty-nine wives, Brigham Young, who succeeded him as president, twenty-six.

The collective personality of the Mormons was another factor creating antipathy toward them. The clannish Latter Day Saints burned with a unique zeal in the furtherance of their cause. They accepted, with utter literalness, such doctrines as Revelation and the Second Coming. The Saints believed in a rigid temperance, denouncing liquor and tobacco, and lorded their purity over outsiders. The Mormons were proselytizers through and through, sparing no effort to enlist new converts. To midwestern gentiles in the 1830s and 1840s, the Mormons were fanatical and relentless, always persuading, pushing, growing, and expanding.

The Saints' palpably admirable qualities received little acknowledgment. Not only were they a friendly, generous people who built strong families and communities but in addition to their temperance, they were industrious to a degree rivaled by few societies. Yet the violence and harassment directed against Mormons continued apace in Nauvoo after the murder of Smith. When Brigham Young and the Council of Twelve decided in September 1845 to depart Illinois, the Saints knew there would be many burdens during their journey. But they also knew they would reach a new place, a much better place, a place of their own, a place far beyond the bigotry.

They began yet another exodus, their largest of all, from Nauvoo in February 1846. The Mormon Trail, 1,200 miles long from Nauvoo to Salt Lake City, holds a distinctive place in the westward expansion. Young and other church leaders planned the expedition to the nth degree. It became a study in discipline, obedience, and cooperation, not an advancing wave but a back-and-forth effort with a constant flow of eastward-moving Saints to report, pick up supplies, and give aid to oncoming wagon parties. Even then the hardships were many. Hundreds died en route, some in winter storms, many others from malaria, cholera, and an epidemic of black canker, with its gangrenous mouth sores.

That the Mormon westering experience had its tragedies should not obscure the larger truth that the Mormon Trail fulfilled the Saints' objectives to an extraordinary extent. Almost immediately Salt Lake City began to sprout: within two days after their arrival in July 1847 Mormon farmers were planting irrigated fields, and shortly thereafter, Young laid out plans for Temple Square and a downtown with 88-foot-wide streets and eight lots to a block—"a city clean and in order." By the time the transcontinental railroad was completed in 1869 and rail traffic became preeminent, 68,000 Saints, many of them from Europe, had traveled the Mormon Trail to Zion. "They were," Wallace Stegner concluded, "the most systematic, organized, disciplined, and successful pioneers in our history."

Brigham Young possessed, if anything, even more ambition than the organizational abilities he demonstrated so brilliantly on the Mormon Trail and during the settlement of the Salt Lake Valley. Determined to make an empire for his people in the Intermountain West, in 1849 he proclaimed the existence of the Provisional State of Deseret. In the *Book of Mormon,*

# Deseret

the name Deseret meant honeybee and Young employed the term to embody the beehive, symbolizing industry and community.

Deseret, stretching from the Continental Divide in the Colorado Rockies to Los Angeles, from southern Idaho to Arizona, was no mean venture. Embracing nearly one-sixth of the continental United States, it included all of Nevada and Utah, most of Arizona, one-third of California, and parts of Oregon, Idaho, Wyoming, Colorado, and New Mexico. The Provisional State of Deseret did not last long, but by any standard, save perhaps Young's, the Mormon land base remained impressive. In 1850, in a compromise, Congress created Utah Territory, which encompassed present-day Utah, almost all of Nevada, western Colorado, and the southwestern corner of Wyoming. Eventually, gentile settlers in the regions far from Salt Lake City, with no allegiance to the church, wanted their own territories and states. By 1868, chunks and slices had been carved off and Utah Territory's boundaries became the same as the state that ultimately was created.

The failure of Deseret to become the nation-state that church leaders envisioned did little to deter them. Instead, they would make Utah a state of the Union, a Mormon state. Surely it possessed all the paper qualifications. Within a very few years after the opening of the Mormon Trail, Utah had the minimum population to qualify for statehood: by 1864 the territory exceeded 60,000, the benchmark at the time, and it soared to 86,000 by 1870. Further, the commitment of church and territory to farming ran deeper than in any other part of the country—normally a huge plus in the homesteading era, premised on the Jeffersonian ideal.

Yet Congress remained staunch against admission. Utah Territory was a thinly disguised Mormon theocracy, after all, with the LDS Church exercising broad influence over government affairs, including appointments to political offices. Opposition to statehood was rooted in the same Mormon bias—with a particular emphasis on polygamy—that had burned so hot ever since the church's founding. (There was an occasional ray of levity among gentiles, however, as when, shortly after statehood, one member of the United States Senate addressed the issue of whether Reed Smoot, a supporter of polygamy but not a practitioner, ought to be seated in that august body. The senator, looking knowingly around the chamber, pronounced: "Gentlemen, I would rather have a polygamist who does not polyg, than a monogamist who does not monog.")

Finally, on October 14, 1890, LDS Church President Wilford Woodruff announced what is known simply as "The Manifesto." This dramatic pronouncement, made after Woodruff had received a revelation from the Lord that plural marriages must cease, ended official church sanction of polygamy and broke the logjam over statehood. The Mormon Church still was far and away the largest political force in Utah (and would remain so more than a century later), but now its power would be exercised through persuasion and the ballot box of a new state, not through a church-appointed government. The Utah Constitution, submitted by the citizens of the territory and approved by Congress, prohibited the practice of polygamy. Utah was admitted in 1896.

**D**uring Utah's half-century struggle for statehood, Brigham Young and the LDS Church developed and executed an unprecedented plan— the Hole-in-the-Rock Expedition was one part—to expand Mormonism's sphere of influence. Brother Brigham, as the faithful respectfully and affectionately called him, was the greatest colonizer in the nation's history. Whether or not there would be a government called Deseret, he strove to build an empire by settling "every arable valley."

As new settlements were decided upon, Young made "mission calls" announcing names of members at general conferences or local meeting-houses. When a call was made, nearly everyone responded and whole families would obediently pack up and move to some new land—often, especially in the early days, unknown and unsettled. Largely through the work of Young and, after his death in 1877, through his inspiration, five hundred Mormon communities had been established by 1900 over most of Utah, much of Idaho, Nevada, and Arizona, and in many other locales including Alberta in Canada and the Mexican state of Sonora. By the new century, the membership of the LDS Church stood at 268,331. In 1900, Utah as a state was 85 percent Mormon, a figure that would drop, but not much, to 70 percent by the end of the twentieth century.

Brigham Young wanted to expand his yeoman farmer's theocracy to all corners, but from the earliest years he had fixed especially on the warmer climes to the south where the sun would have many more months each year to bring crops to life. He succeeded in founding two settlements near the far southwestern corner of the Colorado Plateau, Cedar City in 1851 and, in 1863, St. George, an area that is still called Utah's "Dixie." Even given the church's tenacity for opening new lands, the interior of the Plateau was considered singularly unsuitable for settlement: treacherous to reach and, even if reached, virtually uninhabitable.

By the mid-1870s, Young saw things differently. Ranchers from western Colorado were beginning to run their stock in parts of southern Utah. There was talk of Texans moving their longhorns to the area. Gold had been discovered in the San Juan Mountains of Colorado in the 1870s, and a few miners were beginning to prospect in Utah. The LDS Church faced a growing danger that gentiles might take over southern Utah and northern Arizona. Moreover, Mormon converts from southern states had willingly come to Salt Lake City but were making clear their yearnings for warmer places.

Native Americans played a critical role in the Mormon Church's rising interest in the Colorado Plateau. Mormon doctrine was emphatic on the special place of Indians. American Indians are the descendants of Lamanites who came to this continent in 600 B.C. The Lamanites were Jews, one of the "Lost Tribes," having left Israel sometime before 721 B.C. They were a "wild and ferocious and a blood-thirsty people" who, among many other sins, killed off the more worthy Nephites. Because of this, the Lord cursed the Lamanites with a skin of blackness. Mark down the God-given words from the *Book of Mormon* that describe them: "filthy," "loathsome," "full of idleness and all manner of abominations." This was the "curse"—the word comes up repeatedly—of the Lamanites and, by extension, the American Indians. As the church saw it, the curse had boiled up in southwestern Utah, where Navajo and other tribes had raided the tiny Mormon settlements at Kanab and Pipe Springs. Clearly a larger force was needed to keep the peace.

But church doctrine toward Indians had another, more beneficent, side. The Lamanites could be saved by conversion to Mormonism. When that conversion occurred, the curse of black skin would end and Indians would become—this was taken literally—"white and delightsome." Thus scripture commanded the LDS Church to reach out and convert Indians, and Mormons faithfully complied from the beginning. Here, then, was another pressing reason for the church to renew its efforts in the difficult land to the far southeast. Lamanites—Hopi, Navajo, Zuni, Ute, Havasupai, Hualapai, and Paiute—needed to be saved, made white, and entered on the LDS rolls.

The mission calls for Saints to execute Brigham Young's long-standing plan to settle southeastern Utah, along the San Juan River close to the Four Corners, came less than two years after Young's death. The clerks read out the names, including Cornelius Decker's, in Parowan on December 28, 1878, and in Cedar City on March 22, 1879. This kind of sacrifice and adventure in the name of the church ran in both Lizzie's and Cornelius' blood. She had been born in England and, when her parents were converted to Mormonism, the family set sail for the United States in 1862, when Lizzie was just six. They made the long overland trip to Salt Lake City, then settled in Parowan. Cornelius' father had served with the Mormon Battalion, the crack outfit that marched from Fort Leavenworth to California in 1846. We know that Cornelius felt enthusiasm for this mission: "Everybody was bragging the San Juan up saying what a good country it was for farming and raising stock, so I concluded to . . . go to the San Juan country." Yet Lizzie, and even Cornelius, must have felt some pause. Cornelius had lived his whole life in Parowan, and Lizzie nearly all of hers. Their two boys were still toddlers.

The church had laid out a basic strategy for the expedition of men, women, and children who would dutifully pack up and leave forever their established lives to settle a new and rough land. The Council of Twelve designated Silas S. Smith to lead the effort. A reconnaissance party would travel to the San Juan country and establish a route while the others, along with church helpers, would pack and otherwise make ready for the journey.

The advance party swung far south, crossing through Hopi and Navajo land, before turning north to the present site of the town of Montezuma Creek, which they found satisfying for settlement, in the southeastern corner of the state. They then returned by a northern loop, completing a thousand-mile circuit in six months. Most of this time had been spent examining the Montezuma Creek area, making filings on the land, building a dam and irrigation ditches, and planting crops. The actual travel time was eight weeks on the southern route, six on the northern.

The explorers, with a rashness uncharacteristic of LDS enterprises, recommended a route that had not been part of their travels. Their southern leg, they said, was too difficult and fraught with danger from the tribes. The northern way was simply too long—more than 400 miles. As it turned out, either would have been far preferable to the route chosen—the "Escalante shortcut"—but the Mormon expedition bound for the Four Corners set out for Escalante in late October, 1879.

On the trip east to the tiny settlement of Escalante, and even for a number of miles afterward when the route turned southeast toward the Colorado River, "shortcut" seemed a reasonable description. By the time they had settled in at Forty-Mile Spring in the midst of a frigid winter, of course, the condition of the land and the reports of the scouts had put the lie to any idea of a shortcut.

There was no known route across the canyons of the Colorado River in this area. To cross one of these gorges, there had to be the fortuitous combination of a way in on the entrance side and a way out on the exit side. Forty-five miles downriver, Fathers Escalante and Dominguez had made a crossing a century earlier, in 1777, on the return leg of the Dominican priests' fruitless thousand-mile search to find a route from Santa Fe to the Pacific across the canyon country. But the "Crossing of the Fathers" was unfit for wagons. The only other crossings between Green River, Utah, and Yuma, nearly in Mexico, were at Moab far to the north and Lees Ferry, founded by John D. Lee a few years earlier, to the south. These were the routes used by the expedition's advance party earlier in the year, and both had already been rejected. Brigham Young's dreams, a series of miscalculations, and their own devotion and resourcefulness had taken them on the Escalante shortcut and brought them to Forty-Mile Spring.

Initially, the only person who believed the Colorado River could be crossed here—and that a way out could be found on the far side even if a crossing could be made—was George Hobbs, one of the scouts that the party sent out from the base camp at Forty-Mile Spring. The others sharply disagreed. Yet turning back had itself become increasingly difficult. Heavy December snows had fallen in the higher country they had already traveled, making it hard for their wagons to operate in that terrain. After an agonizing, late-night discussion on December 3 among the men in Silas S. Smith's tent at Forty-Mile, Smith announced the Lord's decision: press ahead. So, placing trust in their leaders, who had been given advice from their God, and concluding that they had come too far to turn back, the pioneers put aside the shrugs of the scouts who didn't see a way across the river or over the tangled ground beyond. The party packed up from Forty-Mile Spring and pushed ahead.

The cavalcade had to traverse increasingly treacherous gullies. Modern-day testament to this is made by a plaque at Carcass Wash where seven Boy Scouts and three of their parents, returning home from a rafting trip down Glen Canyon before it was flooded by Glen Canyon Dam, were killed when their truck overturned on June 10, 1963. In the frigid winter winds of 1879, part of the Hole-in-the-Rock group made camp at Fifty-Mile Spring while other wagons moved on to the edge of Glen Canyon.

At Fifty-Mile camp, food supplies were low but overall conditions improved because the weather broke and the temperature climbed. Lizzie Decker (employing the services of horseback riders going back and forth between the expedition and Escalante) wrote home: "We have just sent our last five dollars to Escalante to get some pork and Molasses." Yet their two boys were doing fine: "Genie and Willie are as fat as little pigs and just as full of fun as they can be." Three days into the new year, a blessed event, the first of three on the journey, took place at Fifty-Mile camp. Lizzie's sister-in-law, Anna Decker, gave birth to a girl, Lena Decker. The baby's middle name was Deseret.

The pioneers broke camp and, 9 miles beyond Fifty-Mile, the expedition was confronted by Glen Canyon, a deep, sheer-sided cleft that is mostly impassable except by climbers with ropes. Although the lower part of the cliff had been eroded away, leaving a narrow gully down to the river bottom, access to the gully was blocked off on the uphill side by great slabs of Entrada Sandstone. The only entrance was through a narrow slit barely wide enough for a person to wriggle through—the Hole-in-the-Rock. On the other side of the Hole-in-the-Rock, the "route" was an out-and-out cliff for 40 feet, where it angled into a boulder-strewn 45-degree chute running down 1,800 feet to the bottom of Glen Canyon.

After more than six weeks of construction work, the Mormon explorers bound for southern Utah made it through the Hole-in-the-Rock. Employing a ton of dynamite carted down from Escalante by the church (the Territorial Legislature had appropriated $5,000 for the expedition), the pioneers blasted away at the niche and expanded it enough to work the wagons through. Even so, the improved opening was still only about 2 feet wider than the wingspan of a long-armed man.

The steepest part of the trail was conquered by the construction of "Uncle Ben's Dugway," which ran along the cliff. Chip by chip the pioneers cut a ledge, wide enough for a wagon wheel, into the cliff. Below that they drilled holes—still visible today—into which they drove stakes from oak trees cut high on Kaiparowits Plateau, 30 miles away. Then they laid poles on top of the stakes and piled rocks and brush on the poles to create a passageway. The pioneers had attached a shelf of a road to a cliff. Even in this land of the dugway—primitive passageways cut into canyon walls—Uncle Ben's was the ultimate.

The rest of the trip down the side of Glen Canyon to the river was not much less arduous. The pioneers lowered people, wagons, horses, cows, and supplies down by ropes and chains. To guard against runaway wagons, the rear wheels were "rough-locked"—the technique of freezing the two rear wheels by wrapping them in chains. Sometimes drivers would hitch a horse, pulling uphill, to the back of the wagon. Lizzie Decker explained it in one of her letters back home to her parents:

> It nearly scared me to death. The first wagon I saw go down they put the brake on and rough locked the hind wheels and had a big rope fastened to the wagon and about ten men holding back on it and then they went down like they would smash everything. I'll never forget that day. When we was walking down Willie looked back and cried and asked me how we would get back home.

There were all manner of near-catastrophes—slips, slides, and falls, cuts, bruises, and breaks—but, incredibly, no actual catastrophes. Not even a horse or cow was lost to the rocky sides and floor of Glen Canyon. And any modern visitor who goes to this blasted-out, chiseled-out, monster of a path and is amazed, as everyone is, at how anyone could run wagons down it, avoiding disaster no less, should consider that they have seen only the top one-third of the trail. The rest is now buried under Lake Powell.

The Hole-in-the-Rock itself was the single most difficult part of the trail and rightly lent its name to the expedition, but in total, the portion of the trail that lay beyond the crossing of Glen Canyon was even more grueling. Certainly there was no hope of following the San Juan River, which came into the Colorado several miles below their crossing point. Steep cliffs came right down to the river making a high-ground trail the only alternative. Lizzie Decker wrote to her parents that this seemingly endless slickrock expanse was "the roughest country you or anybody else ever seen; it's nothing in the world but rocks and holes, hills and hollows. The mountains are just one solid rock as smooth as an apple." Still the band of Mormons pushed on, cutting numerous dugways to surmount the east side of Glen Canyon, then moving across the top of Gray Mesa, then swinging north to skirt long Cedar Mesa.

After crossing Cedar Mesa, the expedition dropped down into Comb Wash and stared up at the vertical, 800-foot west face of Comb Ridge—a cliff. Initially it seemed that the Mormons had no need to scratch out yet another dugway: their destination, Montezuma Creek, lay to the south, so they could turn down sandy but flat Comb Wash and bypass Comb Ridge by following the wash to the San Juan River. Having gone beyond the southern tip of Comb Ridge, they could then travel east along the river-bank the last 20 miles to their new townsite.

Comb Wash turned out to be sloggy, slow going in deep sand. By this time the pioneers had run short on food. Lizzie Decker's husband, Cornelius, recalled: "The night we got down into Comb Wash, just before we got to the San Juan River, our meat and everything else had give out on us. My dear wife and my two little boys had to eat dry bread for their supper. There is where I thought my heart would break; to see them go to bed with nothing but dry bread to eat." Worse yet, they were not done with their road construction work. They had assumed they could finish their trek down Comb Wash and make an easy left turn where the nose of Comb Wash hit the San Juan River. But the south edge of Comb Wash was a cliff tight up against the San Juan. It was impossible to drive their wagons between the base of the cliff and the river.

The exhausted troop built one last series of dugways up and over San Juan Hill, as the tip of Comb Ridge is called. Charlie Redd, the son of Lemuel Redd Jr., one of the Hole-in-the-Rock company, wrote this of his father's travails:

*Aside from the Hole-in-the-Rock itself, this was the steepest crossing on the journey. Here again seven span of horses were used, so that when some of the horses were on their knees, fighting to get up to find a foothold, the still-erect horses could plunge upward against the grade.*

# BEDROCK

*On the worst slopes the men were forced to beat their jaded animals into giving all they had. After several pulls, rests, and pulls, many of the horses took to spasms and near-convulsions, so exhausted were they. By the time most of the outfits were across, the worst stretches could easily be identified by the dried blood and matted hair from the forelegs of the struggling teams. My father [Lem Jr.] was a strong man, and reluctant to display emotion; but whenever in later years the full pathos of San Juan Hill was recalled either by himself or by someone else, the memory of such bitter struggles was too much for him and he wept.*

Yet, almost incredibly, during the backbreaking construction job up and over San Juan Hill, which took another eight days, the group continued to keep their spirits up by dancing to the fiddles each night, just as they had at Dance Hall Rock. On April 6, 1880, more than five months after setting out, they pulled into Cottonwood Wash, 6 miles to the east of San Juan Hill. For the exhausted, bedraggled pioneers, going on to Montezuma Creek was out of the question. Although the farming would be harder in this spot, they founded Bluff and decided to make it their new home. These Mormons had a way of submerging their own individual suffering in the pursuit of a much larger cause. Eliza Redd, who came on the Hole-in-the-Rock Trail and helped establish one of southern Utah's largest families (when I checked the San Juan County phone book, there were more Redds than Smiths or Joneses), seems to have caught the prevailing spirit. "Who goes through life without a little hardship? We came here to learn, not to suck a silver spoon."

The Hole-in-the-Rock Trail was just one part of the settlement of southern Utah and northern Arizona by Mormons. Between about 1875 and 1880, Brigham Young's determination, carried out by his successors, led to the establishment of dozens of communities from the Little Colorado River and the "Arizona Strip" (northwestern Arizona above the Grand Canyon) up to the Ute Reservation below the Uinta Range.

This was big country, and the Mormon population was small and their towns widely separated, but it was a time when a large population was unnecessary to gain control. Except for the Indian reservations, the federal government owned virtually all of the land, which was available to homesteaders on a first-come, first-served, basis. Mormon settlers homesteaded the bottomlands near the rivers for farming and obtained other prime parcels for townsites. The open range was there for the taking by whichever cattle or sheep outfit got there first. In southern Utah, the Mormons had to buy out some gentile sheepherders and cattlemen, but by the end of the century their cattle were running on tens of millions of acres.

The Saints took political control as well. Salt Lake City was watching the Hole-in-the-Rock Expedition closely; in February 1880, when the wagons were still struggling in the slickrock country west of Grand Gulch and before there were any settlements in the area, the Utah legislature created long and wide San Juan County, which was under Mormon control from the beginning. These rural areas, large in land, small in people, spoke loudly in the statehouses. Until the United States Supreme Court announced the "one person, one vote" requirement in 1962, the states allocated legislative seats equally to counties, not on the basis of population. In real terms, though the word "Deseret" was not spread across maps of the American West, the idea of Deseret and the vision of Brigham Young had played out with astonishing success. Much of the Colorado Plateau, especially in southern Utah, was Mormon country.

It remains so, one of the most distinctive cultural regions in the country. Monticello, Blanding, Escalante, Kanab, Price, and dozens of other small towns all bespeak the beehive and remain 70 or 80 percent or more Mormon. Ironically, Bluff is not one of them. The site did not contain enough arable land for all of the Hole-in-the-Rock families, and the San Juan River flooded too high and too often, regularly blowing out diversion works for irrigation. Most of those families moved on to establish other settlements—Lizzie and Cornelius Decker were called to Snowflake, Arizona, in 1885 and then to Colorado's San Luis Valley in 1887—and today Bluff has a population of just a few hundred, mostly gentiles.

Polygamy still plays a role in contemporary Mormon country. The taking of plural wives was official church doctrine when the Mormons staked their outposts on the Plateau, and the early towns had strong polygamous traditions. After the 1890 Manifesto, the practice declined but did not vanish. On the Plateau there are still scattered polygamous families, a few settlements consisting of clusters of families, and one substantial polygamous community—the adjacent towns of Hildale, Utah, and Colorado City, Arizona, which straddle the state line south of Zion National Park, built under a striking stretch of the Vermilion Cliffs.

Colorado City and Hildale, however, are aberrant. In the mainstream Mormon towns, traditions are reflected in tithing and an extraordinary commitment of time to church activities. Most young people go on two-year missions and, as in the Deckers' and Brigham Young's time, adults are sometimes called away for service in some far place, which today is likely to be overseas.

Mormonism continues to be a culture as well as a religion. Mormon settlements are the tidiest communities around. It seems as though they must send the teenagers out on youth activity nights, held on Tuesdays or Wednesdays, to clean the streets with toothbrushes. If Americans subconsciously equate well-tended lawns with worthiness, then these towns are the most worthy. You find here the maximum of hard, honest work, father–son barbeques, mother–daughter sewing bees, church dances, and across-the-back-fence conversations.

The stance of the Mormon communities of the Colorado Plateau toward the outside world is a different matter. All of the pain, commitment, and sacrifice from the Hole-in-the-Rock Expedition and the many other journeys of the 1870s and 1880s, and all the accomplishments since, are as tangible to these inhabitants as the slickrock itself. People were uprooted from their homes to come to this once uninhabited and inhospitable land. In their minds, they were the ones, chosen by the Lord, who brought civilization here, and it was hard. As one long-time rancher, Hardy Redd, told me, they were the people "who built the roads, set boundaries for the Indians, built the hospitals, and kept the peace."

The federal government—never mind that it owns most of the land—can stay out. So can the gentiles, including, to be sure, outside lawyers pressing Indian rights. This is Zion. From the inside, these communities are nurturing and industrious to a new and higher degree. But to many outsiders, including the Navajo, whose lands run up to the south bank of the San Juan River, the Mormon settlements more closely resemble clenched fists. And they continue to hold more ground, and control more decisions, than their numbers would ever suggest.

# COYOTE

**I**f the San Juan County school case could trace its origins in part to the cauldron of the Mormon experience, the history of Indian education also helped explain the substandard schools on the Navajo Reservation, the long bus rides to Anglo towns, and the assimilationist curriculum. Education of Indians in white America has been mostly an exercise designed not just to instruct the minds of Native American children but also to change their minds by erasing their Indianness. A few Indians obtained good educations from this campaign, but until recently American education has been a confusing, battering experience for Native people. Learning mathematics or English literature, after all, does not require that an Indian child forsake a traditional hairstyle, the Gray Horse Dances, or grandfather's Coyote sto-

Coyote

ries. Nevertheless, assimilation into American society and conversion to Christianity dominated education policy toward Indians for well over a century. The Navajo children of San Juan County were no exception.

In the early 1800s, Christian denominations bent on converting Indians began establishing mission schools in Indian country. Congress regularly appropriated funds for these ventures—ignoring the separation of church and state during an era when Indians seemed beyond the Constitution. Although many of the treaties called for the United States to provide reservation schools, this approach had mixed results. (At Navajo, the 1868 treaty called for a schoolhouse but the Navajo simply refused to go.)

The federal government instituted a new and ambitious program in 1879 when it created a system of off-reservation boarding schools for Indian children. The elderly Pawnee men I met in Oklahoma faced typical, not aberrational, treatment in these Bureau of Indian Affairs (BIA) schools when they had their braids cut off, their mouths washed out with yellow lye soap for speaking their native language, and the earrings torn from their ears. Forced assimilation was official policy from the beginning in the BIA schools. "Kill the Indian in him," preached R. H. Pratt, the first superintendent of the Carlisle Indian Boarding School, "and save the man."

This potent combination of religion, education, and assimilation has been a main force in Indian affairs. The influence of the churches, both in Congress and on the reservations, has been pervasive. Christian reformers, for example, lobbied for the allotment policy of 1887, which cost Indians at Navajo and elsewhere tens of millions of acres by locating them on smaller agricultural plots: large hunting grounds would no longer be necessary, the thinking went, since Indians would be transformed into farmers—and Christians. Today, virtually every Christian denomination has a church on the Navajo Reservation.

Despite the persistence of the churches' campaigns, the impact of outside religions has been surprisingly limited. In fact there is a resurgence of traditional Indian religions all across the country, certainly at Navajo. Indians commonly joke about how they may go to the Christian church on Sunday morning, mainly to please their local minister, whom they like, but how they then head home, don their traditional garb, and hold the old ceremonies. As one scholar explains, this is powerfully true among the Navajo, where the traditional worldview remains vigorous:

> *The overwhelming majority of the Navajo today share a consciousness of belonging to a national reality, the Diné, "The People." . . . Navajo concepts concerning their own time and space—the primeval four cosmic ages and the four corners of their universe, all rich in symbolism— are full of vigor today. This explains the emotional attachment each individual feels for the sacred universe he inhabits, Navajoland. . . . [A]lthough Christianity has made some inroads, most Navajo have their spiritual roots in their ancient beliefs and practices, of which their language is the conveyor of meaning.*

Once I observed a conversation about how the Navajo and Anglo worldviews interact. A non-Indian man, sincere and intellectually curious, asked Peterson Zah, by then tribal chairman, to explain the Navajo creation myth. Pete paused. "It is not a myth. But I would be glad to tell you about it." He explained the location of the four sacred peaks, speaking, as many Indian people do, with his hands as much as his voice. With the gentle rolling motions of his hands, palms down, it was as if he were caressing the land within the peaks on the imaginary map on the ground in front of him. Then he pointed carefully to each of the sacred mountains, beginning in the east. Mount Taylor (*Tsoodzil*), outside of Grants, New Mexico. The San Francisco Peaks (*Dook' 'o' ooslid*) to the south, near Flagstaff. Hesperus Peak (*Dibé nitsaa*) to the west, above Cortez and Durango in the La Plata Mountains. Mount Blanca (*Sisnaajini*) to the north, across Colorado's San Luis Valley.

"That is Navajoland. Man and First Woman rose up from the earth into this, the Fourth World, from a place near Huerfano Mountain, which is not far from Chaco Canyon."

There was a silence. Then the non-Indian man asked how this could be true in light of the scientific evidence that the Navajo are Athabaskans who came to the Southwest only about six hundred years ago.

# Coyote

Pete paused, to show respect, I think, rather than to reflect. Then he replied: "Both versions are true."

"How can that be?" the non-Indian asked.

"It depends," Pete said, "on where you are, in what context you are in."

This conversation took place deep within Canyon de Chelly, on the dusty canyon floor where the rose-colored walls enveloped us, moved us with their dignity, and became a participant in the conversation. Here, in this land, which had shaped Pete's thinking as much as his formal college education at Arizona State University, Pete's explanation, once given, seemed reasonable—inevitable really. Reality depends on what place you are in and what the people there believe.

The zeal of the LDS Church to change the Navajo worldview has configured a long and exceptional saga. The Mormons, with their fixation on Indians, the Navajo in particular, have expended more energy, with more impact, on Navajos in the Utah part of the reservation than has any other religion. Beginning in the 1870s, Jacob Hamblin, the "Apostle in Buckskins," proselytized incessantly among the Navajo, who in his view, along with the Hopi, were the "nobler branches of the [Indian] race."

Thousands of Mormons have followed in Hamblin's tracks. The most aggressive Mormon thrust into Navajo culture since World War II was the Indian Student Placement Program. Church members recruited Indian parents to allow their children to live in Mormon homes during the school year—and often during the summer as well. Navajo children, the argument went, would benefit from being in schools of a higher caliber than they could attend at home. However well-meaning the participating families, the program was aimed, of course, directly at the children's minds: in addition to being removed from their homes and tribes, the children faced intense pressure to convert.

The Indian Student Placement Program reached its height during our work on the school case, with some five thousand Indian children from various tribes living in Mormon homes. The president of the LDS Church, alluding to longstanding Mormon doctrine on skin color, proclaimed the program a success: "The children in the home placement program in Utah are often lighter than their brothers and sisters in the hogans on the reservations." (A few years later, in 1979, the reference in the *Book of Mormon* to converted Indians—Lamanites—becoming "white and delightsome" was changed, in one of the few textual revisions ever made, to "pure and delightsome.")

In the early 1970s, there were nearly fifty LDS congregations on the Navajo Reservation, with more than 120 Mormon missionaries advocating Mormonism in general and the Indian Student Placement Program in particular. In terms of numbers, the crusade had considerable success. One writer estimated that the Mormons had baptized forty thousand Navajos, nearly 20 percent of the tribe. The same writer, however, along with others, doubted the depth of those figures: only a small percentage of Navajos actually "use that faith to guide their lives." The Indian Student Placement Program drew heated criticism from Indians and non-Indians alike, however, and has now been reduced to fewer than five hundred children living in Mormon homes.

**B**y the summer of 1974, I was spending more than half of my time on the San Juan County school case. In addition to Eric Swenson, Herb Yazzie, and Rick Collins at DNA, John Wabaunsee, a Potawatomi Indian who had just joined NARF, was on the case. Robert Anderson, an attorney in Monticello, represented the school district. I liked and trusted Anderson, a fair-minded man who would try to reach an agreement with us, rather than litigating, if he thought our case had merit. In the hope of settling the case without a lawsuit, we told Anderson that we would hold off filing our complaint until we had completed our research and held settlement discussions.

We had a long trail to walk. In addition to legal research, we had to sift through boxes of school district records copied by a DNA paralegal. To present a complete picture of the school district's practices, the idea was to put basic data for every student into a computer—race, age, school, miles from school, days missed from school, absences from school, and school-year results (promotion, dropout, or retention)—so that we could quantify the disparities between Navajo and Anglo students. For the elementary schools, we wanted to make comparisons, again by computer, between the reservation schools and the northern schools using a whole range of categories—teacher salaries, student/teacher ratios, square footage of buildings, and expenditures for libraries, materials, school lunches, and building maintenance—to show the inequality between the schools.

We expected substantial disparities—at least as egregious as the chart Paul Smith presented in the Gallup-McKinley case—and believed these statistics would give the district an incentive to settle. We also needed to analyze all the school district's records, everything from school board minutes to grant proposals to the correspondence files. NARF hired paralegal Rick Nordwall, a Pawnee, to work full-time on the case and Ken Red Horse, a Navajo computer expert, to input the statistical data Rick had organized. Poor Ken. This was before keyboard entry. He had to enter the data by punching holes on those old-fashioned computer cards.

After exchanging correspondence with the lawyers for the school district, we had one negotiation session in Monticello. By now Robert Anderson, the local school board attorney, had retained as cocounsel Brigham Roberts, one of the best trial lawyers in Utah and a direct descendant of you-know-who. But Roberts was a "jack" Mormon—one who no longer practices the faith—and went by the name of Bob. Negotiating in good faith, both sides agreed on quite a number of matters regarding the process for sharing and analyzing the data that were now starting to pour out of Ken's computer.

But obstacles to settlement had begun to emerge. For our part, we were determined that the district must build two high schools on the reservation. We were flexible on the details, but the Navajo parents were unwavering on the unacceptability—the immorality—of the busing and on the need for those schools.

# BEDROCK

On its side, the school board was, as we learned from teachers who sided with the Navajo, becoming ever more intransigent. Although the two Navajo board members empathized with the students, this was a five-person board. We never examined whether the voting districts for the school board were gerrymandered, but it sure looked that way. In a county where the electorate was split almost evenly between Navajos and Anglos, two districts up north were virtually all Anglo, two in the south even more heavily Navajo. In the middle was a mostly Anglo district that included part of Blanding and all of Bluff, with nearby areas of high Navajo population carved out and assigned to one of the southern districts. This arrangement assured an Anglo majority on the school board. However collegial their lawyers might be, the three Anglo school board members were not interested, thank you, in being told by a bunch of lawyers—and Navajo—how to run the San Juan County, Utah, School District.

Official opposition to building high schools on the Navajo Reservation extended beyond the school board. In those days, San Juan County politics was the domain of County Commissioner Calvin Black, the prototype for Edward Abbey's Bishop Love who led the furious chases after the Monkey Wrench Gang. Black, the ultimate period piece, personified a deep current in southern Utah culture. He hated environmentalists—outsiders who were out to deny him his living (Black made a fortune in uranium and selling relics obtained by digging up archaeological sites) and San Juan County its destiny (its considerable tax base rested primarily on mining). He wore a bolo tie with a hunk of uranium ore as its centerpiece and once drank a uranium cocktail at a public hearing to show his disdain for the environmentalists' "pantywaist" arguments. Indian lawyers from out-of-state, every bit as much as the environmentalists, were outsiders. So, for that matter, were the Navajo. Black was not in the least amused by the idea that the school district might use its hard-earned uranium tax revenues to build schools south of the river. As far as he was concerned, San Juan County Anglos, and no one else, would run San Juan County.

When we told the two school district lawyers about our impression of mounting opposition on the school board and county commission, they admitted the problem but wanted to continue the negotiations. The school board still could be persuaded if our evidence were strong enough and, in the last analysis, the county commission, even Cal Black, would defer to the school board. Eric wanted to sue immediately, but he reluctantly agreed that we should try one last time for an out-of-court settlement. He acknowledged the wisdom in Pete Zah's belief that the complicated matter of actually building the schools would go much more smoothly if we were on a cooperative basis with the district.

We scheduled a negotiating session with the two school district lawyers for November 4, 1974, in Salt Lake City. In my briefcase I had the complaint, so that we could file the lawsuit if the negotiations failed. Anderson and Roberts made a long statement on why we should hold off longer. They explained the school district's situation at length. Until the 1950s, the district had no responsibility at all to educate the Navajo children. Before then, the BIA educated Indian children through government boarding schools and day schools. The Navajo Reservation alone had some fifty day schools. Then, during the termination era of the 1950s, in an attempt to bring Indians into the mainstream, Congress shut down many of the BIA schools and gave to the states the funding and responsibility for educating most Indian children. At that point, the lawyers emphasized, the two high schools had already been built in Monticello and Blanding.

Further, they argued, the school district was caught off-guard by the rapid increase in Navajo school attendance. In 1958, the first year in which Navajo enrolled in district schools, there were only 142 Navajo students, just 6 percent of the total enrollment. Even ten years ago, the figure was only 12 percent. In the past decade, however, because increasing numbers of Navajo children were deciding to go to school and because of the high birthrate among the Navajo, the figure soared to 46 percent.

Robert Anderson, who lived in the community and knew all the board members well, said he was convinced that the district was making progress. After all, lawyers for the Navajo had contacted the district less than a year ago. The board was determined to equalize the elementary schools if a study, due to be completed within a few months, showed that inequities existed. As for the high schools, that was a complex and expensive matter. Putting two high schools on the reservation might do nothing more than create schools too small to be educationally viable. And if you pull the Navajo children out of San Juan High School in Blanding—where almost all of the Navajo were—that school, too, might lack the critical mass necessary to function at a high educational level. Last, the board doesn't yet know the will of the people. Do the Navajo really want their own segregated schools? Do the Mormon communities support this? And suppose the Justice Department finds that these two high schools would be illegally segregated under *Brown v. Board of Education?* Would that mean some Anglo children would have to be bused down to the reservation to equalize things?

Anderson and Roberts had, I thought to myself, most of their history right. Indian education had traditionally been left to the BIA, and the numbers of Navajo children in district schools definitely had accelerated over the last ten to fifteen years. Our review of the school district files, though, showed a notable lack of concern—in some cases callousness and outright hostility—about the reservation. Several reports warned that future population growth in the district would be on the reservation and more educational facilities would be needed. The hardships of the busing were well known. Delegations of Navajo parents had gone to Monticello to complain to the board. No recent school construction at all, elementary or secondary, had taken place on the reservation. As for the will of the Navajo parents, there was no doubt about that: they wanted reservation schools for their children.

When the attorneys finished, Eric asked: "You know, the uranium boom in San Juan County has made you the richest or second richest school district in Utah, one of the richest in the West. Your assessed valuation is unbelievably high. But right now you have the lowest mil levy in the state. How sympathetic is a federal judge going to be with that?"

Robert Anderson replied: "You have to make your decision about filing based on your judgment as to what is best for your clients. I wish this were moving more rapidly. But I am firmly convinced that substantial progress is being made and I think the board will soon make some meaningful decisions about additional facilities."

We ended the meeting and Eric, John Wabaunsee, and I went outside on the sidewalk to decide what to do.

Eric spoke up immediately. "Charles, we've got to file this lawsuit. I know you think those lawyers are playing straight with us, and I don't disagree with that, but it's the school board that makes this decision. And I'm telling you they are not about to build some new schools on the Navajo Reservation. If they do come around, it'll be for one reason and one reason only, which is that they're staring down the barrel of a lawsuit. We've waited too damn long already."

I knew that Eric was right and told him so. Besides, filing a complaint just begins a lawsuit. This particular complaint would generate a lot of anger in the northern part of the county, but over the course of a few months, that initial reaction would taper off. We could revisit a settlement then. It was getting late in the afternoon and Eric told me to go ahead and get my plane. He'd take the complaint, styled as *Sinajini v. Board of Education,* and file it in federal court.

**Y**es, I thought to myself on the plane ride back to Denver, Eric was definitely right. The statistics coming out of the computers were devastating. Some 209 Indian students were being bused to San Juan High School. Their average roundtrip distance was almost exactly 100 miles. Indian students living at Red Mesa were bused 112 miles roundtrip, those in Oljato 166 miles. The average student spent three hours a day on a bus, traveling 15,000 miles a year. This was the equivalent of ninety student days physically riding to and from school. The students at the end of the longest bus routes traveled 30,000 miles each school year—a distance greater than the earth's circumference.

Moreover, I had seen with my own eyes that the disparities between the elementary schools were far worse than I had first supposed. The schools

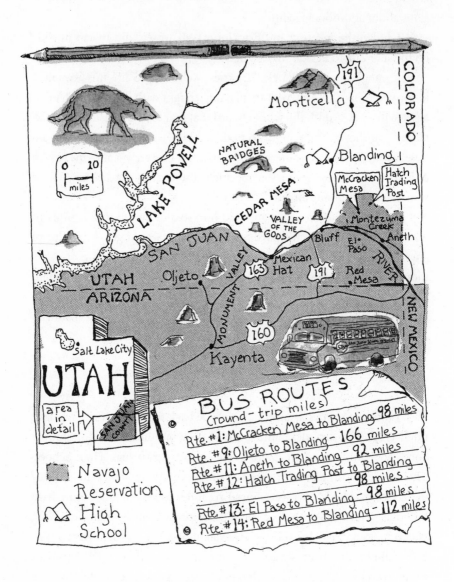

COLORADO

191

Monticello

NATURAL
BRIDGES

0    10
miles

LAKE POWELL

CEDAR MESA

VALLEY
OF THE
GODS

Blanding

McCracken
Mesa

Hatch
Trading
Post

Montezuma
Creek

Aneth

SAN JUAN

Bluff

El
Paso

RIVER

Oljeto

MONUMENT VALLEY

163

Mexican
Hat

191

Red
Mesa

NEW MEXICO

UTAH
ARIZONA

160

Salt Lake City

UTAH

area
in
detail

SAN JUAN COUNTY

Kayenta

Navajo
Reservation
High
School

BUS ROUTES
(round-trip miles)

Rte. #1: McCracken Mesa to Blanding- 98 miles
Rte. #9: Oljeto to Blanding- 166 miles
Rte. #11: Aneth to Blanding- 92 miles
Rte. #12: Hatch Trading Post to Blanding
- 98 miles
Rte. #13: El Paso to Blanding- 98 miles
Rte. #14: Red Mesa to Blanding- 112 miles

# Coyote

in Monticello and Blanding were superb facilities: attractive, roomy, and well equipped. The elementary schools in the south were demonstrably—depressingly—run-down and inferior. They were all overcrowded, and all used mobile classrooms. They variously lacked separate libraries, lunch rooms, and gyms. Our preliminary computer numbers showed that they received sharply lower expenditures in every spending category: instructional, facilities, school lunches, and so forth. I knew the statistics just scratched the surface, but my trips to San Juan County as well as reports from parents, students, and Navajo elders, made me appreciate how deeply the busing tore into the children's educations, the family structure, and the sense of community.

The busing sapped the energy from the children. The length of the bus routes actually understated the burden because most of the children lived miles from the bus stops. Either they walked to the bus stops or were bounced along unimproved, four-wheel trails in their parents' pickups. Rain or snow made the dirt roads even slower going; the twisty asphalt roads turned treacherous. Children had to leave home by 5:30, 6:00, and 6:30 A.M. On many days, children would leave home, and arrive back, in the dark. Eating was prohibited on the buses. One student said: "They should put reclining seats on these buses so we can sleep." Another groaned, "I wish they'd just let us eat a roll or something."

The long distances kept most of these children out of sports and other extracurricular activities. For years no activity buses served the reservation. By the early 1970s, the district did run two activity buses but only as far as Mexican Hat and Montezuma Creek. The buses arrived at 6:00 or 6:30 P.M. One track student, who lived 10 miles from the Mexican Hat bus stop, ran home each night. A boy over on the Montezuma Creek side did the same thing. Most just took the regular bus home and did without sports and the other after-school activities.

This was not just an ordeal of a day, a month, or a year. For every single Navajo child on the Utah part of the reservation, getting a high school diploma from San Juan County was a long-distance endurance run. Students on the Mexican Hat–Oljato side had to do it for four years; children over by Montezuma Creek and Red Mesa (where elementary school was K–6) did it for six years.

And it was just as bad, in some ways worse, for the huge numbers of Navajo children, especially in the outlying areas, who did not ride the buses. The busing drove children out of school: many dropped out (San Juan High School had the highest dropout rate in Utah) and others never enrolled at all (compulsory attendance laws counted for little in that big country). Many parents sent their children away to BIA boarding schools so they would not have to endure the busing.

The specter of busing was a perfect entrée for the Mormons who so persistently pushed the Indian Student Placement Program. Spare your children this. Let them spend the school year with a good family in Blanding . . . or Monticello . . . or Price . . . or Salt Lake City . . . or Orange County, California. It will be best for the children. Do your duty for your children.

All of this ate away at Navajo family traditions. Nearly 75 percent of the homes had no electricity or running water. Children had always been part of the rhythm of tending the sheep, hauling water, sweeping out the hogan, gathering the juniper. But now the long school days left them too exhausted to do their chores.

And uncounted numbers of Navajo children missed the Coyote stories. The grandfathers tell the stories to the children, but by strict tradition they can be told only when the days grow short, between the first killing frost of autumn and the first lightning strike of spring.

Coyote is a little of everything. No—he's a lot of everything. He's the smartest guy in the world but also the stupidest. He is a trickster, outsmarting the other animals and humans, too. He is a fool. Coyote has yellow eyes. This happened when he threw his eyes up in the air so they would come back down with long-range vision but, when they came down, the only difference was that they had pine pitch all over them. He is curious, which always gets him in trouble, like with the porcupine and the skunk.

Coyote is lazier than anybody. Even if it takes him all day and all of his energy, he will steal food so he doesn't have to do the dishes. His appetites

# Coyote

for food, sex, and fun far outstrip his abilities to think his way out of the predicaments those appetites get him into. In one story he explodes from all the food he stole from someone. He's always chasing around after women, and the brothers of the virgins he deflowers find him and punish him.

Coyote has a streak of wisdom. When the people entered this above-ground world, they wanted to know what would become of them. So one of them threw a stick into the water and said: "If it floats, we will all live forever. If it sinks, we shall all die someday." It floated, and they were happy. Then Coyote picked up a stone and said: "If it floats, we will all live forever. But if it sinks, everybody will die sooner or later." Then he threw it in and it sank. The people got angry and wanted to throw Coyote in, too, in hopes that he would sink. But he said: "If we all went on living and the women kept on having babies, pretty soon there would be no room for anyone here. Isn't it better that we live for a while and then die and make room for the younger people?" The people had to agree that he was right, so they let him alone.

New Coyote stories keep emerging. One Indian friend told me one of his. "I was sniffing the bushes one day," my friend began, "and came nose to nose with Coyote. We had a chit-chat and some latté. I asked him how he felt about all those Santa-Fe-kerchief-wearing-kewpie-doll coyote images you see everywhere now. 'Isn't that demeaning?' I asked Coyote."

"'Well,' Coyote drawled, 'it's a helluva lot better than a tailful of double-aught for being a mangy, chicken-stealing mongrel. Besides,' he showed his teeth in a grin, 'the chicks all think I'm a star and won't leave me alone.'"

Some of the old Coyote stories are among the raunchiest, bloodiest stories anyone can imagine. They don't seem to be children's stories, as we think of them, but they are. They alternately amuse and frighten children into remembering the cultural principles hidden in the stories. Coyote is the best and worst in all of us.

Some Coyote stories are also skinwalker narratives. Skinwalkers are people who dress themselves in the skins of various animals, notably coyotes, and travel around doing harm to people. They cover ground with the speed of a wolf. So you might see a skinwalker in one town and when you drive to the next town, the skinwalker is already there even though he doesn't have a car. Skinwalkers are witches and they own the night, all over Navajoland, one-fifth of the Colorado Plateau.

The Navajo use skinwalker stories to frighten their children into the correct behavior. If the kids are not good, skinwalkers will get them when they are out at night. Skinwalkers know who is being bad. "If you know about skinwalkers," one Navajo told me, "then you know why those kids were scared to walk a couple of miles in the dark to meet those buses."

The Navajo parents all complained about busing and Coyote. So did the medicine men, tight-lipped, smoldering. The children who rode the buses were too bone-marrow tired to keep their eyes open, even for grandfather, even for Coyote. There were no grandfathers in the boarding schools. Coyote was unwelcome in the prim Mormon homes where Navajo children in the Indian Student Placement Program were placed. You can only tell about Coyote during the winter. How can you have educations without Coyote? Educations without grandfather?

**W**ith the complaint filed, we requested an early trial date and stepped up our preparation. Depositions were the next order of business. We wanted to take sworn testimony from school district administrators and board members and, as well, to depose Navajo witnesses on the reservation. This would preserve their testimony for use at trial. For the Navajo, some of whom had never left the reservation, it was a long way to Salt Lake City, where the trial would be held.

Robert Anderson and I talked about depositions and he said that he would cooperate in setting them up. There were many logistical details. Since we planned on deposing about forty witnesses, we would need as much as two weeks. Some depositions would be in Monticello and Blanding, some in various locales at Navajo. We agreed to begin on February 26, 1975. Anderson would make available all the witnesses from the school district. As a last matter, I asked him whom he recommended as a court reporter.

"I was thinking you might get to that," he said.

Sensing a smile at the other end of the line, I asked him what he meant.

"Well, there isn't a private court reporter in San Juan County or, for that matter, as far as I know, in southern Utah. The local judge's court reporter usually has some time free but couldn't possibly schedule a job of this size. As a matter of fact, as far as I can tell, there's never even *been* a deposition taken on the reservation in San Juan County. I suppose you'll have to bring somebody in from Salt Lake City or Denver."

We did get a court reporter from Denver, and on February 24, John Wabaunsee, Rick Nordwall, Dan Rosenfelt (a cooperating attorney from the Harvard Center for Law and Education), Carol Wickham (our court reporter), and I got on a plane to Grand Junction. We had enough baggage—clothes for two weeks, several cartons of files, and Carol's court reporting equipment—that we rented a station wagon at the airport and headed out in high spirits through the crisp air on the three-hour drive to Monticello.

Although depositions are used mainly to gain information from the other side and sometimes, as here, to preserve testimony for use at trial, we had another objective in mind as well. We all agreed on the advantages of settling the case, if we could do it on the right terms. We decided to use these depositions to show the strength of our case. As a trial strategy, this carried some risks. (I remember taking a deposition in San Francisco and scoring what I thought were many points. Then, at the deposition's conclusion, I was treated to the gray-haired opposing attorney's outstretched hand and salutation, "Thanks, counsel, for previewing your trial strategy.") Still, we decided to gamble. A good series of depositions might set the stage for resolving this case and getting the schools built.

The first week of depositions did go well. School district officials had little luck justifying why, with the obvious surge in school-age children on the reservation, they hadn't taken some action or at least commissioned a serious study. They had no luck at all in explaining why a district with such a solid tax base and so little bonded indebtedness couldn't now get started with construction. District staff also testified that the two schools on the reservation probably would be large enough to be educationally viable.

On Saturday we worked in the DNA office in Mexican Hat to prepare for the next week's depositions, which would be held on the reservation. Late in the afternoon, Eric suggested we take some time off. "I've got a place I want to show you." His grin, almost as broad as John Echohawk's, spoke absolute assurance.

**M**oki Dugway takes off from the sagebrush, blackbrush, and bunchgrass high-desert floor just north of Mexican Hat, Utah. This is the steep, switch-back route, widened and improved over the years, angling up the 1,500-foot-high east side of Cedar Mesa, which runs north and south, 30 miles long, 5 to 10 miles wide. Geographically this mesa is at the center of the Colorado Plateau. Emotionally, too, Cedar Mesa is at the center: the heart-land for the Old People, the Ancestral Puebloans who lived for centuries in the canyons that drape down off Cedar Mesa.

We ascended Moki Dugway in Eric's station wagon. The burnished redrock residents of the Valley of the Gods look up from directly below. Out to the east lie clay cliffs with patterns that cause them to be called Nav-ajo Rug and, far beyond them, the foothills of the mountains of Colorado.

Once on top of Cedar Mesa, the low, scrubby piñon-juniper forest gives some cover. We turned off Moki Dugway onto a rough dirt road that heads toward the southern tip of Cedar Mesa. As we drove, the piñon and juniper rose up just high enough, and the bumpy road was tucked down in a shal-low indentation just low enough, that I was not much aware of distances. Eric parked and we walked toward a lip of rocks, just this side of the edge of Cedar Mesa.

When I came over the lip, my whole body started. It was as if some invisible person had placed the flats of his or her hands, gently but firmly,

# Coyote

up against my chest, straightened me up, and stopped me in my tracks. I imagine Eric felt the same. I imagine everyone has, back through all the deep millennia.

For you are looking out at the whole world.

This point sits directly above the most distinctive stretch of the San Juan River, one of the largest tributaries of the Colorado. The Goosenecks is a 20-mile stretch of the San Juan where the river weaves and bends and meanders and wraps back and forth through the limestone formations. In a few places, at the very bottom of the winding, deep-cut canyon that is the Goosenecks, you can catch glimpses of the red-brown San Juan itself, nearly a mile below.

By then I'd spent several weeks, off and on, in San Juan County, and I'd met with many Navajos, who almost always talked about the land. I had done a lot of driving and begun the practice of pulling over and exploring around. Yet we'd been working so hard on the school case that I had not given enough attention to the landscape. Now, with some time and a chance to survey so much, I began to consolidate the pieces of information I had learned.

Straight out to the south, beyond the Goosenecks, lies Monument Valley, on Navajo land. Dozens upon dozens upon dozens of orange and red monuments—massive, free-standing sandstone formations, hundreds of feet tall. North Mitten. South Mitten. Squaw Dance Mesa. The Three Sisters. *Natani Tso*—"Big Leader." The Dancers—Yei-bi-chai Formation. The Castle. Thunderbird Mesa. They don't seem to be 20 miles away, as in fact they are. From the tip of Cedar Mesa, Monument Valley is close up, intimate.

I scanned the whole vast country, all the places I had picked out on the maps or seen from ground level, all now taking on new meaning as parts of this sweeping tableau. There's the tip of stately Shiprock—the Rock with Wings—80 miles to the east. Even farther out, the high, hazy San Juans of the Colorado Rockies. The Carrizo and Chuska mountains across the southeastern sky. On the distant rim to the southwest, San Francisco Peaks, one of the Navajo's four sacred mountains. Spread across the south horizon is broad Black Mesa, the mystery within all the mystery, the sacred homeland of the Hopi.

Quietly I told Eric that I was stunned, without words, had never seen anything like this.

"Look," he said, "go off by yourself and just take it in. Take as long as you want."

Gratified by the suggestion, I walked over to a sturdy ledge that reached out into the void and sat down, my legs dangling over the edge. One by one I picked out the settlements, mesas, and monuments that Eric and the Navajo people had mentioned so often. The low, slanting sun, which did its best work at the end of the day, turned the west-facing sandstone walls into a smoldering red.

I found time, too, looking out from the southern tip of Cedar Mesa onto this seemingly boundless landscape, most of it still Indian country, to reflect about other things. Now, two years later, I held even more dearly the realization I had received in the shower in Albuquerque. Doing this work, doing it in the West, was fulfilling beyond anything I could have dreamed of as a boy, in law school, as a young lawyer. It was such a gift, so tangible, as real as my hands or my voice. Now, my thoughts as free as a hawk riding the wind currents, gliding at the same level as my high-mesa ledge, I realized something else. Now I knew why it had happened: why I was here.

My father was a passionate man, but racism seemed to draw out his deepest emotions. He grew up in the Old South, in Atlanta. Yet virtually alone among his peers, I would imagine, he had seen the treatment of blacks for what it was. He must have had bitter arguments with his grade school friends, even with his colleagues at medical school, for bigotry was nearly as rampant in the post–World War II North in the South. He must have said to many of them, and in the same fervid way, what he said to us kids. "Wrong, just as wrong as it can be," he would say, striking a fist on the dinner table. "Don't ever look down on another person because of their skin." Even as a little boy, I could sense the fire raging in him. Now, looking out from my ledge across the expanses of a hundred miles and the thirty-four years of my life, I fully understood that his passion had become an inspiration for me.

Unwilling to forgive his other side, the beatings and the ridicule, I was reluctant to concede so much to him. But it was true. His fire had brought me here, to the southern tip of Cedar Mesa, to Navajo, to the Colorado Plateau.

**D**uring the second week of depositions, the Navajo witnesses testified for two full days in Mexican Hat and one at the Chapter House in Red Mesa. Many observers, as well as witnesses, turned out. Robert Anderson had brought two Anglo board members so they could form their own impressions. Twenty-five Navajo people—students, parents, grandparents, medicine men—quietly and patiently told their stories under oath, mostly through interpreters. Everyone from the outside was moved. The Navajo's long and dignified procession constituted a powerful testament to their people's determination to preserve for Navajo children both the old stories and modern education. This was *their* case. The lawyers were just another kind of interpreter.

Afterward, outside the Red Mesa Chapter House, Robert Anderson called Eric, Herb, and me over. A decent and sensitive man, he knew it was time to settle this case. "Let's get together tomorrow morning in my office up in Monticello and see what we can figure out."

The negotiations took several meetings and numerous letters, back and forth, but finally we reached an agreement. The district would equalize the expenditures and facilities between the northern elementary schools and the reservation schools. It would adopt a bilingual program. It would build the two high schools on the reservation "at the earliest possible date." The school board was to use its own judgment as to how to achieve these and other objectives. In October 1975 Federal District Court Judge Aldon Anderson approved the Agreement of Parties. Pete Zah's hope of avoiding a contentious trial and seeking cooperation had been fulfilled.

# BEDROCK

The school board referred the issue of construction funds for the new schools to the voters in a bond election. We thought the judge would probably require the district to spend the funds even if the bond issue was defeated in the election. But that was the question of judicial power we wanted to avoid from the beginning. The election was set for November 11, 1975.

For the Navajo in southern Utah, this was their moment. The Navajo chapters, working with DNA, put top priority on the bond election. It was a powerhouse of an information, voter registration, and get-out-the-vote drive. Herb Yazzie held bilingual community meetings to explain the issues in the election. Even though the ballot description was set out in Navajo as well as English, not all Navajo speakers read the language. So the Navajo put up signs all around of a Navajo man, his hair tied in the traditional bun, with a thought cloud of a school over his head. On top of that was "Yes." Next to him was the same man with the same thought cloud but with a slash through it. "No" was on top.

Navajo drivers rose early on election day. All the pickup trucks were activated. Fleets of them headed out from Mexican Hat, Montezuma Creek, all the little settlements, trucks peeling off at every rutted road to visit every last hogan, to give every last Navajo a ride to the polls to vote for the children. The turnout was unbelievable. A huge, though ultimately unknowable, percentage of Navajos had registered—and nearly every registered voter voted that day. At 98 percent, Navajo Mountain had the highest voter turnout.

When the votes were tallied, the reservation had gone overwhelmingly in favor of the school bonds. Up north, the schools received a one-third favorable vote—within the range that Pete Zah had hoped for from the beginning. Overall the bonds passed easily, by a 61–39 percent margin. The first school to open was Whitehorse High School in Montezuma Creek, in August, 1978. Monument Valley High School opened two years later.

There have been some continuing problems for Navajos in the San Juan County schools. The Monument Valley school had faulty construction; part of the foundation had subsided and cracked. Worse, as one Navajo woman told me, the school was built on a burial site. Eric, who was left to carry the laboring oar (Herb Yazzie went off to law school and then to the Navajo Attorney General's Office, Rick Collins and I to teaching law), was convinced that the district never did fully equalize expenditures and facilities in the elementary schools. Twice he went back into court, asking the judge to enforce the consent decree's provisions, and twice he came out with mixed results. We may have erred in allowing the school district so much discretion in the agreement. Still, the elementary schools are vastly improved, the millstone of busing is gone from the necks of Navajo children, and at all the schools the imprint of Navajo culture is unmistakable.

In the years since, one thought keeps nudging into the corner of my mind, a thought about the relationship between the course of human events and the Colorado Plateau itself. What would the voter turnout have been in that big, rough country if winter weather had hit that November election day? How many pickups would have slid off the back roads into mucky red sand up to their axles? How many Navajo drivers, taught the polite way all their lives, would have thought, no, I can't push the elders into a long drive to town in this kind of weather? Could sly Coyote, wanting his name in the lights of grandfather's stories, have tricked that gathering storm into taking a detour?

I did not see either of the new high schools until 1990. Ann and I had managed to get away on a pleasure trip, the boys safely at home with our best babysitter. We went to Hovenweep National Monument on the Utah–Colorado line. March: such a fine time of year on the Plateau. Mesa Verde is still quiet then, and once I spent nearly a whole day at Chaco Canyon and saw just three other people.

This afternoon Ann and I had Hovenweep all to ourselves. We wandered among the square and circular watchtowers and dwellings. They faced east from this tight canyon, straight toward Sleeping Ute Mountain, now with its top third snow-covered. We talked about how the Ancestral

# BEDROCK

Puebloans might have felt about the mountain, whether it was calming or threatening or mystical, or some combination.

Montezuma Creek was well out of our way, but we both wanted to go by the school. Our reverie at Hovenweep had given us the gift of a slower pace. We were in no rush.

We came into Montezuma Creek late in the day and spotted White-horse High School right away. It is a fine-looking complex, much better built than most. The track team was still out practicing their many events. We parked and stood by the fence. In a while, the coaches called the boys and girls in, held a short meeting in the center of the field, and dismissed them after a rousing team cheer.

One girl stayed to work on the 110-meter hurdles. The shadows had lengthened out, but the air was warm enough that she needed no sweat-suit. She ran the hurdles, eased across the finish line, ran them again, then again, her long brown legs carrying her forward. She wasn't pushing her-self, just working on form. When her last run was over, she walked to her sweats. She picked them up, tucked them under her arm, and jogged toward the locker room, toward a hot shower, toward some homework—and per-haps, since the first lightning of spring had yet to streak the dry Navajo sky, toward her grandfather and his terrifying, electrifying, side-splitting tales of Coyote.

# VIJHNU

In 1975, after four years at NARF, I joined the law faculty at the University of Oregon. Academic life had gradually become more attractive as, each summer at NARF, I taught a course at the University of New Mexico to Indian students about to begin law school. I wrote my first law review article, a piece on Indian treaties. Another factor was the traveling, once a joy at NARF, later a mixed blessing: Seth, my first son, was a year and a half old.

Leaving NARF to teach law turned out to be much less of a transition than I expected—far less a defining personal event, for example, than meeting Paul Roca or going to NARF in the first place. In addition to teaching Indian law, I continued to work for Indian tribes on a consulting arrangement with NARF and did other projects outside the law school involving Indian issues. Chapin Clark, my dean, assigned me to teach federal public land law and water law, two fields critical to the West. So, both before and after the move, my professional work focused on Indians and the West.

I came into these fields of law at an opportune time. Few law schools included Indian law or public land law in their curricula at the time. Until the 1970s, the assumption was that Indians—and their legal issues—would fade away. Public land law, even though federal lands constituted one-third of all lands in the United States and one-half of the American West, raised few public issues until modern environmental law began in about 1970. Similarly, water law had dealt mostly with narrow, private issues. Without realizing it, I began my academic career just as these western issues began to burgeon and take on new significance to lawyers and the public alike.

Indian law and public land law both needed updated textbooks to capture the many new developments. By 1980, I had published an Indian law casebook with Dan Rosenfelt and David Getches, the former NARF director then teaching at the University of Colorado, and a federal public lands casebook with George Coggins at the University of Kansas. In 1982, nine of us updated Felix S. Cohen's great 1942 treatise on Indian law. Doing a casebook or a treatise is an exercise in learning as much as writing. Those efforts, along with various articles, gave me a much better sense of the broad sweep of public land law and Indian law—and of how these two fields, and others, particularly water, interrelated in the American West.

Traditional legal research was invaluable in giving me a foundation for what I came to think of as the "Law of the American West." But I was increasingly coming to see law less in terms of particular legal rules and more in terms of its relationship to societies and the land itself. Just as I understood Indian hunting and fishing rights much better after visiting Menominee and seeing Warren Kakwich's freezer stocked with wildlife, so too did I gain a context for the controversy over clear-cutting in the national forests by long hikes in the deep Pacific Northwest woods and talks with people in logging towns like Oakridge, Oregon, and Quincy, California. Ranching issues became much more vivid upon a visit to a working ranch, mining law more real after a tour of an operating mine. Environmental groups, tribal organizations, universities, and government agencies invited me to give talks; I tailored my presentations to the place, causing me to read and learn about the local area. Usually I took some hike or tour and seldom failed to benefit from the experience.

Although my reading about the West had not slackened, it had become somewhat more systematic after Paul registered his disgust over my preoccupation with Bancroft's *History of California*. I began to see how "nonlegal" books fit in with my writing and teaching about the law. Good western literature—not only traditional writers such as Jack London, Bernard De Voto, Willa Cather, and John Muir but also the newer breed like William Kittredge, Vine Deloria Jr., Edward Abbey, and Ivan Doig—wrote accurately and evocatively about the people and the land. The distinctive western laws made much more sense when you understood where they came from.

Wallace Stegner, the historian-novelist-essayist who wrote more than thirty books about the West, especially advanced my comprehension of the nexus between the law and the West itself. Although he rarely mentioned law explicitly, his writing on the western character explained all the statutes. The land and water grabs, which the laws encouraged, trace to the get-rich-quick mentality, the quest for "the big rock candy mountain." That impulse usually, though not always, overwhelmed the subtler urge for community that many westerners also held. In all of Stegner's writing, the land was an actual character, part of every episode, holding out the allure of quick riches, resisting the boomers with its aridity and roughness, offering magnificence and the relief of solitude.

Laws rise up from societies and the terrain. This was particularly true in the American West, where the big land and scarce water have always been uniquely entwined with material well-being and with the human spirit. I read these words of the Cherokee legal historian, Rennard Strickland, in 1980 and they are among the best I know: "For law is organic. Law is part of a time and a place, the product of a specific time and an actual place." Law, in other words, has a habitat.

# BEDROCK

Capitalizing upon these realizations would require me to undertake a great amount of on-the-ground inspection, that is, hiking and fishing. Granted a person—a narrow-minded sort—could say that this was a rationalization, a ruse, a frivolous and potentially dangerous attitude for a serious academic. But how better to live a life than on the edge? Besides, by then I had tenure.

I began to explore the unique characteristics of the vast land regions in the West and organized my reading and traveling accordingly. The Upper Great Plains. The Greater Yellowstone Ecosystem. The ancient forests of the Pacific Northwest. The Klamath Mountain region lying in coastal Oregon and California. The Sierra Nevada. The Basin and Range Province. Repeatedly my mind turned to the canyon country that Paul had drawn in the sand and that I had looked out on from the southern tip of Cedar Mesa.

I went down to the Colorado Plateau several times. One visit, in the summer of 1984, was to an innovative four-day dispute resolution session hosted by Robert Redford at Tsaile on the Navajo Reservation. A major conflict had arisen in Indian country over taxes that tribes had levied on companies extracting tribal coal, oil, and gas. The companies cried foul because they were already paying the tribes royalties. The tribes responded that they, as sovereign governments, could both receive royalties and levy taxes. Beyond that, the tribes pointed to the inequities of the original leases, which were far below market value. Numerous lawsuits were in the courts.

The gathering focused on Navajo taxes, but representatives from other tribes, including the Hopi and Ute, were also in attendance. All the mining companies, as well as the big utilities that marketed the energy, were represented, mostly by top-level executives. The issues were, to say the least, divisive. The Navajo taxes alone amounted to more than $100 million.

The talks were productive in that the principals got to spend time with each other in a retreat setting. The more formal, roundtable discussions were often heated, but the two sides defined their positions and came to understand the opposite points of view. The session was not designed to produce any agreements on the spot; it was meant, rather, to lay the groundwork for later negotiations. And that objective, as later events bore out, was achieved in several cases.

One high point of the session was a daylong trip, traveling by jeep with Navajo drivers, down into exquisite Canyon de Chelly, a national monument administered by the Navajo Nation. A shallow, year-round stream meanders past the sheer and rosy de Chelly Sandstone walls. For thousands of years the Ancestral Puebloans made this open, inviting canyon their home. Now Navajo farmers tend small garden plots along the stream.

The long, relaxed day in Canyon de Chelly gave the energy executives an appreciation for the land and the Navajo's tie to it. I rode out of the canyon at dusk with Pete Zah and his wife, Roz. Pleased with the way the trip had gone, Roz said quietly, "I'm glad they got to be down here all day. To begin to understand this, you have to get all of the sun's slants. You have to see the colors of the rocks change as the light changes. You have to get the sand in all of the wrinkles of your face."

The day in Canyon de Chelly reinforced my determination to see more of the vast, complex backcountry of the Colorado Plateau. I had many places in mind, but inevitably the Grand Canyon was near the top of the list. Although I had hiked into the upper end of the Grand Canyon by way of Jackass Canyon, I had never been into the Inner Gorge. Back when I lived in Phoenix, a trip to Havasu Canyon had taken me to within 5 miles of it. Foolishly, I had turned back.

Out of the blue, David Getches called me one day and invited me on a raft trip down into the canyon. The outing had been planned long ago, but a vacancy had come up and I could have the open seat. We would depart from Lees Ferry and, seven days and 88 river miles later, hike out Bright Angel Trail up to the South Rim. David was really enthused. He knew several of the people on the trip, and they had brought together some of the best guides on the river. "Charles, you *have* to come. You'll never have another opportunity like this."

# BEDROCK

I have an approach/avoidance complex about river trips. My real choice, I tell myself, is to hike. I love the hard work of it, the sense of personal accomplishment, the way my hiking boots mold to the trail or the rocks. I love the sweat, all of it, on my chest, all through my hair plastered down under my battered cowboy hat, away from the evaporation. Then, too, if you are traveling by river rather than trail, you are denied the strong, sweet fragrance of sagebrush. If I'm getting somewhere by some mode of transportation other than hiking, a part of me is longing, another part guilty.

River trips, on the other hand, are so much easier, especially if you are a passenger rather than a guide; they take much of the challenge out of getting into remote country. The group experience can make a crowd out of what should be solitary. Then there is the class issue: the Grand Canyon trips remain the province of the middle class and above. The tariff is too high for most people and breeds exclusivity. I should backpack, not float, into the canyon.

Then there is the approach side to my approach/avoidance complex. A good raft trip is so relaxing on the tranquil stretches, so bracingly exciting on the whitewater rapids: your mood changes with the river's moods—calm, lazy, reflective, exhilarated, stormy. You can cover such good distance on a float, often penetrating into country that is nearly inaccessible on foot. The guides know so much lore that the journey becomes a floating university. And the meals are unfailingly terrific.

I convince myself that the daily side-canyon hikes, and the stiff climb up Bright Angel Trail on the way out, will give me sufficient sweat and sage. I call David back and accept.

A couple of days later, I waded into the Colorado River at Lees Ferry, the old Mormon outpost 15 miles below Glen Canyon Dam, helping to push our raft off. The water ran cold and clear against my legs, the Colorado no longer a warm, silty desert river since the dam went in: the silt collects behind the dam and the released water comes from the deep, cool recesses of the reservoir. Self-consciously uncertain, not wanting to make some foolish mistake, I concentrated on following the steady, low-key flow of instructions from the guides. Soon I and the other twenty passengers had clambered aboard the gray rubber rafts and begun our journey downriver, carried by the current and oar thrusts of the guides.

The river guides play a special role in this canyon. Even with all the millions of visitors each year to the rim high above and the thousands of passers-through on the river down here, most of us have obtained just a fleeting understanding. Only a tiny percentage of us know the depths of the Grand Canyon with any intimacy. Among those few intimates are the people who have run the river a great many times.

These guides are mightily competent at their diverse work of packing and unpacking their burdened-down craft (among other things, a float down the full length of the canyon requires food, much of it kept fresh, for up to eighteen days), cooking gourmet meals (coffee must be ready before first light and the steaks may be sizzling beyond dusk), practicing first aid (broken limbs and the sting of rattlers and scorpions are not common but neither are they rare), and working their craft through some of North America's most challenging rapids. They cut colorful figures with their bright shirts as they lead long side-canyon hikes in their Teva sandals designed to go easy on the rubber rafts but also to claim a firm grip on the slickrock. And they are irreverent. The guides not-so-privately root for raven when he raids a raft's stash of halibut or transports the sandwich of an inattentive customer to a ledge several hundred feet up.

The guides' greatest hero is John Wesley Powell. By the late 1860s, when Major Powell arrived on the scene, most of the Colorado Plateau was still a blank space on the maps. Decorated in the Civil War—he had lost his right arm at Shiloh—Powell generated immediate respect and kept it. (Unless you happened to be a western senator during the last decade of the nineteenth century and you believed, as all western senators did, that the West had no limits.) Powell trained his formidable intellect on the American West. As would befit an explorer and visionary, he determined to plumb knowledge from depths previously beyond all reach: he would learn of the Grand Canyon through traversing its entire length by water. No one in written history had ever done it—probably no one in history, period. Although Indian people once farmed the fertile bottomlands where the canyon widened out, they presumably had the good sense to choose activities other than careening a wooden craft down brutal stretches of wild river, narrow canyon reaches, and massive boulders that together made run after run of treacherous, deadly rapids. Remember, in Powell's time this was the original, unrestrained river, long before the calming influence of Glen Canyon Dam.

Against all advice, Powell floated the Colorado River twice, in 1869 and 1871. When he put in at Green River, Wyoming, in 1869, no one expected to see him, any of his crew of ten, or their bodies, again. But Powell made it and so did his colleagues—except three who quit (one can understand this, for all the explorers were miserable and nearly out of food) and were killed, perhaps by Mormons, perhaps by Paiutes, up on the rim. At that point no one had any way of knowing that the expedition was less than one day from the lower end of the Grand Canyon.

Powell published his report on his journeys to a nearly electrified public. He was a scientist, a geologist, and thus his report was accepted as proof about this mysterious region. But Major Powell could also turn a phrase, and he managed to express some sense of the wonders that no other white person had ever seen.

The adventurer went on to serve the country in many other ways. Engrossed by the many Indian people he had known and respected, Powell became head of the Bureau of Ethnology and compiled ethnological reports on Indians that remain valuable today. He learned, for example, from the Ute how fire had carved the deep canyons that held his soul. A Ute chief had lost his wife and wanted to visit her in the Spirit Land. The Creator, Sinawahv, came to the chief and fondly granted him one visit. The Spirit Land, though, was unreachable and Sinawahv found it necessary to create a route. This he did by rolling a great globe of fire through the mountains to make a trail. After the chief had completed his visit with his wife, Sinawahv, fearing that the Ute or others might try to use the trail again, "rolled a river into [the] trail—a mad raging river into the gorge made by the globe of fire, which should overwhelm any who might seek to enter there."

# Vishnu

Concurrently with his position at the Bureau of Ethnology, Powell held the directorship of the U.S. Geological Survey and supervised extensive mapping expeditions of the West. Based on his broad experiences, he developed strong ideas about how the federal government ought to proceed with the settlement. He set out his views in 1879 in his famous *Arid Lands* report. The land and water laws Powell had in mind would be premised on the limits imposed by the region's aridity. He urged that the westward expansion—this was the time of the Great Bar-B-Q, when every federal acre, nearly all of the West, was up for grabs by the railroads, mining companies, timber and grazing interests, speculators, and ordinary homesteaders—be scaled back, made more orderly, and organized around local, self-sufficient farming communities. Powell knew the West but he seemed not to know its politicians. In 1891, western senators and boosters forcibly tabled his *Arid Lands* report and by 1894 had drummed him out of office. Nevertheless, his insights were luminous, then and now, and he stands as one of the leading nineteenth-century public figures in the West.

For all the weight of the *Arid Lands* report and his later career, it was Powell's 1869 expedition down the Colorado River and through the Grand Canyon that is his best-remembered accomplishment and constitutes a grand historical marker for the Southwest. This was the intellectual opening of the Colorado Plateau. By no means was there a rush to the Four Corners. The Hole-in-the-Rock Expedition, for example, did not make its journey until a full decade later. But after Powell at least the maps were filled in and the idea had been established that this interior sector was within the reach of Americans.

As much as today's guides may strive to run the Southwest's largest river in the spirit of Powell, not even the major himself is immune from their irreverence. Perhaps Powell's most memorable passage was written in the Grand Canyon just below the entrance of the Little Colorado from the south, just before the river plunges finally into the depths of the world. Powell described the awe he and thousands of latter-day visitors have felt: "We are now ready to start on our way down the Great Unknown . . . we but pigmies, running up and down the sands or lost among the boulders."

# BEDROCK

These words spoke directly to the imaginative and athletic guides, and they have since formed a new tribe. The river guides are the Butt Pygmies.

B. J. Boyle is in the direct line of Kokopelli, the Ancestral Puebloans' romantic flute player, working his harmonica, skipping over river boulders and canyon rocks with his daypack and Tevas. He loves the Old People and their petroglyphs, granaries, dwellings, and stick figures, constructed by soaking coyote willow branches in water and tying them together in the shapes of tiny animals and people. Lorna Corson, one of the first boatwomen of the Grand Canyon, hired on in the 1970s, just after the companies began to breach their rigid no-female-river-guides dictate, is a carpenter from Wilson, Wyoming. The call of the canyon grows too strong each summer and she heads south for a trip or four. Her musculature is unbelievable, and it is a thing of beauty and power to watch this lithe, brown, 95-pound woman insinuate a bulky raft down through the pounding whitewater. (I intentionally avoid, out of modesty, any description of our trip leader, Dave Edwards, a dashing fellow considered one of the best on the river. Others on the trip agreed that we are nearly dead ringers for each other. Even taking away our hopelessly ratty cowboy hats, they said, it was as if we were brothers. When another tour landed on our beach as we were leaving, the trip leader clapped me stoutly on the back: "How the hell's it goin', Dave?" Later, B. J. yelled out at me: "Hey, Dave, give me a hand, will ya?" I never, not even once, disclaimed the resemblance.)

I found myself gravitating to Matt Kaplinski, another one of the guides. Ever since discovering John McPhee's *Basin and Range,* I have been fascinated by geology. Matt is blocky, square in the face and torso, reminiscent somehow of the granite he studies as a geologist and pursues as a lover.

Matt has what you might call a restrained exuberance. He is a professional who picks out his words with care, but just below the surface burns a red-hot passion for this old land. His ardor permeates his lectures to the group and erupts in his "yee-*hahs*" through the blasting rapids. Matt's fire had gradually grown hotter as the trip moved down into the deep time, each layer representing scores of millions of years: Kaibab Sandstone, Toroweap Formation, Coconino Sandstone, Hermit Shale, the Supai Group.

# Vishnu

On our third day, we reached the stretch of water where the river cuts through the Redwall Limestone deposits of the Mississippian Period.

We rowed over to a beach near Nautiloid Canyon and pulled our rafts up on the sand. Lunch was still an hour away. Some of us followed Matt up into the canyon. "We know quite a bit about what it was like here some 340 million years ago." The Redwall Limestone, he explained, had trapped and fossilized marine animals of many sorts. Then with his squarish hands he pointed out fossils of brachiopods and crinoids. He showed us yard-long nautiloids shaped like ice cream cones and related to squid and octopus. The nautiloids were one of the first animals to pursue their prey. Matt explained how the abundant remains of these ancient species in this layer of limestone tell us not just about them, but about their surroundings as well. "This must have been a calm, warm sea. Those are the conditions that create the highest preservation potential for fossils."

After Matt finished, I made a short climb up to a rock ledge and sat down, my back against a cool rock wall. Some 340 million years ago I—although my species was 339 million years away from being a gleam in anyone's eye—would have been looking out, not on the river and the far canyon wall, but on a tropical sea.

None of the quadrillions of tons of rock now stacked up above me existed then. All the coal, oil and gas, oil shale, and uranium, all those minerals that have given us so many opportunities and so much combat and danger, would be formed much, much later. The sea I tried to imagine while sitting on that ledge represented, I knew, the state of the Colorado Plateau for most of the time since life appeared on earth during the Cambrian Period. During that stretch of 500 million years, in stark contrast to its current physiography, the Colorado Plateau mostly has been low, level, and marine, or intermittently so.

I knew the outlines of how this Mississippian sea had been buried by layer after layer after layer. The Plateau itself remained placid, but violent events beyond the Plateau began to affect it. The Emery Uplift rose up along the western edge. More important, a massive upthrust, probably caused by the collision of North America with the combined continent of

Africa and South America, created a great mountain range to the east, northeast, and north: the Ancestral Rocky Mountains reached from Texas and Oklahoma up through Colorado and Wyoming.

The visible parts of the Ancestral Rockies had mostly eroded away by the end of the Paleozoic Era, 225 million years ago. This range, however, gave much to the Plateau. We instinctively think of the great mountain chains as having been here forever. But in fact the dramatic features of mountains inexorably give way to rain, snow, wind, and gravity. They soften and fade, in time becoming plains and seabottoms.

So these first Rockies—and the mountains on the other side of the Colorado Plateau that had been pushed up in present-day Nevada by the Emery Uplift—gradually wore down. Rivers carried rocks, pebbles, soil, and sand, spreading them out in broad fans on the flatlands down below, which during the Paleozoic were sometimes covered by sea, sometimes not. The older Mississippian Redwall Limestone and other layers were covered by successive horizontal sheets of mud, clay, silt, and sand that in time became shales and sandstones. The winds blew fine sands from the shrinking mountain ranges into dunes, eventually hardening into sandstone deposits. The seas also left their mark during the late Paleozoic. The advancing and then receding seas laid down sheets of salt deposits.

This melting of the highlands beyond the low, level Colorado Plateau, playing out in various ways in various times and places across the Plateau, continued through the entire Mesozoic, "the age of middle life," the era of the dinosaurs that ended 65 million years ago. It continues today as the Wasatch, the Uintas, and the modern Rockies imperceptibly contribute their elevation to the lands below. This old Mississippian sea, and younger seas overlying it, too, have been buried and reburied.

**B**. J. hollered out a lunch call, and I worked my way down the rockslide to camp. "Beach sandwiches," my mother used to call them: ham, turkey, tomatoes, lettuce, onions, mustard, mayonnaise, and heavy with spices—

pepper, oregano, and thyme on that Atlantic beach, jalapeños on this very different one.

Lunch over, we pushed off in our five inflatable rubber rafts. I did the rowing during this next stretch, a gentle one. We were deep in Marble Canyon now, the sheer limestone walls a rusty red. This is where the energy and water developers wanted to put in the Marble Canyon Dam in the 1960s. It would have flooded the canyon all the way up to Lees Ferry, 40 miles, the full length of the float we've made so far. You can see the drill marks on the wall and the engineers' marks, "1A," "1B," and so forth. A few miles further, three bighorn sheep had come down to river's edge to drink and eat the sweet beans of the mesquite. We ran through President Harding Rapid—the strong-rowing and expert Lorna took over the oars here—and pulled into the beach below for the night.

Our group, including the guides, had by now developed the kind of easygoing camaraderie you usually find on river trips. The sun, the wind,

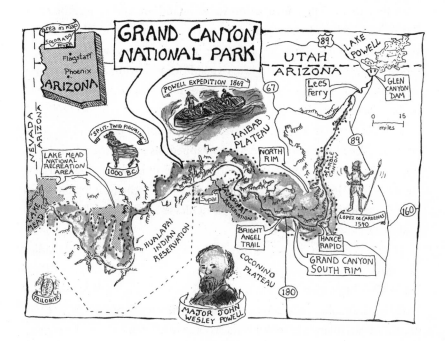

the rain (this is the monsoon season, and we had a drenching, magnificently furious sky-crackler last night), and the gritty sand are equalizers, but the luxury of time is critical, too. Away from the rush of duty, you can ease up, approach people with some slack, without concern for efficiency of words, listen to another's story, tell some of yours. A river instills this pace. For every free river has had a great deal of time and its confident flow tells you that. This one has had millions of years already.

David Getches and I—once young lawyers together at NARF and now with our families entwined (Ann and I gave our second son David's first name and his twin daughters are big sisters to our boys)—spread out our tarps and laid down our sleeping bags. No need for a tent: the skies had cleared and last night's torrent would not be repeated. Three men from New England, themselves long-time friends before the trip, came over. The five of us sprawled out on the tarps and lapsed into talk. They had eagerly anticipated the trip. But they hadn't expected so much from this gorge, and I said that I hadn't either. David and I explained the contours of our lives, they theirs. The conversation went on and on, and so did the river. Rarely had I felt so free to visit in an open-ended way since those dorm-room bull sessions of my freshman year in college. There were other clusters of talks, as well, among the low, riverside forest-shrubbery of mesquite, tamarisk, and coyote willows. Later on dinner—this was Mexican food night—rocked with hilarity.

I sought out Matt after dinner. We found a couple of beers and sat down on a boulder next to the water. Matt wrapped his arms around his knees and looked out at our river, dark in some places, lit up where the big rising moon hit it. He was an intriguing person to me, quiet, understated, yet fiercely dedicated to geology and in particular the geology of this canyon. I asked him how this came to be.

He explained that he had grown up in Jackson, Michigan, and studied geophysics as an undergraduate at Western Michigan in Kalamazoo. Early on in his studies, he did summer fieldwork in Montana and became captivated by the geology of the West: "I knew I'd be out there, somewhere past the 100th meridian." He took his master's at Northern Arizona University,

# Vishnu

a place that emphasizes the study of the Colorado Plateau, its geology, biology, history, literature, and Indian cultures.

"Geology stretches your imagination to a whole other order of magnitude. That's what first drew me. You start out by learning the geologic time scale. At the beginning, it's all memorization. You make up mneumonic devices. Then you start thinking. You go: 'Jurassic. That's 144 million to 208 million years ago. What does that mean? Well, let's see. I'm twenty . . .'"

"You ask me," he continued, "whether I try to imagine *being* there. I don't. To me that's just not realistic. But I do try to imagine what it was *like* then."

Yesterday, when Matt was giving us a one-hour, sandbar lecture on the canyon's geology, his voice started to rise and he started pumping his hand when he began talking about the Vishnu Schist in the Inner Gorge. I inquired about that.

"Well, there's no question about it. I do get excited about the Vishnu. There's nothing in the world like it. That stretches your mind to still another order of magnitude. I mean, it's exciting, no doubt about it, to see a fossilized nautiloid and imagine a scene that existed 340 million years ago.

"But in the Vishnu you're talking about 1.7 billion years. 1.7 billion! You know that the Redwall Limestone is limestone and that the Tapeats is sandstone. In the Vishnu, you don't really *know* what the hell the original rocks were. They've all been metamorphosed—completely changed. They had incredible extremes of pressure, temperature, and time all working on them at once. The pressure amounts to 3 to 4 kilobars. A bar is the pressure pushing down on you on the earth's surface by the weight of the atmosphere. So the subterranean pressure on the Vishnu was three to four *thousand* times heavier. The temperature was 300 to 500 degrees centigrade, much higher in Fahrenheit. This went on for 10 to 50 million years. All that stuff down there was just crushed and twisted and melted in a way we can't really imagine.

"So the great thing about the Vishnu Schist," Matt continued, "is that, the farther you go back into time, the deeper you go into time, the less you

93

know, the more cryptic it is. The Vishnu's been around more, seen more, and we don't know all that it's seen. There's a mystery, a long and deep mystery, about it. And, of course, the other thing is that it is just incredibly beautiful country down there. No place on earth like it. God, I love it.

"Well, you'll get to see the Inner Gorge for yourself day after tomorrow." Then he looked up at the moon, now straight overhead and lighting up all the river we could see, swallowed down his beer, grinned across his blond-red stubble of a beard—this was no place for shaving—and laughed. "Well, actually it's late enough that by now it might just be *tomorrow* that we'll be in the Vishnu. I'm going to bed. Think I'm going to sleep on the raft and feel that river under me."

**M**att wanted to sleep right on the river for all the reasons our species loves rivers—their magic and movement and mystery—but he loves it for another reason as well. This river is the force that cut down through and exposed all of this canyon's geological layers, right down to the Vishnu Schist. Tributaries of the Colorado, small and large, did that same work all across the Plateau and helped give it the face it has today.

For until very recently, the place that would become the Colorado Plateau remained low, quiet, and mostly flat, its upper crust composed of more than a mile of horizontal sheets of sediment laid down over hundreds of millions of years by seas, rivers, and volcanos. The Plateau began to develop its current shape with the inception of one of the great events of its history, the Laramide Orogeny. This convulsion ("orogeny," however racy the term may sound to the ear, means a mountain-building event) began 75 million years ago and continued for 25 million years. The largest visible consequence was the formation to the east and north of most of the dozens of dramatic ranges that compose the modern Rocky Mountains from New Mexico to Montana.

The Laramide event also impacted the Colorado Plateau by shortening the crust, compressing it, fracturing it into blocks. The sideways pressures then forced many of these blocks up, creating mountain ranges on the margins of, and within, the Plateau: the Uintas to the north; the east–west running San Juans in southwestern Colorado; the Chuska Mountains and Defiance Plateau to the southeast along the Arizona–New Mexico line.

These powerful compressive forces also laid the foundation for other major features that define the topography of the Plateau today. Most of them trend north–south: 150-mile-long Waterpocket Fold, now within Capitol Reef National Park; Cedar Mesa; Comb Ridge, paralleling Cedar Mesa to the east; the Coconino Plateau in the northwestern corner of the Navajo Reservation, abutting the Colorado River from the south; the Kaibab Plateau across the Colorado River on the north; the Circle Cliffs west of the Henry Mountains; and the San Rafael Swell to the west of the Green River in northern Utah. There are many more.

No one knows how the Colorado Plateau looked after the Laramide Orogeny finished its work about 50 million years ago. The best the geologists can say is that some of these features had not broken the surface by the end of the event and that others had. Of those that had risen up, most had not yet attained their present elevation. Further, they were rounded, not sharp as they are today. After the Laramide Orogeny, therefore, the mostly flat plain still would have been a fairly easy crossing for human beings if we had existed then. The surface was not yet cut by any of the deep canyons that lace the country today. But all manner of Laramide obstacles lay submerged or partly exposed, soon to be unveiled by the workings of uplift and erosion.

The Colorado Plateau was essentially rimmed off on all sides. The tall Rocky Mountains rose up on the north and east. The lower-lying areas of Arizona's Salt and Verde River valleys lay to the south, the floor of Utah's Great Basin to the west. The high country to the northeast and the low country to the southwest made the intervening terrain—the Plateau—a prime candidate for a great southwesterly-trending river. Apparently no such river existed throughout most of the Tertiary Period (beginning 65 million years ago), because during that time the waters of the Plateau drained mostly into various lakes in the Plateau's interior. The stage was

BEDROCK

set, however, for the River of the Southwest, which would be created by another epochal progression of events.

The terrain we know today—the radical verticality, the myriad canyons and draws—did not result, as one might think, from earthquakes tearing the land apart and creating deep fissures. Rather, in late Cenozoic times— sometime between 30 and 7 million years ago, perhaps even more recently, the geologists are not in accord on this—the whole Plateau began to rise, part of a vast regional uplift that stretched across the whole western interior, from west Texas through Canada to the Arctic Ocean. The Plateau rose imperceptibly, probably never more than a few hundredths of an inch a year. Over those millions of years, however, the uplift was so momentous that the whole landmass was elevated a full mile.

The Colorado River and its tributaries, which swelled as the mountains lifted to higher elevation and collected snowfields that produced increased spring runoff, would have none of it. The torrents held their ground against the rising dome, eating into the upswelling intruder, tearing away rock and soil. The surrounding lands, continuing their gradual upthrust, evolved into high plateaus and left behind deep clefts, as much as a mile down, in the stretches claimed by the insistent currents.

All over the Plateau, whether or not there were rivers running all or most of the time, the sides of the rising fault blocks were eroded away by flash floods, rain, wind, and frost. The stripped-away vertical canyonsides exposed all of the old horizontal layers of sandstone, limestone, shale, igneous rock, and deep metamorphic rock, the Vishnu Schist itself. This long progression of disparate events, large and small, opened up an incomparable natural university of geology: a conspectus of the deep history of the earth. Thus were born the gorges of the Goosenecks, Glen Canyon, Canyonlands, Havasu Canyon, and dozens of others, including the Grand Canyon, one of the seven natural wonders of the world.

The geological history has shaped the human history. Beginning with the first Spanish explorers in the sixteenth century, Indians were a deterrent to European settlement of the Colorado Plateau. Even more fundamentally, the big and harsh land has been a resistance force all of its own.

# Vishnu

People from the outside world were above all thwarted by rock—the way it was laid down, then later thrust up and deeply eroded. Now, more than a century after the Hole-in-the-Rock Expedition, this geology has been breached in some places. Lonely I-70 moves across the northern part of the Plateau. Some 250 miles to the south, I-40, the Old Route 66 that I used to drive, crosses the far end. And I-17 (after construction crews had made a good many road cuts and long, sweeping curves in order to surmount the Mogollon Rim) runs up from Phoenix to meet I-40 at Flagstaff. We have made state highways, some county roads, many jeep trails.

Despite the extraordinary press of human population and our many and various vehicles, the remoteness is still mostly intact. The long north–south ridges—all at least 100 miles—have been punctured by roads in only a handful of places: the San Rafael Swell; the Cockscomb; the Waterpocket Fold; Kaiparowits Plateau; Comb Ridge. Between Moab and Hoover Dam, a run of more than 500 river miles, the Colorado River allows crossings only at Hite Crossing, Glen Canyon Dam, and Navajo Bridge at upper Marble Canyon. Literally hundreds of other major cliff, mesa, and canyon formations prohibit or impede human travel. The Plateau's largest towns, all on the edges, are Flagstaff (58,000), St. George (46,000), Farmington (45,000), and Grand Junction (41,000).

Remoteness, which leaves empty spots on the map, has always been an enemy to our society, a condition to be eliminated. Now we are discovering the value of remoteness. And this is where we have the most of it in the contiguous forty-eight states.

The hardest place of all to reach is the Inner Gorge of the Grand Canyon. To be sure, the Old People had their ways and we have found ours. But the fact that tens of thousands of us run the canyon by river or hike to it by trail each year should not diminish our wonder at the remoteness and rarity of the place. This is where the river has cut the deepest, where the canyon walls are the highest, where the bedrock is the oldest.

# BEDROCK

The day after my early-morning talk with Matt, our river trip reached Hance Rapid, just below the point where Powell stood in awe of the depths ahead and authored his "Great Unknown" passage. Powell had countless more challenges than we: he with his stiff wood dories so vulnerable to punctures from the rocks, we with our broad rubber rafts, nearly immune to the boulders; he with no knowledge of what lay ahead, we with expert guides who could count hundreds of trips among them. Still, Hance Rapid had been a gathering roar in our ears and now it was thunderous, a 10, the highest rating on the Grand Canyon Scale.

The guides pulled into the beach above Hance to scout the rapid. Following them, the rest of us climbed a rise and looked down on a cluster of tangled, jagged boulders interlaced with boiling whitewater. Like all the big rapids, Hance lies at the mouth of a side canyon where blasts of water coming down steep chutes dislodge huge boulders and power them into the main river channel below. The water—again the water—of Red Canyon had done well.

As the guides inspected the river for possible routes through Hance Rapid, it occurred to me that, in addition to being the entrance to the Inner Gorge, this is the stretch of river that Lopez de Cardenas looked down upon when, it is said, he discovered the Colorado River in 1540. While at Hopi in his search for the fabled Seven Cities of Cibola, Francisco Vasquez de Coronado learned of a large river and canyon to the north and dispatched an exploring party under the command of Cardenas. Led by Hopi guides, Cardenas became the first non-Indian to reach the Grand Canyon, which he inspected from the South Rim. European "discoveries" on this continent have acquired a shiny patina of irony, and none more so than this one. Michael Kabotie, the Hopi poet, has his facts right in "Grand Canyon National Park":

> A spiritual place
> our symbolic womb-kiva
> the place of emergence

# Vishnu

through which we
enter our underworld
                heaven

"The Grand Canyon
discovered in 1540
by Pedro de Cardenas"
                The National Parks pamphlet read

I smiled
knowing that my people
always knew
the Grand Canyon was there
and didn't need to be discovered

Cardenas came with
Hopi guides and
I learned how lies
are twisted to sound
                true

Cardenas and his men stayed on the South Rim for a few days, looking down into the gorge toward a distant river. On one occasion, Cardenas' "three lightest and most agile men" tried to find a route down into the depths but returned at four in the afternoon. They had made it just a third of the way down, finding the going "very hard and difficult." Then they departed, ignorant both of the canyon's interior and its thousand village sites dating back more than three thousand years into antiquity.

In thinking of Cardenas, who also came to the canyon in September, it hit me once again how wildly different the places of the Colorado Plateau can be—and how dramatic its verticality. Cardenas, his men, and his Hopi guides stood on firm soil at 6,800 feet among ponderosa pines and bunchgrasses. Down here in the hot desert, nearly a mile below, my boots are sunk into sand and my companions are the prickly pear and the spiny yucca. The seasons are different: up on the rim this afternoon it will be a brisk autumn day, while here the temperature is in the mid-90s, sun-block mandatory; in the winter, the rim is snow country, while daytime temperatures on the river will average in the 50s, 60s, and 70s. The Colorado River has cut down so incomprehensibly far that Cardenas, from his vantage point on the rim, estimated its width at 3 to 6 feet.

Yes, it is completely different down here—and not, at this moment, a particularly comfortable difference. I've never been much of a thrill-seeker. High diving off cliffs, technical rock climbing, and, away from the natural world, roller coasters have never appealed to me. And, as for the chances of my signing up for bungee-jumping or sky-diving . . . My goal was not so much the excitement of running the rapid as the chance to experience the Inner Gorge, the Vishnu Schist.

The guides, I realized, almost certainly would find a safe way through, but I didn't see where. To me, Hance Rapid was an indecipherable confusion of boulders, drops, churning and racing water, spray, noise, and violence. My sense of security had grown shaky. After fifteen minutes or so, the guides had made their selection. Dave Edwards announced, "Okay. Let's see what happens."

I wanted to be with Matt on this one. We walked down from the knoll together, pushed the raft off, and jumped in. Matt grabbed the oars. Sitting next to me was Lynn Curran, a businesswoman from Pennsylvania with dark hair and broad, marvelously expressive features. Martin and Betsy Rosen from the San Francisco Bay area took up the posts at the far end of the raft. The look of the eagle doesn't begin to describe what was in Matt's eyes.

Matt went down a narrow on the right side, cut left, and then for me it was a twisting, spinning kaleidoscope of boulders, bumps, waves, lurches, shouts, jolts, blue sky, and torrents of ice-cold Colorado River water, all punctuated by Lynn's wide-open eyes, wider than wide. White-knuckle, all the way, but we made it through Hance without capsizing, without coming close.

Released from the monster rapid, we settled into a moment of peaceful

# Vishnu

release. Now we were in the Vishnu Schist, the dark Inner Gorge. Yes, you can see how all the depth and pressure and twisting and heating and battering—and all the time, too, 1.7 billion years of time—has made a whole new kind of rock. The Vishnu Schist, made up now of mica, quartz, various crystals, and many other minerals, and shot through with dikes (crosscut layers) of granite, dominates this interior world. The rock is so hard that when the midday sun hits it right, as now, it looks like vast slopes of black, polished steel.

The passage of Hance Rapid was the moment we had anticipated for days. It was a moment that Matt had prepared us for and that he had waited for. Finally free of the rapids, having done his job for his passengers, all of Matt's passion and spirit and fire ignited. He burst up from his oars, landed on the aluminum seat on his knees and, face and fists upward, cried out: "Yee-*ha!*" "Yee-*HA!*" "*YEE-HA!*" "One point seven!" "One point *seven!*" "One point seven *billion.*" "*Billion.*" "BILLION!" "VISHNU!" "VISHNU *SCHIST!*" "*YEE*-HA!" "High fives!" "High *fives!*" "*Every*body, high fives!"

And then we four passengers—though we were far from Madison Square Garden or Chicago Stadium, though we were far beyond the appropriate age for such an activity—spontaneously and irresistibly found ourselves initiating, then accelerating, the chanting rhythm that has become so familiar in the most recent stretch of geological time: "VISH-*NU,* VISH-*NU,* VISH-*NU* . . ." And on. And on. Down the river, down into the earth, down into history, down into time.

Part Two

# CONFLICTS AND CONQUESTS

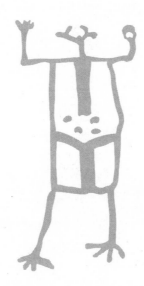

Chapter 6

# KYKOTſMOVI

The small, propeller-driven Frontier Airlines plane took off to the east from the Phoenix airport, rose up above the dry bed of the Salt River, banked, and turned north toward Flagstaff. It was January 1985, and I was headed toward the Hopi Reservation on Black Mesa. Although I'd often been to Navajo, this would be my first visit to Hopi. Less than two months before, the Hopi Tribal Council learned that the law firm representing the tribe had filed a brief in the United States Supreme Court, on behalf of Superior Oil Company, arguing against the right of Indian tribes to tax energy companies. The case involved the Navajo Nation, the Hopi's long-time antagonist, but many council members wondered whether it wasn't a conflict of interest for their own lawyers to participate in an assault on tribal sovereignty.

# CONFLICTS AND CONQUESTS

The past few weeks had been hectic. The Tribal Council contacted three law professors to give written legal opinions on the propriety of the attorneys' actions: Geoffrey Hazard of Yale, one of the nation's foremost authorities on legal ethics; John Leshy of Arizona State, who taught Indian law and federal public land law and was well respected by the Tribal Council; and me. The council gave the matter top priority and moved quickly. The tribe had telephoned us about a week before Christmas and wanted our opinions by mid-January. John Leshy and I had decided, with the approval of the Tribal Council, to submit a joint opinion letter. Now, a week after completing the opinion, I was on my way to a Tribal Council meeting, open to all tribal members, where I was to make a presentation on the complex ethical issues.

When the Hopi called, I immediately thought of John Boyden, the prominent Salt Lake City lawyer who had been general counsel to the Hopi for decades. Boyden had his strong detractors—both within the tribes he represented and among Indian lawyers. Ute tribal members had complained about conflicts of interest when he represented the Ute Tribe in the settlement of its water rights. At Hopi, Boyden had negotiated the lease of the immensely valuable coal deposits under Black Mesa to Peabody Coal Company back in the 1960s. Charges persisted that he had represented Peabody at the same time he worked for the tribe. If this was true—if Boyden had actually represented both sides without consent from the Hopi—it would have been unethical conduct of the worst sort.

Hopi traditionalists, livid over the idea that sacred Hopi land would be mined, sued to overturn the lease. The case, which the courts finally dismissed on technical procedural grounds, had been John Echohawk's first at NARF. By the time I was called in, Boyden had died but his partner, John Kennedy, had continued as chief attorney for the Hopi Tribe. Although Kennedy and I were law school classmates, we barely knew each other.

I had read and heard a good deal about Hopi, but I had no idea what to expect. Many people counted the Hopi as the most traditional Native American group in the country. John Echohawk, who had gone to Hopi many times and spent long hours with traditionalists, spoke in awe of the religious societies and the elaborate dances. I remember him saying that there always seemed to be some ceremony or observance going on, that everything at Hopi seemed to be related to the traditions, that Hopi was just plain different from anywhere else he had ever been. Black Mesa, the remote homeland of this ancient pueblo people, seemed a distant and impenetrable mystery.

If the Hopi and Black Mesa seemed a mystery, so did John Boyden. I had almost no firsthand knowledge of Boyden at the time, having met him just once, years before, at oral argument in the federal appeals court in Denver. This was the case Yvonne Knight and I had brought to protect the right of Pawnee boys to wear traditional, braided hair in school. Boyden, on behalf of the Ute Tribe, had written a friend-of-the-court brief supporting the boys. His presentation to the court was effective—probably more so than Yvonne's. She was just a year out of law school and this was her first appellate argument. Tall, graying, and courtly, Boyden was a leading practitioner, well known to the judges, and they obviously were impressed with him.

For all I had heard of his supposed conflicts of interest, there seemed to be no real evidence of them. John Echohawk always was careful to avoid passing judgment on these allegations against Boyden: "You hear a lot, but I don't think anyone really knows." Although I knew little about the episodes at the time, I instinctively discounted the charges: it seemed unlikely to me that a lawyer of Boyden's standing would do such things. Certainly I had no inkling, as I flew north toward my meetings at Black Mesa, that the matter I had been asked to work on would be entangled with the most contentious events in the modern history of the Hopi and the Ute as well. Nor was I aware that both Black Mesa and John Boyden would be at the very center of the extraordinary machinations of the big urban centers to develop the energy and water resources of the Colorado Plateau in order to fuel the post–World War II boom in the American Southwest.

**P**eople from the Hopi Tribe would be meeting me at the Flagstaff airport. There would be briefing sessions with tribal officials tomorrow. The open Tribal Council meeting would be held the day after. So this plane flight offered a last moment to thumb through the file and reflect. The sun was going down, the Verde River shimmering out to the right, beyond that the rocky canyon of Tonto Creek, where I had often fished, back when I lived in Phoenix. In half an hour, we would leave the piñon-juniper and saguaro cactus landscape below, cross the Mogollon Rim, and reach the pine country on top.

In 1984, four years after John Boyden's death, John Kennedy and his

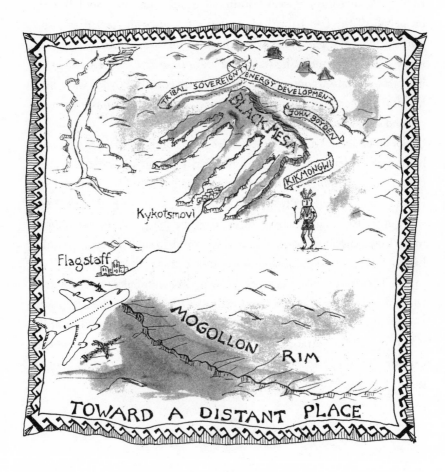

# Kykotsmovi

associates merged with Nielsen & Senior, a larger Salt Lake City law firm. They took with them the legal work for the Hopi Tribe, which, as it had been during Boyden's lifetime, continued to be a very remunerative client. One of Nielsen & Senior's existing clients was Superior Oil Company, owner of several wells at Navajo. In analyzing conflicts of interest under the ethics rules, a firm is generally treated as a single lawyer, so that the firm had to be concerned about potential conflicts even if (as was the case) Kennedy handled the Hopi matters and other Nielsen & Senior lawyers did the work for Superior Oil.

Federal policy and tribal governance had changed fundamentally in Indian country, even since I first worked at the Native American Rights Fund during the early 1970s, even during the past few years. Termination was now in disrepute—it had been as disastrous for other terminated tribes as it had been for the Menominee—and Congress began adopting programs designed to support tribes, not put an end to them. The tribes became much more aggressive in asserting their sovereignty—their right to act as governments. Dispensing with the outside paternalism and their own passivity that had built up over the course of a century, tribal governments took charge of their reservations during the 1970s and early 1980s. The BIA's dominance began to fade. These changes also remade energy development in Indian country in the Southwest.

The Navajo (beginning the series of events that were taken up at the retreat sponsored by Robert Redford) took the lead. In 1978, chafing under the inequitable mineral leases of the 1960s, their Tribal Council adopted tax ordinances assessing millions of dollars annually on energy companies doing business at Navajo. In addition to four huge coal mines, companies had drilled hundreds of oil and gas wells. When the tax notices arrived in the mail, the energy companies loosed cries of indignation. This was not the way tribes were supposed—or allowed—to act.

The indignation quickly translated into lawsuits, a great many of them. The first big decision came in 1982. The United States Supreme Court ruled that the Jicarilla Apache Tribe in New Mexico could indeed tax the companies. True, the Jicarillas were already receiving royalties on the very oil and gas leases the tribe was now trying to tax. But the court explained that governments, including Indian tribal governments, can do that. A city, a state, or the United States can own property (a building, a parking lot, or a coal deposit), obtain a financial return as an owner (through monthly rent or a royalty), and then also levy an income, possessory interest, or sales tax for profits made or activities conducted on that same property. A sovereign government can act both as a property owner and as a regulating or taxing authority. Nor did it matter that the Jicarilla Apaches had no tax ordinance in place when the leases were signed. Governments can change their laws: "Indian sovereignty is not conditioned on the assent of a nonmember. . . . [S]overeign power, even when unexercised, is an enduring presence that governs all contracts subject to the sovereign's jurisdiction, and will remain intact unless surrendered in unmistakable terms."

The *Jicarilla Apache* opinion was one of the strongest pro-Indian decisions ever handed down. It was a beacon of tribal sovereignty, the tribes' ultimate authority to control their reservations; Felix Cohen, the great Indian law scholar, described tribal sovereignty as "the most basic of all Indian rights." The decision—which involved a very large amount of money for the Jicarilla Apache and other tribes—squarely established that tribes, like all governments, must have the means to raise revenues to provide for law enforcement, education, health, environmental protection, and the many other responsibilities of governments. Otherwise, the court pointed out, those under the jurisdiction of Indian tribes, including non-Indians and the energy companies themselves, would not "benefit from . . . 'the advantages of a civilized society' that are assured by the existence of tribal government." To Indian people, who for centuries had regularly been called "uncivilized," it was delicious that the Supreme Court would make reference to the tribes' providing the "advantages of civilized society" to non-Indians. The opinion was written by Justice Thurgood Marshall, who, compared with most other judges, may have had a better-than-average eye for the irony here.

The *Jicarilla Apache* case settled the basic tribal right to tax, but it did not necessarily apply to all tribes. The constitution of the Jicarilla Apache Tribe, adopted under the Indian Reorganization Act of 1934, contained a clause requiring that all tribal council ordinances must be approved by the Interior Department. In upholding the Jicarilla tax, the Supreme Court had noted that these "federal checkpoints" assured fairness by tribal councils when regulating non-Indians. It was still an open question, then, whether an Indian tribe could tax non-Indians without federal approval. A number of tribes had constitutions allowing them to adopt ordinances on their own, without Interior Department review. The Navajo Nation had enacted an elaborate tribal code but had never found the need to adopt any constitution at all. Navajo ordinances did not require federal approval. Could the reasoning in *Jicarilla Apache* be extended to allow the Navajo taxes even though there were no "federal checkpoints"?

Several different companies challenged the Navajo taxes. Superior Oil filed two lawsuits. The case that went to the Supreme Court, however, was *Kerr-McGee Corp. v. Navajo Tribe.* Nevertheless, now the paths of Superior Oil, the Hopi attorneys, and the Hopi Tribal Council began to converge. Nielsen & Senior, the firm representing the Hopi, filed a friend-of-the-court brief on behalf of Superior Oil supporting the Kerr-McGee Corporation and challenging the sovereign authority of the Navajo Nation to tax non-Indian companies.

*Kerr-McGee* was a much-watched case. By now the back taxes for all companies operating at Navajo exceeded $100 million. Many other mineral-producing tribes had enacted tax ordinances and others, including the Hopi, were in the process of adopting them. The Hopi Tribe was at an especially sensitive point. The Hopi, like the Jicarilla Apaches, had adopted a constitution under the Indian Reorganization Act and it too had a federal-approval provision: any Hopi tax would be subject to "federal checkpoints." In a narrow sense, then, the Hopi Tribe, at that moment, was protected by the *Jicarilla Apache* opinion and was not dependent on a favorable ruling in the *Kerr-McGee* case.

But the Hopi Tribe, like many other tribes, was in the process of trying to get out from under federal supervision and expand its tribal sovereignty. At the very time the *Kerr-McGee* case was in the Supreme Court, the Hopi Tribal Council was exploring with its lawyers—the Nielsen & Senior firm—whether to amend its constitution to eliminate the provision that tribal ordinances had to be approved by the Interior Department. So, in real terms, the issue in the *Kerr-McGee* case had direct relevance to the Hopi.

But, beyond that, tribal sovereignty is the foundation that undergirds all tribal authority, whether it be taxation, environmental regulation, child welfare, tribal court jurisdiction, or a host of other specific powers. Supreme Court opinions dealing with one aspect of tribal sovereignty often are written broadly and affect a panoply of sovereign tribal powers. The opinion in *Kerr-McGee* could have a far-reaching impact, for good or ill, on all tribes, including the Hopi. The law firm representing the Hopi, but acting in its capacity as lawyers for Superior Oil, left no doubt about the potential breadth of the issues in its broadside attack on tribal sovereignty in its friend-of-the-court brief in the *Kerr-McGee* case:

> *This case is a watershed in the history of tribal sovereignty. If the decision of the Ninth Circuit is to be affirmed, this Court will turn away from its own decisions extending over 170 years, which have restrained tribes from regulating their external relations with non-Indian citizens.*

The requirement that a lawyer cannot have a conflict of interest while representing a client is, of course, an age-old ethical obligation—one of the foundations of the legal profession. United States Supreme Court Justice Joseph Story wrote a classic statement on the subject:

> *An attorney is bound to disclose to his client every adverse retainer, and even every prior retainer, which may affect the discretion of the latter.... When a client employs an attorney, he has a right to presume, if the latter be silent on the point, that he has no engagements, which interfere, in any degree, with his exclusive devotion to the cause confided to him; that he has no interest, which may betray his judgment, or endanger his fidelity.*

Thus a lawyer cannot represent both sides in a contract negotiation or in a lawsuit except in the rarest circumstances—as when both clients give full and informed consent to the dual representation. A lawyer can, however, under certain circumstances, take conflicting positions on legal issues for different clients so long as the lawyer is not representing both clients in the same lawsuit or other matters. Here the Hopi Tribe was not a party in the Supreme Court case so that the lawyers' brief for Superior Oil against the Navajo tribal tax did not directly oppose any action taken by their client. The two clients that the lawyers represented—Superior Oil and the Hopi—had no direct dealings with each other.

The legal profession, however, has grown increasingly concerned about the propriety of "positional conflicts"—a lawyer taking a position for a client in one case that is contrary to the interests of another client, even though the other client is not involved in the case. This was the situation with the Hopi's lawyers: they were arguing a position in the *Kerr-McGee* case—that Navajo tribal sovereignty does not include the right to tax non-Indians—which might well hurt the Hopi. One "Ethical Consideration" of the American Bar Association (ABA) requires that a lawyer, before arguing a point that would be a positional conflict, "should explain fully to each client the implications of the common representation." The lawyers for the Hopi did not give the tribe such an explanation. Nonetheless, there was not necessarily an ethical violation: the ABA's Ethical Considerations are recommended but not mandatory. The Hopi Tribal Council would have to sort out whether it considered this a conflict of interest, what it expected of its lawyers, and whether it wanted to continue with these lawyers under the circumstances.

I could tell from reviewing the documents the tribe sent me how determined the Hopi were to protect their sovereignty. The law firm's brief on behalf of Superior Oil in *Kerr-McGee* was filed on November 23. The Tribal Council learned of it on December 5. On December 7, a tribal delegation headed by the vice-chairman, Eugene Kaye, was in Salt Lake City conducting a tough, focused meeting with attorneys from Kennedy's law firm. Witness Kaye's opening statement: "There are many concerns about our relationship, . . . but the straw that broke the camel's back is your conflict of interest in this Amicus Brief filed by your firm. . . . We are not going to discuss details of this brief [and] we are not going to argue with you. However, we are here to listen to your explanations and take this back with us. You have an hour to respond to us."

When John Leshy and I got together in Phoenix to write our opinion letter to the tribal council, both of us remarked how surprised we were by the attorneys' posture at the December 7 meeting. The lawyers could have been candid. They could have explained that the position taken by other lawyers in the firm in the *Kerr-McGee* brief in fact ran contrary to the Hopi Tribe's interest in protecting its tribal sovereignty, that it was a mistake, and that the law firm would set up internal procedures to avoid such problems in the future. Instead the lawyers argued that they "thought [the brief] was supporting the position that the Hopi Tribe would take," that there was nothing "detrimental to or contrary to the interests of the Hopi people," and that "[t]he brief ultimately is in your best interest as far as we're concerned or we [would not] have filed it."

To support this contention, the lawyers repeatedly played on the antagonisms between the Hopi and Navajo—two tribes that had undergone a century of bitter conflict over land the government had set aside for their "joint use":

> [T]he Navajo Tribe . . . shouldn't ignore the Secretary of Interior anymore than the Hopi people want to ignore the Secretary of Interior. . . . [The Hopi] have always been very, what I consider to be loyal and deligent [sic], working with the Federal Government. Unfortunately, Navajos have not wanted to become associated in that respect with their organization just as I would say they have not wanted to be cooperative in their dealings with the Hopi Tribe, and what this brief says is that Navajo people are not above the law and that they must follow the law if the Hopi people follow the law. . . . Apparently the Hopis have decided through Constitutional mandate in your organization at least through law, that you are going to work with the Secretary. . . . Navajos are saying no. Navajos are thumbing their nose.

# Kykotsmovi

When John Leshy and I worked on our opinion letter, we discussed at length how discordant the lawyers' comments were with the attitudes of modern tribal councils. The Hopi delegation to the Salt Lake City meeting did not need to be reminded about their tribe's grievances with the Navajo. They had, however, quite precisely separated their struggle with the Navajo from their struggle to protect Hopi tribal sovereignty. They knew very well that the Supreme Court could announce general principles of tribal sovereignty and that the tribal sovereignty of the Hopi and all other tribes was at risk in the *Kerr-McGee* case.

Why would the lawyers think that the Hopi wanted to be "cooperative" with the federal government by allowing their laws to be subject to federal approval? Many tribes were in fact attempting to eliminate federal-approval provisions from their constitutions in order to expand their independence—including the Hopi, as Kennedy knew very well. During the December 7 meeting the lawyers never mentioned that, earlier in the same year, their firm had advised the Hopi Tribe on removing the federal-approval provision from the Hopi Constitution—which would eliminate the distinction between the Hopi's situation and the Navajo's in the *Kerr-McGee* case. As my plane made its way north toward Flagstaff and my meetings with the Hopi, I still could not fathom why the lawyers had responded to the Hopi delegation with such condescension.

In our opinion letter, John Leshy and I concluded that the law firm's *Kerr-McGee* brief was contrary to the interests of the Hopi Tribe. We found that the lawyers had not, as required by the Ethical Consideration on positional conflicts, explained "fully to each client the implications of the common representation." Instead, in our view, the lawyers' statements to the tribe (both at the December 7 meeting and at an earlier meeting when the merger of the law firms was discussed) were "substantially misleading." We did not believe, however, that the state bars of either Arizona or Utah would necessarily discipline the lawyers. In our opinion, since the concept of positional conflicts was still relatively undeveloped and the Ethical Considerations are recommendations only, not mandatory for lawyers, the actions probably would not result in disciplinary action by a state bar.

# CONFLICTS AND CONQUESTS

John and I emphasized that the canons of ethics set minimum standards and that the Hopi could decide, in accordance with tribal traditions, that its lawyers should meet a higher standard. Geoffrey Hazard, the ethics expert from Yale, reached similar conclusions in his opinion letter. He believed that a state probably would not discipline the attorneys, but he underscored the importance of the matter:

> At the same time, it is my opinion that the potential conflict . . . is sufficiently serious that the Hopi Tribe may justly ask that the firm refrain from continuing the concurrent representation of the oil companies in matters such as those involved with the Navajo Tribe. The conflict involves a very sensitive issue that goes to the heart of the Hopi Tribe's sovereignty as such. If the firm refuses to terminate the concurrent representation, the Hopi Tribe is justified in terminating the employment of the firm.

**N**ow the plane was up above the Mogollon Rim, the abrupt southern edge of the Colorado Plateau. The lights of Flagstaff broke the black expanse ahead. Hopi was a two-hour drive beyond.

J. C. Smyth, a non-Indian who was the legislative analyst for the Hopi Tribe, met me at the airport. In our drive across open country toward Black Mesa, he told me that the conflict of interest issue had become the talk of the reservation. There were many Boyden, and now Kennedy, loyalists. Considerable numbers of them had been converted to Mormonism, the religion of both Boyden and Kennedy. There were also many who had never forgiven Boyden for ramrodding the Black Mesa coal lease through the Tribal Council and even now, twenty years later, there was steady talk about Boyden's supposed ties with Peabody Coal. The Hopi, Smyth said, were determined to find out, one way or the other, whether the tribe's current lawyers had a conflict of interest in filing the *Kerr-McGee* brief. But John Boyden, tribal attorney for more than thirty years, a dominating presence on the reservation even in death, was part of this current controversy too.

The next morning, the air chill and dry, I went to the tribal offices. Kykotsmovi lies just below the tip of Third Mesa, one of the branches of Black Mesa, with wide-open views of the flatland–plateau–mesa landscape. This village, founded in the late nineteenth century, is recent by Hopi standards, but in time Kykotsmovi became the tribal headquarters. The tribal office buildings are relatively new: adobe, low, sprawling, and neatly maintained. When I was shown in the front door, the first thing I saw was a large, formal, color portrait of John Boyden holding the *Book of Mormon*.

I had a few short, get-acquainted meetings with the tribal staff and then was given a vacant office where I could work on a briefing to the Tribal Council, which was scheduled for the late afternoon; the open public meeting would then be held the next day. The council was in session, deliberating on other business, but during the council's mid-afternoon break the tribal chairman, Ivan Sydney, came by the office. The Hopi are known for their open, welcoming way and Sydney, handsome and fortyish, was friendly yet businesslike also. "Our only objective is to get to the bottom of this conflict of interest matter. We want to be fair to everybody. It is a very important matter for the Hopi Tribe." Thanking me for doing the opinion letter, he then went back to the Council meeting.

The Hopi Tribal Council sits by virtue of a written constitution authorized by the Indian Reorganization Act, passed by Congress in 1934. For thousands of years the Hopi villages had governed themselves. A Kikmongwi, or traditional religious leader, had special prominence in each village. In 1936, the Interior Department pressed the Hopi to adopt the constitution. It was an agonizing time of confusion. Most Hopi simply refused to vote, but a majority of those who did approved it. The constitution, by vesting authority in one council, greatly weakened village autonomy and altered the authority of the Kikmongwi.

Traditional Hopi have not forgotten the way in which this tribal government was formed at the white man's behest, and in his image of how a government should look. Nor have they forgotten the Tribal Council's most controversial action: the approval of the Black Mesa lease. Yet from what I had heard from John Echohawk and others, the council had, over the years, gradually gained credibility and support. Now council members regularly consult the traditional people in the villages. The white man's constitution was an aberration in this old culture, and the tribe may well amend it to reflect the traditional system more fully, but in the meantime the Hopi grudgingly have begun to live with the constitution and the Tribal Council it created.

At 4 P.M., I was taken down to the Tribal Council chambers for a briefing session before the next day's public meeting. John Kennedy was already there. We had seen each other just once, in passing, in the twenty years since law school. He had read our opinion letter, but he was friendly and introduced me to three younger men, colleagues from his law firm. Then we took our seats. The wide, low-ceilinged room had perhaps ten rows for spectators. The nineteen-member council, seated in two elevated semicircular rows, one behind the other, was still completing other business.

At 6 P.M. the council turned to the matter of the *Kerr-McGee* brief. Chairman Sydney announced that the council would go into executive session with the attorneys and staff.

"Shall we break for dinner?" someone asked.

"We'll send out for hamburgers," said the tribal chairman. "Just pay the tribal secretary. We need to push ahead."

At the chairman's request—and with the admonition that I should be brief because the council members had read the two opinion letters and there would be an entire day's public hearing tomorrow—I began to summarize our findings. Halfway into my presentation, hamburgers, french fries, and soft drinks arrived. "You can continue," instructed the chairman. "We'll talk over our food."

After I finished, John Kennedy spoke at length. He vehemently disagreed with the opinion letters, making many of the same points he and his partners had made at the Salt Lake City meeting. He retraced John Boyden's long career with the Hopi Tribe. As for the *Kerr-McGee* brief,

# Kykotsmovi

Kennedy said he had never even seen it before the meeting with the tribal delegation in Salt Lake City on December 7. He argued that the *Kerr-McGee* case did not threaten any Hopi interests and, raising again the specter of the rival Navajo Nation, asserted that a decision for the energy companies in *Kerr-McGee* might actually benefit the Hopi by restricting Navajo powers. He acknowledged that his firm should have advised the Hopi of the *Kerr-McGee* brief and said the firm would do "everything to make sure that won't happen again."

Kennedy repeatedly brought up John Boyden's name. I was taken by the extent of this when I read the transcript of the Salt Lake City meeting, but it was even more striking here in Kykotsmovi.

Kennedy delved deeply into the mining of coal on Black Mesa, the many struggles with the Navajo, and other episodes in Boyden's long relationship with the Hopi. Now I began to realize that those events and John Boyden—and all of his loyalists and accusers—were organic parts of this controversy two decades later. The room was thick with it, even though every Hopi face was expressionless. He did so much good for our people, he fought so hard for us against the Navajo, he was so loyal, how can we begin to measure all that we owe him? He was so disloyal, so paternalistic, how much more must our people endure? I realized that these questions and many others had been asked over and over in the villages for nearly forty years and that, although the words were never spoken, these were the real questions being asked in this room this evening—and would be asked for a great long time to come. For John Boyden had become part of the stories that would be told and retold, part of Black Mesa itself.

Kennedy continued. After he finished, a few other lawyers and staff members spoke briefly. None of the council members made any comments. At about 9:45, the chairman gaveled a break. He went back into his office, I learned later, to confer with other council members. At 10 P.M. they came back. "Thank you all very much. We will now go into executive session with Professor Wilkinson."

Before the break, the proceedings were mostly in English, with a few translations into Hopi, but afterward the council went almost completely to Hopi, pausing a few times to ask me a question. Occasionally, sprinkled in among the guttural phrases I could not begin to understand, I heard "Weel-kin-son." This late-night meeting in Kykotsmovi on Third Mesa, remoteness within remoteness, utterly unlike any other I had ever attended, went on. One hour, two hours, three. I worried about how the lateness of the hour would affect the council members, many of whom were elderly, and their ability to attend the public meeting the next morning—this morning, now. Some of them lived, I knew, many miles away over back roads. Yet I was rapt, leaning forward, straining my mind, struggling somehow to obtain some understanding from the foreign words and the stolid, dark faces. At last the chairman gaveled the meeting to a close and the council members filed out. The chairman thanked me and told me he would see me at 8:30 A.M. It was 2:30 in the morning.

The public hearing did begin at 8:30 A.M. sharp. The chairs were all taken and Hopi people stood two- and three-deep in the back of the room and along the sides. After a long opening prayer in Hopi, the chairman called me to the podium and I nervously presented our opinion. I know that I stammered, although I don't know how much.

More important, because of the complexity of the issues, I didn't finish my presentation. When my allotted forty-five minutes had elapsed, Ivan Sydney, who chaired the meeting, told me he was sorry but I would have to finish up. Yet I had not reached one of our major conclusions: that the attorney had failed to live up to the recommended (although not mandatory) level of disclosure about the firm's positional conflict between the Superior Oil brief and the Hopi Tribe's interests. Nor had I addressed the ultimate issue: that even if a state bar association did not discipline a lawyer under these circumstances, the Hopi Tribe had every right to form its own conclusion on the acceptibility of this conduct.

John Kennedy had forty-five minutes to respond to the opinion letters. Pounding on the firm's long association with the tribe, regularly citing John Boyden's name, the tribal lawyer forcefully disagreed with our conclusion that the brief was contrary to the tribe's interests. The problem, he said, was only a matter of the law firm's internal procedures: "The tribe should have been advised of [the cases], and we acknowledged that. . . . We don't think that's a conflict of interest if we don't handle procedures right." Then Chairman Sydney opened the floor for statements by tribal members. Hopi people spoke passionately, sometimes in English, sometimes in Hopi. The impassive council members listened.

After the lunch break, during an open discussion period, one of the council members asked Chairman Sydney if I could be permitted briefly to finish my presentation. Relieved, I took five minutes or so to do that, then returned to the place where I was standing, against one of the side walls.

Next to me was an older man on crutches. As soon as I took my place, he asked to be called upon and the chairman said: "Yes, go ahead, Mr. Sekaquaptewa." I knew immediately that this was Abbott Sekaquaptewa, former tribal chairman, still an influential person on the reservation, deeply knowledgeable about the tangle of events in the Hopi's modern history. He had suffered from debilitating arthritis since youth.

Sekaquaptewa, who had been close to John Boyden, gave an impassioned defense of Kennedy and his current colleagues—and of John Boyden. Leaning forward on his aluminum supports, brushing my left arm, his thick shock of hair rolling rhythmically, he made point after point with precision and eloquence. Boyden and Kennedy, he said, both had been warriors for the Hopi and their land. He cataloged several of the causes they had fought on behalf of the tribe. The problem with Superior Oil could be easily explained and nothing like that would happen again.

Sekaquaptewa had made a brilliant defense of Kennedy and Boyden. I remember to this day the heat of his body against my arm, making me feel weak and small, though I was the taller of us, making me know that I was a raw newcomer, new to these issues, new to this land.

Still, why did the lawyers not forthrightly admit that the brief made a dagger thrust at Indian—and Hopi—sovereignty? Why would they be so patronizing as to pretend that the brief would actually benefit the tribe? Was this the relationship of candor, respect, and trust that the Hopi surely expected of their lawyers?

After the hearing, J. D. Smyth drove me from Black Mesa back to

Flagstaff. We talked at length about the controversy. Bringing in the independent law professors had, he felt, been useful even though our opinions did not offer conclusive answers. Kennedy had many supporters, and it helped him a lot that one of them was Abbott Sekaquaptewa. Even so, he believed that the Hopi were more sensitive to moral and ethical issues than any group of people he had ever met. He was sure that the Tribal Council understood that, in the end, the decision had to be made by the Hopi, by their own standards of conduct, not by the rules of Anglo bar associations. But he had no idea how the council would handle this. "You have to have been around here a lot longer than I have to figure out how the Hopi make decisions."

Eventually a resolution emerged. Perhaps out of respect for a dead and revered tribal attorney, it seems there was no specific time or place at which an official decision was announced. Yet, a year later, the Hopi had new lawyers. I knew they believed in proceeding deliberately, in planting the seed of a decision deep in the soil, then caring for it and letting it grow slowly and finally mature, like the corn plants that Hopi farmers tend so painstakingly. There must have been thousands of discussions in the villages on Black Mesa. The Kikmongwi must have played a major role. The tribal council members, as they should have, rejected the tribal lawyers' views. In a sense, they also rejected ours. For this matter had to be decided, not by the advice of Anglo law professors, but by the Hopi's own standards. Their decision, the way they made it and the reasons for it, lodged in the deep mist of uncountable centuries of people and ideas and propriety, was more ethical and profound than our opinion letter ever began to be.

The experience at Kykotsmovi was only a beginning. I had so many questions, and for years they kept coming back to me: in discussions with people who knew the Southwest, in hikes across redrock country, in my readings about the West. Once John Echohawk had told me that some of the Hopi traditionalists were convinced that the vast energy deposits under

# Kykotsmovi

Black Mesa held the key to urban development all across the Southwest. Could Black Mesa have played that kind of role in the making of the modern desert cities from Albuquerque and Phoenix over to Las Vegas and southern California? What did Black Mesa mean to the Hopi? What did it mean to the Navajo, for whom Black Mesa was also sacred ground? What forces had caused the coal leasing to come about? And what exactly had John Boyden done?

Never had an old saying of Paul Roca's seemed so apt. When asked how long it would take to complete a complicated research project—whether it involved business law or the Spanish missions of Sonora—Paul would reply: "How long is a ball of string?" I had only the tip of the exposed strand between my thumb and forefinger.

# C h a p t e r 7

# JACK

**J**ohn Boyden grew up in Coalville, Utah, 50 miles northeast of Salt Lake City in the Weber River Valley. The town was founded in 1859 as Chalk Creek but its name was changed when Englishmen, who had come to Utah as Mormon converts, discovered coal in the area in the early 1870s. The mines were located outside of town and the valley continued to be settled for farming and cattle ranching. By the time John Sterling Boyden was born on April 14, 1906, Coalville had about twelve hundred residents, nearly all of them Mormon.

The Boydens were one of the leading Coalville families, active in government and church affairs. John's grandfather, a dairy farmer, served as mayor and county selectman. His father, who managed the family's farm and ranch properties rather than worked them directly, was a school-teacher, principal, and superintendent. He also served on the city council and on the State Dairy and Food Commission. The family owned "Boyden Block." Their handsome, three-story brick home, the largest in town, was just a few paces from the combination drugstore and soda fountain operated by John's uncle. The townspeople led outdoor lives and as a boy John did a good deal of hunting, fishing, and trapping muskrat in the Weber River, which ran through the family property. He also became an avid reader. The home was filled with books. Young John's favorite was the leather-bound complete works of Charles Dickens.

At Coalville High School, John was a popular and respected student. Mr. C. B. Copley, one of John's high school teachers (and still active at ninety-five years old when I met with him in 1994), describes him as a "better than average, hard-working student," but "not an intellectual giant." He was a boy of "very high integrity." Mr. Copley liked and respected John—and years later was proud to vote for him twice for governor of Utah. John was a skilled debater, the leader of the small-town team that nearly won the state debating championship. Upon his graduation in 1924, the *Summit County Bee* wrote this in an article headlined "A Splendid Young Man":

> *Perhaps John Boyden believes what Henry Ford says, that "work is not only the life of the body, but the builder up of the mind." However, when it comes to AMBITION, we will all certainly have to take our hats off to this boy.*

John entered the University of Utah in Salt Lake City and, after just three years, began the study of law there. He became active in politics, holding high positions in both the Junior Democratic Clubs of Utah and the Young Democratic Clubs of America and campaigning for Al Smith during his presidential bid. Along with twelve other graduates, he received his law degree in 1929.

His hometown newspaper was right about his ambition. Despite the Depression, the young lawyer made a go of it in private practice in Salt

# CONFLICTS AND CONQUESTS

Lake City for four years. Then, in 1933, when the Democrats came back into power, United States Attorney Dan B. Shields named him as assistant U.S. Attorney, a position he held for thirteen years. The office assigned him diverse, interesting cases, and he acquired heavy responsibilities. John masterminded the 1944 raids on Short Creek, the polygamous community on the Utah–Arizona border. The Mormon Church wanted the crackdown in order to avoid still more criticism over polygamy, and Boyden threw himself into the raids and prosecutions. His picture was splashed on the front pages and the affair became known variously as "the Boyden Raids" and "the Boyden Crusade."

John also was assigned many Indian cases because of his interest in Indian matters. The U.S. Attorney's office represented tribes and individual Indians in litigation, and John had the chance to meet leaders from the Ute, Hopi, and Navajo tribes.

The relationships grew. John was a big man, well over six feet tall, handsome and outgoing with an infectious smile. He was genuinely drawn to Indian people, and they liked and respected him. In June 1938, John and his new wife of two years, the beautiful and intelligent Orpha Sweeten Boyden, bundled up their six-month-old baby, John Jr., for a summer vacation. They headed southeast, down to Shiprock and Window Rock, in Navajo country. Then the Boydens drove on to Black Mesa. "We did," Orpha wrote later, "all the tourist things, bought many Indian-made articles (which later became very valuable), and visited with any Indians who would talk to us. . . . The roads were hazardous, hence very few travelers, but we were undaunted." Orpha Boyden observed that "as John visited with Indians and Bureau of Indian Affairs people, he had no idea it would lead to a lifetime relationship with the Hopi Tribe."

Boyden left the U.S. Attorney's office in 1946 for full-time private practice in Salt Lake City. In the same year he took on his first tribal client, the Uintah and Ouray Ute Indian Tribe of Utah. Boyden came to the Utes at a pivotal time. The United States was making money payments to the tribes—not money that would seem big to mainstream Americans but the kind of money that looked very big indeed to dirt-poor people still living

# Jack

mostly off the land in the subsistence way. Big, perhaps, but wrapped in confusions. Suppose the money was hooked to termination—to the end of tribal life? Suppose it was blood money—payments for the old living and hunting grounds?

In May 1950, John Boyden, with his cocounsel from Washington, D.C., stood before the Utes in an old schoolhouse on the Ute Reservation in northern Utah at the foot of the Uinta Range. The lawyers had come to talk about money and land, about a final payment from the United States for the tribe's ancestral land in western Colorado, land guaranteed to the Utes by treaty but forcibly taken by the federal government during the 1870s and 1880s. The lawyers had a proposal, a settlement. But the room held more than the list of attendees would suggest. The men of so many exploits, the heroes of those terrible times when the land was lost—Ouray and Jack—were there, as well, right there in the schoolhouse room, and so was the land.

The tenure of the Ute people on the northern Colorado Plateau traces back farther than we can fully imagine. Some anthropologists think they migrated into the region between A.D. 1000 and 1300. Others believe that the modern Utes emerged from the Fremont people. The Fremont, who date back at least four thousand years ago, lived both in villages and on the move, hunting and gathering, and leaving behind housing sites, baskets, pots, and magical pictographs and petroglyphs. In turn, the Fremont probably evolved from hunters and gatherers who lived on the Colorado Plateau beginning some twelve thousand years ago or more.

The Ute have their own explanation. At the beginning of time, Sinawahv, the Creator, had all the peoples of the world in a bag. He opened the bag and placed the Ute in their mountain, plains, and desert country: in the best place. By any account, the current of Ute blood runs very, very deep out here.

A dominant event in Ute history took place in the early 1600s when tribal members acquired the horse from the Spaniards. Vastly increased numbers of horses were later freed up by the Pueblos' revolt against the Spanish in 1680. With this fantastic new animal, the Ute became extraordinarily mobile. Bands of Utes ranged from the Wasatch Front all the way to the Colorado Front Range—from present-day Salt Lake City to Denver. They established a lasting trail system, including what is now Trail Ridge Road through Rocky Mountain National Park, the highest paved road in the United States. With the horse, these master horsemen traversed all the territory they wished, speeding across open plains, ascending to the high-mountain hunting grounds, dropping down into steep washes, draws, and canyons in that rough country.

Ute people today look back on this period as the time of times in all the centuries since Sinawahv released them from the bag. To be sure, in many ways life was hard. The winters, even in the lower-lying valleys, were brutally cold. A head injury, broken leg, or serious tooth infection could be a life-threatening event. Loved ones were lost in battles with the Shoshone, Navajo, and Plains tribes to the east. The Ute signed a peace treaty with the Spanish in the 1600s, but a treaty was of no use against the smallpox, measles, and other European diseases against which the Ute lacked immunity.

Yet the horse shut down so many threats and opened up so many options, so many freedoms. The curse of hunger, or outright famine, was essentially eliminated by the large-area hunting now made possible. The balance of power with other tribes and the Spanish shifted. The horseback Ute could escape, pursue, and fight so effectively that the other cultures conceded the Central Rockies to the Ute as their mountain stronghold.

This was especially true for the White River Band of Utes, who lived in the White and Yampa River Valleys in what is now northwestern Colorado. The mountain buffalo inhabited the high parks across the mountain spine to the east. With the horse it became almost a routine matter, for a productive hunt in the late spring, summer, or early fall, to head up the Yampa, cross the Continental Divide at Rabbit Ears Pass, and drop down into North Park. Or to ride up the White, traverse the level plateaus of the Flat

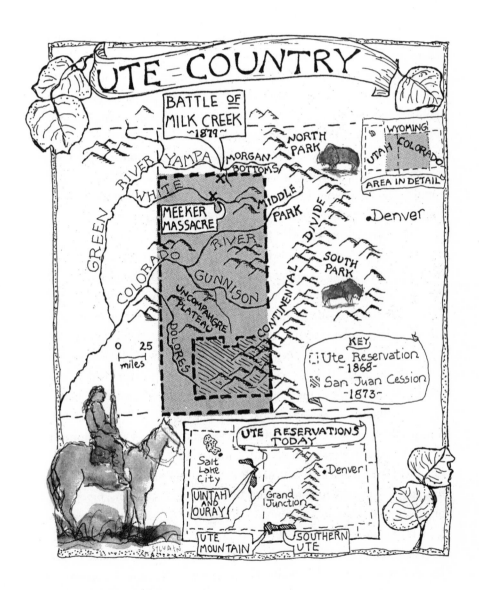

UTE COUNTRY

BATTLE OF MILK CREEK ~1879~

YAMPA

GREEN RIVER

WHITE

MORGAN BOTTOMS

NORTH PARK

MEEKER MASSACRE

MIDDLE PARK

COLORADO

RIVER

GUNNISON

UNCOMPAHGRE PLATEAU

CONTINENTAL DIVIDE

SOUTH PARK

DOLORES

0  25
miles

Denver

WYOMING

UTAH  COLORADO

AREA IN DETAIL

KEY
Ute Reservation
~1868~
San Juan Cession
~1873~

UTE RESERVATIONS TODAY

Salt Lake City

UINTAH AND OURAY

Grand Junction

Denver

UTE MOUNTAIN

SOUTHERN UTE

SILVAIN

# CONFLICTS AND CONQUESTS

Tops, descend their eastern flank, and then move up the mainstem Colorado River and the Fraser River to Middle Park. Yes, the Creator had chosen well and blessed the Ute: other than parts of the Pacific Northwest, Ute country held more kinds of mammals, and in greater numbers, than anywhere else in western North America.

The hunt was a time of heightened excitement. Ute hunters were splendidly arrayed in buckskins adorned with beads, fringe, paint, porcupine quills, and elk teeth. Eagle feathers flowed from their braided hair. Some of the hunting was done from stationary positions, behind cover, but when necessary the athletic hunters worked at top speed, united with their horses, using bows and arrows and, later, rifles. The whole community celebrated when the hunters returned in glory from a hunt, their pack horses trailing behind, weighed down with buffalo and elk meat.

What prizes the mountain buffalo were. They made a wonderful food—meaty, nutritious, delicious—whether cut into thin strips, smoked, and dried for the winter or put right on a spit. Their huge bodies yielded thick, versatile hides, which the Ute used for teepee exteriors (about ten hides were needed) and personal clothing. Sleeping robes made from the shaggy animals, along with the teepee fires, kept away the winter's bitter cold. The women tanned the hides. They scraped the fat off the fleshy side with a deer-bone knife, soaked the skin overnight, applied a mixture with a base of boiled brains, sunned the hide for several days, soaked it again, stretched it (a difficult and tedious job), smoked one side over an open fire, and then finished the hide by softening it through vigorous rubbing with a stone or rope. These hides were warm, pliant, durable, and handsome when decorated with paint, beads, and fringe. Buffalo hides were valuable in trade, too, allowing the Ute to obtain items from the south: clay pots, pipes, and bridles from the Apache and Navajo and steel fishhooks and brass bracelets from the Spanish. Although the Ute preferred mountain buffalo, the abundant deer, elk, antelope, and mountain sheep met most of the same needs.

The Ute made use of virtually the whole land. The cottonwood forests at Morgan Bottoms, an 11-mile stretch along the Yampa River near Hayden, Colorado, serve as a good example. For fuel, the Ute preferred cottonwood, especially in the summer when light, rather than heat, was the main objective: the cottonwood could throw out its bright flame with few sparks and a relatively low temperature. The cottonwood was also best for smoking meat since the smoke, not the heat, dried the meat. Cottonwood leaves were suited for wrapping tobacco as the smoke coated the throat and added flavor to the tobacco. The smoke on the singers' throats enhanced the quality of their voices, giving a stronger range. The White River Utes, employing squawbush and willows as the key materials, put their sturdy, tightly woven baskets (they rarely made pots) to many uses. They ate serviceberries raw or else cooked them and dried them into cakes. An important Ute food, found near Morgan Bottoms, was a succulent tuber of the carrot family that grows in northwestern Colorado and gave the valley its name: the Yampa plant.

Morgan Bottoms, then as now, was spectacular wildlife habitat. The Ute hunted the deer and elk that wintered there. They had less interest in the fish since big game was so plentiful, but they did take some cutthroat trout, suckers, whitefish, and chub with spears, weirs, and their Mexican-made fishhooks. The White River Utes prized eagles for their feathers and bones, which they used as whistles.

Black bear had special importance, too, and used the thick underbrush of the cottonwood forests as cover. Ute dancers wore the bearskins during the Bear Dance, the major festival held in the early spring when the leaves began to turn green. Bear Dance celebrated a new, hopeful year and a good hunt.

Morgan Bottoms was one of hundreds upon hundreds of places integral to the Utes of northwestern Colorado in their intricate life. They camped there for extended periods and used it as a stopover point along the Yampa corridor on the way to and from the mountain hunts. A vivid reminder of the Ute way of life can be found just upstream from Morgan Bottoms. On a vertical cliff up above the river floor is a panel of Ute pictographs with many burnished-red figures, including a rider on horseback.

This horse tribe controlled its domain, apparently with little competition, for more than two hundred years. Then events beyond the Utes' homeland began to take a toll. Americans discovered gold in faraway California in 1848 and, in the same year, the United States wrested territory that now comprises all or part of seven states, including much of the Yampa and White country, away from Mexico. In 1859 and the early 1860s, gold was struck all along the Colorado Front Range, drawing would-be miners from the east and from the mining camps in California and Nevada. By the late 1860s, although few non-Indians had entered Ute country yet, the Ute were caught in a vise.

**O**uray is renowned as the great nineteenth-century hero of the Ute. He is praised in all the history books, honored in all the lists of leading figures in Colorado history. Raised partly in an Apache family, he came to his own tribe as a young adult and quickly assumed leadership in the Uncompahgre Band, which lived in the Gunnison and Uncompahgre Valleys south of the Yampa and White. Eventually he came to be tacitly acknowledged as a spokesperson for the seven Ute bands at treaty time. Federal officials respected him as an able diplomat, a man of transcendent judgment, skill, and reliability. Ouray was quadrilingual, fluent in Spanish, English, and his two Indian tongues.

In 1868, despite facing relentless pressures for Ute land, Ouray was the principal negotiator in what was, from the tribal side, perhaps the most favorable Indian treaty in American history. The Ute domain recognized by this treaty encompassed 16 million acres, one-fifth of Colorado, 120 miles west to east, 200 miles south to north, from the New Mexico border nearly all the way to Wyoming. Most of the high mountains, the place of the summer hunts where the animals must have seemed limitless, lay within the reservation. So did the lowlands, where the Ute and the big game wintered. The government, as well, assured the Ute they could hunt on aboriginal lands that lay outside the reservation, which included the White River watershed but not the Yampa. The Ute owned the whole reser-

# Jack

vation—guaranteed by the 1868 treaty and by settled principles of United States real property law—forever.

Although a skilled hunter and horseman, after the 1868 treaty Ouray gradually began to take on many of the trappings of the whites, their dress, wines, and cigars. He acquired a Mexican servant, worked at a formal desk, and took rides in a carriage given to him by General Edward McCook. He encouraged his people to farm. Ouray had his policy reasons—he felt that coexistence with the whites was essential and wanted to demonstrate some of the benefits of non-Indian society—but his assimilationist ways did not sit well with many Utes.

Photographs of Ouray display a figure of dignity and respect. His clothing is always neat and prim, his broad face open and soft, welcoming. One can see how the Indian agents, the governor of Colorado, even presidents of the United States, were drawn to him. Ouray inspired trust, affection, and comfort in the new people who were so keenly interested in Ute land.

Not Jack. This ultimate leader of the White River Utes, who rode the White and Yampa Valleys, to the north of Ouray's Uncompahgre Band, was born Goshute and taken in for several years of his youth by a Mormon family in Utah. That life was too shackling: the wrong clothes, the wrong schooling, the wrong god, the wrong land. He fled to the mountains in his teens and took up with the Ute, who were closely aligned with the Goshutes. In the early spring, just as the cottonwood leaves were turning green, he lived the Bear Dance for days and a young Ute woman took him as her husband. The Ute welcomed him into the tribe: the custom was to take in Indians from other tribes and, if they became fully part of the society, grant them tribal status.

Jack became so completely accepted by the White River Utes, the most unrelenting Ute band, because his personality so completely matched. He loved the hunt. He rode with abandon. He was fierce: photographs show a lean, leathery man with a hatchet of a face. Jack had no desire at all to be conciliatory. Yes, he had signed the 1868 treaty along with Ouray and seven other Ute leaders but he did that out of strength and an exact knowledge of the treaty's provisions: the treaty had set aside a reservation that included most of the hunting grounds, and the United States guaranteed the Ute access to those traditional hunting areas, such as the Yampa Valley and North and Middle Parks, that lay outside the reservation. And the words of the treaty, which Jack knew by heart, stipulated that no white people, except authorized federal agents, could enter Ute country without permission of the tribe. Jack had no desire to settle down and coexist with white people as a fellow farmer, which was what the white people wanted. He had the opposite desire. Ute country was for the Ute and for the Ute alone.

Some of the older White River Utes, believing that cooperation with the whites was inevitable and necessary, thought Jack too abrasive, but the younger people, and most of the elders, idolized him. He became spokesman for the White River Utes, the band most determined to hold onto the Ute way—the way of the horse and the hunt.

The fury that would descend on Ute country in 1879, or something like it, became inevitable on May 10, 1878, when Nathan Meeker arrived at the White River Agency as the new federal Indian agent, soon to be joined by his wife, Arvilla, and daughter, Josephine. Tension hung in the air like cottonwood smoke. The Ute felt betrayed by the 1873 Brunot Agreement, which had removed 4 million acres, including most of the San Juan Mountains in southwestern Colorado, from the reservation after gold and silver had been found in the San Juans. The White River Utes did not hunt much in those southern mountains, but they knew their band was directly threatened by the precedent of ceding away Ute treaty land. They hated mining: it promoted a sedentary lifestyle and was an affront to the land they revered. Why should a whole mountain range be given over to such people? Then, too, the 1873 agreement seemed a clear threat to the status quo that Jack, Ouray, and many other Utes had tried so hard to achieve. How firm were the solemn promises made in the great 1868 treaty?

And events had worsened since 1873. In 1876, Colorado became a state and the event of statehood seemed to signal to the non-Indian residents

# Jack

that local, rather than Ute, prerogatives were paramount. Frederick Pitkin, who made a fortune mining in the San Juans, was the governor. Prospectors continued to look for gold and silver on the reservation, and homesteaders came through to assess its worth for farming. Jack had gone to Denver on behalf of his people to meet with Pitkin. The governor's views were clear and oft-stated. He addressed the issue in his first inaugural speech and regularly thereafter: Pitkin wanted the Ute out of Colorado.

In his own mind, Nathan Cook Meeker had nothing but the best interests of the Ute at heart. Idealistic through and through, Meeker had become captivated by utopian agrarian communities and after the Civil War wrote an agricultural column for Horace Greeley's *New York Tribune*. With Greeley's encouragement and financial backing, Meeker went west to Colorado and in 1869 founded Union Colony, one of the most famous communal farm societies. The nearest town was named Greeley, after Union Colony's benefactor. The colony prospered as irrigation canals were built, crops raised, and produce shipped to Denver and other markets.

Meeker's own star, however, fell. When Horace Greeley died, his estate called in as a debt the seed money that Greeley had advanced to Meeker. Soon thereafter, the members of the colony voted Meeker down as leader. He was out of a job and, perhaps even worse, bereft of a pulpit for his fervid views on the verities of farming and the hardworking, worthwhile communities it built. Senator Henry Teller of Colorado, however, saw the right fit for Meeker and arranged for his appointment as Indian agent at White River. The sixty-year-old Meeker plunged in, full-spirited and determined to assist the Ute in the high-minded objective of making the necessary transition to a civilized, that is, agricultural, life. His way of using the land was better than the Utes' way and he would convince them of that truth.

Meeker's first move was to relocate the White River Agency about 15 miles downstream to a site (now the town of Meeker) where the valley widened out and the level ground and good topsoil would make for much better farming. There were political rivalries among Ute leaders. Quinkent and the medicine man Canalla, both older and more conciliatory toward the whites, were willing to move. Jack was adamantly opposed. The new location was farther from the mountains and the hunt, and he argued strenuously that the treaty had mandated that the agency be at the existing site. Although the treaty had no such requirement on its face, the provisions regarding the agency are sufficiently extensive (requiring, among other things, the construction of several buildings) as to suggest that the original site was to be permanent. And Jack, as a treaty negotiator in 1868, may have known of assurances made during the negotiations. In any event, despite Jack's understanding of the treaty, Meeker was not to be deterred. In an action that probably seemed to him routine rather than momentous, the federal installation was relocated.

The summer of 1879 came in hot, dry, and tense. Governor Pitkin was beginning his second term and Ute removal remained at the top of his list of priorities. Terrifying fires broke out on Colorado's tinder-dry Western Slope, burning valuable timber stands and sending homesteads up in flames. Pitkin trumpeted as "facts" the complaints of settlers that raiding parties of Utes had set the fires:

*Reports reach me daily that a band of White River Utes are off their reservation, destroying forests and game near North and Middle Parks. They have already burned millions of dollars of timber, and are intimidating settlers and miners. . . . These savages should be removed to the Indian Territory, where they can no longer destroy the finest forests in this State.*

The governor was giving the Ute-hating segment of his constituency what it wanted. For them, the great 1868 treaty reservation was a travesty, allocating an absurd amount of farmland and valuable minerals to the tribe, and they welcomed any justification for removing the Ute from the state. Never mind that it was common knowledge all over the West that miners and loggers were notoriously careless and their fires regularly ravaged the forestlands and threatened settlements. Never mind that the reports of Ute aggression from white settlers were not substantiated (and, even after federal investigation, never would be). Settlers began to issue reprisals. At least one Ute hunter was shot down as an arsonist on suspicion only, the West's version of a lynching. Fair recompense, many settlers thought. The Ute did not belong in Colorado.

Nathan Meeker was growing increasingly jittery. The fires and the pressure from the governor and the settlers—which intensified when gold was discovered on reservation land to the south and miners promptly rushed in—were coupled with severe difficulties at the agency. Meeker wasn't gaining the respect of the Ute. Moving the agency headquarters had caused deep bitterness. Quinkent and Canalla had relocated their camps to the new agency, but Jack and his followers remained 10 miles upstream.

Further, the annuities—the treaty had elaborate provisions guaranteeing annual shipments of food and goods such as blankets and clothing—were late. The goods were important to the Ute: not only could tribal members use them, but Ute hunters could trade them to settlers for rifles and ammunition. Although the delay in the arrival of the annuities was not Meeker's fault (the Union Pacific rail shipments to Fort Steele, at present-day Rawlins, Wyoming, 150 miles north, were being held in a warehouse pending government payment), he was branded with the problem regardless.

**M**eeker's personal foibles added to his problems. He insisted that the Ute call him "Father," which plainly irritated them. Behind his back, and a few times to his face, they called Meeker—who to a non-Indian's eye was handsome, erect, and dignified—an "old lady" because he seemed so inept in Ute country, so out of harmony with the place. Moreover, fearing conflicts with settlers, he told the Ute that they should not leave the reservation—which the Ute knew to be contrary to federal policy and assurances given at the time of the 1868 treaty. Meeker saw himself as a good man headed in the best direction for both the Ute and his own people. But at the same time he knew that his problems were spiraling, and he began to fear for his own safety and, worse yet, for that of Arvilla and Josephine.

# CONFLICTS AND CONQUESTS

The Indian agent had been able to put nearly 200 acres under the plow. In early September 1879, he ordered two additional parcels to be plowed and made ready for irrigation the next spring. One of the areas was a track where the younger Utes raced their horses. The other was the field where Canalla, the old medicine man who had tried to cooperate with Meeker, pastured his ponies.

Meeker's mandate threw the Ute into an uproar. They didn't like plowing to begin with—it tore up the earth and symbolized the new life the white people were trying to force on them—and these were not places where plowing made any sense. The races were good for the young riders and showed off the magical skills of the horse. Canalla needed his pasture for his many ponies. Still, this was not a time to anger the white people. Danger was in the air. There was a great deal of talk among the Ute, some with Meeker, much more in the teepees with elder-stem pipes and the tobacco wrapped in cottonwood leaves.

Meeker decided to go ahead with the plowing. Canalla, who was not a volatile sort, went to the agency and confronted the Indian agent, who was having his lunch. Pushing and jostling ensued between the two older men. Canalla pushed Meeker through the open door and the agent landed in a heap outside the building. His body seemed not to be hurt, but his dignity was. On September 10, 1879, Nathan Meeker shot out fateful calls for assistance to Governor Pitkin and the Interior Department. The telegram to Washington reported:

> I have been assaulted by a leading chief . . . forced out of my own house, and injured badly, but was rescued by employés . . . life of self, family, and employés not safe; want protection immediately; have asked Governor Pitkin to confer with General Pope.
>
> N. C. Meeker, Indian Agent

Interior referred the matter to the War Department, which on September 15 ordered troops to be dispatched to Meeker's aid. The nearest installation was Fort Steele in Wyoming, where troops were under the command of Major Thomas T. Thornburgh. Thornburgh did not take immediate action. This was autumn in the Central Rockies and the major was out on an elk hunt. The Indian forts in the West had become somewhat low-key operations in recent years. The Sioux and the Nez Perce had been subdued and the general assumption was that the last Indian war had already been fought.

But enough telegrams, reports, and rumors were flying around Colorado in general and Ute country in particular that Jack became concerned. He decided to travel north to Fort Steele to talk matters through. Jack and ten of his men headed up Coal Creek Canyon to the divide between the White and the Yampa. This divide, where Milk Creek begins to flow north, was the northern boundary of the reservation. When the riders dropped down into the bottomlands of the Yampa, they learned that federal soldiers were in the area. The Utes sought out Major Thornburgh's camp.

On September 26, Jack and Thornburgh discussed the situation at length. Jack said that he and the Ute wanted only peace and to be left alone: "I told them that I never expected to see the soldiers here. I told him we were all under one government, Indians and soldiers, and that the government at Washington ordered us both; that we were brothers, and why had they come?" Thornburgh truthfully said that he, too, wanted peace and that his orders were to avoid combat. He related the federal government's concerns about the fires—concerns that had been aggravated by still more reports from Pitkin.

Jack, exasperated because he thought he had cleared up the matter of the fires during a meeting just a few months earlier with the governor in Denver, explained that the fires absolutely were not set by Utes. Further, ever precise, ever focused on the language of the hard-negotiated treaty, the Ute leader argued that any entry into the reservation would be in violation of the treaty and an act of war. Ute land was, according to the treaty, "set apart for the absolute and undisturbed use and occupation" of the Ute. The treaty also said that "no persons . . . shall ever be permitted to pass over, settle upon, or reside" on the reservation.

Thornburgh had some treaty words on his side. There was an exception for "officers . . . of the government as may be authorized to enter upon

Indian reservations in discharge of duties enjoined by law." Thornburgh showed Jack his official orders. Jack understood Thornburgh's point but pressed his own position that there was no reason why federal troops, for the first time ever, should encroach on Ute land. The Ute had never engaged in combat with the United States. The fires were not set by Utes. Canalla had done no damage to Meeker.

The next morning, Jack returned to Thornburgh's camp to offer a compromise. Leave your troops in the Yampa Valley at least 50 miles from the agency, well north of the reservation line, and proceed with just five men to the agency. You can investigate the circumstances and will see that there are no possible grounds for bringing in your army. Jack hurried back to the agency on the same day, September 27, and Meeker promptly sent Thornburgh a message by runner supporting Jack's proposal. The agent urged the major to proceed with just five men and said that "the Indians are greatly excited" and "seem to consider the advance of troops as a declaration of real war."

Thornburgh initially acceded. He seemed satisfied with the talks with Jack. After their first meeting, the major wired his superior:

*Have met some Ute chiefs here. They seem friendly and promise to go with me to agency. Say Utes don't understand why we have come. Have tried to explain satisfactorily. Do not anticipate trouble.*

On September 27, Thornburgh wrote to Meeker that he would follow Jack's plan: he would camp down on Milk Creek, well north of the reservation, and then "come in, as desired, with five men and a guide."

But after discussions with his officers and scouts, Thornburgh's hierarchical sense of duty prevailed. He had been ordered to proceed with troops to the reservation. Leaving his army fifty miles distant did not conform to his orders. On September 28, Thornburgh formally reversed himself and sent a letter by horseback messenger to Meeker, saying that he would enter the reservation, leave the force "within striking distance of your agency," and then come in with a guide and five soldiers.

Meeker replied on September 29 at 1 P.M. It was an ambiguous response.

# Jack

He endorsed the march onto the reservation: "I like your last programme, it is based on true military principles." But he also downplayed any trouble and sent a clear signal that he was safe:

> *I expect to leave in the morning with [two Ute leaders] to meet you; things are peaceable, and [Quinkent] flies the United States flag. If you have trouble in getting through the cañon [on upper Milk Creek] today, let me know in what force. We have been on guard three nights and shall be to-night, not because we know there is danger, but because there may be.*

Perhaps something in Meeker's letter might have caused the major to reconsider his decision to march his troops into Ute country. We do not know, for Thornburgh never received the message.

**A** mixture of fear, despair, and determination had settled in among the Ute. No one knew what Thornburgh had in mind but they did know from Jack's reports that the major and his troops had reached the Yampa. And every single Ute knew the horrors of the Sand Creek Massacre east of Denver in 1864 when Colonel John Chivington led his murderous, irresponsible, and unnecessary charge on Black Kettle and the Cheyenne. Two hundred Cheyenne, most of them women and children, were slaughtered. Thomas Thornburgh was not remotely a John Chivington, but the Ute did not know that. They knew only that he was marching toward their land and that there seemed to be no reason for it.

On September 27 and 28, young Ute men began to move up toward the headwaters of Milk Creek, at the north edge of the reservation, and made camp on high ground. Below them was the trail over which Thornburgh might be advancing with his troops and wagons. Down at the agency, most of the old men, women, and children moved their camps south across the White River, away from the federal installation. Dancing and singing went on nearly all night.

# CONFLICTS AND CONQUESTS

Jack, who spent the night near the agency, was on his way before first light on September 29. He rode up past the autumn-yellow cottonwoods along Coal Creek as he had a few days before, but this was different from that exploratory mission to meet with Thornburgh. His scouts had reported that troops were moving up Milk Creek. Would Thornburgh honor his request to leave the troops on lower Milk Creek? The Ute leader could not be sure. But his approach remained the same as it had been over the past few days—indeed over the many years that he had held responsibility for his tribe's future. Look for solutions but be firm. See that the treaty is honored. Preserve Ute land. Preserve the hunt.

Jack crossed over Yellowjacket Pass, rode through the narrow Milk Creek canyon, and arrived at the large bowl just below. He found, as he knew he would, some fifty Ute young men camped at the high edge of the bowl among the sparse junipers. Jack's wife and children had come over from their camp. The young men, many in their early teens, were singing solemnly. Most wore Ute war paint, yellow and black. They were edgy. Jack, the young men, and Colorow, another Ute leader, gathered. They talked, telling each other what they knew, and waited to see what would appear on the trail down below.

At midday, Major Thornburgh and an advance column broke into view on the sagebrush-lined trail at the far end of the bowl. They proceeded on, followed by a long line of soldiers. Now Jack knew that Thornburgh did not intend to abide by Jack's request. He directed his wife and children to return to the camp. Thornburgh waved to the Utes and Jack waved back. Wanting to confer with the major and slow things down, Jack told his men to hold their fire and moved his horse down the side of the bowl toward the troops.

A shot—no one knows whose—exploded and filled the bowl with instant sound and history. Jack shouted out to both sides, "Hold on! Hold on!" but full-scale combat was already raging. Within minutes, Major Thornburgh was dead, shot in the head. The Utes kept his troops pinned for five days until relief forces rescued them. In all, twelve United States soldiers were killed and forty-three wounded. Thirty-seven Utes died.

# Jack

At the moment firing broke out, Ute riders raced down Coal Creek to the agency to warn their people of the danger. At about 2 P.M., Quinkent and perhaps twenty other Utes, furious at Thornburgh's march on Ute land and releasing more than a year's pent-up anger at Nathan Meeker, took immediate action. They killed Meeker (who had just dispatched his ambiguous letter to Thornburgh), all six other agency employees, and eleven other white men. They drove a stake through Meeker's mouth so, they said, his lies would finally cease, even in the afterlife. Twelve Utes, led by Quinkent, then kidnapped sixty-three-year-old Arvilla and daughter Josephine Meeker and a Mrs. Price, holding them for twenty-three days. The hostages initially reported that their captors had treated them well. Later, Mrs. Meeker testified that Quinkent had forced her into sexual intercourse on one occasion. Josephine said that she suffered the same from a Ute named Pah-sone.

Outrage and panic over the battle, the killings at the agency, and the kidnapping and asserted rape of the women spread all over Colorado, on the front pages, in the public lecture halls, over the dinner tables. Governor Pitkin inflamed the anti-Ute hatred with his telegrams to the Western Slope: "Indians off their reservation, seeking to destroy your settlements by fire, are game to be hunted and destroyed like wild beasts." In the months to come, Josephine Meeker made sure the furor did not die down. She took to the lecture circuit and gave detailed descriptions, far more lurid than anything she said to federal officials, of the indignities she suffered during her captivity.

Federal hearings were held promptly in Colorado and Washington to investigate the situation. Ouray, who had been at his home in Uncompahgre Park far to the south at the time of the battle and had struggled to keep both sides calm during the ensuing days and weeks, acted as what amounted to chief counsel for the Ute. The proceedings, especially those in Washington, seem generally to have been open and fair, due in good part to Ouray's vigorous and skillful representation. Jack and the other Ute soldiers were exonerated. (The Battle of Milk Creek was seen as a misunderstanding, ripening into combat, between two governments.) The killings at the agency and the treatment of the three women were viewed differently, however, and Quinkent and the others would have to face federal charges.

The investigations, which drew out all of the tangled circumstances of this clash of cultures with such disparate worldviews, could theoretically have led to a balanced resolution of the Ute's situation. Perhaps the tribe could have retained a substantial, albeit smaller, reservation in Colorado that omitted the agricultural and mineral lands coveted by the settlers. Perhaps that smaller reservation could have been coupled with off-reservation hunting rights in the mountain hunting grounds so dear to the Ute. But that kind of history did not match the passions of the times—that is, the passions of the settlers, whose passions counted. It was impossible for the Ute to remain in Colorado.

**W**hen the Utes were ordered back to Washington for the hearings in early 1880, they were told they would have to negotiate still another "agreement." All the Utes knew what this meant. It would be much worse than the Brunot Agreement in 1873. All the land—almost all of it, anyway—would go. So would the hunt. Jack balked at making the humiliating journey to sign papers of conquest. He considered traveling to Dakota Territory to join Sitting Bull. In the end, Jack did go to Washington.

The final 1880 agreement, passed by Congress in June, erased the treaty signed twelve years earlier. The Southern Utes were to be located on a strip of low-lying land in southern Colorado adjacent to New Mexico Territory. The government would try to find unoccupied land for the Uncompahgre Utes in the Grand Valley. (This arrangement proved unacceptable to the settlers and the band was moved to the reservation of the Uintah Band of Utes in Utah.) Years later, a reservation was set aside for the Weeminuche Band in barren country in southwesternmost Colorado. As for Jack and the other White River Utes, the 1880 agreement was terse: "The White River Utes agree to remove to and settle upon agricultural lands on the Uintah Reservation in Utah." For all of the Ute bands these terms were dictated, of course, not negotiated. Jack was present but refused to sign. A photograph shows him gaunt and glowering, the leader of a horse people who had lost the hunt forever.

He had reason to glower. For we betrayed Jack and the Ute people in countless ways. We took away the land and the buffalo. We took away the hunt. We betrayed the trust lodged in the great 1868 treaty, a device of our making that embodies the solemn word of nations. Jack tried to hew to those words, those promises, in a precise and honorable way, but the promises were stamped out by an onrushing society that would not pause to negotiate.

We betrayed Jack in other ways. In our stampede to assimilate the Ute, we changed nearly all the Ute's names, including his. The man we called Jack was called Nicaagat by his own people. Nicaagat. It is a song of a name, with the *"c"* and the *"g"* pronounced with a soft guttural clip, with all the syllables pronounced equally, flowing like mountain water over pebbles. Ni-ca-a-gat. It means "leaves becoming green," the time when the cottonwoods come out, the time of the spring Bear Dance when he met his wife. Jack. Nicaagat.

And, in the end, we betrayed Nicaagat by driving a wedge between him and his people. Back in 1879, at the end of the commission hearings in Colorado, General Hatch announced that there would be no charges with respect to the battle with Thornburgh's troops but Quinkent and the other men involved in the killing of Meeker and the abduction of the three women must stand trial. Ouray, old and dying, outfitted once again in his buckskins in defiance of his former white friends, flashed out a last burst of rage. There would be no trial of Utes in Colorado. "All the people of Colorado and New Mexico are our enemies." The government, on the word of Interior Secretary Carl Shurz, whom the Ute trusted, agreed to a trial outside of Colorado. But the Ute would have to produce Quinkent and the others.

The Ute leaders at the hearing went into council. They agreed to the trial. They selected Nicaagat and Colorow to bring Quinkent in, which they did. But Quinkent's followers, who were few, never forgave Nicaagat.

# CONFLICTS AND CONQUESTS

Though most of the White River Utes revered him, it seems that Nicaagat could never again be safe among the Ute. In a sense, his destiny had become entwined with that of Ouray, who at times slept with guards at his door as a precaution against rivals who objected to his attempts to appease the whites. Eventually Nicaagat struck out with his wife and children, probably for the mountains, never to return to his people.

General Ranald MacKenzie was sent out with troops in May 1880 to superintend the removal of the White River and Uncompahgre Utes to Utah. The government soldiers rounded up approximately 1,800 Ute people and brought them to the junction of the Grand (later named the Colorado) and the Gunnison Rivers, now the site of Grand Junction. The White River Utes tried to resist one last time, saying they would not go. Utah was not their kind of country. That land already belonged to the Uintah Band and no additional land had been set aside for the White River Utes. The White and the Yampa country was their home. General Mac-Kenzie explained again and again that the move was inevitable.

In the spring of 1881, the despondent Ute failed to hold the Bear Dance for the first time since Sinawahv opened the bag. General MacKenzie had two difficult jobs, marching the Ute out and, in the meantime, restraining the rapidly gathering numbers of settlers wanting to stake their claims on former Ute lands. With the Ute he became more and more insistent. They wanted permission for one last hunt on the Yampa to put in meat for the winter. He refused. The Ute needed to be on the Uintah Reservation before winter broke and the settlers needed to beat winter also.

In late August 1881, the Ute and their persistent military keepers began final preparations for the move. MacKenzie held the settlers at bay. On September 6, the Ute moved out. On the last day the sky was marked by two large, separate clouds of dust. One was created by the White River and Uncompahgre Utes, slowly pushing west with their military escort and what was left of their belongings and their ponies. The other was created by the land rush of anxious settlers, released from the soldiers' restraint by a bugle call, pounding into the Grand Valley, now free of the Ute, to open it for settlement and farming.

# Jack

In the fall of 1993, Ute people came back to the site of the Battle of Milk Creek to dedicate their own monument. This monument tells the story of 1879 as they believe it, and it now sits next to the one the non-Indians erected many years ago to honor Major Thornburgh and his fallen soldiers. The powerful ceremony drew a gathering of more than a thousand people, Ute from Utah and southern Colorado, National Public Radio and Channel Four from Denver, numerous citizens from Meeker and the surrounding area, and many from around Colorado, such as myself and my son David. We all listened intently to the speakers, trying to search out meaning from their words about the whirl of events that descended upon this place more than a century ago. Luke Duncan, erect and dark and in braids, said simply: "We were removed to a country not our own. We still feel that loss today. It was very cruel." Then the eight Ute men seated around the deer-hide drum pounded out an honor song and the old sharp sounds pierced the autumn air of the White and Yampa country once again, and the overlay of the Ute experience hung thick over the sagebrush and juniper bowl.

Conquerors, as well as the conquered, are diminished when a trust is broken. We know now that we came on too hard and fast for the Ute. We could have accommodated settlement by non-Indians and also allowed for the White River Utes to hold good land in the Yampa and White country. We could have allowed for the hunt.

Betrayals, and all the lasting lessons we learn from them, die out when our memories die. This is why the forceful but careful and restrained, even gentle, reminders from the modern Utes matter so. These reminders hold our memories, they keep us fixed on truth, on Nicaagat, who may or may not still travel down the Yampa from the mountains, past the red horseback pictures drawn by his forebears, past the trees whose leaves turn green at the time of the Bear Dance, riding with precision, riding with his best eagle feathers and his finest pony, back from the hunt.

# UINTAH

**B**y the end of September 1881, federal troops had completed their task of marching the White River and Uncompahgre Utes 200 miles north and west to the reservation of the Uintah Band of Utes in Utah. Most of the Colorado Utes knew this land from their travels, but the drier, lower country could not compare to their chosen homeland. Moreover the removal of the two bands to Utah angered the members of the Uintah Band: the federal government never consulted them as to whether they wanted to share the scarce resources of their reservation with the arrivals from Colorado.

The assaults on Ute land continued. Now, however, the implements of conquest shifted from straight-shooting carbines to convoluted and insidious federal laws. The technical complexity of these new devices would prove every bit as difficult for the Utes to defend against as the violence of war. In time, needing legal representation for guidance and protection, all three Ute bands turned to John Boyden. During the 1950s and 1960s, in the climax to a tumultuous century of dealings between the Utes and the United States, Boyden would preside over a labyrinthine series of transactions that cut ever more deeply into Ute land, water, sovereignty, and culture.

The government's relocation of the White River and Uncompahgre Bands to Utah was one more blow to the Uintahs. They too had seen their world nearly obliterated within just a few years. The Uintah Band is the name given collectively to the several Ute bands whose aboriginal territory included Utah. Their most intensely used area reached from the abundant hunting grounds of the Wasatch Front to the Uinta Mountains. (The mountains, river, and basin are spelled Uinta, but you add an "*h*" for the band and the Uintah and Ouray Tribe.) The Wasatch Front received a steady stream of new inhabitants during the 1840s and 1850s. As the church made mission calls, Mormon communities—Coalville, Parawan, many others—sprang up.

Despite Brigham Young's policy of talking before fighting, conflicts with the Utes did break out. Chief Walkara repeatedly led raids on the encroaching Mormon settlements. In 1861, Abraham Lincoln signed an executive order setting aside the whole Uinta Basin (the watershed of the Uinta and Duchesne Rivers, including the area draining the south slope of the Uinta Range) as a reservation for the Utes of Utah.

Lincoln's reservation—over 2 million acres—might seem large, but to the Uintah Utes, who had never agreed to it, it was confining. They had lived on most of the land in what the whites now called Utah, and they refused to move to this limited reservation. In 1865, federal officials persuaded Ute chiefs to negotiate a formal treaty that guaranteed them about $1 million, as well as cattle and the construction of schools and homes. The Spanish Fork Treaty required the Utes to give up all of their land in Utah except for the Uinta Basin, which the treaty confirmed to the Utes, as had the 1861 executive order. Reluctantly the Utes moved to the Uinta Basin.

The problem with the 1865 treaty was that Brigham Young supported it. He wanted the Utes out of the way of Mormon settlement and, as far as he could tell, the Uinta Basin was one place the church could do without. Young had dispatched an exploratory party and their verdict was unanimous and firm: the Uinta was "one vast 'contiguity of waste,' and measurably valueless, except for nomadic purposes, hunting grounds for Indians and to hold the world together." Exactly right for the Utes, from Young's point of view. But Congress—at odds with Utah over the polygamy controversy—was not impressed by Brigham Young's blessing. This left the Uintah Utes, who had bargained in good faith and given up most of their land, caught in the middle of the United States/Mormon controversy.

Under the Constitution, a treaty, even though formally signed by official federal representatives, does not go into effect until the Senate approves it. And the Senate never ratified the Spanish Fork Treaty. Although the reservation in the Uinta Basin remained in place under the terms of the 1861 executive order, the Uintahs never did receive the payments and other promises in the treaty. While the United States could disavow the Spanish Fork Treaty, as a practical matter the Uintah Band could not: its members had already moved to the Uinta Basin and federal soldiers would not allow them to return to their former lands, where homesteaders were beginning to settle. The Uintahs had a homeland, but it was a homeland made of force and deceit as well as soil.

When the two bands of Colorado Utes arrived in Utah in 1881, both the Uintahs and the White Rivers deeply resented the new arrangement. From the Uintahs' side, the reservation was already too small. Now they had to share it with 550 members of the White River Band. The White Rivers, of course, were despondent at the loss of Colorado, and this was a poor substitute. The valley floor, where they were expected to live and farm, was a dust bowl. The one mildly redeeming feature was that the Uinta Range offered elk and deer hunting. But the reservation was minuscule compared to the Central Rockies, and it had to be shared with the Uintahs.

# Uintah

The government treated the third group, the Uncompahgres from Colorado, differently and this bred still more tensions among the bands. Although, like all of the Ute bands, the Uncompahgres had been decimated by disease and warfare, they were the largest band: they had a population of some 1,250 when they were marched to Utah. The Uncompahgres' numbers, along with the United States' gratitude to Ouray, who had died in Colorado in 1880, caused the government to create a separate land base. In 1882, President Chester Arthur set aside the Ouray Reservation, southeast of the Uintah Reservation, for the Uncompahgre Band.

The Ouray Reservation, most of it located on the high East Tavaputs Plateau, was rugged country. It was bounded on the west for 50 miles by the Green River, but here the waters stampeded at the bottom of a steep and rough gorge that cuts the Tavaputs Plateau in half. A soggy and chastened John Wesley Powell, after capsizing and losing guns and a barometer, named the canyon Desolation. Tavaputs East had good deer, elk, and bear

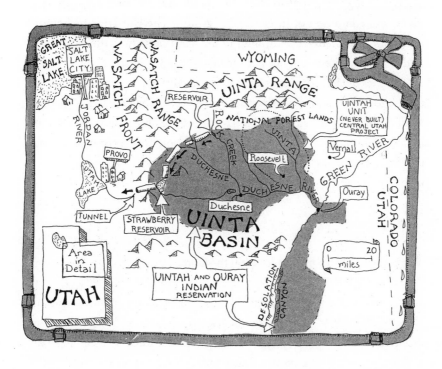

habitat, but the Indian agents were pushing the Uncompahgres toward farming and the reservation had a short growing season. This was no Colorado, but at least it was remote, away from the white people, and the Ouray Reservation was slightly larger than the Uintahs'.

The size of the Uncompahgres' lands enraged the Uintahs. The White Rivers needed no new reasons to be embittered toward the Uncompahgres: they still blamed the Uncompahgres for the Brunot Agreement of 1873, which eliminated the San Juan Mountains from the original Colorado reservation. Federal Indian agents aggravated jealousies among the bands by making unequal distributions of food rations and the small money payments.

The government now referred to all of these Indians collectively as the Ute Indian Tribe of the Uintah and Ouray Reservation, or the Uintah and Ouray Tribe, and administered the two separately created reservations as one. There was, however, no avoiding the fact that the Uintah and Ouray Tribe, although required to share one land base and one tribal government, was composed of three distinct groups. The Ute Tribe had always been a loose confederacy. Loyalties to the band came first, the nation second: it was like the difference between family and country.

The Utes of Utah, disoriented and split, had little time to gain any appreciation for the potential of what they still had left. The Uintah part of their landholdings amounted to 2 million acres and the Ouray part slightly more than 2 million. In all, the three bands held about 8 percent of Utah. But that homeland could not hold in the face of still more conquests—grabs of land, water, and other tribal rights, grabs of freedom, really.

The pressures from non-Indians on the Uintah and Ouray Ute lands were relentless and came from many different directions. Even the federal Indian agents—who, after all, were presiding over the breaking up of reservations all across the West—were taken aback. In 1887, T. A. Byrnes gave this incensed report: "These cattlemen have given me more trouble than all my Indians. . . . They have pastured their cattle for years on this reservation and swindled these Indians at every opportunity." Chief Happy Jack who, like Nicaagat and most other Utes, had his name changed by BIA agents, raged: "You [white people] are just like a storm from the mountains when the flood is coming down the stream, and we can't get help or stop it."

The flood came in the form of miners, farmers in the Uinta Basin, water users on the other side of the Wasatch Range, cattle and sheep ranchers, the Bureau of Reclamation, and the Forest Service. The key to opening up the Uintah and Ouray Reservation for non-Indians was allotment, which became official federal policy when Congress passed the General Allotment (or Dawes) Act in 1887. Allotment, ultimately applied to more than half of the nation's tribes, resulted in a drop in Indian landholdings from 140 million acres to 50 million between 1887 and 1934, when the allotment policy was abandoned in the Indian Reorganization Act.

The Utes, despite the complexities and subtleties of allotment, understood it well enough to resist it. Allotment had two parts, both deadly for an Indian reservation. True allotment, the first part, meant that 80-acre or 160-acre parcels of tribal land would be transferred to individual tribal members for farming or ranching. The stated purpose of allotment— sincerely held by some non-Indians, a homily for others—was to "civilize" Indians. For most Utes, this made no sense at all: why would the Utes, so committed to a hunting life, want to settle down on small, square, flat pieces of ground and farm? More often than not, Indians could not hold onto their allotments. Sharp-dealing non-Indians bought them up or they were lost at tax sales.

The second part of allotment was even more debilitating. Since Indians were going to become farmers and since each individual Ute's allotment would be ample for farming, then clearly the rest of the tribal land must be "surplus." Most of these "surplus" lands—including the bottom lands along the Duchesne River, the very best lands—would be opened for homesteading by non-Indians.

Congress, in 1902, enacted a statute calling for allotment of the Uintah and Ouray Reservation, but it was contingent on Ute consent. Despite government pressure, the tribe refused. Ute leader Happy Jack explained why there would be no consent: "The Indians understand the white man pretty well. . . . When the Indians take their land in allotments, they will lose everything they have. That will not be good." No matter. Congressman George Sutherland and his allies pushed another statute through Congress in 1905. This time there was no consent requirement.

On August 28, 1905, the Uintahs were exposed to their first land rush, the White Rivers and Uncompahgres to their second. The General Land Office found that Ute "surplus" lands had so many homestead applicants, no fewer than 37,702, that it had to set up a tent city in Provo to house them. A much-publicized drawing was held. The early-drawn names would have first choice of parcels. Then the floodgates opened.

But not before a critical presidential proclamation was issued. Gifford Pinchot, chief of the Forest Service, who had Teddy Roosevelt's ear and knew how to work Washington as well as anyone before or since, had his eye on western forestland. The high country in the Uinta Range would make a perfect acquisition since it was "surplus" to the Utes' needs—meaning that the land had little agricultural value, even though it was the Utes' only remaining hunting ground. A presidential proclamation, signed in 1905, added more than 100,000 acres of Ute land to the Uinta National Forest (today the Ashley National Forest).

In the space of just a few years, the landholdings of the Uintah and Ouray Tribe were decimated in the most literal sense: the Utes lost more than 90 percent of their land. By 1909, the tribal estate of more than 4 million acres was reduced to just 350,000 acres. The "vast contiguity of waste" had become, as one promotional ad exclaimed, "The Last Great Undeveloped Agricultural District of the United States and One of the Best."

The Utes, as well as other critics of allotment and related land policies in Utah, have customarily aimed their anger at "the Mormons." It is true that nearly all the active proponents of opening the Ute Reservation were Mormons. The problem with singling out Mormonism is that Congress, responding to local pressures for Indian land, was breaking up Indian reservations all across the West. It is hard to conclude, for example, that the Utes in Utah fared any worse at the hands of the Mormons than the Utes in Colorado did at the hands of gentiles.

# Uintah

One positive trend, however, developed for the Uintah and Ouray Tribe in the 1930s. As studies exposed the extent of land loss and poverty in Indian country, allotment became discredited and Congress halted it. Now federal policy turned and began to support tribal land acquisition. This brought important benefits to the Utes, who succeeded in restoring more than 600,000 acres to the Uintah and Ouray Reservation, which grew to 1 million acres, nearly one-fourth its former size.

But the land acquisitions did not close the many wounds of the down-trodden Utes. The acquired land was mostly nondescript grazing land, and tribal members were angered that most of the money to purchase the land came from the meager tribal funds (there were mineral leases on some tribal lands). The whites occupied all the best lands, along the river bottoms and the highways, and had use of most of the water. Mormon towns— Roosevelt, Duchesne, others—had been established inside the reservation boundaries. The federal government still held the hunting grounds in the high Uinta Range.

All of this history had become part of the fiber of Ute life when John Boyden became tribal attorney just after World War II. The elders told stories, the same stories that had been told to them, about the whole chain of events, back to Ouray, Nicaagat, and Walkara, all the way back to when Sinawahv opened the bag. For the Utes, though, this long experience was not exactly history. It all was so tangible, so close, so immediate, the past/ present of landscape and people that Kiowa author N. Scott Momaday calls "the remembered earth."

The old divisions among the bands had continued—if anything they had multiplied and grown deeper. The White Rivers still resented the Uncompahgres because of the Brunot Agreement of 1873. The Uintahs resented both the White Rivers and the Uncompahgres because the Colorado bands were interlopers. The White Rivers and Uncompahgres resented the Uintahs because the Uintahs had been much quicker to intermarry with the whites and hence had many more "Mixed-Bloods," as they were derisively called. Each band believed the government had favored the others in dispensing money, goods, and favors. The Uintahs took reasonably well to agriculture, the Uncompahgres took up ranching, the White Rivers never liked either much. Yet they were all Utes, bound together by blood, language, religion, and worldview, a commonality that made the layers of grievances even more intense.

The three bands, too, were bound together by a wrenching poverty. Some Utes lived in log cabins, but more made do with dirt-floor shanties nailed together out of whatever scrap could be found. Indoor plumbing and electricity were rare, mortality and alcoholism high, income and employment low.

Boyden had associated with Ernest Wilkinson, a leading Indian law specialist from Washington, D.C., and future president of Brigham Young University, in representing the Utes. Wilkinson achieved good results for some tribes, but he became controversial in Indian country. Some of this notoriety was due to his Mormonism and his paternalistic and domineering personality. Moreover, he was a "claims lawyer," which refers to various statutes allowing tribes to sue the United States over past wrongs for money damages—but not for the return of land. Indeed, Ernest Wilkinson authored the principal money-damage claims statute, the Indian Claims Commission Act of 1946, which explicitly ruled out the tribes' ability to recover lost land.\*

* I wish I could count how many times—surely more than a hundred—I have been asked if I am related to Ernest Wilkinson. My ordeal of fire over being named Wilkinson (there is no relationship between us) took place on a winter's morning in Neopit, Wisconsin, in December 1974. The Menominee Tribal Council had asked me to present to a general tribal meeting the tribe's plan for transferring its land back to the United States in trust. The Menominees had been terminated from federal status in 1954, but Congress had restored the tribe in 1973. The lengthy and complex restoration plan, which would be submitted to Congress for approval, was the dominant issue then facing the tribe. Presenting the plan was as weighty a responsibility as I have ever had. The gymnasium in Neopit was completely filled.

The tribal chair introduced me and I began. It would be an all-day meeting. Halfway into my first sentence, an old Menominee woman stood up in back and shouted, "Mr. Wilkinson!" "Yes?" I replied. "How," she asked, "can we trust you now when we couldn't trust you during the termina-

# Uintah

Wilkinson and Boyden called a general meeting of all White River and Uncompahgre Utes on May 29, 1950, at the old schoolhouse in Fort Duchesne. As the gathering coincided with the beginning of the Bear Dance, members converged from all corners of the reservation, riding their horses, beaten-up pickups, and Model Ts. The meeting was open to the Uintahs, but they could not vote because the White Rivers and Uncompahgres had to make a major decision on their claims case, pending for fifteen years, against the United States for the taking of their land in Colorado.

Wilkinson began by introducing a writer and photographer from *Life* magazine and announcing: "This is probably the most important meeting that you Ute Indians have had since you were forced to leave the state of Colorado." He then proclaimed triumphantly that the attorneys had won the largest Indian claim ever obtained, nearly $32 million. They also had negotiated a settlement agreement with the government attorneys, who would agree not to appeal the $32 million award if the Utes approved the settlement.

The two tribal lawyers, the short bulldog Wilkinson a sharp contrast with the lanky Boyden, presented their proposal at length, and all their words were painstakingly translated into Ute. Their initiative had several aspects. Some provisions dealt with dividing the award with the Southern Utes and Ute Mountain Utes of southern Colorado, where reservations had been created for other Ute bands. These provisions were noncontroversial. The White Rivers and Uncompahgres understood that this award—compensation for the Colorado land taken during the 1870s and early 1880s—

---

tion?" "I had nothing to do with termination, Ma'am. I was only thirteen at the time. That was *Ernest* Wilkinson." I paused, resumed, but after getting just part of my sentence out, the same woman jumped up again and inquired even more loudly, "Young man, how can we trust you if we couldn't trust your *father*?" Good and nervous now, I answered that, right or wrong, this plan should be judged on its own merits. And Ernest Wilkinson had nothing to do with it. I had nothing to do with the man, nothing. On the third try I did get a full sentence out but just one. Then my tormentor in the back row stood up and had the final word. Shaking her finger at me, she sternly admonished, "Young man, you should get to know your father *better!*"

The Menominee restoration plan finally won the approval of the tribe, Congress, and even the woman in the back row.

had to be shared by all of the Colorado Utes. The proposed division among the bands, as set out by the lawyers, seemed fair.

The attorneys then explained the remainder of their proposal. From now on, all the claims and property rights of the Uintah and Ouray bands would be combined and shared equally by the three bands. The Colorado claim of the White Rivers and Uncompahgres would be shared with the Uintahs; all Uintah claims, including a claim (a good one, Wilkinson assured them) for land taken by the Strawberry Valley Reclamation Project, would be shared with the White Rivers and Uncompahgres. Beyond that—and the two lawyers spent little time on this part of their plan—all tribal reservation lands would become the equal property of the three bands.

Boyden and Wilkinson were proposing a financial transaction of indeterminate but stupendous proportions. All the claims—some not decided yet, some not even filed—would be lumped together. All the bands would share equally, even if a claim involved just one or two bands. Clearly this aspect of the lawyers' program—combining all of the claims—benefited the Uintah Band, though no one could say by how much, because the Colorado claim was easily the largest.

But the Uintahs would lose a great deal from lumping ownership of all the current reservation land together. The Uintahs' lands, with oil leases and known coal and oil shale deposits, were far more valuable than the Uncompahgres' high-plateau grazing lands. The White Rivers had never obtained any rights at all to land in Utah; the band had no executive orders, no treaties. They were simply force-marched there, placed on the reservation belonging to the Uintahs, and told to survive. Now the White Rivers would be one-third owners in a million acres. This might be fair to the White Rivers, who had seen little fairness over the past three-quarters of a century, but was it just for the Uncompahgres and Uintahs?

The Utes in the schoolhouse had to consider so many imponderables: of culture, of history, of disputes among the bands, of land, of money. How would Ouray judge us? How would Nicaagat? Even leaving aside the intangibles, it would be impossible to estimate, let alone calculate, the financial impacts without long and detailed expert studies. Yet the Utes' lawyers, eminent and imposing, were urging this arrangement on them strenuously. And the lawyers wanted a decision immediately. There were questions from the audience.

Why do we have to act so quickly? Because "if we can get the judgment entered this June, we can get an appropriation before this Congress adjourns."

The tribal business committee knew of this proposal, but why didn't the rest of the tribe know until today? "Now the reason you haven't heard anything about this from your Business Committee before," Boyden responded, "is because, when they left Salt Lake I asked them not to say anything to anyone about it because if they had told everyone about it at that time and it had then gotten in the news papers, it would have disturbed our negotiations with the Department of Justice."

As a final—or was it a first?—factor, Wilkinson invoked the name of Arthur V. Watkins, the powerful United States senator from Utah. Watkins served on the Senate Interior Committee, with jurisdiction over Indian affairs, and had the keenest interest in Utah Indians. He took a firm, no-nonsense approach and the Utes viewed him with apprehension.

"I want to say to you," Wilkinson said, "that I talked over with Senator Watkins this proposed settlement, and he is very, very much in favor of it and in fact is somewhat surprised we can make as good a settlement as this. I want you to know that."

The lawyers' complicated proposal was too large and too much to decide. Each band needed time and its own separate lawyers—and economists—to parse out all the ramifications from each band's own point of view. Shareholders in a corporation would never be asked to make a decision of this size in this fashion.

The Utes refused to vote on May 29 and then again on May 30 and 31 also. Instead, leaders of each of the bands broke off by themselves, trying to sort things out in small circles of men under the cottonwood trees. Women and men not involved in the deliberations played card and stick games nearly around the clock. On the second day the young people began that high celebration of early spring, the Bear Dance, where some, like Nicaagat, would find their mates for life. Wilkinson and Boyden, meanwhile, continued to push for approval of their plan. These were formidable men and they said they needed a decision at once so that the mysterious, faraway wheels in Washington, D.C., could begin to grind.

The vote went ahead. On June 1 the resolution supporting the lawyers' program passed with 121 tribal members voting in favor. Most of the Utes in the stark meeting room stolidly refused to vote—rendering a no in the Indian way, but being counted as just an abstention under Roberts Rules of Order. Many had already walked out in protest. In all, some eight hundred tribal members had come to Fort Duchesne for the meeting. Only 15 percent had actually voted for the resolution. Nevertheless, by the next year Congress had transformed their vote into binding federal law. Indeed Congress ratified not just the reallocation of the claims awards but also the fundamental alteration of reservation landownership—now "share and share alike"—among the bands:

> The resolution adopted June 1, 1950 . . . as to ownership of land within the Uintah and Ouray Reservation and income issuing therefrom by providing that the same shall become the tribal property of all the Indians of the Ute Indian Tribe of the Uintah and Ouray Reservation without regard to band derivation is hereby ratified, approved and confirmed.

One cannot possibly pinpoint all the forces that generated such rapid-fire, pressure-packed decision making. Perhaps the attorneys were motivated by the fact that they could not receive their fee, 10 percent of the total award, until the claims case was settled and Congress had passed an appropriations measure. Perhaps, although the Uintahs had filed a disclaimer in court of any interest in the claim for Colorado land, the Justice Department had concerns about a suit from the Uintahs if the band was excluded from the Colorado claim.

And perhaps Senator Watkins insisted on the settlement. By this time he was beginning to incubate termination, an assimilationist policy even more far-reaching than allotment. Termination—a sell-off of the Uintah and Ouray Reservation—would be cleaner and quicker if all the bands had equal ownership interests and all the loose ends of nearly a century of conflict and confusion were tidied up.

What we know for sure is that everything proceeded on the fast track. About half the proceeds of the Colorado claim were distributed to the Ute Indians—and lawyers' fees paid out—in 1951 soon after Congress codified the "share and share alike" resolution. The report of the Senate Indian Committee contained an ominous statement no doubt authored by Arthur V. Watkins: "It is anticipated by the committee that this bill will provide the initial impetus in our program to place the Indians of [the] Uintah and Ouray Reservation in a self-reliant position where they no longer will be dependent on the Federal Government for their welfare."

This was perhaps the first officially sanctioned statement of the philosophy behind the most draconian Indian program of the twentieth century: the soon-to-be announced congressional termination policy. Designed by Watkins, it would mean the sale of tribal lands all over the country, the severing of ties to the federal government, the end of special social and economic programs, the elimination of immunities from state taxes and criminal laws, the shutdown of sovereign governmental authority, and the beginning of the charges from other tribes, "You've sold your heritage, you're not an Indian anymore." Tribal land estates—and, effectively, tribalism itself—would be liquidated in favor of rapid assimilation into the American mainstream. By the early 1950s, Watkins had become the national leader in Indian policy. He meant to prove his sincerity by showcasing his Utah tribes in this bold experiment.

Watkins was a complex man. He may well have been sincere about termination. He once not-so-indirectly declared himself the Abraham Lincoln of Indian affairs: "Following in the footsteps of the Emancipation Proclamation of ninety-four years ago, I see the following words emblazoned in letters of fire above the heads of the Indians—'THESE PEOPLE

SHALL BE FREE!'" He played a courageous and historic role during this same era by becoming the first senator to condemn the excesses of the anti-Communist crusade of Joseph McCarthy.

Whatever his motives, Arthur V. Watkins was a bludgeon against Indian tribes and their landholdings during the campaign that terminated some fifty tribes from California to Wisconsin. He bulled the congressional process by badgering witnesses, hectoring tribes to gain their "consent," and pushing bills through with little study of issues that mattered dearly to affected tribes but drew scant attention from congressional colleagues who had many other things on their minds than the byzantine affairs of a few Indians. Until the policy was discredited in the late 1950s and officially repudiated in the 1970s, Watkins had the field to himself and effectively became a one-man Congress on tribal termination.

Watkins wanted to terminate the whole Uintah and Ouray Reservation. The 1951 act dealing with the Colorado claims award set this in motion. It required a three-year tribal planning process designed to make the tribe self-sufficient—that is, ready for termination. John Boyden, by now working closely with Watkins, was deeply involved in this process, for the planning stage included substantial funds for attorneys' expenses. Watkins kept the Utes under pressure to complete the plan on time. There was ample financial incentive for the Utes: Watkins had seen that the whole Colorado claims award, rightfully the Utes' money, would not be paid out in 1951. The government withheld $13 million from the 1951 distribution and would disburse it to the Utes if and when Congress passed a Ute termination act that satisfied Arthur V. Watkins. The Ute were not the only tribe coerced in this way; Watkins also withheld a claims payment due to the Menominee until the tribe voted in favor of termination.

Surprisingly, because Watkins had such a steel grip on Indian policy, especially in Utah, Ute termination did not work out exactly as he wanted. Watkins' idea of termination—sell off the entire reservation and divide up all the tribal assets among the members—made sense to some members of the Uintah Band. Most of them had gotten their educations, high school at least, and about two hundred had left the Uinta Basin altogether. Some of

162

the four hundred or more Uintahs who were "Mixed-Bloods"—less than half Ute—thought they might as well relinquish their tribal affiliation and collect their checks. The White Rivers and Uncompahgres, though, resolutely opposed termination of their tribal existence. The White Rivers had no Mixed-Bloods, the Uncompahgres only a handful. They would be more than happy to see the Mixed-Bloods go, but they wanted to keep what was left of their land. No amount of pressure from Watkins, United States senator or not, was going to change that.

It was close. Events were moving quickly by 1954, and the whole reservation could have been liquidated. Congress had officially adopted the termination policy the year before and Watkins and his collaborator in the House, E. Y. Berry, were rapidly moving bills through hearings. The deadline for the Utes' three-year termination plan came due and Watkins wanted action from the tribe.

But the White Rivers and Uncompahgres remained adamant. Watkins and tribal representatives finally reached a compromise that would terminate the Mixed-Bloods and call for a development program leading to the eventual termination of the Full-Bloods. At a 1954 Ute general council meeting reminiscent of the "share and share alike" gathering four years earlier—again Wilkinson and Boyden forced the issue, again large numbers of Utes left the meeting, again many remaining in the hall refused to vote—the tribe adopted a resolution consenting to the termination of the Mixed-Bloods.

The Ute Termination Act of 1954 terminated 490 "Mixed-Bloods," almost all of them Uintahs, about 27 percent of the tribe. They would receive their proportionate share of tribal lands and minerals. The terminated members would no longer be tribal members and therefore would be ineligible to vote in tribal elections, use tribal lands, or receive federal benefits. The Uintah and Ouray Indian Tribe of Utah, minus the Mixed-Bloods, continued on. True to his pledge to apply termination in his own state, Watkins also sponsored legislation terminating several small bands of Paiutes near Cedar City and St. George at the southwestern edge of the Colorado Plateau.

# CONFLICTS AND CONQUESTS

The termination process required still more complex, high-stakes transactions. The Ute tribal property, including the 1-million-acre reservation, all mineral and water rights, and the remaining $13 million from the Colorado claims, had to be divided up between the terminated members (the Mixed-Bloods) and the Uintah and Ouray Tribe that would continue in existence (the Full-Bloods). Under the resulting distribution plan, which took effect in 1961, the Mixed-Bloods' 27 percent portion of the tribe's mineral rights went to Ute Distribution Corp. (UDC), a newly formed corporation in which each of the 490 Mixed-Bloods received shares of stock. When UDC's stock went on the open market in 1964, most of it was sold to non-Indians. In a major 1972 case, the U.S. Supreme Court found violations of the trade and securities laws due to fraud and deceit by the purchasers. Many of the terminated Utes never understood the meaning of corporate stock and had no realistic chance of holding onto the certificates that represented their tribal land and heritage. The grazing land of the terminated Utes had a different, and perhaps happier, end. The tribe exercised its right of first refusal on the stock of the Mixed-Bloods' grazing companies (separate from UDC), and now the Ute Tribe once again owns these lands.

John Boyden was a dominant figure during the whole elaborate distribution process. As before, he served as general counsel for the Ute Tribe—the Full-Bloods. In addition, the Mixed-Bloods retained his services as their attorney. At least twice, Louis Bruce, then a BIA program officer and later commissioner of Indian affairs, squarely expressed his belief that the two bands should have separate attorneys. One of Bruce's concerns—apart from the skepticism anyone would feel toward the idea of a single lawyer representing all the parties in a complicated and hotly contested negotiation—was simple: "If there were separate attorneys there may be more reason to determine values" of the land and resources. In fact, no one conducted any formal appraisal of tribal lands or timber, generating serious claims of unfairness from the Mixed-Bloods.

Yet Boyden persisted. Supposedly he was completely faithful to two opposing sides—one of which, the Full-Bloods, he would represent for many years afterward. Later, at a deposition, in justifying how he could act as lawyer for both sides in a transaction of this magnitude, Boyden said: "I was trying to be fair with both sides, protecting everybody within those minorities and individuals."

As soon as the Ute termination plan became final, the tribe had to face yet another round of pressures from the outside—this time in the form of water development. Ever since Brigham Young's day, the growing urban society along the Wasatch Front from Salt Lake City to Provo had committed itself to overcoming the natural aridity by maximizing water development. By 1903 a plan had been drafted to import water from the Uinta Basin, where several headwater streams lay just on the other side of the Wasatch Range. The towns on the Wasatch Front and the LDS Church saw major water transport from the Uinta as part of their destiny. The Strawberry Valley Reclamation Project, which tunneled some Uinta Basin water under the Wasatch Range, had been built in the early part of the century but needed to be expanded. By the 1940s, the cities had conceived the Central Utah Project, one of the largest water projects in the West.

John Boyden, general counsel to the Ute Tribe, believed in the effort to bring water across the mountains from the Uinta Basin, the main Utah tributary watershed of the Green River. When he ran for governor in 1948 (he lost a close race in the Democratic primary), he addressed the issue of water development in his platform. He set out this plank, asserting the need of the State of Utah

> *to assume full responsibility in conservation, storage, distribution and use of water and water power. Too few of us realize how dependent we are on water for our use. The Colorado and Green rivers present immediate and vital problems challenging our best efforts in protection of our water rights and in reclamation development.*

# CONFLICTS AND CONQUESTS

During the 1950s he acquired the Big Cottonwood–Tanner Ditch Company, a Wasatch Front irrigation cooperative, as a client.

The Utes, however, stood in the way of the Central Utah Project. Under the 1908 U.S. Supreme Court decision in *Winters v. United States,* Indian water rights are paramount in western states. *Winters,* one of the most significant water law opinions, recognizes tribal water rights dating to the creation of a reservation. On most rivers where reservations are located, these *Winters* rights are the oldest on the river and thus "senior"—superior to all others—under the first-in-time, first-in-right principle that applies in Utah and other western states.

Further, the Utah Utes had their own judicial decision in the Uinta Basin, dating to the 1920s, in their favor. Such a decision was rare for Indian tribes, who seldom had access to lawyers unless a contingent fee in a claims case was involved. Yet John F. Truesdell, a courageous attorney in the Justice Department in Denver, took an interest in the Utes' cause. The Strawberry Valley Project and the Uintah Indian Irrigation Project, both supposedly constructed for the benefit of the tribe, were putting large amounts of Indian water on fields owned by non-Indians. Truesdell labored away and finally secured a 1923 decree recognizing the Ute Tribe's rights under the *Winters* case. When the decision came down, the tribe lacked the financial means to build the dams, diversion works, and other structures necessary to put the water to use. But the 1923 ruling was a solid precedent and remained fully in place. The Utes had the oldest and largest water right in the basin. Their claim was by law superior to the rights of the Wasatch Front developers who wanted to take water out of the Uinta Basin by means of the Central Utah Project.

The Central Utah Project was able to go ahead, however, because of the Ute Deferral Agreement, signed by the tribe in 1965 and negotiated by John Boyden as tribal general counsel. In it the Ute agreed to defer any development of water on 15,000 acres of land for forty years so that the Central Utah Project could proceed immediately. In return, the deferral agreement provided that the Ute Indian Unit, intended to bring water to the tribe, would be "programmed for early authorization" and that substantial tribal water rights, enough to irrigate 60,000 acres, would be "recognized and confirmed . . . without resort to litigation." At the ceremony announcing the deferral agreement, John Boyden proclaimed that: "The Indians signed the agreement as 'good neighbors' to the non-Indians so that the Central Utah Project can proceed in an orderly way."

The Ute Deferral Agreement created abiding problems for the tribe. The promise to "recognize and confirm" Ute water rights was a mirage. The only signatories to the agreement, other than the tribe, were the commissioners of the Bureau of Indian Affairs and the Bureau of Reclamation, along with the Central Utah Water Conservancy District. The State of Utah did not sign and the agreement was not approved by any judicial or legislative proceeding.

John Boyden knew the deferral agreement did nothing to protect the tribe's water rights. Not only was he an experienced water lawyer, but his papers show that he considered filing suit to "quantify" the Ute Tribe's *Winters* rights. Quantification—establishing a client's property right to a fixed amount of water—is the most basic job of a water lawyer when water rights are contested. The methods for quantifying a water right in Utah and other western states are as stylized as those for obtaining a property right in land. You either get a state engineer's water right certificate (directly analogous to a deed) or you get a court decree in a general stream adjudication (directly analogous to a court decree in a quiet title case involving land). The Ute Deferral Agreement never called for either a water rights certificate or decree. The supposed confirmation of Ute water rights was nonbinding: there was no quantification. It was like a lawyer allowing a client in a land dispute with all of his neighbors to settle out of court with just a few of the neighbors—and without getting a deed.

The promise of "early authorization" of the tribe's Ute Indian Unit was another mirage. The idea was to transport water to the reservation from Flaming Gorge Reservoir on the Green River, but the financial and engineering obstacles were overwhelming. Beyond that, water in the Colorado River watershed was extremely tight by the mid-1960s, for the Big Buildup of the Colorado Plateau was well under way. With all the demands for energy, irrigation, and residential subdivisions, where would the water come from to supply the Ute Indian Unit?

The Ute Deferral Agreement of 1965 plagued the Ute Tribe in other ways. The early work on the Central Utah Project—reservoirs and a large aqueduct that transports water under the Wasatch Range and away from Indian lands—significantly reduced the flows of nine different streams in the Uinta Basin. Among other problems, a dam on scenic Rock Creek, which runs through the reservation, released silty water that turned Rock Creek red, destroying the stream's natural beauty and fish habitat. Then, after first speeding ahead, the Central Utah Project began to founder. The financial costs were much higher than expected. The environmental damage raised objections. The Utes repeatedly urged that work on the units benefiting the Wasatch Front be stopped until the Ute Indian Unit was completed. But the tribal project has never even broken ground.

For more than thirty years, the Ute Tribe has gone through bitter, divisive internal debates over the Ute Deferral Agreement—at times flatly disavowing it, on other occasions arguing that Utah and the United States should fulfill their moral, if not legal, duty to provide water to the tribe. In 1992, Congress approved a comprehensive modification of the Central Utah Project, giving the tribe the right to obtain a fixed amount of water and a money payment for the government's failure to build the Ute Indian Unit. The Utes are receiving the annual money payments but have yet to find the water-delivery provisions sufficiently favorable to agree to them, and it is unclear whether the tribe ever will join in.

What is clear is that the Ute Tribe, as the senior water rights holder, had considerable leverage in the early 1960s but did not exercise it. Since then the Central Utah Project has allowed non-Indian urban and agricultural interests to develop still more Uinta Basin water while the Utes have received no additional water. It turns out that John Boyden had the fullest and keenest appreciation of how hard it would be, without a quantification of tribal water rights, to obtain scarce Colorado River water to meet the Ute's needs. And his knowledge had to do with Peabody Coal Company.

# Uintah

**B**y the early 1990s, when I began my work on this book, a great amount of effort had already gone into researching whether Boyden had ever represented Peabody. In the 1970s, a group of Hopi traditionalists requested the Indian Law Resource Center to determine whether Boyden had a conflict of interest by representing the Hopi Tribe and Peabody at the same time. After exhaustive research of tribal, government, and other archival records, the center's "Report to the Hopi Kikmongwis" found suggestions, but no conclusive evidence, that Boyden had indeed represented Peabody on coal and water issues. In the late 1980s, during renegotiations of the Black Mesa coal lease, historians employed by the Hopi Tribe's Washington, D.C., lawyers failed to establish conclusively any conflict of interest.

After those research projects had been completed, the University of Utah's Marriott Library cataloged and made available to the public an additional segment of John Boyden's papers. In 1992, Brian Kuehl, my research assistant, came upon a file that apparently no one had seen before. From Salt Lake City he called to tell me something I never expected to hear: "Charles, John Boyden did represent Peabody. And, as far as I can tell, the conflict involves the Ute as well as the Hopi." Two years later, Cherche Prezeau, another research assistant, came upon still more files in Boyden's papers. These new files would flesh out the full extent of Boyden's double representation, which people had wondered and argued about for decades. But it was Brian's initial discovery that established the fact of Boyden's representation of Peabody on water and coal matters and the tie to the Ute.

John Boyden knew in intimate detail the difficulty of providing water to the Utes. At the same time he was serving as general counsel for the Ute Tribe—and perhaps trying to fulfill his heart's desire to see water tunneled to Salt Lake City and the Wasatch Front as well—he was also representing Peabody Coal Company, which had big plans for developing Colorado River water 200 miles to the south. Peabody wanted to mine coal from the rich deposits under Hopi and Navajo land on Black Mesa. The coal would be shipped by rail to a power plant at an as-yet-undetermined site. The power plant would need water to be heated and turned into steam to turn the electricity-producing turbines. Because of Black Mesa's location in northern Arizona, the plant could be sited in either Arizona, Utah, or Nevada.

In December 1964, when he was negotiating the Ute Deferral Agreement for the Ute Tribe, Boyden appeared in front of the Utah Water and Power Board on behalf of Peabody Coal. An attorney of great stature by now, with thirty-five years of experience, he also was a leading public figure in Utah. (In his second gubernatorial try in 1956, he had run another strong primary campaign but had again narrowly lost.) Boyden's presentation to the board was crisp, informed, and articulate. He wanted to advise the members on Peabody's progress with the project: "I think that you should know what we are trying to do because water is a very precious thing and there is only so much of it." He confided that the State of Utah had a direct stake in this: "If this development goes to Page [Arizona], Utah will have no benefit from it. . . . I would like to see this Arizona coal marketed in Utah." A very substantial water right would be required: "60,000 acre-feet for a 3 million kilowatt plant. This will be a very large plant."

Whether the plant was ultimately located in Arizona or Utah (the site did turn out to be Page), Boyden's proposal on behalf of Peabody in 1964 cut directly against the interests of his other client, the Uintah and Ouray Tribe, because there was only so much Colorado River water. This is the biggest river in the arid Southwest, the lifeline for the region, but every acre-foot, then as now, was sharply contested. All up and down the Colorado, water developers in seven states, searching for ways to take water out of the watershed for cities and irrigation fields, vigilantly and nervously kept a hawkeye watch on every new proposed project because supplies were so tight.

Boyden's lure of a power plant to Utah (with the incentive of providing to the state both jobs and tax revenue) had a doubly deadly impact on the Utes. Under the just-rendered decision of the United States Supreme Court in *Arizona v. California*—which Boyden had discussed with the Utah Water and Power Board that very day—the water right of a Utah coal plant and the Ute water right would both have to come out of the State of Utah's entitlement from Colorado River water. The scarcity of water in Utah was underscored by board member Colten who, at the end of Boyden's presentation, commented: "We as a Board must look at this water situation and we have to recognize that we don't have enough water to meet the applications that we now have on file."

Boyden's representation of both Peabody and the Ute was a direct conflict of interest. It was compounded because Boyden also represented the Hopi, from whom Peabody was at that moment attempting to lease coal and water. Many projects were fighting for Colorado River water over a widely dispersed area in the 1960s, so it is impossible to say exactly how one project played off against another. But it should be marked down that the Central Utah Project and the coal-fired power plant advocated by Peabody Coal promptly got their water and the Ute Indian Unit did not. It is hard to avoid the conclusion that the Utes' lawyer, like other leaders in the region during the 1960s, was much less interested in the welfare of a remote Indian tribe and considerably more inspired by the revolution, in full swing at the time, that was bringing water and energy to the vigorous southwestern cities whose potential seemed unlimited.

Chapter 9

# PHOENIX

**W**hen I lived in Arizona, first getting my sea legs as a lawyer, Phoenix was still a small city. On the day I first drove into town, in the summer of 1965, I wanted to go straight to the firm's office building. Having been told that Lewis & Roca was a "downtown firm," I stopped at a coffee shop to ask directions. "How do you get to downtown? You're smack in the middle of it, young fella." I saw as many ranch hands as attorneys in this downtown, senior lawyers like Paul Roca walked the streets in slacks and no sport jackets, and the perfume of growing oranges had not given way to condominiums and shopping centers. My mother was not alone in asking, "Phoenix? Phoenix *where?*"

# Phoenix

A small city. The moment passed quickly, just as all moments have passed quickly during modern Phoenix's history. When I lived there, ambition was as palpable as Camelback Mountain, the Superstitions, and the South Mountains. Everyone took a personal pride and stake in Phoenix, so young and muscular, and everyone seemed to believe that everything was possible. I knew well that the city had just attracted a Triple A baseball team, the Phoenix Giants, and that the objective was to become major league. I also knew from my law practice that you couldn't begin to keep track of the big development schemes, some honest, some not even close.

I had no idea in 1965, though, of the scale of Phoenix's determined efforts to become a city of the world like, say, Chicago. Nor did I have any idea that Phoenix had long ago outstripped its resource base in the Salt River Valley, that the newly constructed Glen Canyon Dam was just then plugging up the flow of the Colorado River in order to get electricity to Phoenix and other cities, and that Phoenix energy interests, led by the Salt River Project, were heading up various consortiums to build coal-fired power plants in northern Arizona, Nevada, New Mexico, even northwestern Colorado. I never had any real sense of how incredibly effective the civic and industrial leaders of Phoenix had been during the first two-thirds of the century in achieving their announced goals, which equated progress with explosive growth and development. Nor did I know that the other cities of the Southwest had undertaken similar pell-mell races, finally uniting in what I would later call the Big Buildup of the Colorado Plateau.

And I certainly had no comprehension that one of Phoenix's power plants would burn Black Mesa coal, mined from Hopi and Navajo land, or that there was a very real link between Phoenix's efforts and projects like the Central Utah Project, which tunneled Ute Indian water under the Wasatch Range to Salt Lake City. I did not consider, either, the many forms that conquest can take or how much our society can accomplish in a flicker of time.

During my journey since then, I've gained an appreciation of how remarkable the rise of Phoenix has been. I've come to realize also that Phoenix is the best window through which to view an epic series of events on the Colorado Plateau and in the American Southwest during the course of the twentieth century.

**W**hen the year 1900 dawned, Phoenix had a population of 5,500 souls. The town, which had been staked out just thirty-three years before, lacked even a yard of paved road. Arizona had not yet been admitted to the Union.

Nevertheless, during the short life of modern Phoenix, civic leaders had begun to lay the foundations for a population center in the desert. An expansive irrigation system had been created, mostly by excavating and putting back into use the superbly engineered canal system of the Hohokam. This civilization, which inhabited the area from about 2,200 years ago until A.D. 1450 and reached a population between 50,000 and 100,000, had put in at least 175 miles of canals. The Hohokam's main trunk canals—30 feet deep and 75 feet across at the top—are of impressive size even by today's standards. In addition to standard crops such as alfalfa, turn-of-the-century farmers in the area grew specialty produce, including apricots, peaches, grapefruit, lemons, and limes. The orange groves were the most productive of all. And Phoenicians discovered early on that the climate and sweet citrus smells could be combined to boost not only agriculture but a promising real estate market.

The town, in the surge to build a "new Phoenix," had tied itself into the national railroad system. Boosters, realizing the economic consequences of being left off the beaten track, organized a spur line up from Maricopa Wells—the nearest stop on the transcontinental Southern Pacific line—in 1887. Then, in 1895, Phoenix became the railroad hub of central Arizona when the Santa Fe, Prescott, and Phoenix Railroad connected the city to the Santa Fe line to the north.

Now Phoenix had a cost-effective means to get its produce, especially its oranges, to markets from coast to coast. The regular incoming trains meant that the Phoenix business community could establish itself as the distribution center for supplying the farms, ranches, and booming gold, silver, and copper mines in outlying locales. The Santa Fe coaches allowed the area to capitalize upon its sunny, healing winters by affording a comfortable, efficient means of bringing in winter tourists and those afflicted with respiratory ailments.

Still, for local leaders in Phoenix in 1900, the prevailing attitude was to strive for new horizons, to become modern in the fullest American sense. The blunt fact was that Phoenix remained a small, dirt-road frontier town with limited resources. That could be changed, but hard work lay ahead and people would have to pull together.

The city fathers faced two overriding issues. The first was statehood. In 1850, just after the United States and its Manifest Destiny took the Southwest in the Mexican–American War, Congress created the sprawling New Mexico Territory encompassing both Arizona and New Mexico. In 1863, the unwieldy region was divided and Arizona Territory was born. The possibility of statehood, however, lay dormant for decades. Territorial status increasingly chafed. Unlike states, territories were arms of the federal government, not independent sovereignties. Arizona's laws had to be approved by Congress, and the territorial governor and other office holders were appointed back in Washington, D.C. The very term "Arizona Territory" became a symbol of second-class status. With the admission of Utah in 1896, the whole continental United States had now been filled in with states except for the two southwestern stepchildren. Arizona, perceived as lying deep in the Hispanic Southwest, would have to "Americanize" itself to achieve statehood.

Water was the other overarching matter. There was always either too much or too little. With regularity, the spring rains and mountain snowmelt flooded homes and businesses, made quagmires out of the dirt roads, blew out brush diversion dams and headgates, and ripped apart the bridge between Phoenix and Tempe. Then, from 1895 through the end of the century, the Salt River Valley faced a deep, prolonged drought. Crop production dropped, triggering a steady exodus of farm families and wounding the business community. Phoenix needed a major dam on the Salt River to store the floodwaters and put them to good use by releasing steady flows to irrigators during the summers and dry years.

The timing was auspicious. By 1900 the reclamation movement, with a mission of persuading Congress to underwrite dams in the West, had become a powerful force in American politics. Theodore Roosevelt knew the West and ardently supported the idea that the federal government should provide the wherewithal—that is, the money—for irrigation in the arid region. In 1902, Congress passed the Reclamation Act. Phoenix's project on the Salt River was at the head of the line.

From that point on, it was a long ride but downhill all the way. Congress promptly gave official approval to Phoenix's plan. The farmers of the Phoenix area would be the main beneficiaries of the dam. They formed an extraordinarily energetic and effective irrigation organization, the Salt River Project, which took the lead in the congressional lobbying and the planning and building of the dam. Construction—an overwhelming undertaking, one of the greatest in the world—necessarily moved slowly, albeit steadily. Downriver, outside of Phoenix, other workers were putting in the much smaller Granite Reef Diversion Dam. With the big, upstream dam regulating the flow, Granite Reef would raise the Salt River's level enough to divert the river—the entire river—into canals serving the Phoenix area.

The excitement built. In 1909, William Howard Taft became the first sitting president to visit the territory. Taft drew a crowd of nearly fifteen thousand people, the largest ever in Arizona:

> Of course, there is a good deal of soil out here that we wouldn't, at first sight, value in Ohio (laughter), but by your energy and by the applications of modern methods of agriculture you seem to be reducing it to a condition where it brings forth wonderful crops and enriches those who devote their attention to its culture.

The banner headline the next day showed how all the attention to water went hand in glove with ending territorial status: "Statehood Brought Nearer."

The dam, named after Theodore Roosevelt, was dedicated on March 18,

# Phoenix

1911, and TR himself did the honors. He was proud, as he should have been. Roosevelt Dam was, and is, utterly elegant. The face of the dam was made of hand-hewn rocks, installed piece by piece. With Italian stonemasons cutting 350,000 cubic yards of stone, it was the largest masonry dam in the world. The long, graceful arc, 284 feet high, was topped off by electric lamps with globes. Invisible to the eye, installed to create electricity for the Phoenix area, was a state-of-the-art hydroelectric system.

Statehood followed on the heels of Roosevelt Dam and its 19-mile-long reservoir. The long-awaited moment fell on Valentine's Day, 1912. Phoenix, now a town of some twelve thousand strong, had shown it could dream its own actual future.

Ultimately this was true because the town leaders resolutely overcame geographical barriers and apparent natural limits. Essentially Phoenix was a bad place, on its own, to locate a boom-town society that depended on the large-scale use of water and electricity. The Hohokam may have made it for fifteen centuries, through means still not fully understood, but turn-of-the-century Phoenix had far more grandiose plans: a million people, ten times as many as the Hohokam.

So the civic leaders connected the remote desert settlement to the outside world—in a literal sense through the railroad hookups and in a political sense through dogged campaigns in the nation's capital. They also triumphed over the valley's natural scarcity. Knowing that the resources in their own vicinity had to be supplemented, and working mainly through the Salt River Project, they made the whole Salt River watershed—one and a half times the size of Massachusetts—Phoenix's domain. Unlike the Ute, Hohokam, Hopi, or Navajo, Phoenix would not adapt to the land. That would be too confining. Instead, young Phoenix would remake the land, conquer as much desert as was needed.

Most accounts, at the turn of the century and later, remark on Phoenix's single-minded drive and civic self-aggrandizement. One writer called it "aggressive boosterism," and it was. But it was also quintessentially western—that is, of the American West built by Europeans. Anything and everything was possible.

There seems to have been no talk then of the remote canyon country far to the north, above the thousand-foot wall of the Mogollon Rim. The time would come, though, when the Salt River watershed would prove insufficient. The Salt River Project—transmuted from a small farmers' cooperative into an industrial juggernaut—and other central Arizona development interests would have to expand the domain much further. For the dreams Phoenix dreamed at the edge of the century would not just come true but be far exceeded, and energy and water had to be found to fulfill them.

**T**he other towns that ringed the Colorado Plateau a century ago had much in common with Phoenix—or with Tucson to the south, which rejected boosterism in favor of preserving its Hispanic heritage. Towns in the latter category included San Diego and "sleepy Santa Fe." Of the aggressive towns, the largest were Los Angeles, Denver, Salt Lake City, Albuquerque, and El Paso. And all, like Phoenix, successfully attracted the railroads, built water projects, developed dynamic, special-purpose institutions like the Salt River Project, and courted new industry or, in the case of Los Angeles, new homeowners drawn to that sublime, mountain-rimmed bowl by the ocean.

Los Angeles had boomed from a small agricultural village of just 11,000 in 1880 to over 100,000 by the beginning of the century. El Paso, the largest city in the deep Southwest with a population of 16,000 people in 1900, had grown into a thick-chested industrial and mining center along the Mexican border with four separate railroad connections. Albuquerque, with a big "Americanization" push, blazed the way for New Mexico statehood, with the *Denver Republican* urging that New Mexico, with its rapid growth, abundant natural resources, and "intelligent white population," cannot "in justice be much longer denied the rights of statehood." After sixty years of trying, New Mexico joined the Union in January 1912, five weeks before Arizona.

Salt Lake City had become the capital city of a State of the Union. The religious battles now over, at least the overt ones, the town had an established, settled feel to it with the wide streets now lined with mature deciduous trees. The population was 54,000, about three-fourths of whom were Mormon, most of them devout. By 1900, Denver had grown to a city of 136,000, twenty-fifth largest in the nation. A reminder, though, of how fundamentally different that frontier "metropolis" was: Denver had 800 miles of streets, of which just 24 miles were paved. Las Vegas? That future dynamo did not even exist in 1900 nor, after its founding in 1905, did it show up on the census of 1910 or 1920. The cutoff for listing was 2,500 people.

Like Phoenix, these other cities had no designs on the Colorado Plateau in 1900. They had large dreams, true, and were already beginning to look beyond their own valleys. But the canyon country remained too remote and the obstacles laid down by the terrain too great.

**B**y the mid-1940s, the cities had made some changes but the Colorado Plateau had not. Few Americans knew of it and, of those who did, the reaction was about the same as that of the early Mormon pioneers. Nothing but rocks and holes, hills and hollows. One vast contiguity of waste. A way to hold the world together.

Getting there was just too difficult. Once there, it was almost all dirt roads. You had to carry water. A place to spend the night or get gas could be 200 miles away on a washboard road that might be closed off by anything from a crossing herd of sheep or cattle to a flash flood. You had to carry gasoline and perhaps sleeping bags as well. Besides, it was another culture's place. Indian country. There was the Grand Canyon, of course, but even it was an abstraction—a photograph or a painting in an art gallery. Hardly anyone went to the Plateau, and hardly anyone else had much interest. But the urban boosters, and the industrial leaders whose own fortunes depended on urban growth, definitely did know about the Colorado Plateau and its ability to provide the natural resources for the boom they hoped was about to begin.

# CONFLICTS AND CONQUESTS

At the close of World War II, Phoenix was no longer a dirt-road, 5,000-person town. It had become a city of 75,000 people, the center of a metropolitan area with a population of 250,000. Still, the informal western town more closely resembled the territorial settlement of 1900 than it did the megalopolis, pushing 3 million people, that would swarm all over the Valley of the Sun half a century later. The civic leaders at the end of the war, at the beginning of a whole new time, knew what they wanted for the Phoenix area. The same was true for all of the cities that encircled the Colorado Plateau. They all had grown steadily but they all wanted much, much more—expansion of eight, ten, twelve times, more.

This was the time to do it. There would be all manner of opportunities and they would present themselves with breathtaking rapidity. The end of the war unleashed a tremendous, pent-up consumer demand, magnified by a baby boom, for every known product (cars, houses) and many new ones (television sets, electric air conditioners, surfboards). Jet air traffic and the interstate highway system made the West accessible to the rest of the country.

Singularly important was the military budget. The Cold War drove federal expenditures and the Southwest had the asset—open space—that the Defense Department most needed for bases, shipyards, landing strips, and nuclear tests. Civilian support industries, for military procurement and related research and development in electronics and engineering, rose up and boomed. By the early 1950s, defense spending had jump-started all the urban economies.

There was a clarity in the cities. If slaughterhouses and rail hookups could make Chicago hog butcher to the world, then in the Southwest the rivers and fossil fuels, along with transmission lines, canals and tunnels, and freeways, could drive turbines and engines that could make the desert cities national, even international, centers. And the vision was realized. The Southwest's population shot from 8 million in 1945 to 32 million in the late 1990s. Almost all of the growth came in the urban areas, as southwestern cities, with 6 million people at the close of the war, housed a total population of 30 million at the close of the century.

# Phoenix

All the southwestern cities mounted vigorous growth campaigns, but in many ways the success of Phoenix was the most remarkable. The city was smaller than Los Angeles, and its absolute growth during the postwar era was less, but nowhere was the pro-growth movement more effective than in the Valley of the Sun. The long trek for statehood was fresh in the public consciousness, and the end of the war brought a firm conviction that now was the time to shed the mantle of stepchild.

A main civic leader was Walter Bimson, chairman of Valley National Bank. Bimson knew how to choose the bank's borrowers—one aggressive developer, David Murdock, starting out with VNB loans, put in nineteen Phoenix office buildings between the war and 1961—but Bimson also had a flair for building coalitions to promote metropolitan growth generally. He dispatched Valley National Bank executives to other cities to bring in businesses and government installations. Bimson had not only a conceptual grasp of what was happening—and what could—but also the infectious enthusiasm that made him a catalyst. As he put it:

*Most of the reasons for the great population trends in history have been wars or famines, economic reasons. This is a new one—owing to people's desire for the amenities of living. . . . They want to flee from shoveling coal and from shoveling snow.*

Bimson's vision was assisted mightily by the invention of air conditioning. Before the 1940s, homes used fans or "swamp coolers" that blew air through a unit containing wet material, usually tiny slivers of aspen. With modern air conditioning (the many manufacturers in Phoenix made it the "Air Conditioning Capital of the World"), the machines actually refrigerated the air, allowing people to live comfortably in the hot desert twelve months a year.

The Phoenix business community worked together closely and efficiently. Good weather and the expanses of cheap, flat land attracted defense installations and the aeronautics industry. By 1953, military payrolls and purchases reached $200 million, about the same as mining, always a bellwether in the state's economy. When Sperry Rand was deliberating over whether to build two Phoenix plants employing three thousand people in the mid-1950s, the company expressed misgivings over site location and the length of the airport runway. Within three days, Phoenix business leaders had raised $650,000 to acquire suitable land and expand the runway. Sperry Rand moved in. Before long the city had earned the grudging admiration of business leaders in other states. One of them observed that in Phoenix "industrial scouts are met at the plane, entertained, offered free land, tax deals, and an electorate willing to approve millions in business-backed bond issues."

By the 1950s, Arizona had become the fastest-growing state. In 1956, the Phoenix City Council appointed a large (464-member) and diverse Growth Committee to propose capital improvements—roads, airport construction, water supplies, sewer systems, and parks—and the voters approved the committee's recommendations. For its capital improvement program, Phoenix won an "All-American City Award" in 1958. It had already received one in 1950.

Within just a decade after the war, Phoenix had put all the machinery in place for a long, explosive boom. Inevitability was in the air. One business leader enthused: "I don't think . . . that you could keep Arizona from growing if you put a 40-foot wall around it. People are just going to come." When asked what the state needed to grow, Walter Bimson, "Mr. Arizona," answered succinctly with just two nouns: "capital," which Bimson could supply directly, and "water," which he could help obtain through his coalition-building talents.

**P**hoenix, along with Los Angeles, perfected the formula and all the southwestern cities applied it in one fashion or another. The urban areas had another thing in common. Early on in their growth spurts, they had exhausted their local supplies of water and energy.

But from their standpoint, the cities had an ideal target. The Colorado Plateau ranked among the world's best storehouses of natural resources. It

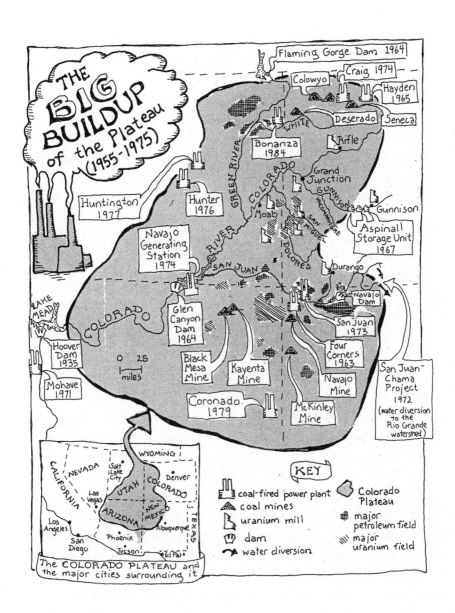

THE **BIG BUILDUP** of the Plateau (1955-1975)

Flaming Gorge Dam 1964

Colowyo    Craig 1974

Hayden 1965

Deserado    Seneca

WHITE

Bonanza 1984    Rifle

Grand Junction

Huntington 1977    Hunter 1976    COLORADO    GUNNISON    Gunnison

Moab    UNCOMPAHGRE

SAN MIGUEL    Aspinall Storage Unit 1967

Navajo Generating Station 1974    RIVER    DOLORES

SAN JUAN    Durango

Navajo Dam

LAKE MEAD    COLORADO    Glen Canyon Dam 1964    San Juan 1973

Hoover Dam 1935    Four Corners 1963    San Juan–Chama Project 1972 (water diversion to the Rio Grande watershed)

0    25    Black Mesa Mine    Kayenta Mine    Navajo Mine

miles

Mohave 1971    Coronado 1979    McKinley Mine

WYOMING

CALIFORNIA    NEVADA    Salt Lake City    Denver    UTAH    COLORADO    Las Vegas    ARIZONA    NEW MEXICO    TEXAS    Los Angeles    San Diego    Phoenix    Tucson    Albuquerque    El Paso

**KEY**

coal-fired power plant    Colorado Plateau

coal mines    major petroleum field

uranium mill    major uranium field

dam

water diversion

The COLORADO PLATEAU and the major cities surrounding it

held huge deposits of high-quality fossil fuels: coal, oil and gas, oil shale, and tar sands. The amount of water was puny (the Colorado River, by far the Southwest's largest, carried just one-sixteenth as much water as the Columbia), but the terrain, with a steep cant to the land and deep canyons, was tailor-made for pouring in concrete dams and storing massive heads of water for electric power generation and for industrial and agricultural use.

There was no one to object. No one lived on the Colorado Plateau except Indians, whose reservations were about to be terminated anyway, and some small Mormon towns to whom a Big Buildup could be made to sound a lot like a beehive. The only people who cared were a few river runners, rockhounds, geologists, and archaeologists.

The national political climate of the 1950s and 1960s was as promising as the canyons and mineral deposits. The country had no environmental laws to speak of, not even the National Environmental Policy Act to require an environmental impact statement. There was no Freedom of Information Act. The federal government owned, or administered on behalf of Indian tribes, nearly the whole Plateau—and the decisions were centralized in one agency, the Department of the Interior. Few murmurs of fiscal restraint were heard in those halcyon days.

Since southwestern water and energy providers had their own interests, one might have thought they would fiercely compete against each other. Similarly, the cities might have gone their separate paths, racing against other municipalities. To be sure, there was some jockeying for position and open conflict. But that is not the larger truth, for the results could not have been achieved through combativeness or going it alone. Instead, private companies and local governments within each metropolitan area bound themselves together through elaborate agreements and understandings, some formal, some informal. These partnerships joined with similar partnerships from other cities to form coalitions, each with the goal of building immense energy or water projects. Then the coalitions locked together in what amounted to an alliance: an alliance unified in the mission of moving upon the Colorado Plateau in order to fulfill the urban areas' dreams.

# Phoenix

Everyone was on the same page. All the governments, federal, state, and local, regardless of party, could be counted upon. The companies were assured of open doors and rapid responses in the Interior Department and anywhere else in Washington, D.C. There would be generous subsidies and minimal regulation. The unknowns might seem imposing but the sense of urgency—after all, the Southwest's destiny hung in the balance—could steamroll any uncertainties or lingering doubts. Everything fit together. It amounted to one-stop shopping from a merchant who was running a fire sale. The Big Buildup of the Colorado Plateau eclipsed virtually every other industrial effort on earth.

The first order of business would be water.

# ROSA

**E**arly in my study of western water, I realized that I needed to get beyond the abstractions of water development—"impoundment," "diversion
works," "project"—and understand the full reality of a dam-and-reservoir
project. The best way to do this is to go to the construction site—the
place—before the dam has been built. Then you can see and feel the free-
flowing river and canyon, and perhaps the human community, about to
be inundated. This way you can begin to learn the true and complete story
of the dam, including the deep emotions that the abstractions dull. If you
love wild rivers, and I am one who does, it is important to know those
stories.

# Rosa

It was too late for me to see the landscape as it was before the Big Buildup. The main water projects had already been built by the time I had focused on the Colorado Plateau. So I was left with visiting once-wild rivers and canyons and trying to imagine them as they were before the dams. I went to all of the water projects on the Colorado Plateau, and read about them, and talked with people who knew about them. Each of the dams had an elaborate story full of gain and loss and ambiguity.

My mind, however, kept being tugged toward one of the lesser-known projects, Navajo Dam. When I pieced its story together, I found that many different and sharp edges of conquest lay beneath the impounded water and the abstractions.

The rear speakers in our van are installed in the hatchback. So when I lifted the hatchback and sat on the back of the van to get set up, the sounds of KTNN drifted down from above. John Echohawk first told me of the trophy trout fishing on the San Juan River in the early 1970s, when word was beginning to fan out from New Mexico that Navajo Dam had created a great fishery. Now, two decades later, I pulled on my hip boots and worked through the familiar ritual of assembling my rod, tugging the loops out of the leader, and threading the line through the guides. Nymph fishing would be the right approach this February day, with its light dusting of snow, and I attached the orange San Juan worm, a fly tied to a tiny size 18 hook, that the owner of the fly-fishing store had recommended. Onto my leader I twisted a piece of soft lead shaped like a book match. This was a time to savor: the old ceremony of getting ready for fishing to the background of country music.

I had learned some things since first hearing of the big rainbows in the San Juan. This river, one of the four main arteries of the Colorado River system, owes its size to the winter storms pushing north from the Gulf of California. They deposit their moisture and build up a deep snowpack in the San Juan Mountains, the massive east–west range in southwestern Colorado. The tributaries—East Fork, West Fork, Navajo, Piedra, Los Pinos, Animas, La Plata, others—flow south from the high country and form the San Juan. From Colorado the river drops down to New Mexico, where it runs mostly west, crossing into Utah near the Four Corners before emptying into what was once the Colorado River but is now 180-mile-long Lake Powell, created by Glen Canyon Dam.

The San Juan produced some good fishing in New Mexico before Navajo Dam was built. A ranger from the New Mexico State Department of Parks told me that "monsters" had been taken out of there before the dam. But the original river was erratic. It was a violent river, unfishable, during the rampaging runoff that the late spring sun sent down the mountains each year. At any time of year, the combination of a light rain and the high desert soils could turn the water red-brown.

Not any more, though, not since Navajo Dam. When the 400-foot earthen dam was completed in 1962, it created one of the tailwater fisheries that have become famous in the West: the South Platte below Cheesman Dam just an hour's drive southwest of Denver, the Big Horn on the Crow Reservation in Montana below Yellowtail Dam, and several on the Colorado Plateau—the Colorado River at Lees Ferry below Glen Canyon Dam, the Green River below Flaming Gorge Dam, and the Dolores River below McPhee Dam in western Colorado. When conditions are right, a dam can do wonders for the trout habitat below the dam. Water is released through the bottom of the dam, and this flow—the tailwater—can make for optimum big-trout conditions. Since the water comes from the depths of the reservoir, during the winter the river is warmer than it would be under natural conditions and during the summer it is protected from the sun, kept cooler than in the free-flowing river. In the case of the San Juan, the tailwater runs at a steady 43 degrees all year. The river runs clear and blue. All the silt is collected behind the dam.

Spectacular trout habitat: big fish, many big fish, and they will take dry flies or nymphs throughout most of the year. The roadway sign is not puffing when it assures fly-fishers that the dam created "extraordinary habitat

# Rosa

for record-sized trout," one of the "prime trout fishing areas in the Southwest," and, the sign could have added, in the nation. The other sign, the lawyers' sign, the one that reminds us of our inability to tame a large wild river with certainty, is an abstraction and only vaguely disquieting. Its black letters read:

WHEN SIREN SOUNDS,

FLOW AND LEVEL OF RIVER

WILL CHANGE QUICKLY

And in red:

WARNING!

GET OUT OF RIVER

CUIDADO

KTNN steadily played out country music as I finished up my preparation. The focused consciousness of this ritual is what has always enraptured me so about fly-fishing. You zero in, with intensity, on the job at hand: holding steady to thread the gossamer leader tip through the eye of a fly; searching the living stream for a likely run of good trout water or, better yet, a feeding fish breaking the surface or momentarily flashing a silver side down below in a dart for a nymph; and setting the hook exactly *now*—for you have only a split moment right when the strike comes.

Another part of your mind fans out over the whole watershed, surveying the river to its source, assessing coming changes in the river from the dark cloud over the feeder creek or from the hot sun melting snow in the high mountains. There is room left in your mind for lazy thoughts of baseball, long-ago lovers, and country music.

There is room, too, for the fishing trips of old. When I was a little boy, no more than six, my father took me out in a rowboat on Higgins Lake in Michigan, where my mother grew up. He cast out the spinner, and let me reel it in and feel the perch's sharp, quick tug—the direct connection with a wild animal—at the other end of the line. Later he got me a handline, sinkers, hooks, and a pound of frozen squid for bait and taught me how to drop the line off a New England wharf, down to the bottom, and then bring up scup and blowfish from the depths of the bay.

To my knowledge, he rarely fly-fished for trout but he mentioned it several times, once telling me that the Au Sable River in Michigan was supposed to be a fine trout stream, that he had seen it, and that it was a beautiful river. In college I bought a flyrod and drove up to the Au Sable, which was, as he said, a lovely place in the Michigan pine country. And so, in this time and place so distant from that fishing day on the Au Sable, my mind played back to my father and what he gave me and what he never did.

Trout fishing, if you have time—and you probably should do it only if you do have time—creates room in your mind.

I was listening to this radio station yesterday, during the drive down to Chaco Canyon and back, and this morning when I made my way up to the riverside parking area. KTNN has country music, yes, but it has other things, too, and the station reminded me once again of what I had learned since I first heard about the trophy trout in the San Juan.

KTNN, the Voice of the Navajo Nation, 660 on your dial, 50,000 watts clear channel. Navajo-language programming had continued to gain popularity since my first trip to Mexican Hat many years before. Now the tribe had chartered its own station. The programming is bilingual, split about evenly between English and Navajo. The morning begins with long, exhaustive news broadcasts, rare on AM. The programming starts out, in Navajo, with the national and tribal news. After that, because the Navajo Reservation is located in three states, KTNN gives the news from Arizona, Utah, and New Mexico. A barrage of words foreign to my ear, grunts, clicks, "eh's" (the Navajo's name for themselves is *Dine*—Din-*eh,* not Din-*ay*). Then, randomly sprinkled through the old language: "Secretary of Interior Bruce Babbitt" and "United Nations" and "Senate Indian Affairs Committee hearings." And the commercials: the un-understood rush of words, then, in the middle of the flow, "Kayenta Burger King," or "Peabody Coal Company," and, once, "acupuncture."

With the long stretch of Navajo-language news done, KTNN did it—all of it, I imagine—over again, this time in English, allowing me to understand Secretary Babbitt's latest proposal and Burger King's opening and closing hours. Following the newscast was an interview with a representative of the Navajo Supreme Court, explaining the tribe's dispute resolution system, where elders held "Peacemakers Court." Then KTNN went into its country music format. Except for the commercials, the broadcast was all in English. No Navajo country singers yet, at least not on this program. I was reminded of my Hopi friend, Elbridge Cochise, a respected tribal judge who could belt out "Cheating Heart" and had recorded and released a couple of tapes of his own country songs.

It occurred to me, sitting on the back of the van, now ready to get started fishing, that once I had conceived of the West largely in terms of its mountain beauty and good trout water. Now the western landscape seems much more complicated. And that is surely the case with the San Juan River.

**O**ne of my former students, Robert Urias, immersed himself in the web of history, law, culture, land, and pent-up emotionalism that comprises the Hispanic experience in the Southwest. He did a research paper on the Hispanics' struggle to reclaim land in the Rio Chama Valley of New Mexico that the Hispanics contend was guaranteed to them in the 1848 Treaty of Guadalupe Hidalgo between the United States and Mexico. The conflict boiled up in 1967 when the charismatic Reies Tijerina led a dramatic, front-page takeover of the county courthouse in Tierra Amarilla. This upswelling of passions inspired John Nichols to write *Milagro Beanfield War*.

Robert told me that he had met Frances Quintana, an Anglo anthropologist who wrote *Los Primeros Pobladores* ("The First Settlers"), a history of the Hispanic settlements in the San Juan Valley. I knew her work, but it had never occurred to me that she might be accessible. Robert gave me her number. "But she might not want to talk," he told me. "Sometimes she just hangs up the phone on people." She didn't hang up on me—probably because I managed to insert Robert's name into the conversation right at the beginning. Mrs. Quintana remembered him and liked him. We set up a time to get together at her home. She suggested that I also talk with her husband, Miguel, and his daughter, Martha.

Mrs. Quintana, in her seventies, is a deliberate, precise woman whose life has been shaped by a prolonged, close-up encounter with injustice. In 1960, her Ph.D. fieldwork took her to the San Juan country, to the Hispanic societies of southern Colorado and New Mexico, where she witnessed the tight-knit cultures and the steady loss of land, water, and community. Later in life, after her children were grown, she married Miguel. In the preface to the second edition of *Los Primeros Pobladores,* Mrs. Quintana acknowledges that she has forged many friendships with the Hispanic people and has come to take their side. "I do think, however," she pointedly wrote, "that I have stayed with the facts." And she has: her factual writing style leaves no doubt of that, and she speaks in the same straightforward way. Yet, in her face, you can see the defiance and a long-smoldering anger.

The Hispanics, who began settling the Rio Grande Valley in the 1500s, eventually moved into the valley of the Rio Chama, a main tributary of the Rio Grande. By the 1700s, the Chama Valley was home to a number of traditional Hispanic communities. The Hispanics mostly stayed out of the San Juan country, a hundred miles to the west, which was Ute and Navajo territory. In the early 1870s, however, it became clear that the United States would remove both tribes from the upper San Juan. When the Brunot Agreement was forced upon Ouray, Nicaagat, and the Ute in 1873, the way was paved for entry by non-Indians. Hispanics from the Chama moved across the Continental Divide and made a number of settlements in the San Juan Valley.

These Hispanic communities were among the few in this New Mexico–Colorado borderland in the nineteenth century. There were the two Colorado Ute reservations—remnants of the vast Ute domain that had, just a few years before, reached nearly to the Wyoming line. Durango and Pagosa Springs were small towns, mostly Anglo, half a day's ride or more to the north. Gold and silver boomtowns like Silverton and Ouray, in the mountains, were much farther north still. By the late 1800s, the upper San Juan was mostly Hispanic.

# Rosa

Rosa, the largest town on the San Juan, was a vibrant, booming community. At the center was the town's namesake—the church of Santa Rosa de Lima honoring the first saint of the New World—an adobe structure that the *pobladores* built collectively. The Hispanics, contrary to the heavy-handed, violent practices of the Americans, had cordial, ongoing relationships with the Ute people, especially those on the Southern Ute Reservation at Ignacio. Fiestas abounded, year-round. The Santiago fiesta in July, for example, featured the *gallos,* or rooster pull, in which horsemen competed to pull from the ground a rooster buried up to its neck. Rosa, Arboles, and the other communities guarded their cultural independence. No school district reached into the valley, but the Hispanics built and operated their own school. They ran a local justice court and managed to bend the jurisdictional rules to keep nearly all of their disputes at home, away from the Anglo-controlled county court in Aztec.

Miguel Quintana, born in 1912, remembers Rosa vividly. The families were large (he was one of seventeen children) and the community was close. Like most, he ran a few cattle, grew some crops, and operated a business—in his case a cantina, then a mercantile store. He loved the fertile land in this broad, sunny valley. "I had," he says, "my silky bottomland." His daughter, Martha, winsome and open, lights up when she remembers her childhood: the dances in the big hall on the third weekend of every month, the wedding celebrations where people from all the nearby towns came together.

Martha talks with reverence about the extended kinship that was the heart and soul of Rosa. "If," she explains, "someone had to stucco a house or build a barn, four or five families would just get together and do it." If a hunter bagged a deer in the piñon-juniper country just up above the farmland, the venison was distributed among the neighbors. If somebody cut some timber from the fine ponderosa pine stands still higher up, many families received firewood. The baking of a pot of beans or a batch of bread was followed by knocks on many friends' doors. When someone took ill, people would fetch a doctor, do the plowing, care for the animals, and take turns sitting up with the invalid. Caring, reaching out, civility, for eighty steadfast years.

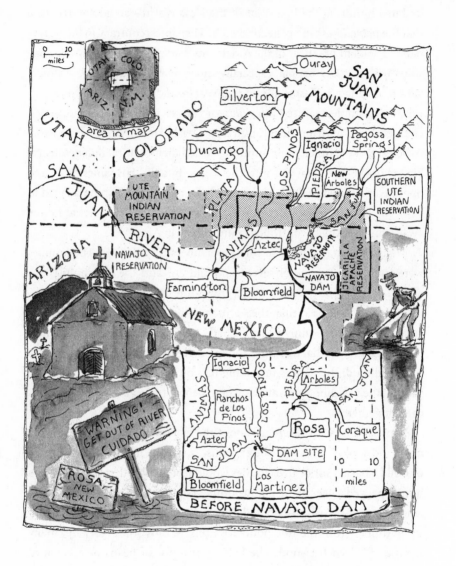

BEFORE NAVAJO DAM

# Rosa

Yet when I met with the Quintanas, it was at their home in Aztec, 20 miles below Navajo Dam, not Rosa or one of the other Hispanic towns. Miguel Quintana resisted the move from his homeland as well as he could. When he and other local residents learned of the impending construction of Navajo Dam and how the reservoir behind it would flood their homes, they protested to the Bureau of Reclamation. They were told only that if people lost buildings or land, they would be paid. A dignified gentleman of few words, Mr. Quintana painted the ending: "I said I would stay until they bulldozed me out and I did."

Martha, just twenty then, was there to help, for the Quintanas were among the last of the 250 families to leave. She explained the last days slowly and softly, almost inaudibly. "The water was coming up, and the buildings had been leveled by the bulldozers. There was no choice. The bridge across the river had been torn down a couple of years before. The remaining families put what we could in our pickups. Then we forded the river, and left."

The water behind Navajo Dam backed up relentlessly and drowned Rosa. Lost also were Arboles, most of Coraque, other smaller communities, and the ranches along the Rio de los Pinos. Los Martinez, just below the dam, was vacated too. People scattered: to Aztec, Farmington, Albuquerque, Los Angeles, Seattle, elsewhere. Most of these subsistence ranch and farm families were rendered landless. There was no reimbursement for relocation costs. The government payments for their land may have met the technical legal requirements, but they were far too small to buy replacement land. Mr. Quintana's old Rosa mercantile building and his silky farmland, of such inestimable value to him and his family, didn't add up to much in an appraiser's eye.

Four families, including Martha's, resettled 30 miles away in New Arboles in Colorado on the shore of Navajo Reservoir. In the traditional spirit of cooperation and community they joined together and built a small white frame church. The cemetery, however, has been a source of continuing bitterness. The Bureau of Reclamation exhumed the bodies in the Rosa cemetery and moved them up to New Arboles: gruesome, yet better than inundation. But some of the oldest graves were unmarked. In the cemetery down in Rosa, people knew them by their location but now everything was rearranged. When relatives come back, often from long distances, they are confounded by rows of markers declaring "Unknown."

The Hispanics remember Rosa. In 1979, Martha organized a reunion on the shore of Navajo Reservoir near New Arboles. No fewer than a thousand people showed up from all over the country. Once again the bright colors swirled all around, the smell of barbequed beef filled the air, and the sounds of the fiesta rang out loud and true on the upper San Juan. Looming over the gaiety, though, was the gray overcast of the bitter loss of a family-oriented community that could be alive every day, not just on reunion weekend. "I'm convinced," Martha says carefully, "that if the dam had never been built, the people who were still in Rosa would have stayed and most of those who left would have come back."

Navajo Reservoir, 35 miles long, covers other eras of human history. Ancestral Puebloans lived in the upper San Juan Valley from five thousand years ago until after A.D. 1000, two hundred generations of human existence. The area is the wellspring of their culture. There is a connection to Chaco Canyon a hundred miles to the south, the large complex of villages that seems to have tied together in some yet unexplained way the economy, worldview, and gods of the Pueblo people of the whole San Juan Basin. Sites submerged under Navajo Reservoir contained goods brought in over well-established trade routes that reached throughout the Four Corners area and over to the Chama Valley. The Old People even engaged in trade from as far away as the Pacific, as evidenced by ornamental beads made from ocean sea shells. Hundreds of ancient sites ranging from campsites to whole villages were inundated.

Four hundred fifty rock art sites on the upper San Juan are gone now, flooded over. Most of the pictographs go way back, but some are more recent, done by Navajo in the 1750s. The "Twin War Gods" were painted on rocks near the confluence of the Los Pinos and the San Juan. Navajo workmen, when they built the dam in the 1960s, knew that the Twin War Gods would be flooded. They were convinced, however, that the 400-foot earth dam, backing up enough water to flood half of Connecticut to a foot deep, would never hold. The Twin War Gods, the workmen said, would eventually win out. In red:

WARNING!

GET OUT OF RIVER

CUIDADO

**N**avajo Dam, a product of the new context, represents how western water policy went bad. Before the Big Buildup, the uses of the Colorado Plateau's rivers were mostly benign and a great deal of good was done. Anglo water use in the Grand Valley, the Uinta Basin, and elsewhere may have originated in blunt-instrument tactics, but the farm and ranch communities that grew up on former Indian lands were almost always industrious, stable, and sometimes modestly prosperous. Many communities, like Rosa, lived off their silky bottomlands and the water that made them spring to life.

Then water use in the Colorado River basin turned to water development. The dominant purpose shifted from small-scale agricultural to crank-it-up-fast industrial. By the time World War II ended, the real estate developers and the corporate executives wanted the rivers, no matter how far they might be from their own locales, and they wanted them immediately. The flows could produce hydropower and water to build waves of new subdivisions.

Traditional western water law, which first arose during the rough-hewn westward expansion of the mid-nineteenth century, was ideally suited for modern, large-scale developers. The law, called the prior appropriation doctrine, granted water users, free of charge, permanent water rights on a "first in time, first in right" basis. Basically, western water law treated the water as a commodity and viewed every river as a commons open for any extractive purpose—mostly mining, irrigation, hydropower, industrial, and household uses—so long as you got there first.

There were other approaches to water that we might have considered. The early Mormon settlements in rural Utah proceeded on a community basis. Ward bishops allocated water to local residents equally—there was no notion of "first in time"—and there were limits: only community members could receive water rights and they could receive no more than their own families could use for their farms. The Hispanics of Rosa and elsewhere had a somewhat similar system, based on the mother ditch that served the whole community: water rights were held not by individuals, but by *acequia* associations, administered by a *mayordomo*. John Wesley Powell premised his 1878 *Arid Lands* report on the idea that water should be set aside for watershed communities. He believed that water must be used carefully and should not be sold, like a commodity, or used outside a watershed. Powell's whole approach toward the West was based upon its aridity—based, that is, on the limits imposed by the land. For Indian people, water was spiritual. Like the land and animals, water was part of the whole natural world and duties were owed: human beings and the rivers were equals. Human beings could use the rivers, but they were required to do so with respect and with prayers. John Muir had his vision. He saw spirituality and beauty everywhere in nature, including water. Nature had its own worth and it benefited humans. Muir passionately believed the rivers and their deep canyons should be preserved.

But in the 1950s such ideas about water were of no moment at all. The original Mormon ideal of share-and-share-alike was long dead; by the late 1800s, the Utah Supreme Court had adopted the competitive and utilitarian prior appropriation doctrine wholesale. As for Indians and Hispanics, who would listen to them? They were societies on the way out. And Powell, not yet memorialized in Wallace Stegner's seminal book, *Beyond the Hundredth Meridian,* was at best just a half-remembered nineteenth-century figure who had been drummed out of his post as director of the U.S. Geological Survey by angry western senators in the 1890s. No one took the conservationists seriously. Muir, like Powell, was just a vague presence. And in the 1950s only David Brower was around to raise Muir's concerns. Brower opposed the Echo Park Dam that would have flooded part of Dinosaur National Monument. But the big interests simply moved the dam farther downriver to Glen Canyon, which was a bigger and better site in any event.

So, instead of borrowing approaches based on respect for local communities and living streams, water policy in the Southwest responded enthusiastically to the boomers' demands. And these demands, coupled with the "use it or lose it" imperative of western water law, made for a rush on the rivers. The states threw all of their weight behind their own developers. Just as the law gave no protection to free-flowing waters or redrock canyons, neither did the system make accommodations for dispossessed people, whether at Rosa or in Indian country. The tribes might have the best water rights on paper, but few tribes had lawyers. When they did—witness John Boyden, the Utes, and the Central Utah Project—the attorneys showed little inclination to stand up to the states and the private interests.

What a combination: free water, vested property rights, ample federal money to fund water projects, infrequent environmental concerns, and little scrutiny. The decisive moments came when the states stopped fighting among themselves and put their combined might behind multi-project, pork-barrel water legislation. All the developers got what they wanted. Looking back on it, Stewart Udall, Arizona congressman in the 1950s and interior secretary during the Kennedy–Johnson years, who saw the buildup firsthand, calls it "water chauvinism. Crazy, crazy river basin management."

The new style of water development on the Colorado Plateau reached its first crescendo with passage of the Colorado River Storage Project Act of 1956. The ideas that coalesced into the 1956 act, which funded Navajo Dam and several other large projects, had been gestating for decades as engineers filed reports selecting the best dam sites and industrial interests began to calculate the dollars that could be generated. With a waning need for irrigation water, the 1956 act's real objective was to provide municipal water and, especially, hydroelectric energy to support future urban growth. To produce the electrical power, the cities needed to have the rivers impounded so that their levels could be raised hundreds of feet and the water allowed to blast down through 15-foot-diameter pipes, called penstocks, to spin turbines.

The separate engineers' reports, when analyzed together, showed that all seven of the Colorado River states shared a broad common interest. What needed to be done was to build a coordinated, basinwide system that would put dams on the mainstem Colorado and the major tributaries to bring the wild Colorado River—from Mexico to Wyoming—under control. (The process of taming the Colorado River had already begun, in the 1930s, with construction of Hoover Dam and its reservoir, Lake Mead, on the lower Colorado, just downriver from the Plateau.) Once the river was tamed, the water flow at each dam could be turned up or down to respond to high and low demands for electricity, drinking water, and farming. In the eyes of the proponents of the Big Buildup, a managed river system was crucial to meeting the needs of the millions of transplants coming to the American Southwest.

The maestro for the 1956 act was Colorado's Wayne Aspinall, the spectacularly accomplished and fervently dedicated chairman of the House Interior and Insular Affairs Committee. No one before or since has run a congressional committee with an iron grip firmer than Aspinall's. Direct, honest, and unflaggingly diligent in his old-fashioned schoolmaster's glasses, Aspinall orchestrated big-dam construction in the Colorado River Basin the way he managed all the business of his committee: attending to every big policy issue, every parliamentary detail, every member's personal foible. The jocular comment that committee members had to obtain the chairman's permission to go to the men's room was nearly as much historical fact as it was bittersweet humor.

Water development in the Southwest was a religion for Aspinall. And he spoke for many others who could see the West's fulfillment of itself on the horizon: "I have always believed the Creator placed natural resources to be used as well as viewed, and to be used by the people generally." Of all natural things, his vision fixed most sharply on the Colorado River: "The river means the West to me. . . . It is the heart of my West."

Glen Canyon Dam, on the Colorado River just below the Utah–Arizona line, was the centerpiece of the 1956 legislation. It stands a full 710 feet high. The project used enough concrete to build a highway completely across the country. The dam has the capacity to back up 26 million acre-feet of water—thereby creating the reservoir, at once the most hated and beloved artificial body of water in America, that has become the revered and reviled symbol of postwar development in the Southwest. Lake Powell, 180 miles long, winding back into side canyons large and small, has a shoreline of nearly 2,000 miles. If the project were superimposed on the East Coast and Glen Canyon Dam were set down in Manhattan, Lake Powell would reach nearly to Harvard Yard.

The Colorado River's main tributaries were brought under control by three major projects and several smaller ones. On the Green River, Flaming Gorge Dam in northern Utah stands 490 feet high. On the Gunnison River in Colorado, the Wayne N. Aspinall Storage Unit consists of three dams. In New Mexico, Navajo Dam and Navajo Reservoir impound the San Juan River.

The four largest structures launched by the 1956 act, one of the most ambitious of all public works projects, were all in place and operating within just a decade. With giant Hoover Dam, 726 feet high, completed two decades before, the dams of the Colorado River drowned more than 300 miles of free-flowing rivers; impounded no less than six times the annual flow of the river behind them; and controlled how much, and when, water would run in the river channels that remained. The Big Buildup conquered the river of the Southwest.

The stakes had gone way up. Navajo Dam, which was not even one of the really big structures by postwar standards, was nevertheless a colossus: it rose a third again as high, and held a third again as much water, as Roosevelt Dam that Phoenix and the Salt River Project had labored to build on the Salt River a half-century earlier. A Hispanic community like Rosa was of no account. The force of it all was unbelievable and it was accomplished in a moment's time. Six short years after Congress had provided the funds, Martha Quintana was struggling to ford the rising San Juan in her pickup, praying that she wouldn't lose her furniture or her fiesta dresses to the current.

Nor is Navajo Dam the San Juan River's only new-style development project. The builders in Albuquerque, on the other side of the Continental Divide, wanted San Juan water for their subdivisions. When Congress authorized another round of Colorado River water projects in 1962, New Mexico got federal funding for the San Juan–Chama Project, which ships water east to the Rio Grande through a complex of giant tunnels 26 miles long. Each year the San Juan is depleted by 100,000 acre-feet—but, incredibly, almost none of the water is used. More than thirty years later, Albuquerque still doesn't need it and still hasn't adopted a water conservation program that would make the San Juan–Chama Project unnecessary instead of a testament to the excesses of the Big Buildup.

Below Navajo Dam, downstream from the blue-ribbon trout fishery on the San Juan River, large withdrawals of water for cities and agribusiness have combined with the San Juan–Chama Project to make the San Juan shallower, warmer, and saltier. Ironically, perhaps, one of these installations is the Navajo Indian Irrigation Project. NIIP was created, not out of any desire of the water barons to get water to dispossessed people, but as a political necessity to satisfy eastern senators. The easterners were wondering quite loudly how anyone could justify all the federal expenditures for non-Indian development when right in the middle of the Colorado Plateau sat the Navajo Nation with the most land and the biggest and oldest water rights. With their other projects in jeopardy, western water interests agreed to support NIIP.

NIIP, the only Indian project authorized during the Big Buildup, was designed by federal bureaucrats, not the Navajo. And from the beginning it was wrought with delays and cutbacks (unlike the San Juan–Chama

# Rosa

Project, which was built promptly to full specifications in order to transport water to Albuquerque). Although Congress funded NIIP's construction, the tribe had responsibility for its operation: the Navajo spent millions upon millions on the poorly conceived project, which yielded few benefits to the tribe and provided far less employment of tribal members than originally negotiated. In the past few years, the Navajo have been able to balance the books at NIIP through their striking ability to create order from the chaos of colliding with a larger society with such a different worldview. One can only guess at the results if all the money for NIIP had been allocated by the Navajo themselves—perhaps for hospitals, the tribal courts, and the impressive tribal education system, preschool, elementary, secondary, and collegiate.

Navajo Dam and Navajo Reservoir, the San Juan–Chama Project, NIIP, and other smaller projects have vitiated the San Juan as a natural river. Evidence is offered by two fish listed as threatened species, the humpback chub and the Colorado squawfish. While the tailwater of Navajo Dam may make good trout habitat, the industrial and agricultural withdrawals farther downriver, which use water stored in Navajo Reservoir, have wrecked the habitat for these less glamorous fish. The squawfish, for example, which once grew to 5 feet in length and is the world's largest minnow, is struggling to survive in today's San Juan River. The lower stretches of the San Juan are so depleted, and the channel so braided, that the squawfish can't make its migration runs up the river to spawn.

This river has been redefined in just forty years.

I got up, pulled down the hatchback, turned off KTNN, locked the van, and took the short walk down the graded trail toward Texas Hole, the most famous fishing spot on the San Juan River. The scattered snowflakes had not discouraged the fishermen. About fifteen of them, in waders, were working the different subcurrents that flowed into the hole. Four river guides had taken their clients out near the center of the river, which is about 40 yards wide here. Skillfully the guides maneuvered their McKenzie river boats, wooden dories specially designed for fishing good-sized trout rivers, into easy casting range of the prime spots that are difficult to reach without a boat. Almost simultaneously, commotion overtook two of the McKenzies.

From one of the boats: "You've got one! Keep your rod tip up! Keep it up or you'll lose him!"

From the other: "See that rise? *Yes!* He's a beauty! Work him—don't force him, take it easy, take it easy."

They landed one of them, the guide scooping the struggling fish from the river with a long-handled net that he operated with both hands. It looked like a nice-sized rainbow: 18, maybe 20 inches. A few minutes later, the boat fishermen had another one on, and then still another.

I made a few halfhearted casts from a position that didn't give me a chance to reach good water. I didn't want to encroach on the other fishermen. I walked up on the bank and saw some promising riffles above Texas Hole, but there were fishermen up there, too, and decided to move on. This was crowded territory and within eyesight of Navajo Dam, as tall as a forty-story office building, two-thirds of a mile wide, reminding me of Rosa.

As I drove the van slowly downriver, I could see numbers of anglers working the "quality water" section of the river, about 2 miles long where fishers can use only barbless hooks and take just one fish a day. The woman at one of the fly shops had told me I'd probably want to stay away from the river below the quality water. "Fish the quality water. That's where the lunkers are."

Still, I wanted to get away by myself, and I drove downstream, past the quality water, and parked. I liked the scramble down the steep embankment and the minor challenge of picking my way through the streamside tangle of red willows, tamarisk, and alder. After breaking clear of the brush, I hit the river just below some riffles that fed out of a likely-looking hole. No one else was around.

# Rosa

It usually takes me a few trips to understand a new river. This is compounded by the difficulties of nymph fishing. You work the nymph underwater and strikes can be hard to detect, unlike dry fly-fishing where the fly floats voluptuously on the surface and a strike is accompanied by a heart-stopping explosion of water. I wasn't surprised when I didn't scare anything up during a couple of hours of casting.

I moved upstream to a point below a side current. Now I was understanding the river better and feeling more comfortable with my San Juan worm. The shallow run was small enough that I would get only one, maybe two, casts before spooking the trout. My first cast hit the water, the worm sank down into the white-green flow, and then the faint orange disappeared in a flash of silver. I twitched my rod and the rainbow was on.

The fish ran up toward the low waterfall at the top of the run and when I put pressure on the line to bring him back, he came straight up out of the water. He fought hard for five minutes or so, and then I brought him into the shallows. A gorgeous, bright rainbow, firm and plump from the rich feed and cold water. This fish was just 11 or 12 inches, hardly one of the legendary San Juan trout, 4 pounds and higher. Still, I was delighted. I slid the barbless hook out and held him lightly in slow current, facing upstream, so he could regain his strength and flip free of my grasp.

I stood by the river looking out toward the place where the rainbow had disappeared into the green. Then I walked to a grassy spot for a lunch of a cheese sandwich, water, and an apple amid the riot of river smells. As I ate my lunch, reflecting on the story of this river, I knew more than ever that a busy managed river, though still a river, is not my choice. My choice is for smaller, remote rivers, less crowded rivers, rivers you have to hike into and break a sweat, rivers where you can fish and think in your own solitude, rivers not managed, rivers that don't exact such heavy human costs.

It was getting time to leave. Otherwise, I wouldn't make it home in time to tuck in the boys and talk with Ann. I made my way back through the brush and up the bank.

My route home took me across Navajo Dam and I got out at the parking area on the dam. I walked across the road and looked downstream. The upper end of the quality water was visible and the fishermen seemed even more numerous than in the morning, dotting the river below, 10 or 20 yards apart. After returning to the parking lot, I stood by the railing and took a good long while to scan the reservoir and the San Juan Valley, trying to imagine Rosa, and what it was like there, before getting back in the van.

# CRETACEOUƒ

In 1963, at the same time the dams were backing up water on the Colorado River and its tributaries, the Four Corners Power Plant started up.
Some of the energy to support the impending boom in the southwestern
cities would come from hydroelectric facilities at the new dams. But electricity from power plants running on coal was another critical prong in the
strategy. Sited within the New Mexico portion of the Navajo Reservation,
20 miles east of majestic Shiprock, Four Corners was the first coal-fired
power plant on the Colorado Plateau.

One can hardly overstate the magnitude of the accomplishment that
began to be realized when Four Corners went on line. It took supreme cre-
ativity and conceptual clarity to imagine and plan a reliable power grid

spanning the Southwest from the Pacific to the Pecos. Implementing the elaborate scheme required the highest measure of single-minded efficiency and industrial brawn. At the same time, the energy development symbolized by the Four Corners Power Plant was hard on the air, rivers, and land. It rolled over dispossessed people. The deals that allowed the Four Corners complex to go ahead were part of a long line of one-sided Indian resource transactions, culminating in the Hopi and Navajo leases of Black Mesa, that made the Big Buildup possible.

**F**our Corners is a mine-mouth power plant symbiotic with Navajo Mine just a few miles to the south. The mine is the sole supplier of fuel to the power facility. To extract the coal, BHP–Utah Minerals International leases 36,000 acres from the Navajo Nation, high-desert land once grazed by traditional Navajo sheepherders.

Strip mining at Navajo Mine begins when giant earthmoving equipment bares the coal seams by tearing away topsoil and overburden—layers of rock, shale, and soil. Then explosives break apart and loosen the tight, dense coal seams for scraping and loading. Each individual blasted strip is 100 feet wide, 30 feet deep, and a mile in length. A "shoot" was scheduled the day I was at Navajo Mine, so I was able to witness a mile-long string of dynamite and nitroglycerin erupt at once in a dramatic crescendo of explosions, debris, dust, and the "whoopees!" of onlooking mine workers and visitors, certainly including myself. Then, to go deeper, the strip will be blasted again and again and again. The company runs several parallel strips at once. The resulting pit is a man-made canyon a mile long, nearly that wide, and 180 feet deep. "What a procedure," the foreman told me. "It takes eight weeks to prepare and three or four seconds to shoot."

The coal is scoured out of the ground by the largest machine I have ever seen. The operator in the cab works what looks like a crane except that the boom is 300 feet long—the length of a football field. The boom holds a dragline: a gigantic escalator with buckets that can lift and dump 65 cubic

# Cretaceous

yards of material each—the equivalent of 6 dumptruck loads. The drag-lines operate around the clock, 365 days a year. To transport the coal to the power plant, the Navajo Mine owns and operates its own 12-mile railroad system. The mine runs two twenty-car trains; every car holds 100 tons of coal. With each train running six full trainloads a day, the mine delivers 24,000 tons of coal daily to the Four Corners Power Plant.

The buildings at the Four Corners Power Plant, up to twenty stories tall, blanket several acres. Like other visitors and workers alike, I am armored in a hard hat, plastic goggles, and earplugs. The boilers, where coal is burned to turn water into steam, amount to buildings unto themselves. These cauldrons create temperatures of 2,500 to 3,500 degrees Fahrenheit. The boilers—operating like gigantic teakettles—shoot out steam and spin generators, 20 feet tall, that produce the electricity. The racket and fury send the electrical power into hundreds of wrist-size wires, held aloft by the 200-foot praying-mantis steel standards, for distribution from Los Angeles to El Paso and points in between. The by-products from energy production at Four Corners—silicon, mercury, aluminum, titanium, iron, sulfur dioxide, nitrogen oxide, ash—are sent aloft through smokestacks that tower 750 feet high.

The coal taken out at Navajo Mine and burned at Four Corners traces to the Cretaceous Period: 136 to 65 million years ago. The Colorado Plateau was then on the western shore of a large inland sea. The climate was mild, with no frosts to stifle the lush vegetation. This coastal regime included vast freshwater coastal swamps, similar to the Florida Everglades, that sup-ported plant-eating dinosaurs and, eventually, today's coal mines and power plants. The organic material for the coal deposits came from vege-tation—large ferns but especially conifers. Some of the plant debris grew in the swamps but even more was carried in by the rivers, sweeping down from the high mountains in what is now Nevada.

As the rivers brought in successive layers of sediment that sealed in the vegetation, the floor of the Plateau was imperceptibly sinking, so that new waves of wood fiber from the upland forests were stacked on top of the older ones. And as more layers of sediment flowed in, the events repeated themselves and the land continued to subside. The vegetation first became peat—beginning a process of breaking the material down to purer and purer carbon (although there are always some trace elements such as those sent up out of the stacks at Four Corners). After the plant material was no longer being deposited, the rivers continued to lay down sediment. These successive rock layers were critical: the increase in temperature accompanying depth of burial is the primary factor for the metamorphosis of the vegetation into peat, then coal.

Two main factors—BTU content and sulfur content—determine the value of coal. BTUs measure the amount of heat the coal can produce: coal from Navajo Mine is rated at approximately 11,000 BTU (highly desirable for power production), while Black Mesa coal registers at 13,000 (nearly off the chart). Sulfur content should be low to comply with air pollution regulations. The historical accident of coal in the western United States forming in freshwater marshes—rather than marine or brackish marshes—made Colorado Plateau coal low in sulfur.

High BTU, low sulfur. The die, molded in the Cretaceous, was cast: coal from Black Mesa and the Kaiparowits Plateau may be the most valuable in the world, and the deposits of the Fruitland Formation, which encompasses the coal at Navajo Mine, are only slightly behind.

You can tell who controls this coal-generated electricity, and where it goes, by the names of the owners of Four Corners Power Plant: Southern California Edison, Arizona Public Service, Public Service Company of New Mexico, Tucson Electric Power, El Paso Electric, and the Salt River Project. This is the same Salt River Project that Phoenix farmers formed in the 1890s to build Roosevelt Dam, but then again it is not. SRP still controls the Salt River and distributes the flow to its customers, but water sales account for just 1 percent of SRP's annual revenues of $1.3 billion. The nation's third-largest public power utility, SRP now runs on electricity.

Like other utilities in the Southwest, after World War II SRP embarked on an aggressive "grow and build" campaign designed to lure more industry to support more growth, construction, and power revenues—an approach that SRP continues today through large contributions to local

Parasaurolophus walkeri

INTERIOR SEAWAY

UTAH

LAND and SEA IN NORTH AMERICA
DURING THE LATE CRETACEOUS

FUTURE SITE of UTAH

LATE CRETACEOUS SEA

COASTAL PLAIN

Alamosaurus sanjuanensis

# THE LATE CRETACEOUS:
The Age of Dinosaurs — and of Coal

chambers of commerce and active recruitment of new companies to the Phoenix area. SRP and the other power providers, both public and private, along with the mining companies and construction firms needed to build plants, transmission lines, pipelines, and roads, accomplished unbelievable things in almost no time at all. When Four Corners went on line in 1963, it provided a capacity of 2,040 megawatts. This means that Four Corners alone, although in fact it spreads its electricity around several cities, could serve a metropolitan area of between 2 million and 3.5 million people.

The dreams of the urban centers became even more expansive after Four Corners started up and the hydroelectric projects authorized by Congress in 1956 were nearly done. In 1964 a group of utilities and municipalities, spanning the Southwest, formed WEST (Western Energy Supply and Transmission Associates). The operative strategy, conceived by James Mulloy of the Los Angeles Department of Water and Power, was called "the Grand Plan." WEST would take the Southwest to an even higher level by spearheading a power network anchored on the building of nuclear plants on the California coast and coal plants in the interior, mostly on the Colorado Plateau.

The Grand Plan was exactly that. WEST spokesmen projected that when completed in 1985, the program would "produce more than three times as much power as TVA, 17 times as much as the Aswan Dam project in Egypt and eight times as much as the Soviet Union's largest power project." Although opposition to the industrialization of the Plateau caused that prediction to fall slightly short, enormous accomplishments were made in the coming years.

The alliance of metropolitan areas spurred an extraordinary spate of power-plant construction. The rush of the 1970s produced eleven major coal-fired power plants across the Colorado Plateau, reaching all the way north to the Hayden and Craig plants in Colorado's Yampa Valley, the Utes' old hunting grounds.

The Grand Plan also created a delivery system: the western power grid. The best hydroelectric sites on the Southwest's infrequent rivers, and most of the fossil fuel deposits, are located far from the cities. Establishing links to distant power sources was essential to realizing the level of development that the region's boomers had in mind. Before Four Corners, it was probably possible to trace an electron from Hoover Dam to El Paso but the interties between individual power sources were weak and unreliable. This all changed with Four Corners and its progeny—and the transmission lines that came with them.

The grid not only delivers huge amounts of power over a vast geographic area; it also gives the utilities flexibility. The Salt River Project's coal-fired power plants provide a reliable base load, for instance, but coal sources cannot be fired up quickly to meet peak demand. Hydroelectric plants, by contrast, can provide immediate peaking power simply by releasing more water through the dam to spin the turbines more rapidly. Thus SRP exchanges some of its coal-fired power from the Colorado plants and receives in return replacement electricity from Glen Canyon Dam to meet peak demands—such as the late morning surge of air-conditioning in Phoenix on a July day.

It may be gilding the lily to claim, as one journalist did, that "SRP has made life possible in semi-arid central Arizona." The Hohokam, after all, made it for more than fifteen centuries and our archaeologists have yet to discover a single air conditioner. But SRP, with its boardinghouse reach into the Colorado Plateau and the alchemy of its swaps on the power grid, has surely made life, as modern Arizonans know it, possible in the Salt River Valley.

The industrial race to the Colorado Plateau that began in the 1950s involved more than water and coal. The same geologic events that created the coal laid down Cretaceous and Jurassic deposits of other organic fuels— oil, gas, oil shale, and tar sands. The San Juan and Uinta Basins both have significant oil and gas production, largely on Southern Ute, Navajo, and Uintah and Ouray Ute lands. Most of the wells were drilled during the 1950s and 1960s. The Plateau holds the nation's (and world's) largest oil shale deposits. Exxon, Unocal, and other companies put in major installations during the late 1960s and 1970s but abruptly pulled out beginning in 1982 when the federal government eliminated oil shale subsidies.

# CONFLICTS AND CONQUESTS

And there is the uranium. Fifty-nine percent of the country's uranium, mostly tracing to the Triassic Period, is found on the eastern side of the Plateau. The rush came on strong after Charlie Steen's discovery—the largest high-grade uranium find ever made—near Moab in 1952. Uranium production involves three different types of sites: the mines to extract the raw minerals, the mills to produce "yellowcake," and tailings piles for waste disposal. Mines, mills, and tailings piles were located all over the area within roughly one hundred miles of the Four Corners. When the bottom fell out of the uranium market in the early 1980s, production plummeted. But the legacy of the uranium rush lives in the form of human casualties and cleanup costs.

Although the Big Buildup met little opposition in the early years, some projects did run into trouble. The first signs of dissent came in the early 1950s with the proposal to build a dam on the Green River near the Utah–Colorado line at the upper end of Whirlpool Canyon. The dam was named after Echo Park, one of the places the reservoir would have flooded, a sublime flat in a tight bend of the Green. In addition to inundating the canyons of the Green, Echo Park Dam would have backed up the Yampa, which entered the Green just above the proposed dam site. This meant flooding half of Dinosaur National Monument, which lay astride both the Green and the Yampa.

David Brower, on behalf of the Sierra Club, led the opposition—the modern environmental movement probably began exactly here—against the Echo Park Dam. It is difficult today for anyone who knows the supremely intransigent Brower to imagine him making an environmentally bad compromise. But this was his first legislative campaign (he had never appeared before a congressional committee) and he made what he still calls his worst mistake. He fought courageously and creatively—at one dramatic moment in 1954 during nine-day House hearings he challenged the Bureau of Reclamation's statistics on a key point and was proved indisputably correct. But the private and public forces had too much might

# Cretaceous

behind them. It was the right time to begin a movement, yet too early to make deep change. Echo Park Dam never came to fruition but in the compromise that became the 1956 Colorado River Storage Project Act, Glen Canyon Dam did.

By the mid-1960s, literally dozens of massive energy, water, oil and gas, and uranium projects were roaring ahead in various stages of study, design, and construction. The high-level bargaining and trading among southwestern states and their developers was building toward another congressional Christmas-tree bill. Then came a watershed event in 1963 when Arizona won the *Arizona v. California* case in the Supreme Court—a decision that finally fixed the state's water rights in the Colorado River. To put the hard-won water to use, Arizona wanted to build the Central Arizona Project. Because of Arizona's insistence on the CAP, and because Arizona was so well placed with Stewart Udall as interior secretary and Carl Hayden as chairman of the Senate Appropriations Committee, the legislative package could not be finalized without the CAP and, as it turned out, Black Mesa.

To Arizonans, the CAP was literally the state's birthright—the primary mechanism for fulfilling Arizona's entitlement to one-fifth of the Colorado River as a result of its statehood in 1912. The $2 billion project, a 200-mile-long system of canals and pipelines, would deliver 1.2 million acre-feet of water every year to the Valley of the Sun and then south to Tucson. The goliath, however, had a hearty appetite for electricity because of the pumping costs associated with the inconvenient fact that part of the CAP route ran uphill.

Although the CAP's take-out point from the river would lie downstream of the Colorado Plateau, the Plateau became directly implicated because the rhetorical question so naturally asked in those frenetic years was: what better way to create a high head of water for spinning turbines to activate the CAP than to dam the Grand Canyon? The utilities and the Bureau of Reclamation pushed for Marble Canyon Dam and Bridge Canyon (later named Hualapai) Dam, which together would make 133 miles of the Grand Canyon into reservoirs.

215

# CONFLICTS AND CONQUESTS

All the competing passions about the CAP and the rest of the Big Buildup, the old ideas versus the new, the drive to make the land over versus the nurturing love to protect it, the belief that Indians were in the way versus the conviction that they belonged there—came together in the person of Stewart Udall, secretary of the interior from 1961 through 1969, longer than anyone except Harold Ickes, Franklin Roosevelt's secretary from 1933 through 1945.

I met Stewart Udall for the first time in 1984, at the retreat that Robert Redford hosted at Tsaile to create a dialogue between tribal leaders and energy executives. Over the years we became good friends and have had many conversations about his life and the fascinating events that marked his tenure, the most dynamic in the nation's history, as interior secretary. From the beginning, Udall captivated me because of his public accomplishments and because of his humanity.

All of his life, Udall—born in 1920 a Mormon but an inactive member of the church by his forties—has been on a mission. His zeal to do good for the people and for the West has burned right on the surface. I've seen him literally jump on to the coffee table to wave his arms and shout out his outrage during a midnight argument over damming the canyons. And he has done good, both as a great conservationist secretary and as a leader of the American conservation movement ever since. But he straightforwardly admits to ruing to the core of his being his great failing: he allowed too much to happen on the Colorado Plateau before he was able to penetrate the thick steel exterior of the wrong but indisputable truths that he and almost everyone else were told about the Big Buildup.

Udall's upbringing bonded him both to the land and to the idea of land development. He came from one of Arizona's oldest pioneer families. One of his great-grandfathers, all four of whom were polygamists, was John D. Lee, who settled at Lees Ferry on the Colorado River just below the Utah line (just below Glen Canyon Dam today). Udall himself grew up in the eastern Arizona settlement of St. Johns. It was a unique town. Founded by

# Cretaceous

Hispanics as a supply base for Fort Apache, soon thereafter it was settled by Mormons after a call by Brigham Young. The west side of St. Johns was Mormon, the east Hispanic, and Main Street was common ground.

"I feel," Udall says, "that looking back over my life, I actually grew up in the nineteenth century. It was still the frontier." St. Johns had no electricity, no tractors. As the eldest son in a Mormon farm family, Udall took on a heavy responsibility: working the horse-drawn plow, baling the hay, milking the cows. When he went to bed during the irrigation season, he fell asleep to the gurgling of water working the fields.

Levi Udall was the patriarch of the family of six children, having broken from the practice of polygamy. (Stewart's grandfather Udall had two wives.) Levi served as president of the local Mormon stake for twenty-four years, much of which time he was also the county judge. A staunch conservative, in 1969 he became a justice of the Arizona Supreme Court and later rose to chief justice.

It was an auspicious setting for a political career for the eldest son, and Stewart Udall made the most of it. When he ran for Congress in 1954, he had a law degree and six years of practice under his belt. He also had the personal qualities: likable, hawk-faced handsome, and athletic, an all-conference basketball player at the University of Arizona. If the young candidate was too liberal for his rural district (he joined the NAACP in 1942 when he was in the military), the Udall family name counterbalanced that.

Congress was not entirely to Udall's taste. Not only was he a first-term congressman in a day when seniority reigned supreme, but the western issues he cared about most fell under the domain of Wayne Aspinall. It was Aspinall who headed the reclamation (read dams and reservoirs) subcommittee of the House Interior Committee until 1958, when he became chairman of the full committee. Udall chafed under Aspinall's tight rein from the beginning.

Udall was a nonplayer when Congress gave the go-ahead to Glen Canyon Dam in 1956. Glen Canyon and the three other big dams authorized by the 1956 statute were all in the Upper Basin and Arizona was a Lower Basin state. Colorado—and Wayne Aspinall—were in the Upper Basin and this was their business. Besides, in the high-stakes swapping and pork-barrel politics of the day, everybody knew that the 1956 statute was a necessary prelude for Arizona's receiving the Central Arizona Project. And *everybody* in Arizona wanted the CAP. It would have been political suicide for Udall to oppose either Echo Park or Glen Canyon. Indeed the thought never occurred to him, nor would it have occurred to anyone else in his congressional seat.

He began to see the world differently in 1961 when Kennedy elevated him, one of the most glamorous members of a glamorous administration, to interior secretary, the first Arizonan ever to hold a cabinet position. Udall then did something that apparently no secretary of the interior has done before or since: he appointed writers-in-residence. Wallace Stegner and Alvin Josephy both served in that capacity. Stegner, who took a leave from his teaching duties in Stanford's English Department for the fall of 1961, urged Udall to take the time to step back and learn about his job by writing a book about the West and the environment. Just before he left Washington to return to Stanford, Stegner presented Udall with a chapter outline.

The result was the well-received *Quiet Crisis,* published in 1963, a treatment of the great American philosophers of the natural world including Henry David Thoreau, George Perkins Marsh, and John Muir. *The Quiet Crisis* formed, along with Rachel Carson's *Silent Spring,* a pillar of the intellectual foundations for the burgeoning interest in protecting the environment. Udall and David Brower liked each other, and the activism of Brower, a regular visitor to Udall's office, buttressed the cabinet secretary's gathering conservationist orientation. "My doubts about all the dams and other development really began to gestate in the early 1960s. Once I was liberated from being a junior congressman and started looking at it from a national perspective, I realized what I had always believed in, what I learned about the world and its creatures growing up back in St. Johns."

Udall became a strong Indian advocate and perhaps the greatest conservationist secretary ever. He got so much out of the power of his office: in addition to accomplishing numerous other reform measures large and small, he facilitated passage of the Wilderness Act of 1964; hatched with

# Cretaceous

Stegner the idea of the Wild and Scenic Rivers Act of 1968 and then spearheaded the lobbying effort; shut down public land selection and mining locations in all of Alaska in order to protect the land rights of Alaska Natives; successfully pushed for Cape Cod, Point Reyes, and six other national seashores; and, on the Colorado Plateau, acheived park status for Canyonlands and Petrified Forest and park additions for Capitol Reef, Arches, and Grand Canyon (Marble Canyon, declared a national monument during Udall's tenure, was incoporated into Grand Canyon National Park in 1975). Still, this was the high crest of the Big Buildup and the Interior Department also approved coal, oil, and gas leases and dam-and-reservoir proposals across the Plateau during his watch.

Feeling a combination of political heat and conscience pangs, Udall broke from the imperatives of the Big Buildup when it came time to make a decision over the two dams proposed for the Grand Canyon in order to generate electricity for the Central Arizona Project. David Brower was raising all possible hell. And then, in 1966, the Sierra Club began running "battle ads" in the *New York Times* against the Bridge Canyon and Marble Canyon Dams. One in particular caught the nation's imagination: "Should We Also Flood the Sistine Chapel So Tourists Can Get Nearer the Ceiling?" Another exhorted readers to write Udall: "Who Can Save Grand Canyon? *You* Can . . . and *Secretary Udall can too*, if he will."

The interior secretary turned his attention to the dams. Rather than rely on the Bureau of Reclamation—which could crunch and recrunch numbers to justify the benefits of any dam—he called on the National Park Service, which took him on a float trip down the canyon through the two dam-and-reservoir sites. On the float, down in the majesties of the canyon, he saw plenty of reasons not to build any dams there and spelled out his findings in an article in *Venture* magazine. Although the public, rallying behind Brower's campaign, had begun to sound loud objections, it was still early for any public official from the West to oppose just about any dam. Udall came down against two: in 1967, he announced that the administration was withdrawing its support for both Marble Canyon and Bridge Canyon Dams.

# CONFLICTS AND CONQUESTS

But the matter could not end there. It may have been nearly unthinkable to dam Grand Canyon, but it remained completely unthinkable not to build the Central Arizona Project. The energy to pump CAP water uphill to Phoenix and Tucson had to come from somewhere.

So, instead of the two dams, the compromise came down in favor of the Navajo Generating Station, to be operated by a consortium of utilities led by the Salt River Project. The power plant would go in at Page, right next to Glen Canyon Dam. The settlement depended on a supply of coal for Navajo Generating Station, but that was no problem. Peabody Coal Company had locked up the coal through leases with the Hopi and Navajo for the rich deposits under tribal lands on Black Mesa.

From the standpoint of the Grand Plan, Navajo Generating Station was a fine substitute: it would more than replace the power lost by cancellation of the two dams. But while the compromise saved the river and the canyon's walls, Navajo Generating Station, positioned as it was at the upper end of the Grand Canyon, dirtied the canyon's air. For all the distance he had come, Stewart Udall still had an Achilles' heel, his longtime, knee-jerk support for what he would later call "that stupid, God, mother, and country project," the CAP.

Stewart Udall, taking David Brower's lead, had fought off the dams. But neither of them, nor anyone else, had yet insisted upon asking the ultimate questions. Must we build the CAP? Is it essential to put in the Navajo Generating Station, the biggest power plant of all? Are there alternative sources of energy? Could we use our water and electricity more carefully and avoid building these mega-projects and incurring their many costs? The Southwest, still imbued with the ambitions and premises of the Big Buildup, was not ready for such questions. The multi-billion-dollar CAP legislation absolutely had to go through.

Time was growing short. Numerous issues, large and small, remained unresolved. It was the summer of 1968 and Udall, who still wanted the CAP, was finishing up his tenure at Interior. Carl Hayden, who had been part of the Arizona congressional delegation since statehood, was retiring.

220

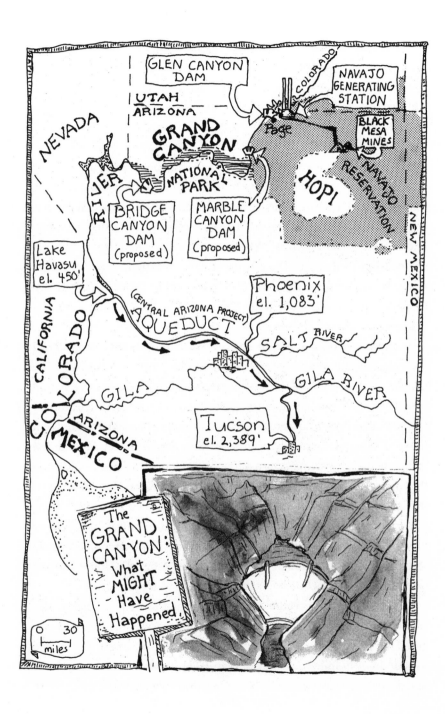

GLEN CANYON DAM

UTAH
ARIZONA

NEVADA

GRAND CANYON

COLORADO

NAVAJO GENERATING STATION

Page

BLACK MESA MINES

NATIONAL PARK

RIVER

HOPI

NAVAJO RESERVATION

BRIDGE CANYON DAM (proposed)

MARBLE CANYON DAM (proposed)

Lake Havasu el. 450'

Phoenix el. 1,083'

NEW MEXICO

CALIFORNIA

COLORADO

(CENTRAL ARIZONA PROJECT)
AQUEDUCT

SALT RIVER

GILA

GILA RIVER

ARIZONA
MEXICO

Tucson el. 2,389'

The GRAND CANYON: What MIGHT Have Happened

0    30
miles

# CONFLICTS AND CONQUESTS

Hayden chaired the Senate Appropriations Committee, which handled this big-money legislation.

Udall saw nothing untoward in the Black Mesa lease arrangements, which resolved the critical issue of a fuel supply for Navajo Generating Station. The mines would bring jobs to poverty-wracked Navajo and Hopi people and royalties to the tribes. Udall had heard the allegations about John Boyden's supposed ties to Peabody Coal but they seemed to him, as to others, like sour grapes. "You have to realize, John Boyden was one of the leading figures in Utah, a highly respected lawyer. He seemed absolutely dedicated to the Hopi's interests. There just wasn't anything that made you question him or his motives." When Stewart Udall told me that, in 1989, I still had not seen any of the Boyden papers that my research assistants would later discover. Udall's reaction to charges of Boyden's perfidy was the same that mine initially had been: skepticism. The ball of string was still to be unwound.

By the end of the summer of 1968, everything had fallen into place. All the state delegations and governors were pulling together feverishly. The industry and government scientists agreed that Navajo Generating Station would be a clean operation, nothing like Four Corners. The environmentalists were on board. So were the tribes. On September 30, 1968, President Johnson signed into law the Colorado River Basin Project Act, the last comprehensive legislative action of the Big Buildup. No dams would flood the Grand Canyon. But the CAP would be funded; Navajo Generating Station at Page, using coal from Black Mesa, would send 24 percent of its power to the CAP; Utah would receive conditional approval for two water projects; New Mexico would have a dam on the Gila River; and Colorado (this bill had to go through chairman Wayne Aspinall's House Interior Committee) would get no fewer than five more water projects.

Almost forgotten, because Peabody Coal had moved so quickly, efficiently, and quietly to complete the tribal leases, was the fact that this grand theater on Capitol Hill all hinged on Black Mesa coal. If you owned it—hundreds of million of tons of high-BTU, low-sulfur coal, maybe the best deposit in the country, maybe in the world—you held the trump card.

# Cretaceous

How you played that card depended on many things. But preeminently it depended on the lawyer to whom you had entrusted your relations with a powerful, complex, and hurried outside world.

The rapid development of the Colorado Plateau took place in a pressure-cooker atmosphere. Confidence ran high, the focus was strictly on achieving results, and little time or care was given to assessing the consequences. Remember that the National Environmental Policy Act—the foundation stone of our environmental policy, requiring disclosure and assessment of the environmental impacts of all major federal actions—did not go into effect until 1970. The tribes, laboring under the threat of congressional termination, were at their most passive. Inevitably, for all the benefits to city dwellers and the corporate developers, the costs of the Big Buildup to the land and Native American people have been many and painful.

The financial transactions became millstones for the tribes. The pattern began with the first installations, Four Corners Power Plant and Navajo Mine, which supplied the coal to Four Corners. The coal lease itself had no escalator clause for royalties, and payments to the Navajo Nation soon dropped far below market value. The tribe also agreed to waive its sovereign right to impose a severance tax on the coal as it was mined. The other transactions of the 1950s, 1960s, and 1970s differed in their details, but the tribes were disadvantaged in every instance—whether it involved coal, water, oil and gas, or uranium. They variously signed away royalties, taxing authority, and land and water rights surely worth hundreds of millions of dollars.

The companies sought the mineral leases in an era when the tribes had no effective means of protecting their interests. Interior Department officials, instead of furthering the agency's duty as trustee to the tribes, saw the development of the Plateau as being in the national interest and gave scant heed to the tribes' interests. Tribal lawyers, while not generally afflicted with conflicts of interest, failed to press their clients' interests aggressively.

These factors no longer apply: today, tribal leaders and their lawyers are sharp at the bargaining table, tribal lawsuits have struck down several of the offensive lease provisions and upheld tribal tax authority, and several leases have been renegotiated. But the early losses under these leases—among the largest financial transactions the tribes will ever engage in—can never be recovered. And the minerals are nonrenewable resources that can be used only once.

The mines and power plants have had profound effects on the lives of Indian people. At the Navajo Mine, thirty-six traditional Navajo sheep-herding people were relocated to other lands. Many Mules Granddaughter, a Navajo from Black Mesa, explained what "relocation" meant to her family: "Where they are mining now is my land. My father is buried there. His grave was torn up in the strip mining." Navajo people—who grew up with turquoise skies as much a part of their world as the sheep, the hogans, and the Coyote stories—grieved. Irene Nakai wrote of her horror at being reminded during a plane flight of what she thought she had escaped for a few days: "Looking south over Dinétah, my people's homeland, I saw it enveloped in an ugly, green cloud—the dreaded smoke from the Four Corners Power Plant in New Mexico." One Hopi woman, a cautious, conservative person, told me the mining and air pollution were like rape.

The Colorado Plateau has always been known as the site of expansive, dazzling views: as much as 200 miles of mind-opening clarity. Yet now, from the southern tip of Cedar Mesa, from Kaiparowits Plateau, from Yovimpa Point, from the flank of Boulder Mountain, from the slope of the Uintas, from Dead Horse Point, from the La Sals, from all the other countless, inspiring viewpoints, our range of vision—our range of comprehension and reverence—is reduced by the particulates in the air down to 120, 100, 80, 60 miles, on some days even less.

Four Corners Power Plant went in first and it was the worst. Its daily emissions, including 1,032 tons of sulfur dioxide and 383 tons of fly ash, exceeded the pollution of New York City. Newer plants gradually became cleaner but the overall pollution steadily worsened. Not only do the power plants send pollution out of their own stacks but, incredibly, the electricity shipped out to urban users causes a second round of pollution. The winds normally blow in from the west and they carry southern California smog—from a metropolitan area made possible in significant part by the Big Buildup of the Colorado Plateau—to the Plateau.

Electricity generated by coal likely contributes to other—perhaps larger and even less correctable—crises. The carbon dioxide emitted from coal plants is a leading greenhouse gas. Whether this will lead to global warming, and possibly a devastating climate change, is not finally known, but the weight of scientific opinion insists that it will. The sulfur dioxide causes acid rain, which increasingly is being detected in the Colorado Rockies. Acid rain appears to be falling in the lakes and snowpack of the Mount Zirkel Wilderness Area at the headwaters of the Yampa River in Colorado. Scientists believe that the primary cause of the acid rain is the emissions from the coal-fired plants at Craig and Hayden. The Salt River Project is a partner in both of these plants: Phoenix has exported its pollution—its waste—more than 600 miles, all the way to Nicaagat's old riding and hunting grounds.

And then there is Glen Canyon Dam. Even with all the mines, coal plants, oil and gas rigs, transmission lines, roads, highways, and other dams, this is the colossus of the Big Buildup: the collision point of all the ironies, competing worldviews, and opposite certitudes.

Glen Canyon Dam created Lake Powell—to many people a beautiful man-made lake—giving access to country that few of us would ever have reached, granting passage along the ferned, red cliffs, into intricate winding side canyons, up to famed Rainbow Bridge itself. More than 2 million visitors enjoy Lake Powell every year. Below Glen Canyon Dam, like Navajo Dam, perhaps even better, the cool, green flows make for trophy-sized rainbow trout.

The turbines also help create homelands in faraway deserts. Children have cool, comfortable rooms to grow in. Businesses have room to grow in, too, giving us what we want: choices, fair prices, quality. "Peaking power" is a gray term, another abstraction. But "brownout" and "blackout" are not. These words conjure up patients in critical-care wards in hospitals starved of electricity. Not with Glen Canyon. Open the gates and the electrons are shot to the cities.

# CONFLICTS AND CONQUESTS

But consider the losses upriver and downriver. Rainbow Bridge, once a place for Navajo to pray, is now defiled by the pool at its base. Gone is the bottom two-thirds of the Hole-in-the-Rock Trail. Gone are tens of thousands of Ancestral Puebloan and Fremont sites. The few people who knew Glen Canyon tell us of other losses. Gone is "a little-known picture of the famous hump-backed flute-player incised in another spot on the same dark red wall. . . . [A] depiction of a man drawing a head on a mountain sheep with his bow and arrow while a friend impatiently dances up and down nearby." Gone are 180 miles of free-flowing river: "Big deposits of gravel and cobblestones in a tremendous variety of color, form, and texture. Rocks from Colorado, Utah, and Wyoming, worn smooth through the ages, seem to exude the romance of far places."

The dams, but Glen Canyon more than any other, have brought the native fish to the edge of extinction. There are eight species native to the Grand Canyon. Four of them (the Colorado squawfish, the bonytail and humpback chubs, and the roundtail chub) are endemic—found nowhere else. The first three are now threatened or endangered and the fourth, the roundtail, no longer exists in the Grand Canyon, although it lives on elsewhere in the watershed. The razorback sucker, native but not endemic, has also been put on the endangered species list. All these fish had adapted to the natural conditions. Glen Canyon Dam changed their whole world. It blocked migration rates. It discharged cold, clear water. This was fine for the rainbows, death for the native fish.

But what about the bald eagles, historically absent from the Grand Canyon, who now come down to Nankoweap Creek and elsewhere to feed on the spawning rainbows? And what about the fact that hardly anyone knew of the Grand Canyon's deep wonders—fewer than a hundred people floated it between Powell in 1869 and the end of World War II—whereas now we can all run the river through the canyon, down into the Vishnu Schist, because Glen Canyon Dam arrests the rampaging spring runoff and discharges water into a riverbed that was often nearly dry in the late summer?

And so we find that this grand-scale reordering of nature has teemed with ramifications and contradictions for the Southwest: a beautiful man-made lake but drowned sacred places; easy access by water to backcountry but trashed-out, crowded backcountry; old animals replaced by new ones through our arrogance, resourcefulness, and luck; impressive efficiency (electricity streaks throughout the Southwest in an instant) but prodigal waste (the desert sun evaporates 600,000 acre-feet of water, enough to serve Phoenix and Tucson, off the top of Lake Powell every year). What can we expect in the years to come? Glen Canyon Dam is completely safe, built to the most exacting standards. Yet in 1983 floodwaters blew out 300 cubic yards—thirty dumptrucks worth—of concrete and sandstone from the spillways. Lake Powell won't silt up for another 150 years or so. Yet people born seventy-five years from now will have to confront that. Now the Sierra Club, inspired still by Brower, and the Glen Canyon Institute want to study the decommissioning of Glen Canyon Dam and the draining of Lake Powell. Is it now time to do the study that we never took the time to do during the Big Buildup?

The uranium mining and nuclear testing may have taken the greatest toll of all. The rush that began in the late 1950s was the world's largest uranium boom. In all, four thousand mines—many of them no more than caverns or pits large enough to walk into—were carved into the Colorado Plateau.

The radioactivity caused uncounted cancers. The tight quarters in the smaller mines were sources of acute problems because there was little ventilation. Some miners, with bravado, scoffed at the "sissy talk" about cancer. Others knew of the risks and chanced it apprehensively. Many, especially in the early years, were unaware of the dangers. Navajos signed up as miners in the larger operations and hundreds of them, without ever being warned, died of lung cancer from breathing radioactive dust. Navajo people, as well as residents of Grand Junction and other towns, were given the radioactive uranium tailings—for free—to use for the foundations in their homes.

The Nevada Test Site for nuclear bomb testing is west of the Plateau, but located downwind are St. George and other communities. There is still no reliable count of the cancers. Since most of the potential victims are stolid, rural Mormons who keep to themselves, official reports fail to reflect the actual mortality rate caused by the tests. Even so, there are known to be hundreds of deaths by cancer among downwinders and the count is steadily growing.

Some of the survivors of the miners and downwinders sued. In the downwinders' cases, several of the plaintiffs were parents who had lost their children to cancer. The suits involving Navajo uranium miners were brought by widows. The plaintiffs' attorney in the miners' case was Stewart Udall. After completing his tenure as interior secretary, he had written about the West, served on boards of public interest organizations (he wryly observes that none of the energy companies ever asked), and took on other causes, notably hardrock mining reform. Yet for all of Udall's public service, nothing moved him as deeply as his fifteen-year crusade to right some of the wrongs from nuclear testing and uranium mining.

There was no doubt, although government attorneys tried to raise some, about the medical evidence. The testing and the mining had killed these people. Federal District Judge Bruce Jenkins found for the downwinders in a 489-page decision, but ultimately the appellate courts ruled that the case could not be heard on its merits. The courts also ruled against the plaintiffs in the Navajo miners case. This was due to the ancient English doctrine of sovereign immunity—"the king can do no wrong"—and related rules that sometimes keep citizens from suing the government even when the government has caused serious injury.

Udall could not bear to go to the Red Valley Chapter to report the final results of the case to his Navajo clients. He sent his cocounsel instead. He was, he said, humiliated and sick at heart:

*And I was ashamed to go because I didn't know how to explain to friends who had trusted me that the government in Washington that had betrayed them—and had needlessly sacrificed the lives of their husbands in the name of national security—could, under the law I had urged them to respect, avoid responsibility for the tragedies that had engulfed their lives.*

# Cretaceous

In the 1990s, Congress finally established trust funds to allow some measure of financial compensation. It was late, pale justice. The only real justice would have come from a government and society caring enough and prudent enough to see that the poison never invaded the land and its people in the first place.

**W**hile Hoover Dam in 1935 represented a reasoned response to modern life in the dry Southwest, we know now that we did not need all the facilities we built after the war. We could have been more prudent. We could have done, for example, without the Central Arizona Project (which by the 1990s saw only one-third of its high-priced water put to use). We could have done without Glen Canyon Dam and Four Corners Power Plant and Navajo Dam and Navajo Generating Station (whose energy and water we could have forgone if we had adopted sensible conservation measures). Yet, in that time and place, certitude ruled the Southwest and restraint was unwelcome.

To appreciate the force and inevitability of the Big Buildup, take David Brower and Stewart Udall, the two greatest environmental leaders alive in America today. Brower: erect, defiant, white-haired, an eagle of a man. Udall: unwavering in his fierce love of the canyon country his family had been born in at Lees Ferry. Brower, with all his many skills and public opinion surging behind him. Udall, first as an Arizona congressman, then as interior secretary, with the power to stop Navajo Generating Station, most of the other power plants, and the mines at Black Mesa. If Brower and Udall couldn't stem the Big Buildup, if they couldn't avoid being submerged by it, who could?

# JUNCTION DAM

There is a widely held assumption that the dynamic westward expansion of the nineteenth century was the West's age of conquest—the era when we remade the land and the peoples who preceded the Americans. I long accepted this tenet. Yet now I see that, in different forms, the conquests have continued. For all the lasting significance of the nineteenth century, our postwar era has had impacts as great, in some cases greater, on the lands and the people than did the century of Manifest Destiny.

On the Colorado Plateau, the legacy of modern times will not be limited to colossal water, mining, and energy projects. In the late 1970s and early 1980s, the winding down of the Big Buildup formed a historical junction with the beginning of another momentous period. This new period—

the age of industrial tourism—has underlying causes eerily similar to its predecessor. First we moved water and electricity from the Colorado Plateau to the cities. Now we in the cities move ourselves to the Plateau. The operative word in both cases is "we."

The early, scattered resistance to the intensive development of the Colorado Plateau gave little indication that the Big Buildup could be stopped. Echo Park was worth fighting for—and, in the 1950s, David Brower and other members of the nascent environmental movement did fight. Yet the momentum for development meant the sacrifice of Glen Canyon. In the late 1960s, despite his own philosophical awakening and the changing times, Stewart Udall's compromise over the dams scheduled for the Grand Canyon turned out to be reminiscent of Brower's accommodation over Echo Park. On the one hand, the country had made a monumental decision, probably for all time: we will not dam the Grand Canyon. But the congressional trading gave the Grand Canyon its ironic sentry, Navajo Generating Station, paid for by the Hopi, Navajo, and Black Mesa. These controversies reflected shifts in public opinion, but the industrial coalitions, with their sights trained on the Plateau, were nothing if not resourceful. The Big Buildup simply moved its projects from one site to another—with comparable or greater effects on the land, air, water, and people.

The outcome at Capitol Reef National Park in the early 1970s was more favorable for conservationists. The long and narrow park encompasses the whole Waterpocket Fold that runs parallel to the Escalante River and the Hole-in-the-Rock Trail traveled by intrepid Mormon pioneers. Southern California utilities wanted to construct a coal-fired plant nearby.

Capitol Reef, where I camped with Ben, my youngest, when he was six, tugs at people in uncommon ways. The main campground is situated under the massive redrock formation that gave the park its name. This campground, a stark contrast to the wilder and more rugged portions of the Waterpocket Fold, happens to be uniquely welcoming for young children. Originally it was a tiny Mormon community settled by one of Brigham Young's mission calls in 1873. Today it is bereft of permanent residents, but its old log buildings are still intact and its orchards of apple, peach, pear, and cherry trees still break out into a profusion of color and fragrance every spring. Deer come down in the evening to graze on the thick grasses in the orchards. Mesmerized, Ben and I watched seven of them swimming across the swift Fremont River at last light on their way to the orchard.

When the coal plant was proposed in the late 1960s, this remote national park was little known. Capitol Reef had been served by a paved road for less than a decade. Still, some conservationists knew of it and their objections carried the day for Capitol Reef, this magical combination of a light pioneer touch inlaid in wild terrain.

The Capitol Reef settlement had some similarities to the earlier compromises at Dinosaur and Grand Canyon. The companies never abandoned the idea of a Utah plant. The location was moved from the site near Capitol Reef to western Utah, near Delta, and the Intermountain Power Plant now sends out 1,600 megawatts of power, mostly to southern California. Yet if a person is willing to condone coal plants and long-range reaches by urban areas under some circumstances, then the Intermountain Power Plant is a reasonably acceptable project. Farmers and other local residents in the Sevier River watershed negotiated with the power companies to obtain conditions favorable to their communities, Capitol Reef was spared, and no protected area was affected by the power plant.

The clearest signal that the Big Buildup had peaked—and that future projects on the Colorado Plateau would be given the strictest scrutiny— was sent out in the mid-1970s by the results of the power plant/coal mine complex planned for Kaiparowits Plateau on the north side of Lake Powell. Rugged and austere Kaiparowits, 1,600 square miles of high plateau country, was still wild, a frontier, perhaps the most remote place in the continental United States. This project, promoted by southern California and Arizona utilities, would have produced the biggest coal plant of all: 3,000 megawatts. Beset with environmental opposition and economic difficulties, the mammoth undertaking collapsed of its own weight in 1976, when the companies pulled out after thirteen years of preparation.

Kaiparowits was proof positive that the context had fundamentally changed. The National Environmental Policy Act of 1970 mandated environmental impact statements—and the new flood of information sparked sharply increased public concern. Meanwhile the public, increasingly interested in the wonders of the Plateau, was losing its stomach for energy and water projects. The tribes began to assert their independence, making their own decisions rather than abdicating to the Interior Department or to their own lawyers. The quality of citizen advocacy, including litigation, burgeoned as old-line groups such as the Sierra Club and The Wilderness Society expanded their operations and new environmental, consumer, and Indian organizations were born: the Natural Resources Defense Council, the Environmental Defense Fund, the Sierra Club Legal Defense Fund, and the Native American Rights Fund, as examples, all came into being in the late 1960s or early 1970s.

And the environmental laws of the early 1970s, including the Clean Air Act, changed the economics for the companies by mandating expensive mitigation measures. The higher production costs were accompanied by a lower-than-projected demand for energy as consumers, spurred by the higher prices after the 1973 Arab oil embargo, began taking conservation measures. As per capita consumption began to level off and fall, the public became ever more suspicious of the utilities' overblown projections of future demand.

Even beyond the cooking of numbers, the Big Buildup's collapse was due in part to the fact that some of its plans were not just grandiose but berserk. Witness Horse Bench Nuclear Center, Project Plowshare, and Junction Dam.

The uranium down in the Plateau's Shinarump and Chinle formations created a carnival atmosphere from the time of Charlie Steen's find in Big Indian Wash in 1952. By the 1970s, even as the uranium boom was dying, there were still people in and out of government inflamed by the possibilities. A serious move was made to locate a "nuclear power park" downriver of the town of Green River, Utah. The Horse Bench Nuclear Center, composed of no fewer than nine nuclear plants, would have generated 11,000 megawatts for the far metropolises. For cooling it would have needed 126,000 acre-feet of water, each year, from the river Powell once traveled.

The nuclear power park proposal was abandoned, but another radical nuclear program, Project Plowshare, did get started before public outrage brought it to an abrupt halt. The idea was to use "atoms for peace" by exploding nuclear bombs in order to crack open deep rock formations holding oil and gas, thus facilitating extraction. The first nuclear detonation, a 29-kiloton blast 4,420 feet down, was set off in 1967 in the San Juan Basin in New Mexico. In 1969, Project Rulison exploded a 43-kiloton bomb 8,430 feet under Garfield County, Colorado. The last salvo of Project Plowshare took place on May 17, 1973, about 50 miles due north of Grand Junction. Project Rio Blanco, as the effort was called, simultaneously detonated three 30-kiloton explosives spaced from 5,800 to 6,700 feet underground. Project Rio Blanco alone was five times larger than Hiroshima. The Atomic Energy Commission quickly abandoned the "atoms for peace" project on the grounds of steep economic costs and health concerns: the nuclear blasts irradiated the oil and gas, making the fuels unsafe for normal handling.

As late as the 1970s, water developers still believed that the Bureau of Reclamation would build Junction Dam. The dam, twenty-five stories tall, would have gone in just below the confluence of the Green and Colorado Rivers in southeastern Utah—in Canyonlands National Park, which was proclaimed in 1964 after a thirty-year campaign. Junction Dam would have inundated more miles of canyon and river than Glen Canyon Dam, backing water 109 miles up the Green into Desolation Canyon and up the Colorado River 93 miles nearly into the state of Colorado. In the process, it would have flooded the town of Moab and the largest wetlands system still left on the Colorado Plateau (now protected as the Scott N. Matheson Wildlife Preserve). And Junction Dam would hardly have been the end of it: just upriver of Junction Lake, the Uinta Basin Lake Dam would have submerged another 150 miles of the Green (including wild Desolation Can-

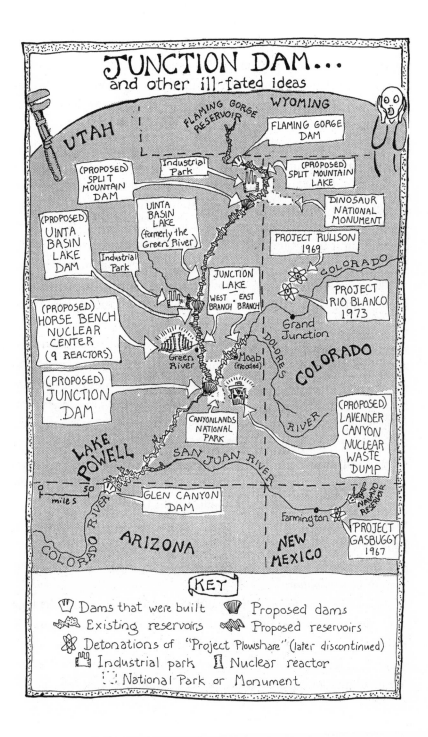

yon) and, above that project, Split Mountain Dam would have created still another reservoir, 80 miles long. The Junction Dam proposal and its brethren, which the Bureau of Reclamation quietly put on the shelf, symbolized the excesses of the past just as the Southwest was beginning to see rivers and canyons in a new light.

It is always hard to track down all the reasons, and give them a weight, when a major shift in public policy occurs at a junction of old and new attitudes. In the case of the demise of the Big Buildup, the public's purse, love of the land, and credulity all were strained. Gradually, public officials began to respond. Western governors, led by Colorado's Dick Lamm, objected on many grounds—not the least of which was their conviction that outside forces were making too many major decisions in their states.

There was another factor—a wild card, utterly intangible and unmeasurable—in the changing of public attitudes: Edward Paul Abbey. Abbey gained a passionate following and an outraged opposition through his novels' monkey-wrenching, high-speed chases, and eco-tirades, but he was first and foremost a fine writer. In addition to being the outrageous, cantankerous, blasphemous, obstreperous—the wild-eyed, fire-breathing—Abbey, he also authored *Desert Solitaire,* one of the great works in conservation philosophy. Among other things, he identified and railed against the phenomenon of "industrial tourism," which now so plagues the Plateau.

Above all, Abbey set out the plain, scratchy, jagged, sun-blistered virtues of the canyon country as no one else ever had. He first came to the deserts of the Southwest in the 1940s and studied at the University of New Mexico from 1947 to 1951. In 1956, he served as a seasonal ranger at Arches National Park, which holds more natural arches than anywhere else, and the largest, and many would say the most wondrous. Arches became the setting for most of *Desert Solitaire.*

Abbey loved the forms of rock and sand, and the drama of the long space, but he also revered the desert's least inhabitants. Take junipers. He had a favorite juniper—shaggy, "ragged," with "a sapless claw"—outside his ranger's trailer at little-visited Arches. On another occasion he paid honor, out of admiration for the staying power of simply making it in the dry country, to "a degenerate juniper tree ... [a]n underprivileged juniper tree, living not on water and soil but on memory and hope. And almost alone." For his best fire of the Plateau, he needed nothing more than some gnarled juniper, a match, and time off by himself:

> *The fire. The odor of burning juniper is the sweetest fragrance on the face of the earth, in my honest judgment; I doubt if all the smoking censers of Dante's paradise could equal it. One breath of juniper smoke, like the perfume of sagebrush after rain, evokes in magical catalysis, like certain music, the space and light and clarity and piercing strangeness of the American West. Long may it burn.*

Abbey changed minds by showing the worth of a place our society had so often deemed worthless.

And so the Big Buildup wound down. No power plant—with the exception of Intermountain Power Plant in Delta, the project that was moved to protect Capitol Reef—has been authorized on the Plateau since Kaiparowits was mothballed in 1976. The same is true for water projects. The only one even limping along (designs have been drawn up and a few test holes have been drilled) is the Animas–La Plata Project in southwestern Colorado, a water project that still has a glimmer of hope because of treaty obligations to the two Colorado Ute tribes.

**T**oday the pace of new industrial development has slowed. Now we are turning to ameliorating the Big Buildup's damage. Our ability to correct the impacts of this modern industrial society on the natural world is being tested as never before.

A great amount of effort has been devoted to improving air quality. The Clean Air Act works mainly through authorizing state governments to regulate their own polluters according to federal standards. The smog on the Colorado Plateau, however, is what we now call regional haze. Thus Utah is limited in its ability to protect the views from Cedar Mesa—and Arizona is hamstrung in its efforts to protect the vistas from the South Rim of the Grand Canyon—because the pollution comes from at least ten states (north to Oregon, Idaho, and Wyoming and southeast to Texas), as well as Mexico. Copper smelters in Arizona and Sonora, oil refineries in Monterrey and on the Gulf Coast, automobiles in southern California, and many other sources all contribute. As a 1993 National Academy of Sciences report shows, 33 percent of all Grand Canyon smog from man-made sources is caused by utilities and other large industries; 16 percent by the engines of gas-powered vehicles; 15 percent by dust from vehicles and construction; 14 percent from diesel-powered vehicles; and the remaining 22 percent from diverse sources including forest fires and woodburning stoves.

Although the 1977 Clean Air Act sets out provisions for dealing with regional haze, the Environmental Protection Agency never implemented the program. As a result of a lawsuit by environmentalists, however, EPA issued regulations in 1991 dealing solely with Navajo Generating Station. This made sense: the plant sits just 20 miles upriver of the upper end of the Grand Canyon and a Park Service report had cited Navajo as a main contributor to the sickening, smudgy pall that hung over the canyon, especially during the winter, making it impossible on some days to see across to the opposite rim. Then, later that year, EPA, Navajo Generating Station, the Grand Canyon Trust, and the Environmental Defense Fund reached a comprehensive settlement with provisions far stricter than EPA's original proposal. Navajo will reduce its emissions of sulfur dioxide by 90 percent no later than 1999.

The improvements will cost the utilities about $500 million. The Salt River Project, which operates the plant, fought against improvements for years, arguing that Navajo contributed only marginally to the problem. Now, having committed itself to the expensive renovations, SRP can afford to take a more sanguine view. Richard Hayslip, manager of environmental affairs for SRP, told me in a reflective moment: "It's irrefutable that Navajo puts out a lot of sulfur dioxide and that it has some effect on the Grand Canyon. It may be that the average tourist won't even notice the difference after we put our scrubbers in. Still, you can't solve a problem collectively if every source can say, 'we don't make any difference.'"

We all are sources. Surely I, in my van, am. The inconvenient fact is that driving the Colorado Plateau is deeply seductive to our kind. Look at that long mesa spread across the skyline! Is that the very tip of Shiprock beyond? Powell was right: those cliffs *are* vermilion! A friend had the spirit exactly right fifteen years ago even if the details seem more complex today. He told me jovially: "The only way to travel the Southwest is in a pickup truck with a cup of coffee in one hand and a can of beer in the other." Even the most rigorous environmentalist will drive to the trailhead. We are all sources.

The power companies contribute plenty of the pollution on their own, and there's no doubt they helped generate the urban growth that causes much of the rest, but we can't rightly put the whole blame on the utilities. The sources are many and diffuse. The answers will lie in some new government regulations, yes, but also in new social and personal ethics.

Meanwhile, in 1990 Congress established the Grand Canyon Visibility Transport Commission to address regional haze in a comprehensive way. The commission is made up of representatives from eight states: the Four Corners states along with Wyoming, Nevada, Oregon, and California. Its job, after an open fact-finding and hearing process, is to make recommendations to EPA. Because its membership includes so many states and because EPA has such broad jurisdiction, the Grand Canyon Visibility Transport Commission has become a main forum for promoting the conservation of natural resources. Conservation plays a big role in reducing energy consumption in the Southwest—thereby reducing both air pollution and the intensive use of water, minerals, and land that accompany power production. This commission is young and has heavy work ahead; we have dug ourselves into a deep hole. Still, its work is one of many encouraging signs.

We have made progress in other areas too. One involves the downriver effects of Glen Canyon Dam on the Colorado River through the Grand Canyon. The dam turned a warm, muddy desert river into a cold, clear mountain river—it once carried an average of 380,000 tons of sediment through the Grand Canyon every day, now just 40,000 tons a day. An intensive interagency scientific effort has been under way since 1982 to evaluate the effects of the dam's flow regime. My geologist and river-guide friend Matt Kaplinski, for example, has made more than twenty extended research trips to gather data on Grand Canyon sandbars and beaches, which are critical wildlife habitat as well as prime camping spots for river runners.

The Grand Canyon Protection Act of 1992 has modified the flow regime of Glen Canyon Dam to give some protection to native fish in the Grand Canyon below the dam and to reduce the scouring out of sandbars and beaches. The changes will mean reduced megawatts and less peaking power: Glen Canyon Dam will become more of a baseload operation. Rates will probably rise by 1.4 to 1.8 cents per kilowatt-hour. Changes in the flow regimes to preserve native fish species have been made at Navajo Dam on the San Juan River and other dams, as well.

As for the whole of the Big Buildup, we seem to have reached a tentative and ambiguous understanding. It went too far and we will not repeat it— at least not in that exact form. We will try to correct the major excesses. We still have not decided, though, how much we are willing to adjust our behavior at the switch, the faucet, and the ignition. Nor have we been willing to confront the attitudes about the rampant population growth in the American Southwest that caused the Big Buildup in the first place.

Exactly what have we learned?

Just as we begin to make earnest if imperfect adjustments to one conquest in the form of postwar development, we discover that another siege is under way.

Land health is in decline across most of the Colorado Plateau, including the backcountry. Part of this deterioration is due to the traditional extractive uses, but today the Plateau also faces conquest of a new sort: the onrush of literally millions of tourists each year. If we have learned that one of the

# Junction Dam

difficulties in scaling down the Big Buildup is that we are all part of the problem, the current recreation boom may present even larger challenges.

For the Colorado Plateau is no longer far outside the nation's consciousness, or godforsaken, or just a place to hold the world together, as it was in 1900 or at the close of World War II. To large numbers of Americans, the Plateau has become chic. Moab is all the rage for bikers and college students, St. George for retirees. It seems that a redrock backdrop has become standard equipment for automobile commercials on TV.

At last we have begun to appreciate the Plateau's profound geological and historical value, and this appreciation will continue to grow. I asked experts in different disciplines about the worldwide significance of the Plateau's special qualities from the perspective of their fields. Two of them responded in strikingly similar ways. An archaeologist said that the Colorado Plateau is an unparalleled resource for understanding the past: "I've seen grown Peruvenists [specialists in ancient Peru] cry over the quality of what we have here." A geologist told me: "When geologists from foreign countries, Germany, Australia, you name it, see the Plateau, they're speechless. I've seen many with tears in their eyes."

This largesse of natural and human history now attracts no fewer than 50 million recreational visits a year to the Plateau's public lands. Fifty million: industrial tourism, just as Abbey warned. They—we—are everywhere. At least the power and water rush manifested itself in mines, plants, dams, reservoirs, and powerlines at a limited number of specific locations.

With annual visitor days doubling to 30 million since the mid-1980s, the national parks are scrambling to react to the new multitudes. The Park Service has been forced to close off some areas in Canyonlands National Park previously open to four-wheeling in order to protect Ancestral Puebloan sites and riparian vegetation. In sublime Canyon de Chelly National Monument, on the Navajo Reservation, 750,000 visitor days a year have compelled Park Service officials to prohibit motor vehicles in about one-third of the park. At Grand Canyon National Park, where 5 million people a year crowd the South Rim, a revision of the park's management plan may well lead to a ban of most private vehicles, with access to the rim allowed only by shuttle. Zion National Park is also sharply reducing vehicle use. The story is the same in nearly every park installation on the Colorado Plateau: pressed to the limits, probably beyond.

Industrial tourism invades the BLM lands, as well, the largest ownership on the Plateau. Perhaps the most dramatic example is the area surrounding Moab, Utah. Once the uranium mining center of the Plateau, Moab seemed on the road to becoming a ghost town when the uranium market crashed in the early 1980s. But then the tide turned with a seemingly insignificant act when two entrepreneurs and out-of-work miners, Robin and Bill Groff, opened Rim Cyclery to offer rentals of trail bikes. In less than a decade, Moab—with its sunny days, hands-off BLM management, and rolling slickrock expanses (slickrock, a misnomer, is sandstone and, rather than being slick, offers welcome traction for tire or sole)— became the mountain-bike capital of the world.

Moab went bonkers. The spectacular Slickrock Trail carries sixty thousand or more bike riders a year. A thousand bikers register every October for the Fat Tire Festival and twice again as many come for the weekend to ride on their own. Four-wheelers, too, revere Moab's surroundings. The Easter Jeep Safari draws two thousand vehicles. Formal events aside, Moab is a high-desert Fort Lauderdale for college students on spring vacation. Arches is just 6 miles north, and Moab is the closest town to Canyonlands to the south. Jetsetters began to look to Moab for their second homes because Aspen was too expensive, too cold, or too . . . Aspen. Three hundred new motel rooms went in during the winter of 1992 alone. Real estate values doubled, then quadrupled, and the rush is still on.

The land around Moab is paying dearly. The BLM, which has adopted fee programs and expanded its patrolling of these public lands, can't keep up. Visitors feel free to ride, camp, and plant "toilet paper gardens" nearly anywhere. A critical part of the natural system near Moab, and across the canyon country, is cryptobiotic soil. This crust grows on top of the sand, holding moisture and storing nitrogen and carbon. If you get down on your knees and inspect it, you can see the minute organisms it comprises:

mosses, fungi, and lichens. It grows, and when it gains enough bulk, larger plants take root in it.

The cryptobiotic soil thus supports the vegetation and the resulting wildlife habitat and prevents the erosion that will destroy this natural system. In a very real sense, the cryptobiotic soil holds the Colorado Plateau together. But all the footprints and bike, cycle, car, and truck tires tear open the fragile soil. Runoff from a sudden rush of rain finds the gashes, widens them, and washes away the underlying sand—and the decades it took for the crust to build up its protection.

These impacts are so many, and so scattered, that there is no way to inventory the total effect on the soils. The pounding we have given the ground cannot be quantified even to the degree that, say, we can measure regional haze. But scientists have no doubts, from their site-specific studies, of the enormity of the loss. It is slow death, but death nonetheless. This erosion—and the accompanying loss of vegetation and animal habitat that depends on the vegetation have become main factors causing the changes to the Colorado Plateau during the second half of the twentieth century: human activities have been an explosive force altering the canyon country far more than the geological events of any comparable time period.

The wounds to the backcountry can be seen in varying degrees all across the Plateau. Another example is the Comb Ridge region, all BLM land, north of the San Juan River. Comb Wash, near the end of the Hole-in-the-Rock Trail, runs alongside the west side of Comb Ridge. The Comb Wash Allotment is grazed by cattle, and the heavy use has badly degraded the land. In Comb Wash itself, the grasses are few and far between. The cryptobiotic crust is long gone. Five canyons drain from the west, off the side of Cedar Mesa. When cattle are released from the floor of Comb Wash into these narrow canyons, they tear out and crush the riparian vegetation. The uplands, too, have been made over: the cattle have taken out the native and highly nutritious bunchgrasses, which have mostly been replaced by invading rabbitbrush, greasewood, and sagebrush.

Without being a range scientist or wildlife biologist, I easily understood what healthy riparian wildlife habitat is by simply hiking, and comparing, the barren sandy stretches of Comb Wash and the revived canyon bottom of Grand Gulch. In Grand Gulch, on the other side of Cedar Mesa, the streamside vegetation has come back vigorously since cattle were removed in the late 1960s and the BLM began administering the area as if it were wilderness. The coyote willow, rushes, and shoots of cottonwood and box-elder trees returned and stabilized the banks. Grasses and flowers took root. To be sure, the vegetation will never be as thick as at Morgan Bottoms, 200 miles to the northeast where the cottonwood forests encompass the Yampa River in Colorado. In Grand Gulch, where it is lower and hotter, the soil is sandier and there is no supply of water to rival the high spring flows of the Yampa River. But the native vegetation of Grand Gulch has grown back thick and tangled enough to make hiking through the dense underbrush a job of the hands and arms as well as the legs.

The reinvigorated plant life in Grand Gulch attracts insects in much larger numbers—and, with them, small birds and animals drawn by the additional feed and cover. On a five-day backpack in Grand Gulch, my boys and I saw the mammals mostly through their footprints, but there were many: mule deer, ringtail cats, rabbits, mice, others we weren't sure of. Frogs and tadpoles abounded. The ravens had a fine food supply, as did two red-tailed hawks we saw diving and playing near the cliffs. You can find most of these plants and animals over in Comb Wash, too, but not nearly in such numbers. (When I last hiked Comb Wash, in 1993, a citizen challenge to BLM grazing management in the area was pending. The effort later turned out to be successful, so today the vegetation and wildlife are probably slowly recovering.)

The human, as well as the natural, legacy is under siege. You can gain a sense of this in the Comb Ridge area, home to stirring Ancestral Puebloan sites. Janet Lever and Ann Phillips, two self-made experts in rock art, took me and a group of my students up into a miscellaneous-looking canyon draining the east side of Comb Ridge. The Ancestral Puebloans had left their pictographs and petroglyphs all up and down the canyon: a birthing scene, many desert bighorn and deer, and a spectacular dream panel with a magnificent Kokopelli figure. Several of the panels contained little six-toed human feet, red in color.

Some of us climbed up out of the canyon—"Tiny Feet Canyon," we called it—to the top of Comb Ridge. Looking across Tiny Feet Canyon now, we saw an eagle's nest of an Ancestral Puebloan village on the far wall. It was on a huge shelf, with several natural amphitheaters and Ancestral Puebloan structures lodged in each one. Down below was what seemed to be a hanging garden. Access to the village seemed nearly inconceivable: we could see no way to get up from the canyon floor far below, and the descent from the crest of Comb Ridge would require the ancient residents to work their way down a 30- or 40-foot redrock cliff. How did the Old People get in and out?

But both Tiny Feet Canyon and Eagle's Nest Village are ripe for injury. Dale Davidson, a BLM archaeologist, showed my students and me an open wound over on the Comb Wash side. We hiked up a thin side canyon to a cave below an overhanging ledge. The site, a very old one, had been looted—all torn up. The thieves must have brought in shovels (some thieves would have brought in a backhoe if access were possible) and dug out the pots—shards were scattered all around—and probably baskets and sandals, which would have been preserved by this dry air. "But," Dale said, "I'm just guessing what was in there. You'll have to ask the thief."

How long the odds, how hopeless the search, to catch this thief of craftsmanship two thousand years old. We stood in the shade of the canyon, peering into the recess under the ledge, trying to implant there, along with the shovelfuls of earth piled up and the rocks strewn about, some notion of "evidence" or "law." But it was hopeless: what could anyone do? The thief was scot-free. The law books say the Archaeological Resources Protection Act reaches into this canyon, but it doesn't.

There is a great deal at risk—the legacy not just of the Ancestral Puebloans, but also the Fremont, Mogollon, Sinagua, and Hohokam—all across the backcountry of the Colorado Plateau. No one knows the exact number of archaeological sites but it is immense. In San Juan County, Utah, alone, where Comb Ridge and Grand Gulch are located, there are 300,000 recorded sites on BLM lands and the estimates of unrecorded sites run into the millions. New Mexico has 120,000 recorded sites and a potential for another one million. All the numbers are conservative. Few private lands have been inventoried. Most of the tribes—not wanting to disclose the locations of their sacred places—refuse to release information on sites within their reservations, one-third of all land on the Plateau. In all, less than 10 percent of land on the Plateau has been inventoried, meaning that the possibilities for future discoveries are thrilling. In 1996, a large fire at Mesa Verde National Park—a comparatively well researched area—burned 4,700 acres of piñon-juniper forest, exposing at least 417 new sites, including several kivas and dwelling units, one of them a 4-room block only 75 feet from a previously known site. A big find, such as a large pueblo, regularly is made on the Plateau. Whole villages, the equal of the most elaborate at Chaco Canyon or Mesa Verde, may lie beneath the sands of all the centuries.

What we do know is that a huge amount of history has been uprooted and sold off. Looting for pots, baskets, jewelry, and other artifacts proceeds at a sickening rate. The site we inspected near Comb Wash probably was the work of commercial looters (the size of the dig suggests a significant amount of equipment, hard labor, and advance planning—and, certainly, a profit motive), and in fact commercial looting is on a sharp upswing. Although the law prohibits the removal or sale of archaeological relics and most of the easy-to-find sites have already been stripped, the market demand for art and artifacts remains strong. Vandalism continues to be a factor. You see, with some frequency, panels of petroglyphs decorated with bullet holes or paint.

Ignorance takes its toll. A group of backpacking Boy Scouts in one of the Cedar Mesa canyons used roof beams from an Ancestral Puebloan dwelling for their evening campfire. The combination of zeal, intellectual curiosity, and arrogance plays a part, too. You can only shake your head in disbelief standing in Grand Gulch under a swooping 500-foot face of

# Junction Dam

Cedar Mesa Sandstone, in front of ghostly, life-size Big Man panel, drawn by the Fremont, who preceded even the Ancestral Puebloans: this gift of the ages has been defaced, heavily chalked over, presumably so that a camera would capture a more vivid image or a piece of fabric would receive an imprint.

More and more people treat the old sites with reverence. But there are so many of us. Too many people, too few ethics: the same basic problem as with the Big Buildup.

**A** main task of our humanity is to learn the lessons of conquest—whether the conquests involve people, such as Nicaagat and the Ute, places, such as Glen Canyon, or life-supporting natural phenomena, such as cryptobiotic soil. We have much more to learn, but there is still time for the Colorado Plateau because it is a broad and distant land. Will we learn what we must, and learn it fast enough, so that the land can hold both its physical health, which is its life, and its remoteness, which is the core of its bold, vivid personality?

I have learned for sure, during my thirty-five years in the law, that the answers, if they come, will be due less to laws than to personal responsibility. And laws are easy compared to personal responsibility.

# Part Three

# ENDURANCE

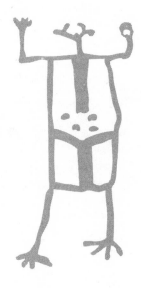

# CEDAR MESA CANYON

**W**hen I went to Kykotsmovi in 1985 for my late-night meeting with the Tribal Council, I encountered a sense of tradition, a feeling of antiquity, unlike any I had ever known. The Hopi people I met then and later had a gentleness and a quiet confidence in their people's way, qualities grounded in the security and stability of a deep and abiding devotion to place: Black Mesa.

One of the Hopi I came to know was Vernon Masayesva. John Echohawk had told me about Vernon in the early 1970s, when John was representing the Hopi traditionalists who tried to block the Black Mesa coal lease. Vernon, then a young engineering student, pursued his studies at Arizona State and spent all his available time going home to Black Mesa for the long meetings of the traditionalists in the old pueblo buildings. Years later, Vernon would become a Tribal Council member and, in the early 1990s, tribal chairman. He jokes that he and I have something important in common: his first meeting as a newly elected Tribal Council member was the one I attended on the conflict of interest issue, causing him to say that it was the first Hopi Tribal Council meeting for both of us.

At once college-educated and deeply traditional, Vernon in effect has taken on the mantle of translator, gathering the wisdom of the Kikmongwi, applying it in the Tribal Council chambers, and explaining it, precisely and patiently and with a constrained but deep-running passion, to the outside world. This translation to outsiders has become necessary because, to the frustration of the Hopi, some aspects of the tribe's future will be decided beyond the edges of Black Mesa.

In my long discussions with Vernon, he burned with resentment at the way John Boyden maneuvered the Hopi Tribal Council into signing the coal lease with Peabody Coal. Yet I was also struck by something else in our talks. Vernon repeatedly made references to Hopi dances and other ceremonies and to the Old People, the ancestors of the Hopi who lived on the Colorado Plateau for millennia. It was clear to Vernon, as I think it is to all Hopi, that tradition and antiquity make up the context for all that the Hopi do and have done, which includes the tribe's dealings with John Boyden. Therefore, while the files that my research assistant, Brian Kuehl, had found among John Boyden's papers explained certain things, and the second batch of files, later discovered by Cherche Prezeau, would establish the extent of Boyden's relationship with Peabody, there was a deep backdrop of Hopi existence and philosophy that counted for much, much more.

The Colorado Plateau has been the Hopi's homeland for longer than we can imagine. Many of the Old People's physical structures, and much of their artistry, remain on the Plateau; their places, and the way they lived many centuries ago, help us understand the modern Hopi. Today the Hopi dance the old dances, displaying over and over the age-old reverence for the earth and for civility among peoples. The dances, too, help explain the Hopi way.

# Cedar Mesa Canyon

The Hopi experience is a long continuity, an endurance. John Boyden disrupted the continuity, perhaps nearly broke it. But, John Boyden or no, the Hopi way has persevered, and it is the best known way to live in the dry and spare American Southwest. The Hopi have endured, and so can the land, and so can we.

Conversations with Vernon Masayesva and others sparked my curiosity about the ancient Pueblo cultures. Although lacking any formal training, I absorbed a good amount of literature and talked with archaeologists, anthropologists, and Indian people. I learned that the actual, physical context was critical. At every opportunity, I hiked into remote areas that friends had told me about or that looked like probable living areas of the Fremont or Ancestral Puebloans. (One issue of terminology needs to be addressed. For a century the Ancestral Puebloans have commonly been referred to by the term "Anasazi," a Navajo word meaning "enemy ancestors." It was used by Richard Wetherill, a southwestern Colorado rancher and one of the first non-Indians to visit the ancient sites, who learned the word from Navajos in the 1880s. The modern Pueblo people, the Ancestral Puebloans' descendants, object to it for the same basic reasons that some Navajo object to their nation being named after a word in Tewa, a principal Pueblo language. At the same time, there is no single Pueblo word for the Ancestral Puebloans; the Hopi word for their ancestors in the Four Corners region is *Hisatsinom,* while in Zuni the term is *Enote:que.* By the mid-1990s, the term "Ancestral Puebloans" had come into common usage. Since it seems to be a sensible approach, I use "Ancestral Puebloans" in place of "Anasazi.")

The ancient civilizations of the Hopi and other Pueblo people thrived in many of the canyons of the Colorado Plateau. Indeed the people seem to have been everywhere. A person must know where and how to look, and be patient, but the rewards are lasting. For these places are palpable with time and give us the chance to transport ourselves far back.

I remember vividly my beginning explorations, in the early 1990s, for

# ENDURANCE

Ancestral Puebloan petroglyphs and pictographs. A Park Service ranger had given me rough directions to a small side canyon, southeast of Canyonlands National Park, that had some petroglyphs. Though she was imprecise about its exact location (the Park Service ethic is to give visitors some, but not too much, guidance in locating backcountry archaeological sites), her description proved sufficient. When I came around a bend in the road at about the location she had charted, a roadless canyon branched in from the west. I got out of the van and began hiking up into this seldom-used draw.

Of course, I was not engaged in some original exploration for these old inscriptions. Yet in my own mind I felt like an explorer, for there were no trail signs, no explanatory exhibits directing me toward the tiny human engravings in the vast, rocky land. This search brought back emotions of hiking into and fishing a far backcountry stream for small, elusive native cutthroat trout.

I knew that the artisans pecked their work on desert varnish, the brown-black coating caused by the leaching of iron and manganese oxides. Using sharp, stone tools, the Old People penetrated through the thin, dark veneer to the underlying red rock, the fire of the Colorado Plateau, leaving a sharp contrast with the darker varnish. The artists liked nearly vertical flat walls.

As I hiked up the rocky bed of the dry creek, I realized that I was borrowing the intensity learned from my visual searches of trout water. Pinprick alert in this waterless stream bottom, I panned over the walls of this canyon. There—and there—I detected the confluence of brown-black and verticality. My jaw tightened. And although I did not shoot my right arm up to set the hook, the taut engagement of mind and body was the same. But no petroglyphs.

Then, at the far boundaries of my vision, above the talus slide on the canyon wall: lines and curves and shapes that seemed different from the designs of wind, water, and rockslides. I tore out of the creek bottom, up the talus slope, banging my left knee in the process, to the bottom of the canyon wall. Yes: six engraved images—petroglyphs, chiseled in stone, as opposed to pictographs, painted on the rock. One had a triangular-shaped body, human, it seemed. The other forms were a row of thick-bodied, rectangular deer, with stick legs and antlers. I'm not one to stand too long at exhibits in art galleries or museums. It makes me self-conscious. But I did stand long here. Three minutes, five minutes, longer. Just me, my first-discovered petroglyphs, and the many centuries.

That day I made other finds. One panel contained three flute players. These were images of the minstrel / fertility figure / bon vivant, Kokopelli, who traveled the Plateau carrying a basket of seeds on his back and often, as in one of these petroglyphs, sporting an impressive erection for planting young maidens as well as the soil. Kokopelli's lighthearted, fanciful, sensual, quixotic tunes have been heard on the Colorado Plateau since the earliest stories. Kokopelli's music lives on, not just on these and thousands of other canyon walls, but in the elaborate fertility dances at Hopi and Zuni and, too, in the delectable improbability of KTNN.

I sketched the musicians' images. I'm not remotely an artist, not even a drawer. Never in my life had I felt compelled to do such a thing before.

My last panel of petroglyphs that first day captivated me even more. I worked my way up the loose talus slope and stood below a panel that the Old Person couldn't have reached by standing on the talus. The panel was up higher and must have been pecked from a narrow ledge about 7 or 8 feet above the canyon debris, 10 or so feet long, and no more than 18 to 24 inches wide. I found myself wanting to sit, or crouch, where the artist or historian or journalist or shaman had made this elaborate set of pictures— four animals, three humans (one a Kokopelli figure with a flute), and a snake. I jumped and pulled myself up, but I couldn't replicate what this person of a thousand years ago or more had done. The ledge was too high, too narrow. It was hard to hold my balance and I was afraid of falling. And my joints were too stiff. In short order, they began to scream out at me.

I couldn't, in other words, do for a few minutes what this artist had done so tediously for hour after hour after hour—very likely for day after day— pecking away the sandstone piece by piece. The panel was not signed, nor, it seems, is any petroglyph or pictograph on the Plateau signed. All that effort, all that time, all that pain throughout the joints, all that and more, not in the glorification of the individual, but in the celebration of something larger: probably the society and the land and the gods all wrapped together. These Ancient People were human beings with a sense of scale.

I pursued this avocation of searching out the places of the Ancestral Puebloans with the kind of passion that we reserve only for those rare, unexpected, and new pursuits in life—pursuits that seem, in a physical way, to transport our minds to different and fresh places. These explorations into the world of the Old People had parallels with my journeys to the underwater world when my father showed me how to drop a handline off a pier and down into the mysteries of the bay. Rewarding though my solitary hikes were, however, my finest quests came when I could bring one or more of my boys, Seth, Philip, David, and Ben.

A few years ago in early May, when Philip was thirteen, tall for his age and blessed with Ann's thick, blond hair, we took a backpacking trip down into one of the Cedar Mesa canyons. Grand Gulch is the most famous of these canyons and rightly so. Grand Gulch has an exceptional diversity of Ancestral Puebloan and Fremont sites; while no single site is as elaborate as, for example, those at Mesa Verde or Chaco Canyon, the sheer profusion of ancient architecture and art may exceed even those places. But Grand Gulch draws numbers of people, especially during the spring, and I wanted for us to have some solitude. So we decided on another Cedar Mesa canyon—a canyon less well known and less well stocked with evidence of the lives of the Old People, though still from all accounts a fine canyon for understanding the Ancestral Puebloans and a lovely one, too.

We headed out in our van from Boulder, where the buds on the maple trees had just come out, toward the Four Corners area, which would be verging on summer. Every other backcountry trip we had taken involved fishing, and Philip had gotten pretty good with his fly rod. I had told him that this was not trout country and was worried he might not be looking forward to the trip or, once there, might be disappointed. But Philip is an

UTAH
area in map

COLORADO RIVER

0        10
miles

ABAJO MOUNTAINS

LAKE POWELL

95

NATURAL BRIDGES

ARCH CANYON

Blanding

RED ROCK PLATEAU

261

HOLE-IN-THE-ROCK TRAIL

GRAND GULCH

CEDAR MESA

WELSH CANYON

OWL CANYON

ROAD CANYON

COMB WASH

COMB RIDGE

191

SLICKHORN CANYON

JOHNS CANYON

LIME CANYON

Bluff

163

SAN

JUAN

RIVER

Mexican Hat

GRAND GULCH
PRIMITIVE
AREA

intellectually curious boy and surprised me with the intensity of his interest in the Old People. Shortly after we drove through Cortez, now in the real canyon country, now with long mesa and redrock views, now with the dial tuned to KTNN, he began to flood me with questions. When did the Old People come here? How did they live? When did they leave? Where did they go?

How did they live? I asked Philip just to wait until we got down in the canyon and actually saw their villages. That would be the best way to get some sense of their lives. As for his other questions, it seemed to me easiest to work backwards in time, since we can be more certain about recent events. We know, I told Philip, that the Ancestral Puebloans left their villages in the Four Corners area between about A.D. 1150 and 1300. Carbon-dating tests, which are very accurate, show that by the late 1200s and early 1300s there is almost no new cut timber for fires or for construction of buildings. Some accounts say that the Ancestral Puebloans "vanished," but all the scholars now agree that this is wrong. They traveled over to the Rio Grande Valley and especially to the pueblos at Hopi and Zuni, settling in with relatives and friends in existing pueblos or founding new ones. Today's Pueblo people are the descendants of the Pueblo people who left the Four Corners area seven or eight hundred years ago.

No one knows for sure why they left. Tree-ring studies establish a deep, prolonged drought from 1276 through 1299. Each year the trees put on a new growth ring. The rings are wide in good growing years, thin in dry years. We know from old trees that the rings were very thin during this period in the late 1200s. Scholars are increasingly skeptical, though, about the significance of the drought. One archaeologist told me: "These folks had lived here a very long time. They knew how to deal with dry country and its cycles." Another possibility is that Ute, Apache, or Navajo, all of whom were in the area, might have pushed them out. Further, a few archaeologists have recently advanced the sensational thesis, which has received sharp criticism from other archaeologists and Pueblo people and cannot yet be considered definitive, that Ancestral Puebloans engaged in cannibalism; one researcher, Christy Turner, hypothesizes that fear of cannibalism may have been one of the factors that sparked the exodus from the Four Corners area. These violence-related explanations, however, run counter to important evidence. The Ancestral Puebloans' departure seems to have been a planned, orderly movement, lacking killings, burning, or other signs of violence. There was no mass fleeing but rather a gradual out-migration of individual families or kinship groups.

Or the departure might just have been a manifestation of deeply ingrained cultural traits. Although we often think of Pueblo people as settled permanently in their villages, the Old People seem to have been only semi-sedentary. They had a pattern of living in an area for sixty, eighty, a hundred years or more, and then moving on. The moving seems not to have been done on a wholesale basis, entire villages all at once; it was incremental, a few families at a time. Often other Ancestral Puebloan groups or descendants of the original inhabitants resettled the vacated pueblos, rebuilding the old structures or constructing their own, sometimes right on top of the previous ones.

We don't know why, I told Philip, they had this habit of settling in for several generations and then packing up. The practice may have had religious overtones. It may have had to do with the capacity of the land to sustain the Pueblo people—to preserve soil productivity, they may have regularly moved on, letting the land lie fallow. Despite the Ancestral Puebloans' thousands of years of residence in the Four Corners region, there seems to be no physical proof they had abused the land—no indication, for example, of salinization, nutrient depletion, or waterlogging. In the Phoenix area, where the Hohokam civilization grew so large (to 50,000 or even 100,000 people) and stayed so long (about the same time span as the Ancestral Puebloans), researchers have found no evidence of soil degradation. Scholars believe that the Hohokam simply rotated their fields to minimize the impact of farming on the land.

The idea that the departure from the Four Corners was a voluntary act of the Ancestral Puebloans would be consistent with the Hopi's own oral history, told and retold over the centuries. The Hopi arose from the interior earth at the sacred emergence place near the mouth of the Little Colorado, not far from the floor of the Grand Canyon. The clans then went out in every direction, experimenting, looking for the best place to live. Finally, after many thousands of years, all of the clans had decided on Black Mesa. One of the Hopi clans, the Badger, is known to have come down from the north and its members consider Spruce Tree House, at Mesa Verde, to be a sacred ancestral place.

So the movement from the Four Corners area, thirty thousand people or more, may have been for the Ancestral Puebloans' own cultural reasons rather than outside forces such as drought or raiding. Perhaps the interior and exterior forces were both at work.

We drove on for a while and Philip broke the silence. "I can't wait to see that perfect kiva." He was referring to an Ancestral Puebloan kiva—one of the classic, circular, subterranean chambers the Pueblo people use for their prayer ceremonies—that a friend had told us about in the canyon we planned on visiting. Most of the kiva roofs have caved in over the centuries, and the term "perfect kiva" describes an ancient kiva that has its roof still in place.

Philip's comment, though, alarmed me. My friend and I had agreed we would get on the phone, each with our topographic maps, and she would give me exact directions. But we'd both gotten busy, she with family matters, me with other last-minute details of the trip. I'd never gotten the final directions. I knew only that the perfect kiva was in the upper half of this canyon, which had several forks. "Yeah," I said to Philip. "I hope we can find it."

We spent the night at a motel in Blanding, Utah. The next morning we rose early, ate our favorite breakfast of huevos rancheros, and did a last shopping at the local supermarket. After another hour on the highway and a bumpy drive over various dirt roads on Cedar Mesa, Philip and I pulled off and parked near an old corral. There wasn't a designated trailhead but this was about the point where a faint trail led to an arm of the canyon. We pulled our packs out of the van and finished loading them up with food, including some stew meat we bought in Blanding.

But there was one final ritual before we could head off. Last night had brought a light rain, and the big smell of sagebrush filled up the meadow. Like most of the Plateau, this was good sagebrush terrain. The corral, identifying the presence of cattle, did not suggest, as it might seem, that the sagebrush would be grazed off. Sagebrush is at least as nutritious as bunchgrass and alfalfa, but the cows won't touch it. Too bitter.

This dynamic between cow and the plant the Navajo call *ts'ah* has put the ranchers, the rangeland, and the cows in a catch-22 ever since the introduction of cattle in the 1880s. The cows overgraze the native bunchgrasses out of their distaste for the sagebrush. But then the aggressive sagebrush plants move in with their deep taproots and sprawling root systems—9 feet or more across for a single bush. With the water and soil appropriated by the invading sagebrush, the grasses can't come back.

So the sagebrush is much more predominant in this cattle and sheep country than it was a century ago. On another day, in another mood, I might complain about this drastic alteration of the natural system, but not today. Grateful for the cow-enhanced profusion of sagebrush and its fragrance, I engage in one of my favorite customs. I tear a bushy sprig, then another, off a tall sagebrush, stuff them in my left shirt pocket with the leaves just inches from my nose, and suggest to Philip that he do the same. He does. We pull on our packs and we're fully ready to hike, fortified by these pale, blue-green leaves. Like Kokopelli, they play out some of the Plateau's best music, a symphony for the nostrils.

After a half an hour of traversing the scrubby piñon-juniper forest on top of Cedar Mesa, we hit the edge of the side canyon and began to work our way down. Within just a few hundred yards, we came across a Pueblo granary, about 4 feet high, set on a ledge and built into the canyon wall. We spent some time inspecting the flat-rock walls and sturdy masonry, nearly a thousand years old. Our topographic map told us we were a good mile and a half from the nearest surface water, a spring down in the side canyon where we planned to camp that evening. Probably, we surmised, they dry-farmed their corn on top of the mesa and brought it down into the side canyon for safekeeping. "Dad," Philip said, shaking his head, "I can't believe we're seeing this."

Enthused by our discovery, we resumed our journey down the side canyon. Philip, hiking a few steps ahead of me on the trail, had more questions. "Dad. When the Old People first came here—how long ago was that?" I gave him my understanding of this. On one level, a person can say that the answer is twenty-one hundred years ago: the beginning point of the Ancestral Puebloan tradition as defined by archaeologists.

The Puebloans did not, of course, just appear twenty-one hundred years ago. These dates are all approximations, categories sketched out by archaeologists. Such classifications have the advantage of providing helpful groupings that show cultural change. They have the disadvantage of arbitrariness—of suggesting fixed boundaries when in fact this was a process of very gradual cultural change. The point is that by about twenty-one hundred years ago the people we call the Ancestral Puebloans had shifted from a mostly nomadic life to a mostly sedentary one. Building settlements that would be lived in for many generations became a main cultural trait.

But these same people had been living on the Colorado Plateau for long before that. Everyone agrees that human beings have been in the region for at least twelve thousand years. We call these early Native Americans the Clovis people, identified by their use of distinctive spear points shaped on both sides, first found near Clovis, New Mexico. The Clovis were hunters who followed big Pleistocene mammals, the mammoth and the *Bison antiguus*. They migrated long distances and the hunters followed them. But by the end of the Pleistocene, about eight thousand years ago, these animals had gone extinct. Their pursuers had no need to continue their long hunting journeys and they became more localized: now they hunted rabbits, other small animals, and, occasionally, deer and bighorn. They also increased their foraging for vegetation such as piñon nuts, berries, and Indian rice grass. The tendency toward settling down became much more pronounced as corn and squash were obtained from peoples to the south.

# Cedar Mesa Canyon

The changeover from foraging to farming was completed about twenty-one hundred years ago. At this time the distinctive culture we call Ancestral Puebloan was in place. Then, over the centuries, the culture evolved from pit houses to masonry pueblo residences with great kivas and reached its widest geographic distribution and highest population numbers between about A.D. 900 and 1100.

We stopped at a bend in the deepening canyon, the rocky walls a hundred feet high, to take a break and drink some water. "But then," Philip asked, "how long ago did the ancestors of the Ancestral Puebloans come here?" That was, I replied, a much harder question. The evidence is limited, and there is a lot of guesswork. Most archaeologists believe it is just a matter of time before hard evidence is found establishing the presence of human beings in the New World long before twelve thousand years ago. Some experts argue that there are already sufficient data to place the true date much, much earlier.

Professor Joseph Greenberg and other linguists believe that the first migration from Asia—called the Amerinds (some of whom evolved into the Ancestral Puebloans, Hopi, and other Pueblo peoples)—took place between fifteen thousand and thirty thousand years ago. The Na-Dene (including the Navajo and Apache), Greenberg concludes, must have come from Asia between ten thousand and fifteen thousand years ago. The third wave, the Eskimo-Aleut, who remained in the north, crossed between six thousand and nine thousand years ago. These linguists do not rely on the physical evidence used by archaeologists. Rather, they believe that the Amerind must have arrived at an early date because the longer time frame is essential to account for the diversity of languages on this continent. Biological anthropologists using molecular techniques have supported Greenberg's findings.

A respected archaeologist, Richard S. "Scotty" MacNeish, may have succeeded in pushing the date back even farther. In Pendejo Cave in southern New Mexico he found stone chopping implements, animal bones gnawed on by humans, human hair, and five pits lined with rocks from outside the caves. He then used accepted carbon-dating techniques to determine their age. MacNeish believes the evidence shows human habitation in Pendejo Cave back to thirty thousand years ago, perhaps thirty-eight thousand. Numerous archaeologists have rejected MacNeish's findings, but he has many supporters also. Robson Bonnichsen says: "My personal conclusion . . . is there had to be humans here before Clovis. Scotty's out there . . . on the firing range with a lot of people taking potshots at him, but he's working hard and doing it well."

The dignity of this long occupation, whatever its exact length, is engrossing. I tried to articulate the profundity of this to Philip as we hiked on. Few non-Indians today can claim four generations on the Colorado Plateau, and only a handful of Mormon families can claim five or six generations, perhaps a few seven. The Pueblo people, tracing back through their ancestors—the Ancestral Puebloans and the gatherers and hunters before them—can show at least six hundred generations and, if Scotty MacNeish is right, perhaps three times that: eighteen hundred generations. And there may well be other discoveries.

**I**t was late afternoon when we reached the spring and set up camp for the night on a bench up off the floor of the side canyon, above the point where the spring seeps out of the sandstone wall. This was stew night, and we filled up our pot with potatoes, carrots, onions, water, the beef, and a pour of red wine. The sagebrush in our shirt pockets, and in this side canyon, was big sagebrush, *Artemisia tridentata,* a member of the sunflower family. *Artemisia,* which dominates half the acreage in the eleven western states, is perhaps the most abundant shrub in North America. Although it smells like true sage—the genus *Salvia,* of the mint family—sagebrush tastes no better to us than it does to cows and I knew better than to use it in the stew. The Colorado Plateau has pockets of *Salvia,* the culinary herb, but having seen none in this vicinity, I seasoned the stew with some true sage—probably grown in the Mediterranean—from my backpacking spice kit. For fragrant authenticity, we sprinkled our fire with local sagebrush, and we ended up with successes of both our dinner and our campfire.

Philip and I crawled into our sleeping bags early. In the middle of the night we were startled out of our slumber by a sudden, violent cloudburst. The monsoon season on the Plateau comes during late summer and early fall, but localized thunderheads can roll in at any time and dump voluminous amounts of water—even though the sky may have been clear a few hours earlier, as it was when Philip and I had turned in. I had almost decided to sleep in the open air without pitching the tent.

The next morning we awakened to a long-distance discussion between two frogs, one in the pool at the base of the spring, the other downcanyon. Philip stuck his thatch of blond hair out of the tent and began his own "bree-deeps." It seemed that on some occasions the frogs responded to this third colleague, avid but bogus.

We pulled on our clothes and descended toward the pool. The sky had cleared and, even though the sun had just entered the side canyon, the sandy soil had mostly dried out from the combination of seepage and evaporation into the dry air. We never did see the frog, but Philip took off his boots, waded into the little pool's cattails and sedges, and had a gleeful time pursuing tadpoles.

We had a hard hike that day. The trail petered out and the bottom of the side canyon, dry except for short stretches below our camping spring and another spring farther down, was mostly boulders. We clawed our way as much as we walked, but there were compensations. The side canyon had cut deeper, a good 500 feet down now, and its sandstone walls became higher, more imposing, more fiery. In addition to the yucca, sagebrush, and occasional bunchgrasses, we found good numbers of foot-high hedgehog cactuses, fully flowered this spring day, some scarlet, some yellow. Still we grew impatient with the bouldering and wondered if we would ever reach the main branch of our Cedar Mesa canyon. At last, three hours later, we did.

I had a campsite picked out about 4 miles upcanyon. The hiking, along a sandy streamside trail, was much easier than in the narrower side canyon. We needed to be especially vigilant now, for this wider canyon was a prime candidate for ancient dwellings. The little stream ran perennially, or nearly so, and would have given the Old People a good opportunity to divert water for their rows of corn. The stream made many deep pools, and in midafternoon we took a swim in the bracing water, finding relief from the high, hot sun. We found two more granaries but no homes. And no perfect kiva.

We camped in a splendid place at the junction of the main canyon and a side canyon, just across from a large balanced rock. Rolling his eyes, Philip observed that the mammoth, egg-shaped boulder, perched a good 50 feet above the streambed, looked like it could topple over at any time, perhaps crashing down in our direction. But he also allowed that the rock seemed like it had remained in its current position a long time.

We had been talking all day about our planned dinner of fresh pasta and sundried tomato pesto, a repast we were experimenting with, gambling that it wouldn't go bad in the heat. We were starving and ate early. It was otherworldly delicious.

During dinner we spied some Ancestral Puebloan structures across the canyon, up on a broad shelf, beyond the balanced rock. The site looked fairly elaborate. Several squares seemed to be windows. With the last bit of his pesto mostly chewed, Philip jumped up. "Let's go! Maybe this will be the perfect kiva!"

We forded the stream and worked our way up to the shelf, which was easy to reach. The Cedar Mesa Sandstone was layered, almost in staircases, up to the site, about 100 feet above the canyon floor. Once on top, we could see that the shelf was much broader than it seemed from below. This may well have been a gathering spot of some sort, perhaps for ceremonies. There were several rooms with windows and a granary with a door of juniper branches. The door was removable, so that we could look inside the storage area. We saw a kiva, but it was half filled with red dirt, its roof long ago caved in.

The task of trying to piece together ancient lifeways is challenging, fascinating, mind-expanding. The Ancestral Puebloans had no written lan-

# Cedar Mesa Canyon

guage and so we have only the hard parts: walls, doors, pictographs and petroglyphs, arrowheads and metates, pots and bowls. But we also have contemporary Pueblo cultures. Although they have been subjected to four centuries of assimilation, we surely can learn a lot about the ways of the Old People through the ways of today's Pueblo people.

We imagined this might have been a year-round living place for three or four families. South-facing and with plenty of sun, the site was near the bottomland where they grew corn. But we knew there were also structures up on top, now a thousand feet above us, on Cedar Mesa. The deer and rabbit hunting, and piñon nut gathering, would be better up there. Perhaps the Old People lived up on the mesa but farmed and held ceremonies down here. Perhaps they lived part of the year above, part below. Perhaps this, perhaps that.

Darkness had begun to gather and we walked down from the shelf. Our campsite was next to a generous overhang, and we spread our sleeping bags underneath. The storm had passed and the sky was clear. Later, I knew, the moon would be full and bright. There would be no weather, but even if there were, our overhang would protect us well. In my sleeping bag, I was left with my stiff joints after our long day. I would always, I imagine, think of the Ancestral Puebloans, who had to be master climbers to live in these canyons, in terms of their supple joints and my stiff ones.

With Philip asleep next to me, I thought back forty years and more. How often had my father taken me off somewhere—just the two of us? The demands of the medical school were heavy, but he had tried. He had taken me fishing on a few afternoons, good afternoons. In 1950, we sat behind home plate at Yankee Stadium, my first baseball game, and we went to a couple of basketball games at Madison Square Garden. Wide-eyed, I got to watch him perform an operation, doing research on monkeys, at the hospital in New York. For a while in the summers we went out sailing in the catboat in the Atlantic off Martha's Vineyard. Then, when I was about thirteen, his medical research and his own demons began to consume him. This, coupled with the surly bravado of my adolescence, led us into the warfare from which we never emerged.

Paul Roca had done much better with his children. Paul and Mariana, his daughter and my friend, were very close, always engaged in spirited conversations. He took his son, Mike, down into the deep Sonoran and Chihuahuan backcountry on many of his freewheeling, celebratory jeep trips in pursuit of forgotten Spanish missions. It occurred to me that my practice of taking one of my boys whenever I can was probably inspired by Paul.

I sank into sleep and hours later awoke to the full moon, straight above Balanced Rock. I hoped we would find the perfect kiva but worried that it was a needle in a haystack.

The morning came in clear and crisp. My muscles and joints had loosened up. This would be our critical day. We would start early and hike the main canyon—6 miles to its upper end and back if we had to—and then return to our camp. Tomorrow we would hike out, going up a side canyon that was a candidate for the perfect kiva. But this main canyon was much more likely and today would be our last chance in it. We made breakfast, packed water and lunches, and headed upcanyon. "We're going to find it today, Dad."

Much of the canyon floor was Halgaito Shale, chocolate and brittle. It came in thin sheets and broke off easily at the edges. The walls of this canyon, deep backcountry, plain old BLM land, were Cedar Mesa Sandstone, a soft, glowing pink.

The fire in this Cedar Mesa Sandstone has pedestrian origins, though, a mineral with the name of hematite: iron oxide ($Fe_2O_3$).

This sandstone originated in the Permian Period some 225 to 280 million years ago. During this time, the Colorado Plateau was alternately covered by advancing and retreating seas and by sand dunes, much like the Sahara. Originally these formations were a pale yellow or white. Then winds carried tiny chemical particles of hematite, the principal ore of iron, onto the Cedar Mesa dunes. Over millions and millions of years, this dust infiltrated the dunes and formed clay rims on the grains of sand. When

# Cedar Mesa Canyon

water intruded, the particles recrystallized into the stable form of hematite. In the course of recrystallizing, these small iron particles turned red. (Big hematite crystals are black.) The process was very similar to rusting. Later, rivers and seas laid down sedimentary deposits that covered the Cedar Mesa desert, sealing in the soft dunes and creating sandstone deposits.

These processes tinted the Cedar Mesa Sandstone walls rising up around Philip and me as well as sandstone and shale deposits across much of the Plateau—the Navajo, Wingate, and de Chelly formations and many others—in an array of reddish tones. Some deposits of the Cedar Mesa Sandstone and the others never received this dosage of color and remain sand-hued, like the dunes they once were.

So this fire of the Colorado Plateau goes back to hematite and time and rusting. Not romantic perhaps, but effective.

By this time Philip had a good feel for this canyon and how the Old People lived in it. The village sites would almost always be on a large, level, south-facing ledge—up off the canyon floor and preferably with a significant overhang. We hiked at a determined pace but made expeditions up the canyon sides when the conditions seemed right. We found more granaries, a site with two rooms, and, high up on a ledge only 20 or 30 feet deep, a multistoried village with many rooms. We then went off on several false leads. One of them took us on a long, winding trek to a precarious perch much closer to the rim than the floor.

Back down on the canyon bottom, we sat under a cottonwood tree for a snack of water and trail mix. Although it was late morning and we had done considerable scrambling to get up to the sites, real or imagined, we both commented on how we didn't feel particularly tired. Then we got up and went back to the trail. We continued upcanyon for another half an hour, mostly in silence, sustained by the trickle of the stream, the fire in the sandstone, and the Old People all around us.

"Dad! Isn't that a door up there? Way up, on the fourth shelf up?"

"Where? Just to the left of that juniper tree?"

"No. Farther to the right, at the end of that long ledge."

My eyes just weren't as good as his. I worked at it but even with further directions I couldn't see a door or any other structure. But I did think I could see a wall at the other end of the ledge. He said, yes, it was a wall.

"Come on, Dad, let's get up there."

Our ledge, well more than halfway up the side of the canyon, would require a stiff climb. Excited, convinced that this could be the place, we tore up the slope as quickly as we could, Philip in the lead. Several sheer rock faces confronted us, but we climbed them or worked our way around them. The slopes were covered with loose rocks. At one time, pushing off with my right foot, I dislodged a good-sized rock, a dangerous practice on such steep ground. The rock, after gathering others and building into a small landslide as it blasted down the canyonside, finally crashed noisily in a cloud of dust on the canyon floor. One of the advantages of having a canyon to yourself is that the solitude can cover your mistakes.

At that point, we stopped on a slope of scree, not far below our ledge, to catch our breath. Even I could tell that there definitely was a granary door. It looked beautifully constructed. We had only about five minutes more.

"Dad, let's go!" Philip went on ahead, scrambling for all he was worth. I stayed below, enjoying his dust and spirit.

Minutes later, from the ledge I heard that cry from the depths of his generation's culture. "Yesss! *Yesssss!! Yesssss!!!* It's the perfect kiva! Dad! *Dad!* Hurry! *Hurry!*"

I did.

I worked up to the ledge and soon stood on it, breathing hard and trembling through all my limbs. The village had numbers of structures— granaries, rooms for living—and the perfect kiva. Perfect because the roof, at ground level, was completely intact and the old ladder, which some good and hardy soul in the BLM had reinforced with aluminum bolts for safety, rose up through the opening. There were hiking-boot prints around, but not many. The canyon saw little traffic and this site was easy to miss. Without Philip, I probably would have.

Philip was desperate to go down into the kiva but I was firm. No, we are going to take our time and enjoy this. You always open the best present last. And we were going to be here a while. Take your time, take your time.

# Cedar Mesa Canyon

We were hungry and climbed up on a high rock to have our lunch of hard rolls, salami, cheese, and ballpark mustard. This village was set in the elbow of a bend in the canyon and, like the Old People, we had long views up and down the canyon. Across the way we could see the piñon-juniper top of Cedar Mesa.

Now that we were beginning to settle in here, in this place, in the company of the Old People, we found ourselves slowing down, a state of mind encouraged by the surroundings. Over the years I have been lucky to spend quite a lot of time with traditional Indian people. Philip has, too. The conversations move along slowly, constructed as much of gaps, pauses, and silences as they are of words. A person always listens when another is talking, with no interruptions, which would show disrespect. In many tribes, when a person is speaking, the listener should not gaze deeply into the speaker's eyes for that would intrude into their privacy. We, of course, are taught just the opposite. For them, it is less the individual than the individual's place in the family, the tribe, the natural world. Surely it was that way with the Old People who once lived here. Slow, steady, respectful.

We finished our meal and began to explore, light steps coming naturally to us now, around the village. There were pictographs: a snake about 2 feet long, a small black animal, white hand marks with red concentric circles on the palms. A white painted man had red arms and legs. We found a pecked-out Kokopelli, playing his songs, spreading his seeds. On top of one of the low pueblo walls, visitors of our time had placed potshards and corncobs, each as small as my pinkie. I was reminded, despite all the looting by renegades, that the far greater number of us in the backcountry have created our own traditions built on respect: it is now our ethic, as well as the law, to leave these remains for other visitors to enjoy.

Corn had been a major influence in Ancestral Puebloan culture. Carbon-dating has placed corn in Mexico 5,600 years ago. Maize apparently did not reach the American Southwest until 3,500 years ago but, when it did, it spread rapidly among the Old People. The cultivation of maize seems to have been the main factor in the Pueblo peoples' move from foraging to farming.

# ENDURANCE

The corn was mostly ground into flour and it seems that Pueblo women spent huge amounts of time grinding—and thinking and talking. Time was spent, too, with the young ones. We had brought several books on this trip. Philip had read Terry Tempest Williams' *Coyote's Canyon* and much of *Wind in the Rock,* by Ann Zwinger, both of which deal with the Cedar Mesa canyons. Philip was still young enough to like me to read to him, and at the village I read him a passage from Mary Sojourner's *Sisters of the Dream,* about Choovio, an Ancestral Puebloan mother, and her small daughter Talasi:

> *Choovio built up the fire, warmed cornmeal soup and fed them both, grateful for the shadows flickering on the walls, for the food in their bellies. . . .*
>
> *She sat for a time with Talasi, smiling down at the round sleeping face. Then she turned to her grinding stones and ground corn far into the night, corn for the ceremonies, corn for the feasts, sacred corn for the sacred work of Soyal. Talasi, drifting in and out of dreams, heard the rasp of her mother's work, the music of the grinding, the music of her mother's songs and saw, behind her closed owl eyes, the Spirits dancing high above, laughing and playing, bounding from star to star.*

This passage made Philip wonder about the Ancestral Puebloan children in this high-ledge, steep-canyon village. He worried that it might be dangerous for them. Perhaps, he reasoned, this shows that they lived on the mesa all year and that only the adults came down to this site, for farming and ceremonies.

I myself have come to think that the canyon sites were occupied year-round. So I suspected there may well have been a wall—a guardrail—along the side of the ledge. We did see many cut rocks down the slope, suggesting such a possibility. Even if there weren't a wall, Indian societies seem to work especially hard at disciplining their children and probably the Ancestral Puebloans would have had an effective way of teaching their children to stay away from the edge. (When Philip and the other boys were little, and Ann and I would take them to powwows, all the Indian people would always be looking after the kids. "At an Indian get-together," one Indian

# Cedar Mesa Canyon

friend had told me, "you've got babysitters all over the place.") But, as is so often the case with the Old People, today we have only the pleasure of speculation, and may never know for certain.

We looked around the buildings. From a discussion with a BLM archaeologist I knew that the Cedar Mesa pueblos in this reach of the canyon had been settled late, during the 1100s and 1200s, when Ancestral Puebloan architecture had become highly refined. These buildings were not, however, as elaborate as those at Chaco Canyon, 150 miles to the southeast, part of the national park system, with their immense size and exquisite detail work. As William Henry Jackson of the U.S. Geological Survey had written in 1877, the Ancestral Puebloans "must have employed a large body of intelligent, well organized, patient, and industrious people, under thorough discipline for a very long time." Our village was not nearly of Chaco's magnitude, the masonry work not so polished, but the same intelligence and industriousness showed through. These buildings were hardy and employed passive solar heating. Even today, the same principles of architecture are used throughout the Southwest.

Their pottery too was exceptional. The Ancestral Puebloans developed many kinds of vessels and artistic styles. One potter told me, "Their work is magnificent. It's amazing they could turn out work like that without a wheel."

It was finally time to go into the perfect kiva. A friend from Hopi had told me that it was permissible to go into a kiva so long as we did not damage it in any way or show disrespect. "You don't have to pray in our way or anything like that. Just be very careful and remember where you are."

Gingerly we descended the old ladder and gave our eyes time to adjust to the dim light. This was not a great kiva big enough to hold one hundred people or more. Rather, this kiva probably was used by a few small villages in the immediate vicinity. Yet we could see that this was a place of great importance. For one thing, it required an enormous amount of work to create. This kiva, after all, was hand-dug seven and a half feet down into the sandstone. It was about fifteen feet in diameter. The ceiling was made of thick juniper beams. All of this was done without any beasts of burden.

We could see, even seven hundred years after the area had been abandoned, that the kiva had been well cared for. The circular walls were coated with a smooth mortar and then painted a dark red. There was a yellow circle on the west side and another on the east. In this protected space, I was reminded that while we often think of the Ancestral Puebloan villages in terms of grays and browns and unadorned sandstone, in fact these were colorful societies. Since gravity has collapsed most of the ceilings, we usually see only the exposed surfaces, weathered by the many centuries. Yet the interior walls, as here, often were elaborately decorated. The great kiva at Aztec, New Mexico, which has been restored with authenticity, is ablaze with color. Several sites, including the Hopi site of Owatobi and Kuaua near Bernillo, have kiva murals covered over and repainted with mineral and vegetable pigments as many as seventy or eighty times.

Philip and I sat down on the floor, backs against the wall, he at the north, I at the east. Out near the middle of the floor was the *sipapu,* the small opening representing the entrance up from the underworld, the sacred emergence place. We've since talked about that trip a great deal, but for whatever reason we've never discussed our thoughts during our silent hour in the perfect kiva. Perhaps it was simply because we moved beyond specific thoughts to a slow, steady flow of reverence for the people, gods, and ideas that made for such a long-lasting way of life in this compelling but difficult landscape.

We got up, climbed the ladder, hugged, and stood for a while on the ledge, looking across the redrock canyon to the top of Cedar Mesa. Then we looked at each other, still not needing words, and began walking, slowly and pensively this time, down the canyonside. By the time we reached the trail, we were talking again as we made our way back to the campsite.

That night after Philip had trailed off, lying in my sleeping bag under our protective sandstone shelf, waiting for the nearly full moon to come up over the canyon rim, I remembered something that had not occurred to me during the day. The kivas were in continual use. And just as Choovio instructed Talasi in her own way as she steadfastly worked her stone mano, grinding the corn to flour in the trough-like metate, so too was the kiva the place, then as now, where the fathers instructed their sons. I imagine, in a society where they caressed time rather than raced against it, the Ancestral Puebloan fathers knew, that to be good fathers, they had to be neither strong nor handsome nor rich. They had only to give their time to their sons. And while my world may be too different, and my own limitations too many, to live that idea as well as they, at least now I have that idea, borne not so much from analysis as from reverence visited in a perfect kiva carved by hand seven and a half feet deep in the sandstone of a Cedar Mesa canyon seven hundred years ago or more.

# BLACK MESA

I am driving west on Black Mesa in my van with four friends as morning first begins to bring light. A man from Hopi told me that this large flat mesa, with several branches, was shaped like a human hand, and it is true. If you place your left hand, palm down and directed to the southwest, on a large U.S. Geological Survey topographical map of Arizona, your hand almost exactly matches this high-desert landform: the back of your hand is the upper end of Black Mesa, your thumb is the high ridge running from Tsegi to Cow Springs, your forefinger is the Big Mountain–Rocky Ridge complex, and your other three fingers, in order, are Third Mesa, Second Mesa, and First Mesa, the most southeasterly extension. You'd have to imagine that the hand is separated at the wrist—signifying the 8,000-foot-high crest and sheer escarpment of the northeastern edge of Black Mesa rising 2,000 feet above the desert floor below. The twelve Hopi villages (except for Moenkopi, which is 15 miles beyond the west boundary of the reservation) are located at the lower end of Black Mesa, on the numbered mesas.

Our journey will take us to Hotevilla for Home Dance, held separately in each village. By all accounts (I had not been to Home Dance before), this kachina dance is a grand, electrifying ceremony, a high point for each village every year. The kachinas come down from their home in San Francisco Peaks each February, when they perform the Bean Dance, bringing fertility both to the cultivated fields and to young families. The last kachina dance, this one, is in late July when they return home, taking the prayers of the people up to San Francisco Peaks. The kachinas leave behind their wisdom and strength, and their bounty, for this is a rain dance.

# ENDURANCE

I turn the vehicle off the paved road into the village, which is on Third Mesa. We are followed by another van, as there are nine of us in our party: myself and a couple from Boulder, two women friends from Flagstaff and St. George, and a couple from Flagstaff, she an archaeologist and he a naturalist, with their two children. Hotevilla's Home Dance is open to outsiders, if invited, and we had received invitations from Vernon and Becky Masayesva and other friends in the village.

Hotevilla has about four hundred permanent residents, but that number will expand by several hundred this weekend as family members return for Home Dance. The village's name, testament to the critical role of water on Black Mesa, comes from the Hopi words *"hota,"* a person's back, and *"veli,"* meaning to scrape or peel—because the village's main spring is located in a cave with such a low ceiling that people would often scrape their backs against it.

Out by the highway, most of the houses—a mixed lot ranging from wood shanties to cinderblock buildings—had electricity. We drove down a sandy street past the last wood power pole and parked. Looking around, I could see that the main part of the village lacked plumbing as well as electricity. We would be using the outhouses today.

As we walked toward the square at the center of the village, the homes grew progressively older, more traditionally Pueblo, low and blocky with few windows. The buildings are made of stone or adobe. The Old People developed adobe, a mixture of sand and clay, because it dries hard without cracking. Most of the structures are covered with adobe plaster, giving the homes a reddish-brown, earthen color.

We started at a commotion to our right. On a rooftop a large golden eagle was flapping on his platform, straining at his tether. We knew that tomorrow morning he would be smothered. His feathers would be removed, to be used for prayers in future ceremonies, and he would be reverently laid to rest and buried, his head facing west. Like the powerful kachinas, this great bird will carry the messages and prayers of the Hopi people aloft.

When we reached the square, several hundred people, mostly Hopi, were already there: up on the flat rooftops and terraces, in the four passage-

# Black Mesa

ways that fed into the square, on the open areas above the slightly recessed square, inside the stuccoed buildings (since homes made up the sides of the square). There were portable chairs all around, down on the sandy ground, up on the roofs and terraces. Each of us moved off to find a place from which to watch. I went to a low rise beyond the southwestern corner of the square and took a spot in the back. The sun still lay below the eastern ridge far beyond the village buildings, and the kachinas had not yet arrived. Good: this ceremony would continue from daybreak till dusk, and I wanted to see all of it.

The square was drenched with anticipation. This feeling came not from the sounds or motion, however, for there was very little of either. People picked their way to their places, and even whispers were rare. Hopi hide their feelings—people should not be conspicuous in a crowd. Only non-Indians, I surely include myself here, leaned forward or cocked their heads. Yet you knew how much emotion was in the air as the Hopi people awaited the entrance of the majestic kachinas, bringing with them all the years, all the people, all the hopes, the remembered earth. Still, for all I could feel and for all I had tried to learn about Home Dance from reading and listening, I had no real idea of what to expect. I waited, drinking in the people, the ancient buildings, the blue sky bare of clouds, the cool early air.

Is that something out past the pueblo structures? It seems like a jiggling, a waving, almost a cornfield in a breeze. Now I realize that they are coming: I am seeing the very tips of the kachinas' masks, the tall feathers and long stems of grain, waving as they walk single file toward us from the east. Now they are coming down the alley, more than forty in all, now into the square with their turquoise masks and white skirts and red belts and the spruce bunched as fluffy collars and draped from their belts and their skirts. They are carrying full armloads of squash, melons, and most of all corn, the most sacred plant, to be distributed to the many Hopi who once again had experienced the elegant arrival of the kachinas, about to begin the day's dances before their long journeys home.

# ENDURANCE

The sprigs of spruce adorning the kachinas had been gathered many days ago—for Home Dance is a ceremony that requires long and rigorous preparation before the entrance into the square—from a grove near a spring in a secret place in the high country of Black Mesa. These spruces must be gathered exactly there, nowhere else. A great deal depends on these spruce trees: contrary to our view, the Hopi do not believe the spruce exist because of the water; rather, the spruce come first and *bring* water. At the end of the Home Dance tonight, people from this village, from other Hopi villages, from Zuni, and from pueblos over on the Rio Grande will come to the kachinas and take some of the sprigs of spruce, which can then be planted in their own fields, so that rain will come to them.

The whole of Black Mesa is a spiritual place to the Hopi. Villages, shrines, and burial grounds from the distant past remain in place. Two weeks before Home Dance, men had constructed *páhos*, prayer sticks made of eagle feathers, and left them in the right places on Black Mesa during their journey to the spruce groves. After the dance, the men will leave more *páhos*. Masauù, the Guardian of this world for the Creator, has told the Hopi that Black Mesa is the center.

Historically the Hopi had used coal for firing their pottery but non-Indians did not become aware of Black Mesa coal until 1909. Initially the find attracted little interest because of its remote location, but the deposits, their extent not yet fully known, gradually gained more attention during the ensuing decades. Mineral companies explored the area to determine its potential for oil and gas as well as coal. They liked what they found and applied pressure on the Department of the Interior to open Black Mesa for drilling. By the end of World War II, the companies and the Interior Department, which also wanted to see Hopi minerals extracted, were both ready to go ahead but faced an array of obstacles.

In the Hopi's eyes, they themselves did not own the land or minerals—no one did—and therefore could not lease them out to someone else. Beyond that, although the Hopi's careful agricultural life was a good use of the land, the intensive extraction that the companies had in mind was not. Masauù had given that message to the Hopi. Beyond that, even if the Hopi did want to lease, who could sign off on it? There was no formal Hopi tribal government. And beyond even that, there shouldn't be. Decisions were made in the villages, each one independent, a separate sovereignty unto itself.

The Bureau of Indian Affairs took steps in 1936 that eventually erased two of the obstacles—village autonomy and lack of any formal governmental structure. John Collier, Franklin Roosevelt's BIA commissioner, brought to the office a long and distinguished career as an Indian scholar and activist. He accurately viewed the early 1930s as the nadir of Native American existence on the continent. Tribes had seen their landholdings plummet by 90 million acres as a result of the allotment policy. Tribal governments were inactive, leaving reservation Indians without any leadership to protect against further encroachments from the outside. Collier drafted the Indian Reorganization Act and by 1934, in the early blush of the New Deal, persuaded Congress to pass it. The IRA ended sales of Indian lands and allowed tribes to organize and adopt federally chartered constitutions.

Collier, who had many accomplishments for Indians during his tenure, committed his biggest error at Hopi. His objectives, if presumptuous, were sincerely intended to benefit Indians: he fervently believed in his vision of tribal constitutions and wanted the Hopi, above all other tribes, to have a written constitution so they could operate more effectively in a changing world. Then, too, acceptance of the Indian Reorganization Act at Hopi would give his program credibility with other tribes who themselves could receive its benefits. Collier, who had lived in the Southwest and had many friends at Hopi, barnstormed the reservation, promoting his plan, which would create a central Hopi tribal council. Then he dispatched Oliver LaFarge to carry on the lobbying effort. LaFarge was loyal to Collier, but in a letter back home to his family, he made it clear that this was an unhappy assignment:

*The Indians didn't think this up. We did. . . . We came among these people, they didn't ask us, and as a result, they are our wards. It's not any inherent lack of capacity, it's the cold fact of cultural adjustment.*

# ENDURANCE

The proposed constitution made several changes, seemingly insignificant to outsiders, that were highly disruptive to the intricate, ordered Hopi way of life. Vernon Masayesva, tribal chairman in the 1990s and translator for the traditionalists, explained to me the cultural context surrounding the constitutional provision that gave the Kikmongwi—the traditional religious leaders of each village—the responsibility of certifying the tribal council members from the villages:

> [T]here are many examples where the Kikmongwis' involvement in the political process has really created serious problems within the villages. The reason, I think, is that the old Kikmongwi system of government used to be very different. It was set up in such a way that the non-Hopi mind couldn't understand it.
>
> The Kikmongwi is like a monk, a religious father figure to all of his children. He is kept separate from the secular world. He is prohibited from getting involved in making secular decisions such as getting involved in a property dispute. That is handled by his advisors, by his lieutenants, and there are several categories of these: his interpreters, his policymakers—there are various types of leadership that support the Kikmongwi. But the Kikmongwi himself is excluded from everything that has to do with secular matters, particularly disputes.
>
> The Hopi Constitution, when it was written up, unwittingly dragged the Kikmongwi into the political process. Probably the people who wrote the constitution thought this was necessary—after all, a leader has to have a role, has to have some kind of power. So, in the constitution they acknowledge the Kikmongwi and define powers for him and that power is certification. In other words, a council member elected by the people to represent a village cannot be seated at the council chambers unless there is an accompanying certification from the Kikmongwi. This gave the Kikmongwi a political power that he never had before. . . . The Kikmongwi office has now been compromised and . . . desecrated.

A great confusion descended. Hopiland swirled with unanswerable questions about the meaning of certification, voting, representatives, and a

282

tribal council. The Hopi, after all, were a people with a wholly different tradition of governance—a people living on an isolated mesa where decisions were not made but, rather, emerged from an age-old rhythm of clan, village, Kikmongwi, and Masauù. The real issue in the election was whether the villages, each an elaborate, decentralized theocracy, wanted to jettison their own ways of making decisions and superimpose the white man's system on their own.

In the end, the Hopi adopted Collier's IRA constitution. At least they voted it in according to the way Anglos count votes. Most of the traditionalists opposed the constitution. The idea of deciding matters by a hard-and-fast vote on a particular day, rather than by the old tested way, was alien to the Hopi. Opponents of the BIA's proposed tribal council system, instead of voting in the BIA election, simply stayed away. Although the constitution "passed" in the 1936 election by a count of 651 to 104, no fewer than 2,000 eligible voters abstained. Oliver LaFarge made it clear to Collier that this amounted to a "heavy opposition vote," but Collier certified the election anyway.

The 1936 election was a watershed event. The creation of a tribal council eliminated the impediments to mineral leasing that had previously flowed from village autonomy and a lack of written governmental structure. Now one single official body had the power to sign a mining lease and bind every Hopi village. The other obstacle to the wholesale development of Black Mesa—the Hopi's own reluctance to allow it—would in time be moved aside by the rise of a "progressive" faction in the tribe, and the resultant capture of the Hopi Tribal Council by pro-development forces.

Though it was not remotely John Collier's intention when he put the IRA through Congress and pressed the Hopi to adopt the constitution, the 1936 election radically changed the centuries-old relationship between the Hopi and their place, Black Mesa. By the 1960s, the constitution would move the Hopi into the middle of the rapid industrialization of the American Southwest. The catalytic force was John Boyden. Over the course of thirty years, Boyden would have a dominant voice in the future of Black Mesa and the Hopi Tribe.

Boyden's first choice for a tribal client was Navajo, not Hopi. In 1947, he applied to the nation's largest and most powerful tribe for the position of claims attorney and general counsel. Instead, the Navajo selected Norman Littell of Washington, D.C. Boyden approached the Hopi in 1950, but he encountered an immediate problem. From the beginning, controversy had simmered in the villages over the new Tribal Council, tarred as the "white man's government." The Kikmongwi regularly refused to certify council members, and the Tribal Council had disbanded in 1943. The absence of an active Hopi governing body was of growing concern to the energy industry. By 1950 the BIA was updating more than a dozen companies on the agency's progress toward reorganizing the Tribal Council.

The Salt Lake City attorney wanted to be general counsel at Hopi and consummate the mineral leases, but the Hopi's claims case had to be dealt with first because there was a deadline. The claims case was itself a significant matter: Boyden knew from his concurrent work at Ute, where he and Ernest Wilkinson pressured that tribe into passing the momentous "share and share alike" resolution in 1950, that the attorneys' fees in Indian claims cases could be very lucrative. The Indian Claims Commission Act, passed in August 1946, allowed tribes to recover money damages for lands taken by the United States. But all claims had to be filed within five years.

John Boyden put in considerable effort to be appointed tribal claims attorney in time to beat the August 1951 deadline. With no Tribal Council in place, Boyden and the BIA decided the best course was to seek separate approval from each village. He held lengthy meetings in the villages and spent a great deal of time on the reservation persuading Hopi individually and in small groups.

Boyden's full-court press during 1950 and 1951 has always been controversial. Did Boyden lead the Hopi to believe that their claims suit would allow them to recover not just money but also land, which is what they really wanted? Under the Indian claims statute, the courts were authorized to award tribes only money, not land. In fact, the award of money damages for confiscated tribal land is a final extinguishment of any claim to that land. Oliver LaFarge, who as John Collier's emissary in 1936 had seen the difficulties inherent in presenting complex legal matters to traditional Hopi, noted the problem a year before Boyden ever came on the scene:

> I find it clear that a great many Hopis are under the impression that the Indian Claims Commission might award them land. . . . I notice that there is a great deal of reference to this Commission as the "Land Claims Commission." The prevalence of the term is, of course, a deception in itself.

No one will ever know exactly what Boyden said, and in what context, at the many meetings and discussions. The minutes of some village meetings do show Boyden making precisely the point that the Hopi could obtain money, and money alone, in the claims case. Nevertheless, angry charges persist that he raised his future clients' hopes that the claims case might somehow result in a return of former tribal land.

Several villages and a rump group, not recognized by the BIA but calling itself "the Tribal Council," finally gave their approval to Boyden. Five villages refused to approve his claims contract. The BIA, however, concluded that he should be installed as claims attorney for the Hopi Tribe. Boyden officially signed the contract on July 12, 1951, just a month before the statute of limitations ran out on the claim.

Boyden immediately turned his attention to being named Hopi general counsel. Although the claims case figured to return a sizable attorney's fee—they almost always did (and in 1976 he would receive $500,000 for the Hopi claim)—the general counsel's contract was even more important to him. The Hopi had no money to pay him in the role of general counsel, but he knew the potential that lay underground. Boyden was candid about his self-interest. He told one village, for example: "If I can do something with your resources, I will get paid. That is the chance that I am willing to take." An internal BIA memorandum in 1952 stated that Boyden "pointed out that remuneration for his services will depend largely on working out solutions to many of the Hopi problems to such a point that oil leases will provide funds." But there was still no officially constituted Tribal Council either to retain him or to sign mineral leases.

Boyden had a strategy. In confidential conversations, he told the BIA that it should wait before formally recognizing the present Hopi Tribal Council. In the meantime, the agency should approve Boyden as general counsel to the tribe. He had a contract signed by the rump-group council and seven of the twelve villages. Approving his contract, he explained, would be "the first step." Then, as general counsel, he could "develop a representative tribal council with whom [the] BIA and outside interest[s] may deal."

Eventually his plan worked—but only after BIA Area Director Allan Harper recommended that the contract be disapproved. Approval, Harper wrote, "would effect recognition of the Tribal Council by indirection, thus reversing the basic Hopi policy which has been worked out in the field." Further, the area director predicted, "there will be a rebirth of bitterness and extreme controversy among the Hopi villages." Nevertheless, Boyden prevailed with Harper's superiors in Washington. In 1952 the BIA approved his contract as general counsel.

The next matter was recognition of the Tribal Council under the Hopi Constitution. Boyden's constituency, the "progressives," had become increasingly active. Many of them had converted to Mormonism, Boyden's religion. The "traditionals," knowing that the progressives wanted mineral leasing, refused to participate. Many of the Kikmongwi withheld the certification of council members. Only nine members out of seventeen had been named. Still the BIA, though facing widespread criticism that such a council could not be representative, reasoned that a "quorum" existed. Finally, in 1955, the Interior Department gave its formal approval to this group as the official Hopi Tribal Council. For the previous twelve years, the Hopi had not convened a single meeting of the governing body created in the 1936 constitutional election.

The new Tribal Council and its lawyer promptly went to work on the task of mining Black Mesa. They encountered even more questions. What minerals did the Hopi own? Above all, who owned the minerals under the high, north end of Black Mesa where the best deposits lay? Was there any validity to the Navajo's claimed right to all or part of the Black Mesa coal? The answers would be found in the Navajo–Hopi land dispute, one of the most heartrending issues on the Colorado Plateau or any other region. For decades two tribes engaged in combat over land, coal, oil, water, and financial revenues, and traditional Navajo and Hopi faced eviction from the land where they had always lived.

The Navajo signed a treaty with the United States in 1868. It came after a collision between the same forces at work at Ute and across the Southwest during the second half of the nineteenth century: Americans irresistibly moving westward into new territory and Indian people digging in, struggling to protect their homelands. In 1864, American soldiers cornered Navajo resisters in the remote bends of glorious Canyon de Chelly. After the Navajo surrendered, the troops marched eight thousand Navajos across New Mexico to Fort Sumner, also called Bosque Redondo. This was the Long Walk of the Navajos. For four years, the Navajo stayed at Fort Sumner, confined with the Mescalero Apaches under brutal conditions. Finally their captors allowed the Navajos to return to their ancestral lands. The resulting Treaty of 1868 set aside a land area roughly one-third the size of today's Navajo Reservation.

The Hopi also had land rights in northern Arizona. The tribe never had a treaty with the United States, but for most purposes an executive order can accomplish what a treaty can. The problem, then, with President Chester Arthur's 1882 executive order creating the Hopi Reservation was not that it was an executive order but rather that it was shortsighted, a recipe for conflict from the beginning.

The Hopi executive order arose out of the need to protect Hopi occupation from encroachment both from the west, where Mormons had established a community at Moenkopi, and from the east, where Navajos returning from Fort Sumner began to build hogans on land traditionally held by the Hopi. The executive order encompassed Hopi heartland: nearly all of Black Mesa and additional lands as well, about 2.5 million acres in all. The terse, one-page document set the land aside for the "Moqui [that is, the Hopi], *and such other Indians* as the Secretary of the Interior may see fit to settle thereon" (emphasis added).

Leaving aside for the moment questions of land and mineral ownership as between the Hopi and "other Indians," in human terms a document expecting two strong, ethnically distinct peoples to share a homeland was a dubious enterprise. To be sure, the historical antagonisms between the Hopi and Navajo are sometimes exaggerated. Many Hopi and Navajo families have lived near each other in amity for generations. Yet the fact remains that these are two very different peoples. The Navajo are a herding and hunting tribe, assertive and aggressive, able to change in order to meet new circumstances, quick to move into new territory and defend it. The Hopi are farmers rooted in one place; Black Mesa. Navajo see their tribal personality as firm and strong, the Hopi view theirs as peaceful. These differences remain evident today. For the change in going from the Navajo Reservation to Hopi is pronounced, nearly jolting—the Navajo proud and impressively aloof, the term "Navajo Nation" a ringing declaration with a hard emphasis on the first syllable of the second word, the Hopi open and friendly, welcoming.

The 1882 executive order never worked in terms of resolving landownership between the two tribes. Navajos moved onto Black Mesa, building their hogans and running their sheep. The Navajo population grew rapidly, the Hopi's much slower. Initially the 1882 reservation established by executive order was west of, and separated from, the Navajo Reservation, but the Navajo pressed the United States for more land to meet their burgeoning population and livestock needs. By 1884 Navajo additions to their reservation bordered the executive order reservation on the east and north. By 1900 another expansion of the Navajo Reservation included lands adjacent to the Hopi on the west as well. By 1934 Hopi lands had become completely surrounded by the Navajo Reservation.

# Black Mesa

Navajo sheepherders continued to move onto Black Mesa. In 1937, Commissioner of Indian Affairs Collier created grazing districts within the executive order reservation. The only Hopi grazing district was District 6—a diamond-shaped area in the southern part of the executive order reservation, including lower Black Mesa and the Hopi villages. All the rest of the land within the executive order reservation was placed in Navajo grazing districts. These designations did not resolve the ultimate question of landownership. But now Hopi land—once a glorious expanse of canyon and mesa country all the way south to the Mogollon Rim and north to the Colorado River in Utah—seemed to be a small diamond-shaped grazing district within a surrounding doughnut of Navajo grazing districts within the Navajo Reservation. The coal fields were mostly within the executive order reservation but also mostly overlain by the new Navajo grazing districts.

John Boyden turned his formidable energies to the conflict with the Navajo over who owned Black Mesa and the untold mineral wealth under it. The Hopi's position was that the tribe owned the entire executive order reservation and all its minerals: this was Hopi aboriginal land and the executive order was intended to give the Hopi a homeland. Boyden negotiated with Norman Littell, still general counsel at Navajo, who also avidly supported a settlement of land and mineral rights so that mining could begin. Boyden and Littell finally agreed on a solution: submit the issue to the federal courts. The lawyers drafted a bill, agreed upon by both tribes, that waived the tribes' sovereign immunity and allowed them to sue each other over the ownership issue. Introduced by Stewart Udall, then a beginning congressman, it passed Congress in 1958. Dewey Healing, the Hopi tribal chairman, promptly sued Paul Jones, his Navajo counterpart.

In 1962, a special three-judge district court in Arizona handed down the epic decision in *Healing v. Jones,* deciding rights to 2.5 million acres of land, an area a third again as large as Delaware. Neither tribe won a complete victory. The court ruled that the Hopi owned District 6, the diamond, outright; this was now the Hopi Reservation. As for the surrounding land, where the Navajo were now much more numerous but the Hopi could show centuries of residence, the Hopi and Navajo had "equal rights" to the land and minerals. After *Healing v. Jones,* these lands surrounding the Hopi Reservation were called the Joint Use Area and the mineral picture was clarified: the Hopi would receive all revenues from the reservation and the two tribes would split, fifty-fifty, any proceeds from the Joint Use Area, where the most valuable coal lay. In 1964 the Hopi Tribal Council, now receiving payments from oil and gas leases on the reservation, paid John Boyden $1 million for his work on *Healing v. Jones.*

Some of Boyden's work for the Hopi in the following years did not directly involve coal. Disputes over Navajo ranchers running their sheep and cattle on Joint Use Area lands used by the Hopi multiplied: the idea of Navajo and Hopi "equal rights" to the surface of the Joint Use Area, created by *Healing v. Jones,* worked no better than the original executive order. In 1977, after fifteen years of court cases and congressional action, with Boyden as the chief strategist, a federal judge (without altering the equal split of mineral royalties) drew lines in the Joint Use Area, dividing it between the two tribes. The ruling, which increased the Hopi Reservation by 900,000 acres, meant that several thousand Navajos, but just one hundred Hopis, would have to be relocated.

Relocation, which still had not been completed by the late 1990s, brought protracted agony to the affected Indian people on Black Mesa. Most of these have been elderly, traditional people and, for both Navajo and Hopi, their land was sacred. For many, it was the only land they had ever known. Health specialists agreed that the stress of removal would be overwhelming, leading to disorientation, sickness, depression, even early death. Still, the relocation program has marched on. Some resisters, most notably Navajos near Big Mountain in north central Black Mesa, simply will not go.

There are many reasons why the Hopi prevailed—if by prevailing we mean partition and relocation in the executive order lands—in this struggle between the Navajo and the Hopi that has continued for some forty years. The single greatest force behind the Hopi movement, however, was John Sterling Boyden. He was known to everyone involved as a person of

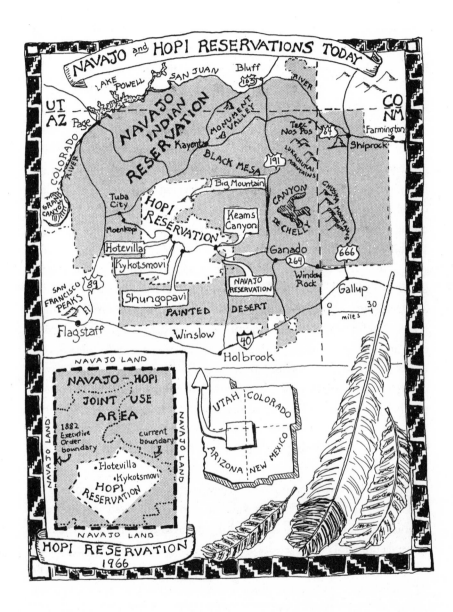

great prestige, in both legal and political circles. He was a superb trial lawyer, a master tactician in Congress, utterly tenacious. An Interior Department spokesman articulated what most knowledgeable observers would say about Boyden's handling of the Navajo–Hopi land dispute from the 1950s until his death in 1980: "John Boyden set the groundwork so well, he had prepared the entire strategy so carefully and it was so clean that [opponents] didn't have a chance. . . . Boyden had everything set for a decade. He was just waiting to move forward and lay down an unassailable attack."

But Boyden also had plenty of time to work on mineral leasing—the primary objective he had candidly targeted from the beginning of his representation of the Hopi. In addition to triggering the eventual relocation of ten thousand Navajos, the 1962 court decision in *Healing v. Jones* had opened the door to Black Mesa coal.

This judicial clarification of joint Hopi–Navajo ownership of the subsurface minerals, with the royalties to be divided equally, came at exactly the right moment. The Big Buildup of the Colorado Plateau's water and energy resources by the booming southwestern cities had moved into high gear. Uranium production was in full swing. The dams authorized by Congress in 1956—Glen Canyon, Flaming Gorge, Navajo, and others—were under construction and Four Corners, the Plateau's first coal-fired power plant, was about to go on line. Now the utility companies wanted to multiply the capacity and efficiency of the western power grid by putting in a new round of power projects. Black Mesa was a key component in the Grand Plan from the beginning. And its importance would grow ever larger as the decade of the 1960s progressed.

On the Hopi Reservation, a bitterness settled in—just as predicted by BIA Area Director Allan Harper when he recommended against Boyden's appointment as general counsel and the de facto recognition of the centralized council. The conversations about coal, water, and the foreign constitution of 1934 went on late into the night in the rectangular, layered village buildings. The traditional leaders wrote many letters to the outside world. As early as 1949 they beseeched President Truman to prevent any mineral leasing. To the traditionalists, as they said in a 1959 petition to BIA

# Black Mesa

Commissioner Glenn Emmons, the work of Boyden and the Tribal Council was a double wrong: the Hopi's sacred homeland, Black Mesa, should not be mined at all; but in any event the matter should be "settled in accordance with our ancient knowledge and with the consent of our Hopi Traditional Leaders." Thomas Banyacya was one of the spokesmen: "You pass all kinds of laws without asking us. You will make us landless, homeless people. This land is the only land we have. This is the land of the Great Spirit. European people can go back to their lands. Native people have no place to go."

On May 16, 1966, John Boyden brought a proposed coal lease for the Black Mesa Mine before the Hopi Tribal Council. Peabody Coal Company would do the mining. (The actual lease was with Sentry Royalty Company, a subsidiary of Peabody, but the parties knew that Peabody would later take over the lease and do the mining. The transaction was commonly referred to as "the Peabody lease.") The proceeds from this lease, on the Joint Use Area, would be divided equally between the two tribes. There would be two mines, Black Mesa and Kayenta. Peabody already had signed a separate lease with the Navajo for the Kayenta Mine, on Navajo land. The coal from the mines would be transported to two undetermined sites where power plants would be built. This took place before environmental impact statements. There were no public hearings. Few people, Indian or non-Indian, in or out of government or business, knew about the transactions.

Nothing on record indicates that John Boyden ever provided the Hopi Tribal Council with any substantial analysis of the Peabody lease. The Tribal Council minutes, which usually were complete, show little discussion of the Peabody lease. There is no indication that Boyden explained the magnitude of the operation and its probable impact—that, for example, the two mines on Black Mesa, directly adjacent to each other, would constitute the largest coal strip mining complex in the country. The minutes reflect no information on whether the Hopi Tribe would be receiving the highest possible financial return—especially in light of the pivotal role of Black Mesa coal in the development of the American Southwest.

Nor was there much mention of water, so scarce on Black Mesa, so central to the people on Black Mesa. Peabody would be slurrying coal to one of the power plants, using 4,000 acre-feet of groundwater annually from under Black Mesa. Boyden briefly mentioned that the Hopi would "benefit" from the lease of water but gave no information on whether the Hopi would receive market value for their water. Nor did the lawyer disclose whether he had any ties to Peabody Coal Company.

The Peabody lease decision, one of the weightiest in the tribe's long history, was now up to the Hopi Tribal Council. But this was a wholly new kind of government on Black Mesa, created in 1936 after an election under the Indian Reorganization Act, dormant from 1943 to 1955, revived by the tribal attorney, John Sterling Boyden, a decade previously.

# KACHINA

The kachinas at Home Dance do successive rounds, continuing all day, of their rain dances and songs. When the kachinas left the square after the conclusion of the first round, which lasted about forty-five minutes, I moved down into one of the passageways to get a closer view. I was now at ground level and when the kachinas returned, I was startled at their size: nearly 8 feet to the tips of the parrot and eagle feathers on their *tabletas*— their tall, dramatic masks. Hopis had explained to me that although their children do not worship kachinas, the kachinas do excite the greatest wonder and awe in them, in somewhat the same way that Santa Claus does for our children.

If the children are in wonder and awe, so is everyone else. These are the

# ENDURANCE

Hemis kachinas, sometimes improperly referred to as Niman (Nee-*mahn*) kachinas because Home Dance is also called Niman Kachina. From here I can see the exquisite detail of the costumes of the thirty Hemis kachinas. Their *tabletas* seem to have slightly different designs, but all use a background of turquoise with cloud and half-moon symbols painted in red, white, black, and yellow. The kachinas carry turquoise rattles and wear white and black rope sashes, red moccasins with white soles, full red fox pelts hanging from the belts, and elaborate red sashes, also hung from the belt. I finally realized that they created the sharp, dry, rattling sound by working in unison the desert tortoise shells each kachina had strapped to his right calf.

The dance includes ten other kachinas, called kachina *manas,* who, with their red and white shawls and black wigs with circular whorls on the sides, kneel in front of the Hemis kachinas. The kachina *manas* are less dramatic than the Hemis kachinas (most things I have seen are), but they drive the dance by scraping painted sticks with cut notches across deer scapulas and ceremonial dried gourds. They begin slowly. At first it seems they are tuning their instruments, but they are making frog sounds. Then their rain noises steadily build up. When they get into full swing, they are metaphorically creating thunderstorms.

The songs, sung by the Hemis kachinas, are a low, driving rumble accompanied by the rasping of the kachina *manas'* instruments. The kachinas are led by a kachina father. It is a great honor in the village to be chosen, and Neil Monongwe has been selected for many years. He is an older man and the responsibilities, which begin in February, are very heavy. The Hotevilla residents all realize that this will be his last Home Dance as kachina father.

The bare-chested kachina father, and a younger man in training, sprinkle cornmeal on the Hemis kachinas as they sing. The father instructs them to come closer, to touch shoulders, like clouds clustering together. He is also encouraging all of us to come together, to be participants, not just observers, in the prayers for rain.

In between some of the songs, the Hemis kachinas pass out the long

# Kachina

stalks of corn they have carried down to the square. The Hopi receiving the bounty do so silently, with no overt thanks. You know they are reverent about the corn, though, if you have seen the cornfields the stalks come from. Almost all of the farming at Hopi is dry farming. The seeds are planted deep, at least a foot, to reach moist soil. The rows are 5 or 6 feet apart and each plant is wide-spaced, so that the root systems won't compete for the scarce water. Black Mesa has a great many of these carefully tended fields, some just a few rows, some an acre or more. The Hopi have been called the world's finest dry farmers, and they grow more corn than anything else.

The kachinas did two more rounds, the air beginning to fill with the smells of roasting chiles and cornmeal, tortillas, and stew from the kitchens near the square. Then it was time for the long—two hours or so—midday break. Our friends from the village had invited us to lunch, so we went by their home. The dark, cool rooms were packed with family and visitors. After lunch we went out to our vans to reapply sunblock and fill our water bottles with ice water from the spigot of our big aluminum container.

That done, we began walking back to the square so that we wouldn't miss any of the rounds. We knew that the Home Dance was accelerating. During the morning, the kachinas' gifts became increasingly elaborate, as some of the cornstalks had tiny, painted bows and arrows attached to them. On our walk, it began to seem that we might get some relief from the intense sun of the late morning. A light cloud cover had formed.

We passed the eagle. He had been gathered from his nest as a chick, and had spent his life in captivity, but seemed nonetheless fierce for it. A gust of wind came up and he rose with it to the height of his 4-foot tether, flapping his wings furiously. He lives for the wind rising up from the desert floor to the mesa. I can't help my ambivalence about his being laid to rest tomorrow. But he is surely the right being to take prayers upward, powerful and true.

I walked into the square with a Hopi man I met at lunch. I asked him whether he thought the village would continue to keep Home Dance open. "The Hopi way," he answered, "is that you trust everybody. If a stranger asks you for something, you give it to him. If he breaks that trust, that's his problem, not the Hopi's problem. The Hopi aren't the victims, other people are the victims."

"But many people have violated our trust. Outsiders act disrespectfully at the dances, or they take pictures, or make drawings, which they are not allowed to do. So, many of the villages have closed their dances. We haven't yet, but we might. It's a matter of whether the people of the village will still be willing to trust."

John Boyden always denied that he ever represented Peabody Coal Company. There were always contrary rumors, however, supported by the fact that in the critical years of 1966 and 1967 Peabody Coal was listed as a client of Boyden's firm in Martindale-Hubbell, the professional directory for lawyers. Boyden himself dismissed the allegations: "You may be sure that I have represented the Hopi Tribe for a good many years and have never represented any other client whose interests in the subject matter were adverse to the Hopi Tribe at the time of such representation." When the charges continued after Boyden's death, John Kennedy, Boyden's law partner, explained that the firm's small amount of work for Peabody "was done by an office mate—and that Boyden was unaware of the relationship." Kennedy angrily denounced the accusations of Boyden's tie with Peabody as "baseless, unfair and inaccurate."

Peabody Coal itself denied any conflict involving Boyden, the Hopi, and the company. In 1979, the Indian Law Resource Center, conducting research for its "Report to the Hopi Kikmongwis" on the Boyden–Hopi issue, wrote Peabody concerning the matter. The general counsel to Peabody responded by saying that Boyden had never represented Peabody. He acknowledged that Boyden had done work for Kennecott Copper in 1968, when it acquired Peabody in a major corporate transaction, but emphasized this was not direct representation of Peabody: "It is important to stress that Mr. Boyden represented the buyer [Kennecott] and its lenders in this transaction and did not represent Peabody." The general counsel added that he had discussed the matter thoroughly with one E. R. Phelps, Peabody's vice president for engineering during the 1960s, with responsibility for the Black Mesa mines:

> *Mr. Phelps does not recall any situations where Mr. Boyden represented anyone other than the Hopi Tribe other than the situation described above where Mr. Boyden represented Kennecott and its lenders in the transaction whereby Peabody was acquired in 1968.*

Yet all the denials now ring hollow. And although I suppose that John Boyden will be on my mind whenever I go to Black Mesa, his dealings weighed especially heavy on me at Home Dance this day. Just a week ago, I had received a phone call, late at night, from my research assistant, Cherche Prezeau. She is quite a proper young woman and I don't believe she had ever called me at home before, much less at such a late hour, after 10 P.M. She was calling from Salt Lake City, where I had asked her to go in order to finish our review of John Boyden's papers.

"Charles, I'm really sorry to bother you so late, but I just had to call. I spent most of the day in the University of Utah library. They recently put out a whole new batch of John Boyden's papers. They've never before been open to the public.

"Charles, there's a whole file on his work for Peabody Coal. I can't even begin to tell you how bad it is. All I can say is, I'm driving back tomorrow and I think you had better read it right away."

I spent the next evening going over the file, and it was a sickening, depressing experience. It literally caused my stomach to hurt and I've had that same feeling every time I have returned to that file.

The Boyden papers that my other research assistant, Brian Kuehl, had found two years earlier were highly significant. They contained newspaper accounts identifying Boyden as Peabody's lawyer and a transcript of his appearance before a Utah administrative board on behalf of Peabody in connection with a proposed power plant that would use coal and water obtained by Peabody from Black Mesa. This was the situation that presented a conflict with his work for the Ute, as well as the Hopi.

These new documents, however, went much further, and were far more detailed and graphic. The file, labeled "Peabody Coal Company," contained correspondence between Boyden and Peabody Coal executives and representatives. It also contained his attorney billings for work done for Peabody between 1964 and 1971.

Boyden's representation of the Hopi against the Navajo in the land dispute may indeed have been loyal and tenacious. His role as tribal attorney in the development of Black Mesa, however, paints a very different picture. There is no longer any question that he violated his high duty to the Hopi by working concurrently for Peabody Coal during the decisive years of the 1960s. The correspondence was very substantive and, as well, showed a close, ongoing personal as well as professional relationship between Boyden and Peabody officials. Several letters to and from Peabody executives discuss water and mineral rights on Black Mesa. His main correspondent at Peabody was E. R. ("Ed") Phelps—the same E. R. Phelps who, in the 1979 letter from Peabody to the Indian Law Resource Center, could not "recall any situations where Mr. Boyden represented anyone other than the Hopi Tribe." The salutations in Boyden's letters to Phelps in Boyden's capacity as Hopi attorney were "Dear Mr. Phelps." In his Peabody role they were "Dear Ed."

Boyden worked actively for Peabody over the seven-year period. Among other things, he reported on his meetings, on behalf of Peabody, with the governor of Utah and the state engineer. The file shows that Boyden represented Peabody in October 1964 at a hearing in front of the Utah State Land Board; he urged the board to sell Peabody land for a proposed power plant that would use Black Mesa coal. The file also contained the transcript (which had also been included in the earlier papers) of Boyden's appearance on behalf of Peabody, before the Utah Water and Power Board in 1964. At this hearing, when the Hopi were deep in continuing negotiations with Peabody over the leasing of Black Mesa coal and water, Boyden forcefully argued Peabody's side on water rights—a presentation that included Peabody's statement that a "possibility is to obtain Indian water rights."

Indeed Peabody did lease water as well as minerals from the Hopi when the Hopi Tribal Council saddled itself with a very bad business deal by approving the lease for the Black Mesa Mine. The tribe received 3.335 percent of gross sales (the royalty for the Navajo Tribe was the same), which was below accepted royalty rates at the time. Even worse, the lease did not have any reopener—a standard provision allowing renegotiation after an agreed period, usually ten years. By 1978, just eight years after Peabody began mining the coal, a confidential Interior Department audit concluded that the royalty rate did not "accurately reflect or compare with current rates." The return was "only a little more than half of what the [federal] government is receiving" for coal leases on federal public lands.

The Black Mesa lease had other undesirable features from the Hopi standpoint. It allowed Peabody control over much more land than was customary or, apparently, legal—40,000 acres as compared to the limit of 2,560 acres in the federal regulations for Indian leasing. For the right to take 4,000 acre-feet of Hopi water each year, in a lease signed at the height of the rush on the Colorado Plateau's limited water supply, Peabody paid the Hopi the laughable rate of $1.67 per acre-foot.

Further issues, all resolved favorably to Peabody and against the Hopi, continued to arise after the 1966 lease. In 1967, Peabody wrote Boyden wanting to complete the formality of assigning the lease from Sentry to Peabody. The Navajo had insisted on a payment of $100,000 for a similar assignment. Instead of trying to bargain for the same payment for his tribal client, Boyden wrote Peabody that he would try to "expedite" the matter. Then he wrote the tribal chairman that the Hopi had no legal basis for objecting to the transaction and opposing any payment from Peabody on "the principle involved in attempting to extract money from the coal company under these circumstances." Boyden then nonetheless gave the Tribal Council a vague assurance that the Hopi would receive the same payment from Peabody as the Navajo had received, but in fact no payment was ever made.

# Kachina

Boyden passed up another opportunity to advance the Hopi Tribe's interests in 1969. The BIA had expressed concern about the low payment rate for the use of Hopi groundwater: "The transportation of coal slurry [the Tribal Council had approved a right-of-way for a coal-slurry pipeline] will require a tremendous amount of water. . . . [W]e feel that a much greater amount should be charged for the water if possible." The council decided to "defer action on the matter" and refer it to Boyden "for further review," but the issue was apparently never raised with Peabody.

Perhaps the most dubious decision flowing from the Boyden–Peabody connection, other than the 1966 lease itself, was made in 1967. This took place in the middle of intense activity, involving all the southwestern states, over the Central Arizona Project. To get the CAP through Congress, Stewart Udall and other leaders, under pressure from the public opinion that David Brower had aroused, agreed that the Navajo Generating Station should replace the two proposed dams in the Grand Canyon; this would provide the energy needed to pump CAP water on its uphill run from the Colorado River in western Arizona over to Phoenix and Tucson. Black Mesa coal would fuel the new power plant: Navajo Generating Station. But the 1966 leases with the Hopi and Navajo could not provide enough coal to slurry coal to Mohave Generating Station and also supply the new project: at 2,250 megawatts, Navajo Generating Station would be the largest coal-fired plant on the Colorado Plateau.

Peabody, working closely with Western Energy Supply and Transmission Associates (WEST), which was coordinating the Grand Plan for energy development in the Southwest, had seen the congressional compromise coming. In 1967, E. R. Phelps, John Boyden's colleague at Peabody, contacted both the Hopi and Navajo chairmen, sending a copy to Boyden, with a request for additional coal-lease acreage. Phelps wrote: "WEST Associates . . . are planning new power plants in the area [which] . . . would contain two 1000 megawatt units." Phelps calculated that existing leases would provide Peabody with 148 million tons of coal but now, with Navajo Generating Station, Peabody would need 230 tons. Thus, Phelps wrote, "there is a deficit of 82 million tons [of coal]." Peabody wanted to expand the lease area on Black Mesa by ten thousand acres, or fifteen square miles.

This was not news to Boyden, who had been working for Peabody on this very project since 1964. He had long known that a major plant might be located, as Navajo Generating Station was, at Page on the Arizona side of the state line. But Boyden's comprehensive understanding of the Big Buildup and the centrality of Black Mesa coal worked to the advantage of Peabody, not the Hopi. With Boyden's support, the Hopi Tribal Council agreed to the expanded lease area. Despite the urgency to Peabody and the tribe's truly significant bargaining leverage, the Hopi received no payments for this major lease expansion other than a continuation of the below-market royalties provided for in the 1966 lease.

Hopi traditionalists opposed the leasing at every turn. In addition to their many letters and petitions to presidents, the Interior Department, and congressmen, they traveled to the cities, the universities, even other countries, to explain how their sacred land was about to be torn apart. "Hopi clans," traditional leaders wrote,

> have traveled all over the Black Mesa area leaving our sacred shrines, ruins, burial grounds and prayer feathers behind. Today, our sacred ceremonies, during which we pray for such things as rain, good crops, and a long and good life, depend on spiritual contact with these forces left behind on Black Mesa. . . . If these places are disturbed or destroyed, our prayers and ceremonies will lose their force and a great calamity will befall not only the Hopi, but all of mankind.

The traditionalists—NARF lawyers Joe Brecher, Bruce Greene, and John Echohawk handled the case—even sued in federal court in 1971. Their position was that the Tribal Council lacked authority to act on behalf of the Hopi people. The council was barely limping along in 1966. Only eleven of seventeen seats had been filled. Of these, just six council members had been certified by Kikmongwi, as the Hopi Constitution required. Boyden argued for the progressives. He claimed that the other five representatives had been validly appointed by various other means and that the rump council's approval of the lease was valid. At best, the legal justification for the Tribal Council's action was ambiguous. For the traditionalists, who seem surely to have represented a majority of the Hopi, this was not merely a council chosen in an election that most voters boycotted. This was a council that was never properly constituted or convened in the first place.

The courts dismissed the traditionalists' suit on grounds of sovereign immunity—the centuries-old British doctrine (also invoked against the widows of the Navajo uranium miners in their lawsuit against the United States) that "the king can do no wrong." Since the Hopi Tribe was a sovereign state, the court reasoned, the Tribal Council could not be sued without its consent even if its action were illegal. To the traditionalists, the judicial ruling was the ultimate study in circularity. In effect the judicial opinions said to them: you allege that the Hopi Tribal Council has no authority to act for the Hopi Tribe; but the Hopi Tribe is a sovereign that cannot be sued; so therefore your suit against its Tribal Council must be dismissed. And so the mining complex on Black Mesa went full steam ahead.

In the past two decades, the Hopi Tribe has taken a number of corrective actions. Spurred in significant part by the conflict-of-interest controversy in 1986 involving Boyden's partner after Boyden had died, the Hopi empowered themselves by taking their government back from law offices in Salt Lake City. Vernon Masayesva speaks from his perspective gained over many decades. Gone are the days, he explains, "when lawyers were father figures, when you don't question or criticize, when you accept their word." Now, at the Tribal Council's insistence, the old centralization of legal representation has been eliminated: the tribe has water specialists for water matters, trial lawyers for the land litigation, and on-reservation attorneys for handling ongoing business and coordination with the firms in Denver and Washington, D.C. Now, instead of pressing decisions on the tribe, the Hopi's lawyers give the Tribal Council options and explain the risks and advantages of each.

In 1987, the Hopi and their eminent Washington lawyer, Reid Peyton Chambers, succeeded in renegotiating the Peabody lease. Until then the

Hopi had never received more than $3 million in any year in royalties—in all, the tribe lost tens of millions of dollars between 1970 and 1987. Under the renegotiated lease, the tribe began receiving a standard royalty (divided with the Navajo) of 12.5 percent of the value of the coal—doubling annual Hopi royalties to more than $7 million. The old figure of $1.67 for an acre-foot of water was scrapped—and replaced by a payment of $300 per acre-foot. In a provision the Hopi insisted upon to give Peabody an incentive for water conservation, the price for water doubles after the first 2,800 acre-feet. The new lease contains a reopener clause: after ten years, the royalties can be renegotiated, but they can only remain stable or go up. The renegotiated lease did not heal all the old wounds—it did not recoup the many lost millions of dollars, nor did it prevent the scouring of sacred land—but the new lease did eliminate some of the bitter taste of financial injustice.

The Tribal Council, organized in 1936 under the new tribal constitution and resuscitated by the tribal lawyer in the 1950s as large-scale mining became a possibility, remains in place. So do many of the tensions built into that document. Yet the Hopi strive to be sure that the old values are embedded in their decisions. Problems, many of them, remain, but they will be addressed by the Hopi themselves. When Hopi people go to their tribal headquarters and walk in the front door, no longer do they confront the image of John Boyden. The Hopi have found a way. And although some of the trappings may be different, underneath it is the same way it has always been.

The mines on Black Mesa embody the contrasts between the traditions and antiquity of the Hopi way and the race-ahead outside world. The costs have been high—both in terms of the impacts on the Hopi's spiritual homeland and in terms of lost revenues due to the tribe's failure to use its enormous leverage to gain economic benefits from the lease and related transactions with Peabody Coal. Yet the two tribes, Hopi and Navajo, also gained many benefits from the mines. This is especially so for the Navajo. The Navajo Nation receives higher revenues than the Hopi Tribe since it splits the proceeds from the Black Mesa mine with the Hopi but also obtains all royalties from the Kayenta Mine on Navajo land north of the 1882 executive order reservation. In all, the Navajo Nation receives about $26 million annually whereas the Hopi Tribe receives $7 million. Peabody, the largest employer of American Indians in the country, has a workforce at the two mines of about nine hundred employees, 93 percent of whom are Indians. These are steady, high-paying jobs, and a few Navajos have moved into management positions. Almost all the jobs go to Navajos, since the entrance to the mine is from the north, where the Navajo town of Kayenta is the closest settlement. From the Hopi villages at the other end of Black Mesa, the only all-weather route is through Tuba City, a drive of 130 miles or so each way.

All the while, as the revenues pour in, the blasting, digging, scouring, pumping, slurrying, and railroading continue at a frenetic pace. The ambiguities and uncertainties continue, too. "It's very simple," one Navajo leader told me. "We're hooked. When you're hooked, you lose your options."

The mining operations may have contributed to a new set of problems. In the mid-1990s, the water situation on Black Mesa took a sharp turn for the worse: the groundwater under Black Mesa is dropping, and springs have diminished or dried up entirely. The many skilled Hopi farmers see the effects every day, and so do the people who haul their household water. The Interior Department and even Peabody agree that the aquifer is going down. It is unclear, though, why. Peabody's pumping may be the cause, but the company's claim that it takes water only from a deep aquifer, unconnected to the shallow surface aquifer feeding the springs, may be correct. The crisis—for the Hopi have no perennial streams on their reservation—may be caused instead by overpumping from the shallow aquifer in the towns of Tuba City and Moenkopi, far to the west.

Vernon Masayesva believes to his depths that the water crisis at Hopi is due to the Peabody pumping. He has seen the long series of modern events. His life changed in the early 1970s when, as a young man, he listened late into the night in the pueblo homes in Hotevilla as Thomas Banyacya, David Monongwe, and the other traditionalists talked about the immorality of leasing sacred land on Black Mesa. For him, Black Mesa, water, and the soul of the Hopi are one. He laments, "All of our songs are about rain. Our poetry, our kachinas, are about rain. The mining of our water violates our beliefs. When you sell something that sacred, it doesn't sit right, it bothers you, it sits on your conscience." Sil Perla, Peabody's general superintendent for the two mines, speaking not directly about water but generally about the whole matrix of jobs and money and culture and Black Mesa, says sympathetically but also matter-of-factly: "The Hopi want to go back to the way they were twenty years ago. That's impossible. Time goes on."

**W**anting to get a view from different angles, I watched the first round of afternoon dances from a flat roof above the northeast corner of the square. I could count six kivas around the village, the distinctive uneven tops of their ladders sticking up through the entrances. The kachinas came in now, using the passageway just below me. Still sluggish from lunch, I was taken aback by their vigor. They had been fasting for four days.

As the kachina *manas* ritually made storm rumbles with their ratcheted sticks and gourds and the Hemis kachinas broke into their chant, I found myself wondering about John Boyden's motivations. He was an accomplished lawyer, in many ways a good man. He came to many Hopi dances and, like myself, tried to bring his boys, and his daughters, whenever he could. By every account he cared deeply for the Hopi, many of whom were his passionate loyalists. At Boyden's funeral, Abbott Sekaquaptewa, then Hopi tribal chairman, spoke with genuine warmth, affectionately referring to him as "Big John." Boyden had two kachinas in his office: the owl, a warning to watch for danger to Indian people, and the bear, the warrior. His collection of Indian art, which included many kachinas, was magnificent and he donated it to Utah State University, where it is on impressive display.

But balanced against the good were incidents that ranged from the heavy-handed to the poisonous: the "share and share alike" resolution in

1950 that reordered the property interests and litigation rights of the three Ute bands in one fell swoop; his representation of two Ute tribal groups at once when they were dividing up the tribal land and other assets; and his machinations as counsel for the Hopi, Utes, and Peabody Coal at the same time—while keeping the Peabody connection hidden from the tribes—when scarce Colorado River water and Black Mesa were at stake.

Good lawyers, almost all of them, avoid even a brush with a conflict of interest. It is a matter of honor, not just a rule in the Canons of Professional Responsibility. Lawyers can use the word "sacred," too, and many would use it to describe their duty to their clients.

I don't think he did it only for the money. The fact that the Hopi made him rich would, if anything, have made him toe the mark even more. The money may have been one factor, but I suspect it was no more than that. Beyond that, there was the ambition his local paper noted back when he was on his high school debate team: the ambition that prompted him twice to seek the governorship of Utah. He certainly coveted his role as one of the main players in the Big Buildup that meant so much to Utah and the Southwest.

Just as important as his ambition, I have come to believe, was his certitude, the absolute conviction that he knew what was best for society. The Utes would benefit from termination by being liberated from reservation life. The water of the Colorado River could better be used by Salt Lake City and a coal-fired power plant than by the Utes or Hopi. The Hopi could be brought into the twentieth century only through the revenue from coal mining. Toward these ends, he might have justified ramrodding some tribal councils and even engaging in some conflicts of interest. This certitude, if not the conflicts of interest, put Boyden in a large body of people from Brigham Young to Nathan Meeker to John Collier to Wayne Aspinall to Stewart Udall—men who knew to an absolute certainty what was right for the Colorado Plateau. Conquest by certitude.

There was, too, his Mormonism. Boyden grew up devout in Coalville and remained so all his life. He was a ward bishop in Salt Lake City from

1953 through 1958. Only the most faithful are called to be bishops, a heavy, time-consuming responsibility. One of the speakers at Boyden's funeral in 1980 was Marion G. Romney of the First Presidency, one of the three highest officials in the LDS Church.

Documents in the file that my research assistant found showed that John Boyden hardly left his religion at home when he went to Black Mesa. LDS officials contacted him on several occasions to ask his help in obtaining tribal support for meeting houses on Hopi tribal land. Boyden professed neutrality. But in his capacity as tribal attorney, he advanced his church's case. Pointing to the freedom of religion clause in the Hopi Constitution, he made to the Hopi Tribal Council "a plea for a right of religious assembly for the over 450 members of the Church of Jesus Christ of Latter-day Saints on the reservation." His legal argument was specious: the right of free exercise of religion would not, for example, require the federal government or a state to lease government land to a church; nor would the free-exercise provision require the Hopi government to do so. After Boyden's plea, the requested LDS meeting house was built near Keams Canyon. In another instance, after the Mormons had constructed a meeting house at the village of Polacca, a church official thanked Boyden for "the tremendous work you have done in getting the site."

In the era when the critical events at Ute and Hopi were unfolding, it was difficult for devout Mormons to disentangle completely from "the Curse of the Lamanites"—the idea that Indians are a special group to be converted to Mormonism, made "white and delightsome," and thereby saved. This seems to have been part of Boyden's thinking. On at least some occasions, he referred to Indians as "Lamanites." To be sure, he had many Indian friends. Still, in the last analysis, did his religion prevent him from treating them as full equals?

But the truest observation about John Boyden came from Vine Deloria Jr., the Sioux historian and lawyer, when I asked him why he thought Boyden had been so paternalistic and overbearing with the Hopi and Ute. Vine has a strong perspective on Indian policy in the 1940s and later because he not only studied but lived those times. He knew Boyden and most of the other key figures personally. After making his usual gratuitous inquiry about the health of my "father, Ernest," Vine grew serious. This subject was serious to him and he had thought about it a lot. He spoke slowly: "Look. To understand guys like Boyden, Wilkinson, and Norman Littell, you've got to understand the historical context. Nobody really believed that Indians had any rights. Nobody thought they would be around very long. 'We'll just try to help that little band of survivors as best we can.'"

Indians, in other words, were not equals—not in John Boyden's mind, not in Mormon society, not in American society. Weak and confused, the Hopi and the other tribes had few ways to combat the many faces of termination—of conquest—during the 1950s and 1960s.

**T**he gift of giving grows more elaborate as the day moves on. During the last few rounds, the square becomes the analogy to Christmas that is often made about Home Dance. For weeks the men at the village have been busy making gifts, mostly flat dolls—kachina-like figures carved and painted on thin boards—and kachina dolls, some small and simple, some large and exquisitely carved. Each of the presents is tied to a cornstalk. There are so many that the kachinas have to bring in several armloads for each round.

The restraint of the children is incomprehensible to me. They stand there and a Hemis kachina—huge, beautiful, powerful, mystical—approaches. These little people remain perfectly still, betrayed only by their eyes, which widen, widen, and widen as it becomes ever clearer that they may be a chosen one. Don't move, the little girl off to my right is thinking, I can't extend my arms just yet. The kachina may be going to the nearby cousin. Then! The kachina is right in front of me, so towering, so strong, so giving. Somehow, miraculously, the corn plant and the tied-on kachina doll are in my arms. I can't run out from the square, but I am allowed to walk. Calmly. Slowly. No show of excitement on my face. Now, I'm past the last row! A few more steps and I can run! I'm off, back to my own living room with this magical kachina that can teach me, inspire me, be with me always.

# ENDURANCE

It was 6:30 P.M. as the kachinas filed out of the square. The last round would be a ceremony where all the young women who had been married in traditional Hopi ceremonies during the past year were presented to the gathering. This was an important moment for the brides. Hopi weddings involve two weeks of ceremony and this was the last time they would wear their wedding dresses.

I saw Becky Masayesva, and we talked about Home Dance. This was a doubly important day for her since her daughter, Denise, had recently been married. She showed her enthusiasm for still another reason.

"Isn't this something?" she said, looking up.

I had been enjoying the clouds for the comfort they brought from the July heat, but I hadn't noticed how they had thickened and darkened, or thought about their significance on this day.

The rain was coming down steadily, though lightly, as the kachinas returned, not to the square but to a street nearby. The crowd had swollen during the last rounds to a thousand or more. All the rooftops were packed. The front door to one of the homes opened and the brides came out into the street. There was no applause, but the brides received the honor of the gathering's pure quiet and attentiveness.

The kachina father and the kachina *manas* started up the songs of the Hemis kachinas. Soon a surrounding lightning storm ignited. Lightning reserves its best displays for high mesas in the American Southwest. The streaks cracked the sky in all directions. Thunder. The rain began coming down in sheets. It was at the tailend of dusk now. No one wanted to leave, although some did. Drenched, my friends and I found vacant eaves and moved under them. A Hopi man next to me said quietly: "This Home Dance will last this village a long, long time."

The kachinas moved into single file for the last time, ready to begin their journey to San Francisco Peaks. This was the time when Pueblo people could pluck sprigs of spruce from the kachinas, who stood in line. The people did their work so deliberately, and took so much longer than I had imagined, that at first I worried for the kachinas, bare-chested, wet, exhausted. Yet they stood in line erect and absolutely still. Then I realized

# Kachina

how exactly wrong my reaction was. This was no ordeal. This was their moment: a chance to extend a final gift of spruce after all the many gifts of the long day.

The rain softened into a drizzle. The people had finished gathering their spruce. The kachina father moved to the head of the line. A flash bright-whitened the street, the square, the village, the whole mesa. The violent thunderclap shattered the air almost immediately. The noise and vibrations came from no specific place, they came from everywhere, from on high, from all sides, up from the ground. Right then the kachina father called out and the kachinas broke into stride, their work done, heading toward home.

# DRUID ARCH

**M**y destination—I was off by myself this week—was the backcountry of Canyonlands National Park in Utah. The story of the Colorado Plateau includes the injuries we have inflicted but it also encompasses the sweeping landscapes of wild country that have endured—and they make a better and happier part of the story. For wilderness hones the body and inflames the mind; it offers the prose of pure biology and geology and the poetry of elegance and rarity. During this journey to Canyonlands, I would find something else in the wilderness. At the far end of Elephant Canyon, I found that wilderness has healing power.

I planned to hike into the historic Confluence, where the Colorado and Green Rivers meet. Another place I wanted to visit was Druid Arch. I had

# Druid Arch

seen photographs of it, imposing and freestanding; this arch must be one of the finest in the canyon country. The name intrigued me, too. My father had claimed to be a Druid priest. I was never clear about what that meant or how seriously he took it. I did know that Druidism, based on the worship of nature gods and including animal sacrifice, was an ancient Celtic religion suppressed by the Romans. In recent times, I knew, there has been a revival and Druid festivals are held today in England and Ireland.

The connection between my father and the arch might have had no rational basis. But I made the connection nonetheless and it gave an added air of mysticism to what by then had become the most mystical place I know: the wild Colorado Plateau, land of Coyote, Twin War Gods, and the Old People, land of canyons and mesas with unknowable secrets, vistas with no limits except the human imagination, and fantastical redrock monuments and arches.

**A**fter getting in late and pitching my tent in the near dark, I headed out the next morning from my campsite in the warm, clear October air toward the Confluence. Early in the century I would have been visiting the junction of the Grand River and the Green River. Below the Confluence, the combined flow of the two branches was, then as now, called the Colorado River; the beginnings of the Colorado, in other words, were in Utah. Above that point, the river flowing down from the state of Colorado was called, not the Colorado, but the Grand.

Then, in the 1920s, Colorado tourism interests—looking for an advantage against their neighbor states—rearranged the geography of the Southwest. They persuaded Congress to jettison the name Grand River and change it to Colorado River, thereby allowing the namesake state to claim the distinction of having the headwaters of the Colorado River within its borders. So the origins of the Southwest's largest river now lie, not in Utah at the Confluence, but in Rocky Mountain National Park in north central Colorado.

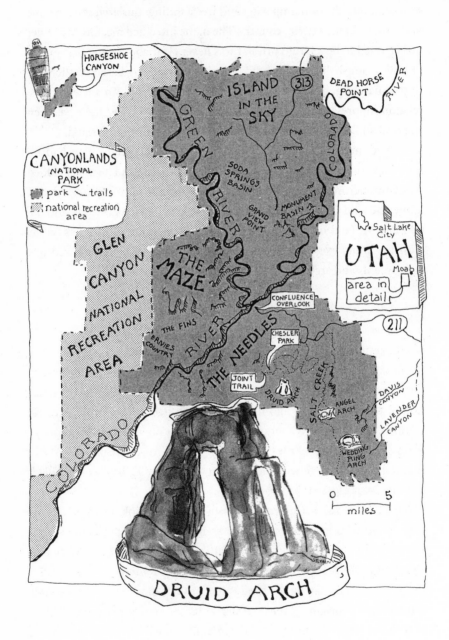

HORSESHOE
CANYON

ISLAND
IN THE
SKY

313

DEAD HORSE
POINT

GREEN RIVER

COLORADO RIVER

CANYONLANDS
NATIONAL
PARK

■ park trails
national recreation
area

SODA
SPRINGS
BASIN

MONUMENT
BASIN

GRAND
VIEW
POINT

Salt Lake
City

UTAH

Moab

area in
detail

GLEN
CANYON

THE
MAZE

NATIONAL

RECREATION

AREA

CONFLUENCE
OVERLOOK

211

THE FINS

ERNIES
COUNTRY

RIVER

THE NEEDLES

CHESLER
PARK

JOINT
TRAIL

DRUID ARCH

SALT CREEK

ANGEL
ARCH

DAVIS
CANYON

LAVENDER
CANYON

WEDDING
RING
ARCH

COLORADO

0        5
—— miles

DRUID ARCH

# Druid Arch

The 6-mile trail to the Confluence crosses north–south ridges made of Cedar Mesa Sandstone and drops down into the valleys between. The long views all around include The Grabens, with its high and wide skyline of parallel rows of sandstone blocks. A dirt road, which allows four-wheel drivers to take a slow, roundabout route, goes within a quarter of a mile of the Confluence overlook. A couple of four-wheel-drive vehicles were parked there. The handful of people didn't interfere with my desire to be alone, for there's plenty of room along the high cliffs above the Confluence.

A thousand feet below Confluence Point, the two greatest rivers of the Southwest come together and form a handsomely carved "Y"—the Green from the left (west), the Colorado from the right, the combined flow the stem. On this day the Green was siltier and the Colorado stronger. The river just below the meeting point was reddish-brown on the west one-third, green on the east two-thirds. (On another day, depending on such things as snowpacks and storms in the headwaters of the two rivers, the effect can be just the opposite.) A half mile below the Confluence, the Grand-Colorado color continued to hold its own, the eastern third still completely clear. Eventually the currents melded into a uniform brownish-green before surging into Cataract Canyon.

There is beauty and strength here along with the symbolism of these rivers joining—you could call the Confluence the heart of the West—but the Confluence also was the site of a surprise moment when new currents began to flow on the Colorado Plateau.

Created in 1964, at the high crest of the Big Buildup, Canyonlands National Park traces to a proposal, made back in 1936, by the Utah State Planning Board. The agency saw significant tourist revenues from a new park in this "wonderland." United States Senator Elbert Thomas of Utah enthused: "I believe it would be a fine thing . . . if we could have another national park in Utah [Zion, Bryce Canyon, and six smaller units had already been designated] based upon this inspiring region." The state's suggested acreage totaled 570 square miles.

In June 1936, just two months after the state's initiative, the National Park Service, under the conservation-minded Interior Secretary Harold

Ickes, upped the ante more than tenfold. Ickes called for a 7,000-square-mile Escalante National Monument. The political climate nationally was such that the blockbuster initiative—the monument would have comprised about 8 percent of Utah—seemed to have a chance, but communities in southern Utah would have none of it and the proposal went dormant. A small group of locals, however, and later Bates Wilson, long-time park superintendent at Arches National Monument and called "the Father of Canyonlands," kept the idea alive.

Then the movement for Canyonlands got a major boost from the unintended consequences of an airplane flight arranged by Floyd Dominy, the dynamic commissioner of reclamation who presided over the dam construction of the Big Buildup. In 1961, Dominy took the new interior secretary, Stewart Udall, up to get an aerial view of Dominy's pet idea: "Junction Dam." This was the impoundment, slated to be built just below the Confluence, that would have created a reservoir larger than Lake Powell and flooded Moab. When Udall looked down to survey the scene, however, his eyes failed to see a dam site: "I saw the Needles and all those monuments and formations and all the rest. I had no idea anything like that existed there. I didn't say anything to Dominy, but to myself I thought, 'God almighty, that's a national park.'" By 1964, Congress had established Canyonlands National Park with Bates Wilson as its first superintendent.

At 527 square miles, or 337,000 acres, Canyonlands is just a remnant of Ickes' original Escalante National Monument idea but a glorious place nonetheless, most of it still wild. My Confluence and Druid Arch hikes were over in The Needles District, the site that first inspired Udall. Across the Colorado River, almost impenetrable, lies The Maze. To the northwest, detached from the main body of the park, is Horseshoe Canyon, holding the Great Gallery: Fremont pictographs that rank among the most elegant rock art panels in the world. The north end of the park, between the Green and the Colorado, is called Island in the Sky—so named because the only access to the broad, long mesa (the "island") is by means of crossing a single neck not much wider than its narrow, two-lane road. Also to the north and within Island in the Sky, on the distant east side of the Green River, is

# Druid Arch

the White Rim Trail, where slow-moving four-wheel vehicles are allowed. Jack Campbell, a self-described desert rat of a geologist, loves White Rim as much as Matt Kaplinski loves the Vishnu Schist: "I can hear the winds of the Permian sea blowing across the aeolian sands."

The walk back from the Confluence went quickly, my mind full of the blendings of river currents and the meetings at history's junctions. My steps were quickened also by the knowledge of dinner, which tonight would be fresh pasta (well, three days old) and sundried tomato pesto.

**U**p early the next morning, I estimated that my hike to Druid Arch would be about 16 miles, in a loop, from my campsite and back. My approach toward measuring distances on hiking trips matured on a long-ago back-packing trip in Wyoming with my younger sister, Martha. I told her our first day's hike would be 8 miles, but I had misread the topographic map, taking a straight-line measurement when in fact the map clearly showed a meandering trail. The real distance was nearly 14 miles. Martha was foot-stomping furious. Initially, at midday, when the miscalculation became obvious, I wrote off her anger. Part of the job description of the firstborn, after all, is to write off just about anything another sibling says. But by late afternoon, her message had become so penetrating that even an insensitive firstborn couldn't ignore it. Carefully chosen and placed terms like "stupid" and "arrogant" can do that. So can the sentence: "No one asked you to guide this trip, smart ass, but if you're going to do it, do it right and don't burden everybody else with your incredible ineptitude." My trail estimates, even for solo trips, have been conservative ever since.

This route to Druid Arch would take me over to Chesler Park. One short leg of my hike was along a jeep trail. Canyonlands National Park is unusual in the way it is designed to accommodate not only hikers but jeepers and mountain bikers as well. The park has 192 miles of four-wheel-drive roads. Most of Canyonlands, however, including Chesler Park proper and the canyon leading up to Druid Arch, is closed to bikes and four-wheeled vehicles. The Wilderness Act of 1964 directed the Park Service to study all of its roadless areas and make recommendations for wilderness designation. In the case of Canyonlands, the Park Service recommended that more than three-fourths of the park, 260,000 acres in all, be declared wilderness. Although Congress has yet to act officially, the Park Service manages all these areas as if they were wilderness.

Coming down into Chesler Park, I passed Elephant Arch, its trunk forming the arch. A smaller, unnamed arch was nearby. With a long, free day, and with Druid Arch my objective, I found myself thinking more and more about my father. I remembered how quick his mind was. He was brilliant: skipping two grades in elementary school, graduating from Georgia Tech at twenty, obtaining his M.D. from Emory, and then joining the faculty of the University of Michigan Medical School. In addition to being Douglas MacArthur's doctor in World War II, he served on a medical team that treated President Eisenhower during his heart attack. In his late thirties he was named chairman of the Department of Medicine at NYU. The position is above the dean of the School of Medicine and, as people at NYU have explained to me, is comparable to president of a major university.

An old family friend once told me, "Don't expect, or want to be, that brilliant, Charlie. You can't be. And it wouldn't be worth it anyway." That was good advice.

I thought back to the time I was twelve or thirteen when he began badgering me. He would humiliate me in front of grown-ups. "Look at his ears, look at how they stick out," he would announce to a dinner-party gathering of his friends, people I liked and respected. "Doesn't he look exactly like a taxicab coming down Main Street with the doors wide open?" One Saturday, in the middle of a Babe Ruth League game, he rushed over from our house and pulled me off the pitcher's mound, loudly cursing me for not mowing the lawn right. I probably hadn't.

Another family friend, a psychiatrist we called Uncle Seth, took me aside and explained how difficult it was for my father to see me moving into adolescence and doing all the things in high school—dating, playing sports—

that he himself had never been able to do because he was so much younger than his classmates. "Jesus," Uncle Seth said, "I don't think when he went to college, even by the time he was halfway *through* college, that he knew why boys dated girls. Try to understand that."

After I was in high school, the combat escalated. My grades, never good, got even worse and several times I skipped school. I did my chores partially, deficiently, or not at all—sometimes because the tasks were unreasonable, sometimes because I forgot, sometimes just to defy him. He cut off my allowance, refused to sign for my driver's license, and dramatically presented me with a copy of his will, which disinherited me. In my junior year, I won the 880-yard run in a track meet. That night, so excited by my accomplishment, I talked to my friends on the phone and several times exceeded the "five-minute limit" my father placed on my phone calls. After a couple of warnings, he charged at me while I was still on the phone and stomped on my left foot, breaking one of my toes and keeping me out of track for the next two months. On other occasions he hit me. Thereafter I began taunting him, calling him "Big Guy," wanting to wound him and succeeding.

By my senior year in high school, he was assigning Martha and Bobby, six and eight years younger, to babysit for me. He refused to contribute to my college education, and my mother went to work to pay my tuition at Denison University. After packing my stuff in Larry Malm's car for the drive out to Ohio, I never went upstairs to say goodbye and he never came down. He had been in bed with what he called angina. Except for a few shouted insults, we hadn't talked in months.

I sat down to take a drink of water, looking out on Chesler Park, several hundred acres, ringed by improbable spires striped with orange, peach, rose, and beige. At one end of Chesler was a formation nearly 200 feet tall, thin at its base, looking like a gargantuan red and gray version of the sought-after statuette in *The Maltese Falcon*. Out in the center of the enclosure was a large island of spires at least as tall, their erect bearing making them look like aristocrats.

In years past, ranchers could bring their cattle in to graze through a narrow opening at the west end of the park. Now, with cattle excluded, the native bunchgrasses in Chesler are hearty, tall above the sandy soil. It is true that this land is fragile. But if you give it some care, and give it some time, it can endure.

I stayed in Chesler Park a good long while, two hours or more. Though there were a couple of small hiking parties, one a family, Chesler's surrounding walls of spires created a closed-off privacy, an interior place, a magic place, and, as the land can do, rekindled deep memories—memories of childhood. My father introduced me to the Oz books when I was a little boy, just nine or ten. I read nearly all of them, not just *The Wizard of Oz* and *The Land of Oz,* but more than thirty others, all telling stories of secret and mystical places—places like the Merry-Go-Round Mountains, the Quadling Country, the Island of Isa Poso, and the Kingdom of Rinkitink—places where danger lay in wait but was always surmounted. The colors, the island by itself out in the middle, the midday air telling of autumn's approach, all made Chesler Park as close a place to the Land of Oz, my boyhood land of dreams, as any place I have known.

**C**ongress may not have yet declared this part of Canyonlands as official wilderness, but land can define itself on its own terms. This land is wilderness: it is healthy and magnificent and remote and roadless, and the few people are swallowed up in it. In addition to its intrinsic worth, it has the value of distinctiveness. We have long thought of wilderness in terms of alpine forests, snow-capped summits, and coldwater streams. This wild desert country—so different from the normal conception of wilderness and only recently understood—expands our minds by causing us to focus on the different virtues found where extreme aridity prevails, where water is scarce, where vegetation is scant. There is more wild desert on the Colo-

# Druid Arch

rado Plateau than anywhere else. Yet we are at the same stage as we are with preserving the work of the Old People: we have given some protection to wild desert lands—the trail to the Confluence and Chesler Park are examples—but we still have not gathered the will to take the kind of stand the wild places merit.

The politics over Utah wilderness are venomous. In 1979, when the Bureau of Land Management declared its wilderness study inventory— this was just an inventory of eligible roadless areas, mind you, not BLM recommendations, much less a bill in Congress—all hell broke loose across southern Utah. Wilderness, perceived by many locals as a lockup of natural resources commandeered from Washington, D.C., was about as welcome as new schools for Indian children.

Within weeks a brigade of Grand County commissioners and local business leaders had mounted bulldozers, taken out the BLM barricades at the mouths of Negro Bill Canyon and Mill Creek Canyon, two areas near Moab slated for further study, and cut roads partway up the canyons. The purpose for bulldozing the canyons was twofold: to make them ineligible for wilderness by eliminating their roadless status and to make a statement of principle in support of local control. The bulldozer brigade added the patriotic touch, since this was the Fourth of July, of draping their D-7 Cats with American flags.

The pitched conflict continued for several years. There were hangings-in-effigy of environmentalists, there were sit-ins, and there were threats of physical violence. By the mid-1990s, the discord mostly had moved indoors to county, state, and federal hearing rooms. Still, the spirit of the 1979 Bulldozer Wars has been kept alive by the oil-and-water relationship between, on one side, the staunch, mostly Mormon, pro-development contingent in southern Utah and, on the other, the wilderness advocates, many of whom live in Salt Lake City and other urban areas, led by the fierce and effective Southern Utah Wilderness Alliance (SUWA).

SUWA was a driving force behind a remarkable document, *Wilderness at the Edge*, published in 1990. In this report, thirty-five Utah conservation organizations set forth their own inventory—head-and-shoulders above the BLM staff work in technical quality—and made wilderness recommendations totaling 5.7 million acres of BLM land. Bills, incorporating the recommendations, were introduced in Congress and gathered significant support in Utah, especially along the urban Wasatch Front. But these bills never moved.

Then what was once a regional issue mushroomed into a pressing national concern. Ironically, the trigger was a 1995 bill introduced by the Utah congressional delegation. Designed to squash the drive for preservation of Utah lands, the bill would have designated a small amount of "wilderness" (many nonwilderness uses would have been allowed) and opened all other Utah roadless lands for development. The proposal, pushed by Senator Orrin Hatch and Congressman Jim Hansen, figured to move through the Republican 104th Congress easily. Yet by the end of 1995 a vigorous national campaign—with the Southern Utah Wilderness Alli-

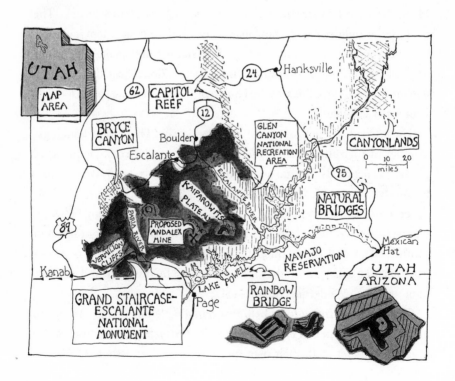

ance taking the lead—had killed the delegation bill. Millions of Americans now understood the virtues of the southern Utah backcountry—once leftover lands, variously ignored and scorned.

My mind played out from Chesler Park to Kaiparowits, the high plateau of BLM land 100 miles to the southwest. The ground I was hiking in Canyonlands personifies certain wildlands on the Colorado Plateau. But Kaiparowits represents a different kind of wilderness: also dry, high desert but much more forbidding and even more remote. Kaiparowits was on my mind not only because I love it but because recently I had participated in events that followed the defeat of the Utah delegation's 1995 proposal and culminated in Kaiparowits being protected as part of a major national monument.

Kaiparowits is a word used by the Ute and Paiute meaning "arm off." The Indians gave the name to the one-armed John Wesley Powell and in time the plateau was named for him. This massive upswelling, 1,200 square miles in all, began to take its current form during the rising and eroding of the Tertiary about 50 million years ago. Kaiparowits is shaped like a giant bell. Utah Highway 12, which passes through Escalante, runs approximately along the north, higher-elevation edge. The landform then flares out: the Cockscomb along the west edge trending southwest and the Straight Cliffs, looming above the Hole-in-the-Rock Trail of the old Mormon pioneers, angling to the southeast. Like the Straight Cliffs, the southern cliffs of Kaiparowits, 50 to 60 miles long, 1,000 to 2,000 feet above Lake Powell, fashion a distinctive part of the lifted horizon of the central Colorado Plateau.

Kaiparowits is, in a word, *wild*—"wilderness," as Raymond Wheeler put it, "right down to its burning core." This is the interior of the Colorado Plateau, itself the interior of the nation. The plateau is so remote and rough that few cattle or sheep have grazed it, leaving more pristine grasslands than anywhere else in the country. Kaiparowits is little visited, perhaps less touched by human beings than anywhere else in the continental United States.

In the red hills of Kaiparowits, the fire in the Colorado Plateau is due to coal, not hematite, the rusting process that reddens sandstone. On Kaiparowits, where 4 billion tons of recoverable coal from the Cretaceous hold more BTUs than all the energy in Saudi Arabia, the rock crust of the earth has in some places been scorched red by the naturally burning coal underneath. You can hike into places where coal seams rise all the way to the surface and smolder, sending up wisps of smoke. It was here, during the 1960s in the heyday of the Big Buildup, that a consortium of utilities proposed the biggest coal mine and biggest power plant of all, only to see the project collapse in the changed economic and environmental climate of the 1970s.

Then, in the late 1980s, came a new, scaled-back proposal. Andalex Resources, Inc., obtained BLM leases to extract 2.5 million tons of coal a year (compared to the 15 million tons previously planned). There would be no power plant on Kaiparowits or, for that matter, any open-pit mining. Rather, Andalex would employ long-wall mining 600 feet beneath the surface. The coal would be hauled out horizontally through portals and the earth above allowed to settle down into the mined-out areas.

The company designed the mine with obvious care to avoid environmental problems. The extraction would be done in Smoky Hollow, a badlands gully 50 to 150 feet deep. Two wilderness study areas are in the vicinity: Wahweap, the nearest boundary of which is 4 miles west of the mine, and Burning Hills, which comes as close as 2 miles to the east. The mine, however, would lie outside the wilderness study areas. The actual mine site itself, then, is nondescript country—no significant wildlife habitat, no special scenic values, no known archaeological sites—on the southern end of Kaiparowits Plateau.

The mine site itself may not be a problem, but there are others. Andalex plans to truck the coal out, making 150 daily roundtrips, 300 individual runs. The road in would be a bear. The probable route would be built in hazardous terrain across crumbly ridges and washes that can receive mighty flash floods. You can see evidence of the force of these floods in John Henry Canyon, which the road would have to cross: on top of a boulder 8 feet above the creek bottom rests a 20-foot-long chunk of cottonwood, 8 feet in diameter, weighing a good ton, deposited there by a rampaging gully washer. The access road would traverse the Wahweap Wilderness Study Area for several miles, and the trucking operation would cause plenty of commotion in that silent, wild country.

The trucking would also cause plenty of disturbance in the local communities. Andalex plans to haul the coal more than 200 miles—the longest coal-trucking venture ever undertaken—to rail spurs near Cedar City, Utah, or Moapa, Nevada. Along the way the trucks would roll through the towns of Kanab, Hurricane, and Cedar City, 300 trips a day, a truck every five minutes, around the clock. And these will be Rocky Mountain double coal trucks, weighing 130,000 pounds loaded, 50 percent larger than western doubles (the standard 18-wheelers). The coal would then be transported to the West Coast, probably for shipment to Japan.

Kaiparowits itself would be at risk from more than the project as now designed. The currently proposed mining operation is only part of the lease area held by Andalex. In thirty years, Andalex could attempt to develop the rest of the lease area to the north, inside the Wahweap Wilderness Study Area. The expanded project, even more than the current Andalex proposal, would cut deeply into the remoteness that is Kaiparowits. Andalex, or a successor lessee, would have to await the results of a second environmental impact study (and a possible denial on environmental grounds). But when a mining company has put in the kind of infrastructure Andalex plans, the company enjoys a great amount of momentum when it wants to expand its lease area. There would be tremendous pressure to mine the wildlands. Mike Noel, of the Kanab BLM, comments: "In thirty years, let's hope we're smarter and that we've got energy sources other than fossil fuels."

Let's try to place ourselves thirty years in the future and imagine how the Andalex project would look from that vantage point. We have a benchmark of sorts. The original Kaiparowits project was being advocated about thirty years ago. That consortium would have built a coal mine—the largest coal mine in the world—in order to supply a power plant on Kaiparowits that would have produced 3,000 megawatts, the largest coal-fired power plant in the world. The companies, to serve the eight to ten thousand employees, would have constructed a town for twenty-five thousand people. There is almost no one around today who would stand up for that project. Kaiparowits Plateau would have been trashed and the air pollution in the Grand Canyon would have been multiplied several times over. And we didn't *need* all that additional energy. With all the environmental and community disruption, how would the Andalex proposal look thirty years hence?

In any event, it now appears that the Andalex mine will never be built. I first got wind of this in July 1996 when I received a phone call from my old friend John Leshy. I had worked with John on the opinion letter to the Hopi Tribal Council about the lawyers' conflict of interest and he later became a coauthor on my casebook of public land law. In 1993, Bruce Babbitt named him solicitor of the Department of the Interior, the top legal position in the department.

Emphasizing that his call had to be kept confidential, John said that the Interior Department, at the request of President Clinton, was preparing documents that, if signed by the president, would include the Kaiparowits Plateau within a national monument. He wanted to know if I would be interested in serving as a special counsel to the Interior Department and participating in a work group that was drafting the proclamation for presentation to Clinton. The monument would encompass some 1.7 million acres in southern Utah. It would reach from the Grand Staircase—the dramatic series of ascending cliffs and mesas, named by Clarence Dutton, the noted geologist who traveled with Powell—east over to Kaiparowits and the Escalante drainage, including segments of the Hole-in-the-Rock Trail. A national monument, while the protections are different than for wilderness, is essentially identical to a national park. Designation would give truly significant preservation status to Kaiparowits and the other lands. Monument status for Kaiparowits, a revival of Harold Ickes' Escalante National Monument, was a stunning proposal—I'd never heard a word of it—and I accepted John's offer immediately.

# Druid Arch

I put my other work aside and, for an intensive three weeks, dedicated most of my time to the monument: doing research and drafting, attending two meetings in Washington, and participating in several conference calls. Our work group, about fifteen people from the Interior and Justice departments and the White House, plus myself, was operating under the Antiquities Act of 1906—a measure that gives the president broad authority to designate national monuments. We knew, since this was during Clinton's reelection campaign, that presidential politics would influence whether the proclamation would actually be signed. But I, and presumably my colleagues on the work group as well, had no doubt that declaring this 1.7-million-acre expanse of fragile wildland—3 percent of the State of Utah—as a national monument would bring much-needed protection to these lands and would, as well, make a bold statement about the values of BLM lands in southern Utah. We finished our drafting work in mid-August and waited.

By early September, when the administration had tentatively decided to go ahead with the monument, the matter still had been kept entirely in-house. Then, on September 3, Frank Clifford of the *Los Angeles Times* broke the story. The Utah congressional delegation and Governor Leavitt loudly cried "foul" (and "land grab") over this use of the Antiquities Act—for, almost unique among the environmental laws, this measure does not require an environmental impact statement or other public disclosure. Clinton wavered in the face of Utah's strenuous objections, but he made no concessions.

The White House announced the impending creation of the Grand Staircase–Escalante National Monument just three days in advance of the ceremony on September 18, 1996. Even so, thousands of people (I was among them) came from all over the Southwest for the gala occasion on the South Rim of the Grand Canyon. The Grand Canyon Trust rented all available buses in northern Arizona to bring people up. Large numbers of Indian people attended, celebrating the sweeping action in the name of land preservation. After a round of speeches and heartfelt cheering, President Clinton officially signed the proclamation on the South Rim of the

Grand Canyon. He was sitting at a small desk at the spot where Teddy Roosevelt proclaimed the original Grand Canyon National Monument (later, of course, made into a national park). The Grand Staircase–Escalante became the second-largest national monument ever created in the Lower 48 States.

Many residents of southern Utah—some, wearing black armbands, held their own anti-monument gathering in Escalante—opposed the monument. Public opinion, though, nationally and in the Southwest, strongly supported the Grand Staircase–Escalante. In Utah as a whole, sentiment was about evenly split. Many Utahans backing the monument, however, thought that the secret process leading to the monument was wrong.

In a sense, I agree. I am sympathetic to the objections based on the lack of public participation: local communities *should* be involved in public lands decisions. Yet, in this situation, the tone had already been set by the Utah congressional delegation's minimalist "wilderness" bill in 1995, which the delegation tried, unsuccessfully, to ramrod through Congress after very limited public hearings. For Clinton to try to reach some sort of compromise on monument status with the Utah delegation, which had taken such a hard-line, anti-wilderness stance, would have been pointless.

The exact effects of the monument designation will be decided during a three-year public study process to determine land use: grazing, recreation visitor facilities, and limited roading. The proclamation gives considerable guidance for this process. The monument's purposes—preserving the area because it is an "unspoiled natural area" and a "frontier"—suggest that this is to be a "wilderness monument." Any roads or other facilities, therefore, must be few and have a light touch.

Thus it seems most probable that the Andalex coal-mining project on Kaiparowits cannot go ahead. Andalex has valid leases, but it has not secured rights-of-way, which must now cross monument lands, or other required approvals. Clearly, the monument's purposes are incompatible with the steady rumble of Rocky Mountain double coal trucks and a large coal mine, and it is doubtful that the BLM would grant the approvals. As a result, Andalex and the Interior Department are discussing a trade for

# Druid Arch

federal coal leases in a location more suitable for mining. The monument does not carry formal wilderness designation—only Congress can do that—but, like much of Canyonlands National Park, most of the Grand Staircase–Escalante inevitably will be managed as if it were wilderness.

As I sat on a low rock ledge looking out on the spires of Chesler Park, I reflected on how far I had come in my understanding of the desert since I gained my first glimmers while hunting doves outside of Phoenix with Paul Roca. I love the whole of the new monument. But Kaiparowits Plateau in particular inflames me because it so starkly represents all the values of the wild desert.

Few people come to Kaiparowits. The conveniences are so few, traditional beauty so scarce, normal recreational opportunities so limited. Precipitation measures only 10 to 12 inches a year. There are just two or three perennial streams, and they carry little water. One dirt road, passable for passenger cars, runs up to Escalante. Otherwise it is all jeep trails. The scattered piñon and juniper trees offer almost no cover from the sun. Cross-country backpacking is for experts only. You have to scour the topographic maps, plan your trip with care (being sure to hit the springs), and stick to your plan. Even a short hike is a challenge. From a distance, Kaiparowits looks flat on top but in fact it is up-and-down, chopped-up, confusing. You can get lost, snakebit, or otherwise injured. There's no one to call.

There are reasons to come, though, in addition to the remoteness and the physical challenges. Kaiparowits is home to hanging gardens, Ancestral Puebloan sites, wildlife from lizards to mule deer, wildflowers found nowhere else, and the burning core that rises to the surface. Higher up, raptors thrive on the wind currents. And from Kaiparowits you are given startling vistas in all directions: vivid views more than 200 miles if the winds have cleared out the haze, panoramas as encompassing as those from the southern tip of Cedar Mesa, the east flank of Boulder Mountain, the high La Sals, or Dead Horse Point. If you climb the rocky promontories on top of Kaiparowits, you can see off to Boulder Mountain, the Henrys, Black Mesa, Navajo Mountain, the Kaibab Plateau, the Vermilion Cliffs, long stretching landscapes of sacred country.

The languid stillness of Kaiparowits turns your mind gently and slowly to wondering about time, to trying to comprehend the long, deep time all of this took, from Cretaceous, from back before Cretaceous, and to comprehend—since Lake Powell and the seventy-story stacks of Navajo Generating Station are now part of the vista—how it is that our culture has so much might and how it is that we choose to exert it so frantically, with so little regard of the time that you can see, actually see, from here. Perhaps somehow, if we take some moments now, here in this stark piñon-juniper rockland place, here in this farthest-away place, we can nurture some of the fibers of constancy and constraint that our people possess in addition to the might. The silence is stunning, the solitude deep and textured.

Kaiparowits makes you decide on the value of wilderness and remoteness. Kaiparowits is where the dreams for the Colorado Plateau collide. Coal, jobs, growth. Long vistas, places to get lost in, places to find yourself in.

In a sense, of course, wilderness is a flawed idea. The term as we define it in the Wilderness Act—"untrammeled by man"—is preposterously inaccurate. The wildlands of southern Utah have been worked, and worked hard. You can see it in the cliffed, well-structured homes and you can imagine all the tended crops and intense hunts over all the years. You find, too, the much more recent ranch and mine trails. Today we surely trammel it with our boots and waste. Nor is the wilderness idea without its unintended consequences. The magic of its name draws people and, ironically, can weaken or even erase land health and serenity. Still, wilderness is the best idea we now have to preserve the tart, savory taste of remoteness.

So put all of the acreage recommended by *Wilderness at the Edge* in wilderness. Southern Utah's economy will benefit, not suffer. The glory lands,

# Druid Arch

and the legacy of the Old People, will be protected, as they should be. Put all of them in: Negro Bill, Comb Ridge, Cedar Mesa and all its canyons, the San Rafael Swell, the whole Escalante drainage, the Henry Mountains, all of them, and all of the many others, too. Put the whole new monument in. And the national park wilderness study areas, too, including Chesler Park and the way leading up to Druid Arch. Put them all in. We will be a far better and richer people if we do. We will have fulfilled deep-running duties to the whole world, and earlier worlds, and worlds still to come.

**W**hen I told my sister, Martha, that I was going to Druid Arch and how it reminded me of our father, she replied that she'd love to come too. She said she would try to meet up with me in Chesler Park. And even though I knew it was unlikely, given her job and her family, I had hoped she'd be able to make it. It was as if I saw her now, a mile away, across the park against the peach-hued southern spires, fit as ever, great hiker that she is, always loving the West though living in Evanston, Illinois. I began hiking toward where I thought she was, across this interior parkland, across Oz, and it was slow-walking country, no rush, a place and time to float as much as walk in the early morning sun.

Martha is the family historian. She is always trying to piece together what we have and what we have lost. In thorough and quite formal sessions, she interviewed Aunt Katy, Aunt Ginny, and other family elders. A few months ago she sent me a copy of William Styron's *Darkness Visible*, his account, originally delivered as lectures at Virginia Medical School, about his long encounter with clinical depression. "Charlie, read this," she wrote. "You'll see for the first time what it was. At least that was my reaction."

After I read the book, I absolutely agreed. Everything that Styron described—the closed-in feeling, the hopelessness, the drinking and the pills, the lashing out, the continuing obsession with suicide, the *darkness*—fit. Finally I understood. My father, like Styron, was a victim of clinical depression before his own medical profession knew what it was or how to treat it.

When Martha and I had talked on the phone, I told her of a trail I'd heard of, called Joint Trail, a narrow, winding corridor that wove its way through the high rock wall on the south side of Chesler Park. A strange name, Joint Trail, and Martha wondered whether it had been named by a psychedelic ranger during the social revolution of the 1960s. But no. It's a trail through a labyrinth of joints: fractures in the rocks, half a mile long from entrance to exit, usually 2 to 4 feet wide at the bottom of crevasses up to 150 feet high. After our trek through Joint Trail, giggling like kids as we squeezed through the narrow places, Martha and I climbed to the rocks on top. A person could leap over the joints in many places. I found one place where I dared to. Martha jumped several.

I envy my friends who can show their East Coast parents the West and, best of all, can take them out into the backcountry if they're in good enough shape. I wondered what Druid Arch would mean to my father. Sailing, beach picnics, and, for me, playing baseball and listening to Red Barber precisely announcing Brooklyn Dodger games were the activities of a summer's day back then, back when the summer days were still good for us.

Would he come to Druid Arch? The shortest route is over 11 miles, some of it slow going in the sandy bottom of Elephant Canyon. To my knowledge he had never done much hiking. But suppose we had all day and laid in plenty of water and a gourmet picnic like my mother always made? Would the sourdough rolls, provolone, Grey Poupon mustard, and water in my daypack be sufficiently tasty fare? He was, after all, a Druid priest. And the Druids, who viewed mistletoe as sacred and held their ceremonies in the darkest oak groves, were nature lovers. Merlin, the prophet and mystic of Arthurian legend, was thought to be a Druid. Because of Merlin's connection with nature and the other world, as well as his ability to embody both good and evil, Nikolai Tolstoy and other scholars believe that Merlin represents the Trickster in Britain's remote past—thus playing somewhat the same role in his landscape as Coyote does in this one. Would the idea of Druid Arch, deep in wild country, so inlaid in the natural

# Druid Arch

world, appeal to my father, move him? If Coyote appeared from behind the sagebrush, would his eyes see Merlin? Would Druid Arch be a place for my father to pray?

Would he come? Would he like it? Would I give him a chance?

Martha was sure he would come and that he'd be on the trail up the canyon to Druid Arch. We hiked to the edge of Chesler Park, sat for a time taking in the upthrusting pillars and colored stripes of this Oz, and walked off together.

And then, just when I had decided that he hadn't come, there was my father, over on the trail to Druid Arch, waiting for us. His hair was full white now, just like the picture of my grandfather. Together the three of us walked up the canyon, along its twists and weaves and bends and turns. The canyon floor was stone dry but water comes through here. The cottonwoods and willows told us that. The surging flash floods brought in sufficient water to seep down to their roots.

Water is always near a person's mind in this country even if, as has been true so far today, you never see a drop outside of your water bottle. Water in this country is rare, powerful, sensual, and, existing as it does mostly in your mind, mystical.

My father was a mystic. He read everything Robert Graves wrote. I imagine that's why he claimed his Druid priestship. I am Charles III, he Charles Jr., and there is a sense of tradition in the family. As we hiked, I asked him about his story—the one he always told so seriously, about the dimple on the chin that he and I shared being the kiss of an angel. Did he make that up or did his father, Charles Sr., tell it to him? How many generations back do the dimples go? I thanked him for taking me on his knee, and with great solemn mysteriousness, telling me that we were both witches and that I would understand what he meant when I grew up. Martha thanked him for sailing her to that secret beach on Martha's Vineyard where she could turn over the scallop shells and find fairies underneath. She also thanked him, as she had when she was six, for naming the vineyard after her.

We walked on toward Druid Arch. The only people here, we settled into the quiet, the shuffling of our boots the only sounds amid our dreamtime as the bad years dropped away one by one by one, scattering behind us, joining the yellow cottonwood leaves of October on the canyon floor. I smiled, as a person always will, at the sharp, exact, descending-down-the-scale *tee-tee-tee-tee-tee* of a canyon wren. I began to look over to my father. For he if anyone, though this land was new and different to him, would understand the mysticism of the canyon country that is its ultimate and truest quality, even more than the geology and archaeology and clarity and beauty. He would understand how Kokopelli and Coyote and skinwalkers and kachinas have always walked this ground and always will, and how it is in the deep backcountry that the mysticism is most likely to be ignited and how that mysticism is the Plateau's hottest flame of all. Yet, when I turned to him, he was gone.

Martha and I kept on. Soon we found ourselves confronted by a 20-foot-high pour-over, dry this day, a waterfall on some cloudburst days. We were in shadows now. She would have to go on alone. She always had, always would.

Martha hiked up the stairs beside the pour-over, just five days past her twelfth birthday, home after school in late September, three weeks after I'd driven off to college. Did the house seem dark to her then? It did to me when I went there a few years ago: so dark. Probably not to her, home after school to see her dad, up in the bedroom where he'd been for so long but always joyful to see her, his little girl. Up the stairs. No noise. We've talked about it a lot but I'll never know all she saw or thought, a girl finding a shotgun on the bed and her father who was but never would be again.

In time I made it up to the head of the canyon, to Druid Arch. It sits on a large redrock island at the head of the canyon, and the expansive floor at the base of the arch is a place to wonder and sort things out. Only 20 to 40 feet thick, the arch is free-standing, not lodged in some larger formation. Its mass is overwhelming, more than 200 feet high. Druid Arch is really three arches: two long, vertical, more-or-less rectangular ones and a smaller opening near the base. No one was down here. There were two climbers, high on the formation. Barely visible to the eye (you needed binoculars to bring them in), they helped give scale to the colossus.

I sat down with my back against a boulder, took out a water bottle, and let out a big breath. Let's put the pieces in place. One piece at a time. No rush.

I didn't kill him. He, and his depression, did that. I didn't even contribute. That was hard for me to say, even to myself. I didn't want to rationalize. But it was true. I deserved to hear those words. I didn't kill him.

I didn't let the sins he visited on me be visited on my own boys. I made myself a promise that I'd never once strike, not even spank, any of my boys and I've kept my promise. There were a few times when the world might have been made a better and more peaceful place if I had given them a good whipping, but I haven't and never will.

I've always believed, but now knew with clarity, that he didn't intend to do what he did to Martha. He loved her unequivocally. He never would have wanted her to come upon that scene. The madness blinded him and didn't allow him to connect one thing to another.

And finally: I forgive him. I forgive him.

Let's run through those sentences one more time, slowly. These are things I have to put in order. I said them again.

In my slickrock seat, I realized there was still one last thing.

Lord, what a sense of humor he had! What an engaging, funny man. I remember, years ago, going through old family papers and coming upon a printed booklet of the proceedings at a ceremony that the medical school held in his honor a couple of months after he died. The moderator, a close friend and colleague, finished it off perfectly:

*I must close this evening by saying that there was only one Chuck Wilkinson and that we will not ever see his like again. To which Chuck would undoubtedly wish me to add, 'and thank God for that.' And he would wish that we would all laugh.*

My father had many stories, each of them new and electric every time he told them. I think his favorite might have been the one—a true one (not always a requisite for his stories)—about the black couple driving from Boston down to New York to get married. This was the early 1950s. Their car had broken down on the Merritt Parkway late at night and my father picked them up and brought them to our nearby home in Westport, Connecticut. They telephoned a garage, but the tow truck couldn't get there until the next morning. My father invited them to spend the evening. Being proper people, our guests could not sleep in the same bed, and so the black man slept in my parents' room. This was a time and place when realtors still would not sell to blacks, and we kids knew hardly any minority people. The next morning, as she did every day, Martha, just six or seven, raced down the hallway, threw open the door, and bounded onto her parents' bed. Then Martha in a fit of surprise—and transformed forever into the principal character in a story about race and civility and youth and a family's favorite baseball team—blurted out: "Are you Jackie Robinson?" Our guest, still groggy with sleep, burst into a belly laugh and told and retold the story that day and in later years too when we saw him and his wife again.

Released into giddiness, I began chuckling, then laughing convulsively, unstoppably, my face drenched and eyes blurred with tears, through which I was quite sure I saw one of the high-above climbers look down from his perch on Druid Arch to see what was causing such a commotion far below in this distant, rocky outpost.

Wilderness. A place for beauty. A place where plants and animals and land and water are protected. A place for song and laughter. Wilderness. A place for mysticism. A place where the work of the Old People is safe. Wilderness. A place where you have to work at it. A place you can lose yourself in. Wilderness. A place you can find yourself in.

# MOUNT BLANCA

**M**ore than a decade after my first visit to Hopi for the late-night meeting in Kykotsmovi, I returned to Black Mesa on a last interviewing trip for this book. Over the course of a day, I met with several people, including Vernon Masayesva. The talk was open, comfortable. They kidded me about how good I was at selecting my Home Dances. "It's been a long time since we've had one like that. Last year we had some rain, but not like when you were here." When we gave our goodbyes, Vernon, ever welcoming in the Hopi way, said: "We hope you can get back for another one of our dances. You could bring your family." I said that I definitely would.

The next morning, feeling refreshed by my meetings on Black Mesa, I drove my van west on Highway 264 toward Moenkopi and Tuba City. I was heading up to Marble Canyon, just across the Colorado River in Utah, to meet up with people from the Grand Canyon Trust. This was early February and the small Hopi farm plots lay fallow along both sides of the road. People at Kykotsmovi told me the villages had not yet held Bean Dance, when the kachinas would return from San Francisco Peaks. Soon, after those dances, with their prayers for rain and a good growing season, Hopi farmers would be out preparing these fields and another cycle would begin.

In American society we are taught that people, and the events and movements we create, make history. At Hopi, the primal force is the steady, reassuring inevitability of land, sky, and seasons. When I first drove across old Route 66 more than thirty years ago, John Boyden was the Hopi's lawyer and termination hung in the air. The Hopi survived both and emerged stronger for the bitter lessons. They had a balance and a continuity to maintain, and they succeeded. Now, in a few weeks, once again the green shoots of new corn will nose up through Black Mesa's reddish soil.

The value of a homeland has become ever more evident and profound to me over the years. Going to Home Dance at Hotevilla, a village mostly without indoor plumbing and electricity, crystallized this. I took to asking Hopis—and Indian people from other tribes who know life both on the reservations and in the cities—a question. Who is happier, the Hopi who live in Hotevilla or the non-Indian people who live in a well-to-do suburb, say, Scottsdale or Boulder? I tell them I know that being happy is a relative and personal concept, but I'd be interested in their answer.

Every last Indian person has told me that they think the Hopi of Hotevilla are happier. Life in the city is so stressful, so fast. The city is a place of steel and concrete, not land. Everything is so impersonal. The only thing that matters there is money. But, I ask: what about the poverty in Indian country and all the pain and troubles that come with it? "All of those things came after the white man. We never had poverty before. We never had trouble with alcohol. We had full, productive lives. And you know what we have learned? The only way to restore the balance we once had is to use traditional means: the families, the medicine men, the ceremonies, the dances.

# Mount Blanca

And we are finding ways to do that." One man from Hotevilla told me that in his village there is family—family everywhere. You go at your own pace. There's always a meal and a bed. People care about you. You can farm and hunt. You can be yourself. You have the land.

I've never seen such permanence. The Hopi's whole way of seeing the world is, and always has been, built on stability, staying power, loyalty to people and place, on endurance. The Hopi will live on Black Mesa a century from now, five centuries from now, and beyond. So will the other tribes of the Colorado Plateau. That's not remotely romanticism or idealism. That's history. Facts. Data.

As I passed across the western border of the Hopi Reservation, entering Navajoland, I wanted to get out of the van, into the open air. It was still several hours before I had to be in Marble Canyon, and there was a place I wanted to go back to. I took a turnoff on a dirt road to a boulder field where the ages had randomly strewn big slabs of Moenkopi Sandstone. Not far from the east rim of the Grand Canyon, this spot lies along a trail that Hopi clans use on their annual trips to the sacred salt deposits down in the depths of the canyon. The deposits are near the Hopi emergence point.

I got out near the boulder field. No one else was here on this chilly, windy day. I began to walk around. Each of the Hopi clans had an area where, over the centuries, they had left petroglyphs. So I passed clusters of bears, owls, parrots, and other clan symbols. I kept on walking, hands dug into the pockets of my jeans, piecing my thinking together, weaving in and out of the slabs and their symbols, some down on flat land, some up on a low hillside.

Instead of conquering the world around them, Indian cultures have taken what it gave them. The Ancestral Puebloans lived one way—farming and living in rock—in the canyon Philip and I visited. The Ute lived another way—hunting and living in buffalo hide—in the higher country to the north, at Morgan Bottoms on the Yampa River. But neither tried to remake their place. They reached certain population levels and held them. Life is a cycle, not an ever-ascending trajectory.

# ENDURANCE

The centuries and millennia have intensified the commitment to a community of people and land, a tribe's place. As the White River Utes know, there is no pain like the pain of a land-based people who have lost their land. Nor have I known a tenacity like the determination of Indian people to hold their places. The elaborate stories passed on by the oral tradition become part of the land: Coyote and skinwalkers are as real as the sand and the sage. Indian ceremonies—and all of the time and work and love that goes into them—express a unity with, and commitment to, the natural world. The ceremonies that honor the place, like Home Dance, are expansive, demanding, indelible on the mind. Knowledge of the place is detailed and widely held: nearly everyone living at Hopi, for example, will know of this boulder field, even though it lies 50 miles west of Black Mesa. Vine Deloria Jr., the Sioux historian, told me: "Indians can be unhappy, but I do not think that Indians are ever lonely. They are never alone. The plains, the canyons, all have so many stories."

I sat down on a boulder near sandstone slabs where Hopi clan members had pecked out cornstalks and coyotes. This small hillside lay only slightly above the landscape out to the west and from this low angle the cleft of the Grand Canyon was barely distinguishable, but I could make it out. How many times, on their way down into the canyon depths to the place where the Hopi emerged from the underworld into this world, have clans come to this boulder field to make their petroglyphs and reaffirm their existence and long continuity?

Thirty-five years ago I saw the West as clean and fresh, open and uncluttered. I no longer see it that way. I love it still, with all my heart, but I fear for it. For it is aging rapidly.

The arid West may be the region that needs a reverence for place the most. This could be viewed as a sad comment about a wondrous land. It could also be viewed as hope accompanying new green shoots rising up out of the oldest, richest soil.

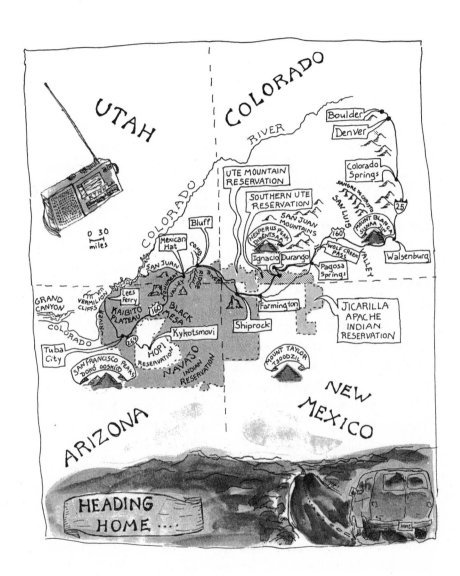

# ENDURANCE

**I** worked my way back to the highway and then headed north toward the Colorado River, the Kaibito Plateau on the right, the late-afternoon brilliance of the Vermilion Cliffs off in the distance. I crossed over the river at Navajo Bridge, just below Lees Ferry, where the float trips bound for the Grand Canyon put in. That night I had more interviews over dinner. It had been a long trip, and tomorrow I would be heading home, a thirteen- or fourteen-hour drive. If I got up early, and had my thermos filled with strong coffee, I could see Ann and the boys before they went to bed.

The next morning I pulled out of the Marble Canyon Lodge in the dark. When I drove over the bridge and passed into the Navajo Reservation, I switched on KTNN. The country music format was going strong. At the end of the 5 A.M. news, the sports update in the Navajo language was broken by "Michael Jordan" and "Bulls 121, Lakers 110." Near Tuba City I turned east on US 160. Most of the reservation highways have Navajo Nation route numbers, but this road apparently hasn't been given one yet. The Navajo have kept a good part of their ancestral land within the four sacred peaks: from this west end of the reservation, you have to drive nearly 200 miles before leaving Navajoland.

Soon the first traces of dawn began to show. Black Mesa rose up off to the right, its tall rim sharp against the early light. This is the high-elevation side of the mesa, the Hopi villages at the far end, 50 miles away as the crow flies. Several pickups were out, probably Navajo workers heading for the mine. I pulled over and gathered a couple of handfuls of sage so that the smell would fill up the van.

I took a detour, though, turning off to the north to go through Mexican Hat. The San Juan Inn, just across the dilapidated bridge over the San Juan River, would put on a good breakfast. I wolfed down a plate of huevos rancheros and then went over to the gift shop. This is one of the two motels, along with Recapture Lodge up the road in Bluff, on this stretch of the river. Both, like the Marble Canyon Lodge, are modest and well-worn but wonderful in their own ways, funky hideaways now part of the desert landscape in their own right. I'd stayed here often, including the trip for the depositions in the school case when Eric Swenson first took me up on nearby Cedar Mesa.

# Mount Blanca

Mike Tong, the manager, always likes to banter. "What didja do, spend the night at Recapture and come by here for a cup of coffee out of guilt?"

"No, I'm coming up from the south. Got to stay at a decent place last night, though, Marble Canyon Lodge."

"Oh, great. You guys from Colorado sure are uptown."

I picked out a couple of small Navajo pots and a wedding basket. The shop also had replicas of Ancestral Puebloan pottery, smooth and designed on the inside, the individual clay coils showing on the outside, and I got one of those. The San Juan Inn sells the best coffee cups around, decorated with a drawing of the old river bridge at Mexican Hat—saggy as can be. We dickered over the price of my purchases, the objective being social rather than financial.

"Come on, you're going to run me out of business. And don't give me that crap about having to send all of your boys off to college. You shouldn't have so many."

I filled up one of my new cups with coffee and headed on. In a few miles I got to Comb Wash and San Juan Hill, where the Hole-in-the-Rock Expedition endured the last of its agony. Then I came into Bluff, a settlement of a few hundred souls out in the middle of nowhere, with the few amenities consisting mostly of the sere dignity of stone pioneer homes and the shade of creaky cottonwood trees, just the way its eclectic canyon-country-loving residents want it: an acquired taste, maybe, but a great place, once you understand it and the country it's set in. My own guess is that someday, maybe soon, someone is going to want to put in a destination resort near Bluff: golf course, swimming pools, condos, airstrip, the whole thing. If that happens, it will open up the heart of the Colorado Plateau and there'll be no going back. I wonder, if such a thing is proposed, whether we'll consider the value of remoteness in a serious way.

I followed the San Juan River up through Shiprock and Farmington. Navajo Dam lay ahead. I thought of the Quintanas, who had lost their homeland to that dam. Then, incredibly, after the reservoir went in, Martha's husband and son—Miguel's son-in-law and grandson—drowned in the reservoir in a boating accident. What a curse. I drove across the top of the dam and worked my way slowly up toward the Colorado line.

# ENDURANCE

This was Valentine's Day and KTNN had designated it "Lovers Weekend." The disk jockey was Navajo but he announced this segment in English, so I could join in the fun: dedications were encouraged but you couldn't give your last name, only your first name and the part of the reservation you were from. Still, even with all the attractions of Lovers Weekend, I was feeling divided radio loyalties now as I drove up the Los Pinos arm of Navajo Reservoir toward the Southern Ute Reservation. So I switched over to KSUT, the Ute tribal radio station, "Four Corners Public Radio," with six different FM frequencies. Now I was in Colorado.

I drove into Ignacio, the largest town on the Southern Ute Reservation. Traditionally, Indian reservations have lacked any semblance of infrastructure. So much poverty: why would a businessperson put in a supermarket, gas station, or clothing store? The trading posts weren't much more than thinly disguised pawn shops and well-situated acquisition points for buying up traditional blankets, jewelry, and baskets at cut-rate prices from the artisans. But the economy of Indian country has been changing since the early 1980s and Ignacio had a solid look to it: a well-stocked grocery store; a bank; a chain convenience store (7-2-11); several other going businesses; a tribal subdivision outside of town with trim new houses, many with expansive views of the pine-layered mountain country. The Southern Utes were doing well, making the best of their oil and gas deposits. They had invested their royalties and established Red Willow Production Company, a tribal oil drilling operation. The Southern Utes had also opened up a casino.

The tribal complex in Ignacio included the reasonably upscale Sky-Ute Lodge and Convention Center. The tribal office buildings were impressive and, on a hunch, I drove in. For years I had been jealous of my friend David Getches, who had a KSUT T-shirt. I was on target: the tribal radio station was in the complex and, after doing a promo for the fundraising drive on why out-of-towners should tune in KSUT and paying a tariff of $10, I walked out with my own T-shirt.

Back in the van and heading east on US 160 with the high San Juan Range my companion to the north, I stayed with KSUT for a while but missed the merriment of Lovers Weekend and switched back to KTNN.

# Mount Blanca

The announcer, a man, asked his audience: "I know I shouldn't give my valentine a toaster or a blender, but what *should* I give? Give me some help." To my ear, the advice, all from female callers on a subject I had not studied enough, sounded excellent. Most callers mentioned flowers. One said: "*Bury* her in flowers." Another commented slowly: "Just make it simple and thoughtful. It shouldn't be anything important or expensive or permanent. Mainly, it should be pretty." One spirited Navajo caller, who may have known the disk jockey, observed: "You know, I realize that you said you know a toaster or a blender is the wrong choice. But anyone who would even *mention* a toaster or a blender for Valentine's Day is beyond hope." "Beyond," she repeated, "*hope.*"

I feared that I was fast moving out of the station's range, but KTNN was still coming in strong when I reached Pagosa Springs. By now I had left the Colorado Plateau. The next stretch of road climbed up the San Juan Range to the Continental Divide and Wolf Creek Pass, the toughest winter pass, I think, in Colorado. The road was icy, snow was coming down hard, and an 18-wheeler had jackknifed. But I made it and eased my way down the east side of the San Juans into the broad, dramatic San Luis Valley. Out in the valley, KTNN's 50,000 watts continued to do fine. I knew that you can get it in Albuquerque and I once heard that you can pull in KTNN at night on the beach in Los Angeles.

The San Luis Valley is defined on the east by the elegant Sangre de Cristo Mountains. As you start up toward La Veta Pass, which allows passage through the Sangres, you are flanked on the north by Mount Blanca, *Sisnaajini,* more than 14,000 feet high, the easternmost of the Navajo's four sacred peaks, unreachable in its distant serenity. The signal was breaking up, the static was annoying, but you could still get KTNN—vibrant, proud, and whimsical, like Kokopelli, all the way to Mount Blanca.

On the way over La Veta Pass, as reception became impossible, I put on a country music tape and continued east. I stopped at sunset in Walsenburg for a vanilla milkshake. When I started up again, I recalled that KTNN was going to carry the Window Rock–Monument Valley girls' basketball game. Monument Valley High School is one of the two new schools built on

347

the Utah part of the reservation to end the long-distance busing in San Juan County. During our work on the school case, Eric Swenson and I often talked about what a defining moment it would be when an Anglo basketball team came down to a full gym in one of the new Navajo schools and, for the first time, the Navajo kids won.

I realized now that Eric and I had the right idea but we were off on the particulars. Sure, it was important to the Monument Valley kids and parents to beat the Anglo schools from up north. But Window Rock was the capital of the Navajo Nation—the whole Navajo Nation! And Eric and I had conceived of these things in terms of boys' basketball. Now the girls' teams were followed with every bit as much passion. One Navajo girl had earned a basketball scholarship at Stanford. Another went off to play at Arizona State.

When I turned the radio back on, now driving north toward Boulder on Interstate 25, I found that KTNN came in nearly as well as on the other side of Mount Blanca. The radio waves were floating tonight. There were two announcers, one in English, one in Navajo. As far as I could tell, their relay-team approach was for the announcer receiving the baton to give the score, quickly summarize the last few minutes' action, which had just been announced in the other language, then pick up with the play on the court. They talked fast and excitedly. The Monument Valley team had a record of 22–2, Window Rock was undefeated at 23–0.

The contradictions. How remarkable, given the bleak state of Indian country, including Navajo, in, say, the 1960s, that a game such as this—between two Indian schools with excellent teams in a packed gymnasium, carried on a 50,000-watt tribal radio station, no less—could ever be played. Yet because of the rush to build hard and fast, such a game would never be played in Rosa or in Meeker in a high school named after Ouray or Nicaagat.

The English-speaking sportscaster told me that Monument Valley fell behind early, by as many as fourteen points. The home crowd, though, never seemed to let up. I got thoroughly into it and yelled along with them, "Come on Monument Valley!" pounding the dashboard with the flat of my right hand when they scored.

# Mount Blanca

The Monument Valley girls came back, but now I was nearly to Colorado Springs and the reception ranged from none to gratingly exasperating to barely decipherable. I thought I heard the Anglo announcer say "tied" and "one minute to go." Then came a commercial in Navajo for good old Kayenta Burger King. Then came the Navajo announcer. Names of girls. An accelerating crescendo of words in a language I couldn't understand. Crowd noise. Then words that had no counterpart in Navajo that the Navajo announcer shouted out in English: "Three *pointer!*" Then: "*Yessss!*" Then: "Monument *Valley* . . ." Then I was left with static, the headlights out on the road ahead, and my own thoughts of what endures, and what does not, and what should.

# Notes

CHAPTER 2: MEXICAN HAT

16    *Menominee Termination Act.*   Menominee Termination Act of 1954, PL 83-399, 68 Stat. 250, 25 U.S.C. §§891–902 (repealed 1973).

16    *United States termination policy.*   See Felix S. Cohen, *Felix S. Cohen's Handbook of Federal Indian Law* (Charlottesville, Va.: Michie Bobbs-Merrill, 1982), pp. 811–818; Charles F. Wilkinson and Eric R. Biggs, "The Evolution of the Termination Policy," *American Indian Law Review* 5(1) (1977): 139–184; Francis Paul Prucha, *The Great Father: The United States Government and the American Indians,* abridged ed. (Lincoln: University of Nebraska Press, 1986), pp. 371–373.

16    *Menominee termination.*   Stephen J. Herzberg, "The Menominee Indians: Termination to Restoration," *American Indian Law Review* 6(1) (1978): 143–186; Gary Orfield, "Termination in Retrospect: The Menominee Experience," in Richard N. Ellis, ed., *The Western American Indian: Case Studies in Tribal History* (Lincoln: University of Nebraska Press, 1972), pp. 189–195.

17    *Tribal sovereignty.*   See *Worcester v. Georgia,* 31 U.S. (6 Pet.) 515 (1832); *Kerr-McGee Corp. v. Navajo Tribe,* 471 U.S. 195 (1985); Charles F. Wilkinson, *American Indians, Time, and the Law: Native Societies in a Modern Constitutional Democracy* (New Haven: Yale University Press, 1987).

17    *Menominee Restoration Act of 1973.*   Menominee Restoration Act of 1973, PL 93–197, 87 Stat. 770, 25 U.S.C. §§903–903(f) (1994).

22    *Navajo Nation statistics.*   See David H. Getches et al., *Cases and Materials on Federal Indian Law,* 4th ed. (St. Paul: West, 1998), pp. 7–23.

24    *Natonabah v. Board of Education.*   *Natonabah v. Board of Education,* 355 F. Supp. 716 (D.N.M. 1973).

25    *"built-in headwinds."*   *Griggs v. Duke Power Co.,* 401 U.S. 424, 432 (1971).

25    *"an even chance."*   NAACP Legal Defense and Educational Fund, *An Even Chance* (New York: NAACP Legal Defense and Educational Fund, 1971).

27    *Court ruling.*   *Natonabah.*

27    *Consent decree.*   *Denetclarence v. Board of Education,* Judgment, N. 8872 Civil (D. N. M. Feb. 15, 1974).

28    *History of San Juan County (generally).*   Robert S. McPherson, *A History of San Juan County* (Salt Lake City: Utah State Historical Society and San Juan County Commission, 1995); Gary Topping, *Glen Canyon and the San Juan Country* (Moscow: University of Idaho Press, 1997).

28    *Monticello.*   Charles S. Peterson, *Look to the Mountains: Southeastern Utah and*

351

# Notes

*the La Sal National Forest* (Provo: Brigham Young University Press, 1975); Faun McConkie Tanner, *The Far Country: A Regional History of Moab and La Sal, Utah* (Salt Lake City: Olympus, 1976).

28 *Blanding.* Gary L. Shumway, "Blanding: The Making of a Community," *Utah Historical Quarterly* 48(4) (Fall 1980): 390–405.

29 *The legal troubles of Peter McDonald.* Jay Rayner, "Little Big Mac—The Navajo Chief Who Split the Nation," *Guardian,* Aug. 29, 1992, p. 4; Laura Laughlin, "Ex Official of Navajo Tribe Wins Court Leniency Plea," *Los Angeles Times,* Dec. 1, 1992, p. A20.

31 *Navajo language radio (generally).* Michael Haederle, "All Navajo, All the Time: With a Homely Mix of Music, News and Gossip, KNDN Binds a Far-Flung Indian Community," *Los Angeles Times,* Aug. 3, 1992, p. E1.

### CHAPTER 3: DESERET

37 *Hole-in-the-Rock Expedition (generally).* David E. Miller, *Hole-in-the-Rock: An Epic in the Colonization of the Great American West* (Salt Lake City: University of Utah Press, 1966); William B. Smart, *Old Utah Trails* (Salt Lake City: Utah Geographic Series, 1988), pp. 121–133.

37 *Elizabeth Morris Decker and Cornelius Decker (generally).* Miller, *Hole-in-the-Rock.* See also the untitled two-page biography of Elizabeth Decker at the Daughters of the Utah Pioneers Museum in Salt Lake City.

38 *Decker's equipment* Miller, *Hole-in-the-Rock,* pp. 192 and 195.

39 *National parks on the Plateau (generally).* Scott Thybony, *Canyon Country Parklands: Treasures of the Great Plateau* (Washington, D.C.: National Geographic Society, 1993).

39 *Dance Hall Rock.* Miller, *Hole-in-the-Rock,* p. 54.

40 *physical description of Lizzie Decker* Untitled biography, Daughters of the Utah Pioneers Museum ("this dainty, curly headed girl with her sunny disposition").

40 *"a new religious tradition."* Jan Shipps, *Mormonism: The Story of a New Religious Tradition* (Urbana: University of Illinois Press, 1985).

40 *Church of Jesus Christ of Latter Day Saints (generally).* Leonard J. Arrington and Davis Britton, *The Morman Experience: A History of the Latter-Day Saints* (Chicago: University of Illinois Press, 1992); James B. Allen and Glen M. Leonard, *The Story of the Latter-Day Saints* (Salt Lake City: Deseret Book Co., 1992); Shipps, *Mormonism,* p. 149.

40 *Joseph Smith.* Fawn M. Brodie, *No Man Knows My History: The Life of Joseph Smith, the Mormon Prophet* (New York: Knopf, 1960).

40 *Mormon doctrine.* Bruce R. McConkie, *Mormon Doctrine,* 2nd ed.(Salt Lake City: Bookcraft, 1966).

41 *"God himself."* *History of the Church of LDS,* 2nd rev. ed. (Salt Lake City: Deseret News Press, 1964), vol. 7, p. 464.

41 *"prophets, seers, and revelators."* D. Michael Quinn, *The Mormon Hierarchy: Origins of Power* (Salt Lake City: Signature Books, 1994).

41 *Number of wives of Smith and Young.* Wallace Stegner, *The Gathering of Zion: The Story of the Mormon Trail* (Salt Lake City: Westwater Press, 1981), pp. 33 and

# Notes

199; Linda King Newell and Valeen Tippetts Avery, *Mormon Enigma: Emma Hale Smith* (Garden City: Doubleday, 1984), p. 333.

41    *proselytizing.*    D. Michael Quinn, historian of the LDS Church, interview with author, Salt Lake City, Utah, March 4, 1994.

42    *Mormon Trail (generally).*    Leonard J. Arrington et al., *Building the City of God: Community and Cooperation among the Mormons* (Salt Lake City: Deseret Book Co., 1976); Stegner, *Gathering of Zion.*

42    *"a city clean and in order."*    Stegner, *Gathering of Zion,* p. 170.

42    *"They were the most systematic."*    Ibid., p. 6.

42    *Mormon pioneer figures.*    Ibid., p. 9.

42    *proclamation of the Provisional State of Deseret.*    Dale L. Morgan, *The State of Deseret* (Logan: Utah State University Press, 1987), pp. 26–27.

43    *meaning of "Deseret."*    Ibid., p. 32.

43    *Deseret and Utah Territory (generally)*    Charles S. Peterson, *Utah: A Bicentennial History* (New York: Norton, 1977), pp. 37–40; Dean L. May, *Utah: A People's History* (Salt Lake City: University of Utah Press, 1987), pp. 68–69; Morgan, *State of Deseret.*

43    *Population figures.*    Edward Leo Lyman, *Political Deliverance: The Mormon Quest for Utah Statehood* (Urbana: University of Illinois Press, 1986), p. 12; Stegner, *Gathering of Zion,* p. 9. See also Remarks of John F. Kinney, delegate from Utah Territory, of March 17, 1864, *Congressional Globe,* 38th Cong., 1st sess., pp. 1170–1173 (March 19, 1864), series no. 74.

43    *Utah Statehood battle.*    Lyman, *Political Deliverance;* Gustive O. Larson, *The "Americanization" of Utah for Statehood* (San Marino, Calif.: Huntington Library, 1971).

43    *statehood population requirement.*    Lyman, *Political Deliverance,* p. 7.

43    *Polygamy (generally).*    Richard S. Van Wagoner, *Mormon Polygamy: A History* (Salt Lake City: Signature Books, 1992); Newell and Avery, *Mormon Enigma,* pp. 130–156.

44    *"gentlemen."*    Morris K. Udall, *Too Funny to Be President* (New York: Holt, 1988), p. 82.

44    *"The Manifesto."*    Gustive O. Larson, "The Crusade and the Manifesto," in Richard D. Poll, ed., *Utah's History* (Provo: Brigham Young University Press, 1978), pp. 257–274.

44    *colonization goals of Brigham Young (generally).*    Leonard J. Arrington, *Brigham Young: American Moses* (New York: Knopf, 1985), pp. 167–191.

44    *mission calls (generally).*    Eugene E. Campbell, *Establishing Zion: The Mormon Church in the American West, 1847–1869* (Salt Lake City: Signature Books, 1988), pp. 57–91; Arrington, *Brigham Young;* May, *Utah,* pp. 72–73.

44    *number of Mormon communities.*    May, *Utah,* p. 73.

45    *Membership of the LDS Church in 1900.*    Shipps, *Mormonism,* p. 168.

45    *the founding of Utah's "Dixie."*    Angus M. Woodbury, *A History of Southern Utah and Its National Parks,* rev. ed. (Salt Lake City: Utah State Historical Society, 1950).

45    *Lamanites and Indians (generally).*    William E. Berrett, *Teachings of the Book of*

# Notes

*Mormon* (Salt Lake City: Deseret Book Co., 1965), pp. 210–216; B. H. Roberts, *Studies of the Book of Mormon*, 2nd ed. (Salt Lake City: Signature Books, 1992), pp. 188–194; Daniel H. Ludlow, ed., *Encyclopedia of Mormonism: The History, Scripture, Doctrine, and Procedure of the Church of Jesus Christ of Latter-Day Saints* (New York: Macmillan, 1992), vol. 2, pp. 804–805.

45  *"filthy," "loathsome," "full of idleness."*   *Book of Mormon*, 1 Nephi 12:23 (1986 ed.).

45  *"curse" of the Lamanites.*   *Book of Mormon*, Alma 3:14–16, 23:5–9, 23:17–18. See also Eugene England, "'Lamanites' and the Spirit of the Lord," *Dialogue: A Journal of Mormon Thought* (18)4 (1985): 25–32.

46  *"white and delightsome."*   McConkie, *Mormon Doctrine*, p. 429, quoting *Book of Mormon*, 2 Nephi 30:6. At 2 Nephi 30:6, the *Book of Mormon* used from 1870 until 1981 contained the phrase "a white and delightsome people." In the current *Book of Mormon* (1986 ed.), this phrase has been changed to "a pure and delightsome people." The reason given for this change, one of the few textual changes ever made, is that "pure and delightsome" reflects language used in pre-1870 editions. See "A Brief Explanation about the Book of Mormon," *Book of Mormon* (1986 ed.). Elsewhere in the current edition of the *Book of Mormon*, the term remains "white." See *Book of Mormon*, 2 Nephi 5:21; Jacob 3:8; 3 Nephi 2:15.

46  *Parowan mission call.*   Miller, *Hole-in-the-Rock*, p. 10.

46  *"everybody was bragging."*   Ibid., pp. 191–192.

48  *President Smith's decision.*   Ibid., pp. 65–67.

49  *"we have just sent."* Ibid., p. 76.

49  *"Genie and Willie."*   Ibid., p. 80.

49  *Lena Deseret Decker.*   Ibid., p. 81.

49  *Dynamite.*   Ibid., pp. 105–106.

49  *"Uncle Ben's Dugway."*   Ibid.

50  *"it nearly scared."*   Ibid., p. 197.

50  *"the roughest country."*   Ibid., p. 197.

51  *"the night we got down."*   Ibid., p. 195.

51  *"Aside from the Hole-in-the-Rock."* Leonard J. Arrington, *Utah's Audacious Stockman: Charlie Redd* (Logan: Utah State University Press, 1993), p. 15.

52  *"Who goes through life."*   This quotation was read to me by Eliza Redd's grandson, Hardy Redd, on March 20, 1993.

53  *purchase of sheep and cattle operations.*   Arrington, *Audacious Stockman*, pp. 29–30, and 37; Robert S. McPherson, *A History of San Juan County* (Salt Lake City: Utah State Historical Society and San Juan County Commission, 1995).

53  *creation of San Juan County.*   Arrington, *Audacious Stockman*, p. 17; McPherson, *San Juan County*, p. 319.

53  *"one person, one vote."*   *Baker v. Carr*, 369 U.S. 186 (1962).

53  *Decker family moves to Arizona and Colorado.* Untitled biography, Daughters of the Utah Pioneers Museum.

54  *people "who built the roads."*   Hardy Redd, interview with author, Bluff, Utah, March 20, 1993.

# Notes

CHAPTER 4: COYOTE

56    *Indian education (generally).*   Francis Paul Prucha, *American Indian Policy in Crisis: Christian Reformers and the Indian, 1865–1900* (Norman: University of Oklahoma Press, 1976), pp. 265–291; Margaret Szasz, *Education and the American Indian: The Road to Self-Determination since 1928,* 2nd ed. (Albuquerque: University of New Mexico Press, 1977).

57    *"kill the Indian."*   Francis Paul Prucha, ed., *Americanizing the American Indians: Writings by the "Friends of the Indian," 1880–1900* (Cambridge, Mass.: Harvard University Press, 1973), pp. 260–261.

57    *Christian reformers.*   Prucha, *American Indian Policy.*

58    *"the overwhelming majority."*   Miguel León-Portilla, *Aztecs and Navajos: A Reflection on the Right of Not Being Engulfed* (New York: Weatherhead Foundation, 1975), p. 20.

58    *Navajoland and Navajo creation belief.*   Stephen Trimble, *The People: Indians of the American Southwest* (Santa Fe: School of American Research Press, 1993), p. 131; Terry Tempest Williams, *Pieces of White Shell: A Journey to Navajoland* (Albuquerque: University of New Mexico Press, 1984), pp. 30–35; Paul G. Zolbrod, *Diné bahanè: The Navajo Creation Story* (Albuquerque: University of New Mexico Press, 1984).

59    *Jacob Hamblin (generally).*   Juanita Brooks, *Jacob Hamblin, Mormon Apostle to the Indians* (Salt Lake City: Westwater Press, 1980).

59    *"nobler branches."*   Steve Pavlik, "Of Saints and Lamanites: An Analysis of Navajo Mormonism," *Wicazo Sa Review* 8(1) (Spring 1992): 21.

59    *Indian Student Placement Program.*   Daniel H. Ludlow, ed., *Encyclopedia of Mormonism: The History, Scripture, Doctrine, and Procedure of the Church of Jesus Christ of Latter-Day Saints* (New York: Macmillan, 1992), vol. 5, pp. 679–680; "Church Modifies Indian Placement Program," UPI (Jan. 13, 1985), available in LEXIS, Nexis Library, UPI File.

60    *"the children."*   John Dart, "Indians Hope to Shift Mormon View of Their Skin Color," *Washington Post,* March 2, 1979, p. A-26.

60    *revision of "white and delightsome."*   See author's note, "white and delightsome," to page 46, above.

60    *Mormon Church and Navajo converts.*   Kendall A. Blanchard, *The Economics of Sainthood: Religious Change among the Rimrock Navajos* (Rutherford, N.J.: Associated University Presses, 1977); Pavlik, "Of Saints and Lamanites."

60    *"use that faith."*   Pavlik, "Of Saints and Lamanites," p. 27.

60    *Criticism of ISP program.*   "Church Modifies."

62    *The Monkey Wrench Gang.*   Edward Abbey, *The Monkey Wrench Gang* (Philadelphia: Lippincott, 1975). See also, James Bishop Jr., *Epitaph for a Desert Anarchist: The Life and Legacy of Edward Abbey* (New York: Atheneum, 1994).

62    *Calvin Black.*   Raymond Wheeler, "Southern Utah: The Trauma of Shifting Economies and Ideologies," in Ed Marston, ed., *Reopening the Western Frontier* (Washington, D.C.: Island Press, 1989), pp. 164–166; Jim Woolf, "Utahn Calvin Black Is in Another Uranium-Related Fight," *High Country News,* March 13, 1989, p. 7.

# Notes

63    *BIA day schools on Navajo Reservation.*   Szasz, *Education*, p. 63.

63    *Transfer of Indian education to states.*   Ibid., p. 89; Francis Paul Prucha, *The Great Father: The United States Government and the American Indians* (Lincoln: University of Nebraska Press, 1986), pp. 352–353.

63    *Navajo children in district schools.*   *Sinajini v. Board of Education,* Civil No. 74-346, Agreement of Parties, pp. 6–8 (D. Utah, Aug. 15, 1975).

65    *Disparity in school expenditures and conditions of Navajo schools.*   Testimony of Jack Hennessy before the U.S. Commission on Civil Rights, Hearings on the Educational System in San Juan County, Utah (Supplement to Oral Testimony submitted on Oct. 23, 1973, at Window Rock, Navajo Nation); Hildegard Thompson, *The Navajos' Long Walk for Education: A History of Navajo Education* (Tsaile, Ariz.: Navajo Community College Press, 1975).

67    *"they should put" and "I wish."*   Navajo children, interviews with Rick Nordwell, San Juan County, Utah, Dec. 1974.

68    *Coyote stories.*   Hilary Groutage, "He Will Tell Stories, But Not in Summer," *Los Angeles Times,* June 25, 1990, p. E3. See also Bernard Haile, ed., *Navajo Coyote Tales: The Curly Tó Aheedlíinii Version* (Lincoln: University of Nebraska Press, 1984); Barry Lopez, *Giving Birth to Thunder, Sleeping with His Daughter: Coyote Builds North America* (New York: Avon Books, 1977).

69    *"if it floats."*   Zolbrod, *Diné bahanè,* p. 82.

69    *Santa Fe Coyote.*   My thanks to Marlon Sherman.

75    *settlement.*   *Sinajini,* agreement.

76    *school bond election.*   "Navajos Carry Utah School Bond Election," *Navajo Times,* Nov. 13, 1975, p. A-1.

76    *Opening of schools.*   "Whitehorse High School Dedicated Saturday," *San Juan Record,* Aug. 24, 1978, p. 4.

77    *Subsequent litigation.*   *Sinajini v. Board of Education,* 964 F. Supp. 319 (D.Utah 1997).

### CHAPTER 5: VISHNU

81    *"for law is organic."*   Rennard Strickland, *Fire and the Spirits: Cherokee Law from Clan to Court* (Norman: University of Oklahoma Press, 1975), p. xiv.

82    *Navajo mining taxes.*   See *Kerr-McGee Corp. v. Navajo Tribe,* 471 U.S. 195 (1985); *Southland Royalty Co. v. Navajo Tribe,* 715 F.2d 486 (10th Cir. 1983).

85    *Colorado River guides (generally).*   David Sievert Lavender, *River Runners of the Grand Canyon* (Grand Canyon, Ariz.: Grand Canyon Natural History Association, 1985); Christa Sadler, ed., *There's This River: Grand Canyon Boatman Stories* (Flagstaff, Ariz.: Red Lake Books, 1994); Michael P. Ghiglieri, *Canyon* (Tucson: University of Arizona Press, 1992); Nancy Nelson, *Any Time Any Place Any River: The Nevills of Mexican Hat* (Flagstaff, Ariz.: Red Lake Books, 1991); Katie Lee, *All My Rivers Are Gone: A Journey of Discovery through Glen Canyon* (Boulder: Johnson Books, 1998).

85    *Major John Wesley Powell (generally).*   Wallace Stegner, *Beyond the Hundredth Meridian: John Wesley Powell and the Second Opening of the West* (Lincoln: University of Nebraska Press, 1954).

85    *Powell's explorations.*   John Wesley Powell, *The Exploration of the Colorado*

# Notes

*River and Its Canyons* (New York: Dover, 1961; originally published in 1895); John Wesley Powell, *Report on the Lands of the Arid Region of the United States, with a More Detailed Account of the Lands of Utah* (Boston: Harvard Common Press, 1983; originally published in 1879); Frederick S. Dellenbaugh, *A Canyon Voyage: The Narrative of the Second Powell Expedition down the Green-Colorado River from Wyoming, and the Explorations on Land, in the Years 1871 and 1872* (New Haven: Yale University Press, 1962; originally published in 1908, 1926).

86    *Death of Powell Colleagues.*    Wesley P. Larsen, "The 'Letter' or Were the Powell Men Really Killed by Indians?" *Canyon Legacy* 17 (Spring 1993): 12–19.

86    *Wonders.*    Powell, *Exploration of the Colorado*, pp. 251–253.

86    *Ute version of canyon creation.*    "Origin of the Colorado River and Its Canyons— A Ute Myth," recorded by John Wesley Powell in John F. Hoffman, *Arches National Park: An Illustrated Guide and History* (San Diego: Western Recreational Publications, 1981), p. 50.

86    *"rolled a river."*    Ibid.

87    *Arid Lands Report.*    Powell, Report on the Lands.

87    *insights were luminous.*    See Stegner, *Beyond the Hundredth Meridian.*

87    *"we are now ready."*    Powell, *Exploration of the Colorado*, p. 247.

89    *Grand Canyon geology (generally).*    Stanley S. Beus and Michael Morales, eds., *Grand Canyon Geology* (Flagstaff: Museum of Northern Arizona Press, 1990); Michael Collier, *An Introduction to Grand Canyon Geology* (Grand Canyon, Ariz.: Grand Canyon Natural History Association, 1980).

89    *Geology of the Colorado Plateau (generally).*    Donald L. Baars, *The Colorado Plateau: A Geologic History* (Albuquerque: University of New Mexico Press, 1983); F. A. Barnes, *Canyon Country Geology for the Layman and Rockhound* (Salt Lake City: Wasatch, 1978).

89    *technical studies of Plateau geology.*    Fred Peterson and Christine Turner-Peterson (leaders), "Geology of the Colorado Plateau, Field Trip Guidebook T130," paper presented at the 28th International Geological Congress, Grand Junction to Denver, Colo., June 30–July 7, 1989; Charles B. Hunt, *Cenozoic Geology of the Colorado Plateau: Geological Survey Professional Paper 279* (Washington, D.C.: U.S. Government Printing Office, 1956).

90    *other sources of the geology of the Plateau.*    Dr. Jack Campbell, interview with author, Denver, Colo., Jan. 18, 1994; interview with Dr. Warren B. Hamilton, U.S. Geological Survey, Jan. 13, 1994; interviews and conversations with Dr. Richard Reynolds, U.S. Geological Survey 1993, 1994, 1995, and 1998.

97    *population figures.*    Population information for these cities (all of which have additional population in surrounding areas) is available on the World Wide Web, U.S. Department of Commerce, Bureau of the Census, *Homepage* (visited Nov. 23, 1998) ‹http://www.census.gov/population/www/estimates/popest.html›.

98    *Grand Canyon rapids (generally).*    See Larry Stevens, *The Colorado River in Grand Canyon: A Comprehensive Guide to Its Natural and Human History,* 3rd ed. (Flagstaff, Ariz.: Red Lake Books, 1987).

98    *Cardenas expedition.*    Herbert E. Bolton, *Coronado: Knight of Pueblos and Plains* (Albuquerque: University of New Mexico Press, 1949), pp. 137–142.

98    *"Grand Canyon National Park."*    Lomawywesa (Michael Kabotie), *Migration*

# Notes

*Tears: Poems about Transitions* (Los Angeles: American Indian Studies Center, University of California–Los Angeles, 1987), pp. 40–41.

99    *"Three lightest" and "very hard."*   Katharine Bartlett, Harold S. Colton, and Jack Holterman, "Spanish Pathways," *Cañon Journal* 1 (Spring 1995): 32 and 37.

### CHAPTER 6: KYKOTSMOVI

109    *firm treated as a single lawyer.*   American Bar Association, Model Rules of Professional Conduct, Rule 1.10(a), explanatory comment #[6]; Geoffrey C. Hazard Jr. et al., *The Law and Ethics of Lawyering,* 2nd ed. (Westbury, N.Y.: Foundation, 1994), p. 640.

109    *Navajo tax ordinances.*   See, for example, *Kerr-McGee Corp. v. Navajo Tribe,* 471 U.S. 195 (1985).

109    *Navajo oil and gas wells.*   Donald R. Wharton, "Resource Development on Navajo: The Dineh Power Project," paper presented at the University of Colorado Natural Resources Law Center's Natural Resources Development in Indian Country Conference, Boulder, Colo., June 8–10, 1988, p. 2.

110    *"Indian sovereignty."*   *Merrion v. Jicarilla Apache Tribe,* 455 U.S. 130, 147–148 (1982).

110    *"the most basic."*   Felix S. Cohen, *Felix S. Cohen's Handbook of Federal Indian Law* (Albuquerque: University of New Mexico Press, 1971; originally published in 1942), p. 122.

110    *"benefit from."*   *Merrion,* pp. 137–138.

111    *"federal checkpoints."*   Ibid., p. 155.

111    *Indian Reorganization Act provision for tribal constitutions.*   Indian Reorganization Act of 1934, PL 73-383, chap. 576 §16, 48 Stat. 984, 987; 25 U.S.C. §476 (1994).

111    *Tribal attorney's advice.*   Scott C. Pugsley, attorney in Nielsen and Senior law firm, opinion letter to Honorable Ivan L. Sidney, chairman of the Hopi Tribal Council (Aug. 3, 1984).

112    *Supreme Court Indian opinions often written broadly.*   See, for example, *Worcester v. Georgia,* 31 U.S. (6 Pet.) 515 (1832); *Lone Wolf v. Hitchcock,* 187 U.S. 553 (1903); *McClanahan v. Arizona State Tax Commission,* 411 U.S. 164 (1973); *Oliphant v. Suquamish Indian Tribe,* 435 U.S. 191 (1978); *Merrion v. Jicarilla Apache Tribe,* 455 U.S. 130 (1982).

112    *"this case is a watershed."*   Amicus Brief for Superior Oil Co. et al. at 21, *Kerr-McGee.*

112    *conflict of interest.*   American Bar Association, Model Rules of Professional Conduct, Rule 1.7, explanatory comments #[8] and [9]; American Bar Association, Model Code of Professional Responsibility, Disciplinary Rule 5-105.

112    *"An attorney is bound."*   *Williams v. Reed,* 29 F.Cas. 1386, 1390 (C.C.Me. 1824).

113    *positional conflicts.*   John S. Dzienkowski, "Positional Conflicts of Interest," *Texas Law Review* 71 (Feb. 1993): 457–540; R. David Donoghue, "Conflicts of Interest: Concurrent Representation," *Georgetown Journal of Legal Ethics* 11 (Winter 1998): 319–328.

113    *"there are many concerns."*   Transcript, meeting of the Special Committee on Organization and Design with Nielsen & Senior, P.C., p. 2, Salt Lake City, Utah (Dec. 7, 1984).

# Notes

114    *"thought [the brief] was."*    Ibid., p. 5.

114    *"detrimental to."*    Ibid., p. 6.

114    *"the brief ultimately."*    Ibid., p. 11.

114    *"the Navajo Tribe."*    Ibid., p. 5.

114    *"[the Hopi] have always."*    Ibid., p. 6.

114    *"apparently the Hopis."*    Ibid., p. 33.

115    *December 7 meeting.*    Ibid.

115    *opinion letter.*    John D. Leshy and Charles F. Wilkinson, opinion letter to Honorable Clifford Balenquah, vice-chairman of the Hopi Tribal Council (Jan. 16, 1985).

115    *Code of Professional Ethics.*    American Bar Association, Model Rules of Professional Conduct, Rule 1.7, explanatory comments #[8] and [10]; American Bar Association, Model Code of Professional Responsibility, Ethical Consideration 5-16.

116    *"at the same time."*    Geoffrey C. Hazard, opinion letter to Honorable Clifford Balenquah, vice-chairman of the Hopi Tribal Council (Jan. 16, 1985), p. 4.

121    *"the tribe should."*    George Hardeen, "Indian Law Professors Criticize Hopi's Lawyers," *Navajo Times,* Jan. 28, 1985, p. 1.

### CHAPTER 7: JACK

124    *Boyden family.*    Orpha Sweeten Boyden, *John S. Boyden: Three Score and Ten in Retrospect* (Cedar City: Southern Utah State College Press, 1986).

125    *Quotes about John Boyden.*    C. B. Copley, interview with author, Coalville, Utah, March 4, 1994.

125    *"perhaps John Boyden."*    Boyden, *John S. Boyden,* quoting "A Splendid Young Man," *Summit County Bee* (Spring 1924): 13.

126    *Mormon involvement in the Short Creek raids.*    Boyden, *John S. Boyden,* p. 33.

126    *"Boyden Raids."*    Martha Sonntag Bradley, *Kidnapped from That Land: The Government Raids on the Short Creek Polygamists* (Salt Lake City: University of Utah Press, 1993), p. 68.

126    *"Boyden Crusade."*    Richard S. Van Wagoner, *Mormon Polygamy: A History,* 2nd ed. (Salt Lake City: Signature Books, 1989), p. 287.

126    *"we did all the tourist things."*    Boyden, *John S. Boyden,* pp. 30–31.

126    *"as John visited."*    Ibid., p. 31.

127    *theories of Ute origin.*    J. Donald Hughes, *American Indians in Colorado,* 2nd ed. (Boulder: Pruett, 1987), pp. 26–27; David B. Madsen, *Exploring the Fremont* (Salt Lake City: Utah Museum of Natural History/University of Utah, 1989), pp. 1–15, 63–64; Charles S. Marsh, *People of the Shining Mountains: The Utes of Colorado* (Boulder: Pruett, 1982).

127    *Ute culture and history (generally).*    Donald Callaway, Joel Janetski, and Omer C. Stewart, "Ute," in William C. Sturtevant, gen. ed., *Handbook of North American Indians,* vol. 11, pp. 336–367 (Washington, D.C.: Smithsonian Institution, 1986); Marsh, *Shining Mountains;* Mark E. Miller, *Hollow Victory: The White River Expedition of 1879 and the Battle of Milk Creek* (Niwot: University Press of Colorado, 1997).

127    *Ute creation accounts.*    Nancy Wood, *When Buffalo Free the Mountains* (Garden

# Notes

City: Doubleday, 1980), pp. xiii–xiv, and 5; For an account citing Coyote as the bag carrier, see Steve Jackson, "Sacred Ground," *Westword*, Oct. 19–25, 1994, pp. 26, and 28–30.

128 *Utes and horses (generally).* Robert W. Delaney, *The Southern Ute People,* (Phoenix: Indian Tribal Series, 1974), pp. 9, 12, 17; Marsh, *Shining Mountains,* pp. 12, 14–15, 34; Anne M. Smith, *Ethnography of the Northern Utes,* Museum of New Mexico Papers in Anthropology no. 17 (Santa Fe: Museum of New Mexico Press, 1974), pp. 31–33, 54, 121–122, 127.

128 *Ute hunting grounds.* David Lavender, *David Lavender's Colorado* (Garden City: Doubleday, 1976), p. 66.

130 *the abundance of mammals.* Callaway, Janetski, and Stewart, "Ute," p. 338.

130 *Utes and buffalo.* Callaway, Janetski, and Stewart, "Ute," pp. 337–338, 341, 346, 348; Marsh, *Shining Mountains,* p. 171.

130 *Ute use of vegetation at Morgan Bottoms.* Clifford Duncan, Northern Ute Tribal Council, telephone interview with author, Aug. 30, 1993; A. Smith, *Ethnography,* pp. 37, 66, 83, 119; Callaway, Janetski, and Stewart, "Ute," pp. 337–338.

132 *Ouray (generally).* P. David Smith, *Ouray: Chief of the Utes* (Ouray, Colo.: Wayfinder Press, 1990); Dee Brown, *Bury My Heart at Wounded Knee: An Indian History of the American West* (New York: Holt, 1970), pp. 367–370 and 387–389; Marsh, *Shining Mountains,* pp. 43, 57–68, 99–104.

132 *Treaty of 1868.* Treaty with the Ute Indians, March 2, 1868, 15 Stat. 619 (1869); Marsh, *Shining Mountains,* pp. 67–68; P. David Smith, *Ouray,* pp. 72–76.

132 *tribal ownership of treaty land.* See Felix S. Cohen, *Felix S. Cohen's Handbook of Federal Indian Law* (Charlottesville, Va.: Michie Bobbs-Merrill, 1982), pp. 471–477.

133 *Ouray's assimilationist ways and difficulties with his people.* Robert Emmitt, *The Last War Trail: The Utes and the Settlement of Colorado* (Norman: University of Oklahoma Press, 1954); Wilson Rockwell, *The Utes: A Forgotten People* (Denver: Sage Books, 1956) p. 104; P. David Smith, Ouray, pp. 139–144.

133 *photographs of Ouray.* Marsh, *Shining Mountains,* pp. 61 and 82.

133 *Jack's youth.* Brown, *Bury My Heart,* pp. 372–373; Emmitt, *Last War Trail,* pp. 39–40, and 301–302; Marsh, *Shining Mountains,* p. 92; M. Wilson Rankin, *Reminiscences of Frontier Days; Including an Authentic Account of the Thornburgh and Meeker Massacre* (Denver: Smith-Brooks, 1935), p. 36.

133 *photographs of Jack.* P. David Smith, *Ouray,* pp. 173 and 177; Marsh, *Shining Mountains,* p. 77.

133 *Jack's attitude.* Brown, *Bury My Heart,* p. 367; Emmitt, *Last War Trail,* p. 55; Marsh, *Shining Mountains,* pp. 89–90.

134 *Brunot Agreement.* Act of April 29, 1874, chap. 136, 18 Stat. 36 (1878); Marsh, *Shining Mountains,* p. 75; P. David Smith, *Ouray,* pp. 91,–117; Brown, *Bury My Heart,* pp. 370–371.

135 *Jack's meeting with Pitkin.* White River Ute Commission Investigation, House of Representatives, 46th Cong., 2nd sess., House Exec. Doc. no. 83 (1880); Marsh, *Shining Mountains,* pp. 89–90; Brown, *Bury My Heart,* pp. 377–378.

135 *inaugural speech.* Emmitt, *Last War Trail,* pp. 21–22; P. David Smith, *Ouray,* pp. 148, and 150.

# Notes

135    *Nathan Meeker (generally).*    Emmitt, *Last War Trail*, pp. 44–52; Marsh, *Shining Mountains*, pp. 87–92; Marshall D. Moody, "The Meeker Massacre," *Colorado Magazine* 30 (Jan. 1953): 91; P. David Smith, *Ouray*, pp. 154 and 157.

135    *White River agency relocation.*    Marsh, *Shining Mountains*, p. 89; Moody, "Meeker Massacre," p. 93; White River Investigation, p. 66; Brown, *Bury My Heart*, p. 372.

136    *"Reports reach me daily."*    Report of the Secretary of the Interior, 46th Cong., 2nd sess., House Exec. Doc. no. 1, pt. 5, vol. 1, p. 84 (Washington, D.C.: Government Printing Office, 1879).

136    *destruction by miners and loggers.*    Marsh, *Shining Mountains*, p. 79; Moody, "Meeker Massacre," p. 93; Albert B. Reagan, "Chipeta, Queen of the Utes, and Her Equally Illustrious Husband, Noted Chief Ouray," *Utah Historical Quarterly* 6 (Jan. 1933): 103 and 105; P. David Smith, *Ouray*, p. 157.

137    *Shooting of Ute hunter.*    Marsh, *Shining Mountains*, p. 89; P. David Smith, *Ouray*, p. 172.

137    *late annuities.*    Testimony in Relation to the Ute Indian Outbreak, House of Representatives Committee on Indian Affairs, 46th Cong., 2nd sess., House Misc. Doc. no. 38 (May 1, 1880); Brown, *Bury My Heart*, p. 374; Marsh, *Shining Mountains*, p. 89; P. David Smith, *Ouray*, p. 157.

137    *an "old lady."*    Emmitt, *Last War Trail*, pp. 78–79.

138    *"I have been assaulted."*    Secretary of the Interior, p. 91.

139    *Jack's meeting with Thornburgh.*    Marsh, *Shining Mountains*, pp. 92–93; P. David Smith, *Ouray*, p. 158; Ute Indian Outbreak, pp. 62–64, 192, 194; White River Investigation, pp. 71–72; Brown, *Bury My Heart*, pp. 381–382.

139    *"I told them."*    White River Investigation, p. 71.

139    *"Absolute and undisturbed use and occupation."*    Treaty with Ute, p. 619.

139    *"no persons . . . shall."*    Ibid., p. 620.

139    *"Officers . . . of the government."*    Ibid.

140    *"the Indians are greatly excited."*    Secretary of the Interior, pp. 92–93.

140    *"Have met some Ute chiefs here."*    Ibid., p. 93.

140    *"come in as desired."*    White River Investigation, p. 38.

140    *"within striking distance."*    Ute Indian Outbreak, p. 64; White River Investigation, p. 39.

141    *"I like your last programme."*    Secretary of the Interior, p. 93.

141    *"I expect to leave."*    Ibid.

141    *Sand Creek Massacre.*    Brown, *Bury My Heart*, pp. 83–94; Marsh, *Shining Mountains*, pp. 93–94; P. David Smith, *Ouray*, p. 158.

142    *"hold on! hold on!"*    White River Investigation, p. 73.

142    *Battle of Milk Creek.*    Miller, *Hollow Victory*, pp. 53–143; Ute Indian Outbreak, pp. 64,–69, 194–198; Brown, *Bury My Heart*, pp. 384–387; Marsh, *Shining Mountains*, pp. 94–95; P. David Smith, *Ouray*, pp. 160–162.

143    *death of Nathan Meeker.*    White River Investigation, pp. 13–16, 21–22, 25, 41–42; Marsh, *Shining Mountains*, pp. 95–97; Moody, "Meeker Massacre," pp. 99–100.

143    *kidnap of Arvilla and Josephine Meeker.*    White River Investigation, pp. 13–19, 21–27, 40–50; Marsh, *Shining Mountains*, pp. 97–100; Moody, "Meeker Massacre," pp. 99–102.

# Notes

143    *"Indians off their reservation."*    P. David Smith, *Ouray,* p. 165.

143    *testimony of Josephine and Arvilla Meeker.*    White River Investigation, pp. 21–27, and 40–50; Ute Indian Outbreak, pp. 71–94; Emmitt, *Last War Trail,* pp. 205–214.

143    *federal hearings.*    P. David Smith, *Ouray,* pp. 168–176; White River Investigation; Ute Indian Outbreak; Secretary of the Interior, pp. 82–98, and 121–125.

144    *Utes ordered to Washington.*    P. David Smith, *Ouray,* pp. 174–176; Marsh, *Shining Mountains,* p. 99.

144    *1880 agreement.*    Act of June 15, 1880, chap. 223, 21 Stat. 199 (1881).

144    *"The White River Utes agree."*    P. David Smith, *Ouray,* pp. 176–178 and 186–200; Marsh, *Shining Mountains,* p. 103.

145    *Nicaagat.*    Emmitt, *Last War Trail,* pp. 39 and 82.

145    *"all the people."*    White River Investigation, p. 76.

146    *Nicaagat's fate.*    Peter Tawse, Diary from May 17 to August 13, 1880 (available at Western History Collection, University of Colorado).

146    *Account of Nicaagat's death.*    See Marshall Sprague, *Massacre: The Tragedy at White River* (Boston: Little, Brown, 1957), pp. 325–326.

146    *Final exodus to Utah.*    Marsh, *Shining Mountains,* pp. 101–107 and 190–193; James Parker, *The Old Army: Memories, 1872–1918* (Philadelphia: Dorrance, 1929), pp. 130–135.

### CHAPTER 8: UINTAH

149    *history of the Uintah and Ouray Reservation and the three Ute bands.*    Fred A. Conetah, *A History of the Northern Ute People* (Salt Lake City: Uintah-Ouray Ute Tribe, 1982); Floyd A. O'Neil, "The Reluctant Suzerainty: The Uintah and Ouray Reservation," *Utah Historical Quarterly* 39 (Spring 1971): 129; Floyd A. O'Neil and Kathryn L. MacKay, *A History of Uintah-Ouray Ute Lands,* Occasional Paper of the American West Center (Salt Lake City: University of Utah, 1979); Joseph G. Jorgensen, *The Sun Dance Religion: Power for the Powerless* (Chicago: University of Chicago Press, 1972), pp. 28–66, and 89–173.

149    *aboriginal location of the Ute bands.*    Conetah, *Northern Ute People,* pp. 24–25; Jorgensen, *Sun Dance Religion,* pp. 29–41.

149    *Chief Walkara.*    Paul Bailey, *Walkara: Hawk of the Mountains* (Los Angeles: Westernlore Press, 1954).

149    *1861 executive order.*    *Executive Orders Relating to Indian Reservations,* 2 vols. (Washington, D.C.: Government Printing Office, 1912–1922), vol. 2, p. 169.

149    *1865 Spanish Forks Treaty.*    O'Neil and MacKay, *Uintah-Ouray Ute Lands,* p. 7.

150    *"One vast 'contiguity of waste.'"*    Jorgensen, *Sun Dance Religion,* p. 36.

150    *Effect of unratified treaties.*    Francis Paul Prucha, *American Indian Treaties: The History of a Political Anomaly* (Berkeley: University of California Press, 1994), pp. 70–79. See also Jennings C. Wise, *The Red Man in the New World Drama* (New York: Macmillan, 1971), p. 249.

151    *decline in Ute population.*    Jorgensen, *Sun Dance Religion,* pp. 37–38 and 48. Utah Utes, for example, declined in number from 4,500 in 1859 to 800 in 1880, ibid., p. 38.

151    *Uncompahgres' population.*    Floyd A. O'Neil, "A History of the Ute Indians of

# Notes

Utah until 1890," (Ph.D. dissertation, University of Utah, 1973, p. 162).

151 *1882 executive order.* *Executive Orders,* vol. 2, pp. 170–171.

151 *Desolation Canyon.* John Wesley Powell, *The Exploration of the Colorado River and Its Canyons* (New York: Dover Publications, 1961), pp. 192–195.

152 *rivalries among the bands.* Conetah, *Northern Ute People,* pp. 115–116; Jorgensen, *Sun Dance Religion,* pp. 48–50; O'Neil, "History of the Ute Indians," pp. 166–168, citing Elisha W. Davis, Uintah Agency, letter to commissioner of Indian affairs (Aug. 20, 1885).

152 *Ute landholdings.* See O'Neil and MacKay, *Uintah-Ouray Ute Lands.*

152 *federal administration.* O'Neil, "History of the Ute Indians," pp. 163–191.

152 *"these cattlemen have given."* O'Neil and MacKay, *Uintah-Ouray Ute Lands,* p. 23.

153 *"You [white people] are."* Ibid., p. 30, citing U.S. House of Representatives, "Grant of Lands for Use of Certain Indians," 58th Cong., 1st sess., House Doc. no. 33, p. 4 (May 30, 1903).

153 *Federal allotment policy (generally).* Frederick E. Hoxie, *A Final Promise: The Campaign to Assimilate the Indians, 1880–1920* (Lincoln: University of Nebraska Press, 1984); Francis Paul Prucha, *Americanizing the American Indians: Writings by the "Friends of the Indian," 1880–1900* (Cambridge, Mass.: Harvard University Press, 1973).

153 *allotment of Uintah and Ouray Reservation.* See David Rich Lewis, *Neither Wolf Nor Dog: American Indians, Environment, and Agrarian Change* (New York: Oxford University Press, 1994), pp. 34–70.

153 *1902 Ute Allotment Statute.* Act of May 27, 1902, PL 57-125, chap. 888, 32 Stat. 263 (1903).

154 *"the Indians understand."* Kathryn L. MacKay, "The Strawberry Valley Reclamation Project and the Opening of the Uintah Indian Reservation," *Utah Historical Quarterly* 50 (Winter 1982): 68 and 83.

154 *1905 Ute Allotment Statute.* Act of March 3, 1905, PL 58-212, chap. 1479, 33 Stat. 1048, 1069–1070 (1905).

154 *1905 land drawing.* MacKay, "Strawberry Valley," p. 86.

154 *1905 National Forest Reserves Proclamation.* Presidential Proclamation of July 14, 1905, 34 Stat. 3116 (1907). See also Joanna Endter, "Cultural Ideologies and the Political Economy of Water in the United States West: Northern Ute Indians and Rural Mormons in the Uintah Basin, Utah" (Ph.D. dissertation, University of California at Irvine, 1987, p. 115); O'Neil and MacKay, *Uintah-Ouray Ute Lands,* p. 32.

154 *Ute loss of landholdings.* Endter, "Cultural Ideologies," pp. 115, 123; O'Neil and MacKay, *Uintah-Ouray Ute Lands,* pp. 32–35.

154 *"The Last Great Undeveloped."* Independent Service promotional pamphlet, March 1916; copy provided by John Shurts.

155 *tribal land acquisition.* Conetah, *Northern Ute People,* pp. 140–144; Jorgensen, *Sun Dance Religion,* p. 151.

155 *Ute stories.* Anne M. Smith, ed., *Ute Tales* (Salt Lake City: University of Utah Press, 1992).

# Notes

155    *"the remembered earth."*   N. Scott Momaday, "The Remembered Earth," in Geary
       Hobson, ed., *The Remembered Earth: An Anthology of Contemporary Native
       American Literature* (Albuquerque: University of New Mexico Press, 1981), p. 164.

156    *Ute poverty.*   Parker M. Nielson, *The Dispossessed: Cultural Genocide of the
       Mixed-Blood Utes: An Advocate's Chronicle* (Norman: University of Oklahoma
       Press, 1998), pp. 64–65; Conetah, *Northern Ute People*, p. 139.

156    *Indian Claims Commission Act.*   Indian Claims Commission Act of 1946, PL 79-
       726, chap. 959, 60 Stat. 1049 (1947), 25 U.S.C. §§70–70V (omitted 1994). See gen-
       erally, Felix S. Cohen, *Felix S. Cohen's Handbook of Federal Indian Law* (Char-
       lottesville, Va.: Michie Bobbs-Merrill, 1982), pp. 160–162, 562–574.

157    *1950 meeting.*   Minutes, General Council Meeting, Uintah and Ouray Agency,
       Fort Duchesne, Utah (May 29, 1950); "Indians: Back Pay for the Utes," *Time,* July
       24, 1950, p. 19; "Ute Indians Hit a $31.7 Million Jackpot," *Life,* July 24, 1950, p. 37.
       See also Nielson, *The Dispossessed,* pp. 36–43.

157    *"this is probably."*   Minutes, General Council Meeting, p. 2.

159    *"if we can get."*   Ibid., p. 7.

159    *"now the reason."*   Ibid., pp. 4–5.

159    *"I want to say."*   Ibid., p. 10.

159    *Utes wait to vote.*   "They Dance and Think before They Take Government
       Offer," *Life,* July 24, 1950, p. 38.

159    *Utes refusal to vote.*   Transcript of remarks by Robert L. Bennett, program offi-
       cer for the BIA, BIA staff meeting on the Uintah and Ouray Program, May 20,
       1954, p. 2. Bennett was a former BIA superintendent of the Uintah and Ouray
       Reservation and would later become commissioner of Indian affairs. See also
       Statement of Francis McKinley, Ute tribal member and coordinating officer,
       Hearings before the Committee on Interior and Insular Affairs, "Tribal Funds of
       the Ute Indian Tribe, Utah," 82nd Cong., 1st sess., (Washington, D.C.: Gov-
       ernment Printing Office, 1951), p. 4.

160    *June 1 vote.*   Nielson, *The Dispossessed,* pp. 40–42.

160    *"the resolution."*   Act of August 21, 1951, PL 82-120, chap. 338, 65 Stat. 194 (1952).

160    *disclaimer by Uintah Utes.*   Peyton Ford, deputy attorney general, Department
       of Justice, letter to Joseph C. O'Mahoney, chairman, Interior and Insular Com-
       mittee (June 15, 1951) in United States Code Congressional and Administrative
       News, 82nd Cong., 1st sess., p. 1704 (1951).

161    *Senator Watkins and the termination policy.*   Charles F. Wilkinson and Eric R.
       Biggs, "The Evolution of the Termination Policy," *American Indian Law Review* 5
       (1977): 139 and 155–156; Gary Orfield, "A Study of the Termination Policy"
       (Washington, D.C.: National Congress of American Indians, 1966), cited in
       Wilkinson and Biggs, "Termination Policy," p. 167, n. 10.

161    *"share and share alike" resolution.*   Nielson, *The Dispossessed,* pp. 36–43 and
       54–55; Remarks of Robert Bennett, p. 2.

161    *"it is anticipated."*   United States Code Congressional and Administrative News,
       82nd Cong., 1st sess., p. 1702 (1951).

161    *termination policy (generally).*   Donald Lee Fixico, *Termination and Relocation:*

# Notes

Federal Indian Policy, 1945–1960 (Albuquerque: University of New Mexico Press, 1986); Wilkinson and Biggs, "Termination Policy"; House Concurrent Resolution 108, 67 Stat. B132 (Aug. 1, 1953).

161 *"following in the footsteps."* Arthur V. Watkins, "Termination of Federal Supervision: The Removal of Restrictions over Indian Property and Person," *Annals of the American Academy of Political and Social Science* 311 (May 1957): 47 and 55.

162 *Watkins' legislative tactics.* Wilkinson and Biggs, "Termination Policy," pp. 155–157.

162 *John Boyden's attorney fees.* U.S. House of Representatives Subcommittee on Indian Affairs of the Committee on Interior and Insular Affairs, "Hearing on H.R. 7390 and S. 2742 to Amend the Act of August 21, 1951, Relating to Certain Payments Out of Ute Indian Tribal Funds," p. 2 (May 7, 1954) (unpublished), disclosing that $432,000 in attorney's expenses was paid to Boyden from the Utes between 1951 and 1954.

162 *claims award and the Termination Act.* Defendant's Exhibit 5 (Minutes, Meeting of the Uintah and Whiterivers *[sic]* at White Rocks on March 14, 1954); *Hackford v. First Security Bank of Utah,* No. C75-278 (D.Utah, Oct. 4, 1977), *aff'd,* 1983 WL 20180 (10th Cir. Jan. 31, 1983), *cert. denied,* 464 U.S. 827 (1983). At the meeting to discuss the proposed termination legislation, Robert Bennett, program officer of the BIA, who had been working closely with Senator Watkins, presented the termination issue—including the distribution of the remaining $13 million from the judgment of the Colorado claims case. The draft termination statute provided for the distribution and division of all assets, including cash, to the Mixed-Blood Utes, but only after a final distribution plan had been developed, approved, and executed. Arthur V. Watkins, U.S. Senator, letter to Joseph A. Workman, Mixed-Blood Ute (Feb. 2, 1955). Mr. Watkins' letter was in response to Mr. Workman's letter inquiring about the distribution of the Colorado claims award. Mr. Watkins explained in his response that the claims award would be distributed only after the termination roll had been prepared and a plan to distribute the tribal assets had been completed. The Utes' termination plan was finally completed in 1961.

162 *Watkins coercion at Menominee.* Vine Deloria Jr., *Custer Died for Your Sins: An Indian Manifesto* (New York: Avon Books, 1969), pp. 71–77.

163 *Mixed-Bloods' support.* Statement of Albert H. Harris, representative of the Mixed-Blood Members of the Ute Tribe, U.S. House of Representatives Subcommittee on Indian Affairs of the Committee on Interior and Insular Affairs, "Partition of Ute Indian Tribe of Uintah and Ouray Reservation, Utah, and Termination of Federal Supervision over Mixed-Blood Members," p. 15 (June 9, 1954) (unpublished).

163 *opposition by the White Rivers and Uncompahgres.* Ibid., pp. 7–8 (testimony of Reginald O. Curry, chairman, Ute Indian Tribal Business Committee).

163 *development program for Full-Blood termination.* Ute Termination Act of 1954, PL 83-671, chap. 1009 §24, 25 U.S.C. §677w (1994).

163 *Ute general council meeting.* Nielson, *The Dispossessed,* p. 57.

# Notes

163    *Ute Termination Act.*   Ute Termination Act, 25 U.S.C. §677–677aa (1994).

163    *Southern Paiute Termination Act.*   Act of September 1, 1954, PL 83-762, chap. 1207, 68 Stat. 1099 (1955).

164    *distribution to the Mixed-Blood Utes, including fraud.*   *Affiliated Ute Citizens of Utah v. United States,* 406 U.S. 128 (1972).

164    *Louis Bruce's concerns.*   Carl J. Cornelius, file memorandum describing the Uintah and Ouray meeting on Oct. 22, 1956 (Nov. 23, 1956).

164    *"if there were separate attorneys."*   Ibid.

165    *"I was trying."*   Deposition of John S. Boyden, *Hackford,* p. 52.

165    *early conceptions of the Central Utah Project.*   Jim Woolf, "Water Plan Devised in 1903 May Be Forefather of Central Utah Project," *Salt Lake Tribune,* Nov. 21, 1983, pp. B1 and B3.

165    *"to assume full responsibility."*   Orpha Sweeten Boyden, *John S. Boyden: Three Score and Ten in Retrospect* (Cedar City: Southern Utah State College, 1986), p. 47.

166    *Indian water rights (generally).*   Cohen, *Handbook of Federal Indian Law,* pp. 575–604; Daniel McCool, *Command of the Waters: Iron Triangles, Federal Water Development, and Indian Water* (Berkeley: University of California Press, 1987).

166    *Winters decision.*   *Winters v. United States,* 207 U.S. 564 (1908).

166    *Non-Indian water use*   See, for example, Endter, "Cultural Ideologies," pp. 133–136.

166    *John F. Truesdell.*   I thank John Shurts, a Ph.D. candidate in history at the University of Oregon, for allowing me to review John F. Truesdell's office files, which amply demonstrate the arduous work done by this U.S. attorney on behalf of the Utes.

166    *Ute water decree.*   *United States v. Cedarview Irrigation Co.,* No. 4427 (D.Utah Mar. 16, 1923).

166    *Ute Deferral Agreement.*   Agreement between the United States, the Ute Indian Tribe of the Uintah and Ouray Indian Reservation, and the Central Utah Water Conservancy District (Sept. 20, 1965); "Indians Okay Water Loan," *Deseret News,* May 7, 1965, p. 8B.

166    *"programmed for early authorization."*   Agreement between United States, Ute, Central Utah Water, p. 6.

167    *"recognized and confirmed."*   Ibid., p. 4.

167    *"The Indians signed."*   "Indians Okay Water Loan."

167    *Boyden's consideration of lawsuit.*   John S. Boyden, letter to E. L. Decker, John S. Boyden Papers (Dec. 10, 1963).

167    *Obtaining of water right*   See, for example, David H. Getches, *Water Law in a Nutshell,* 2nd ed. (St. Paul, MN: West, 1990), pp. 56–71 and 139–153.

168    *CUP delays and agreement (generally).*   Daniel McCool, "Utah and the Ute Tribe Are at War," *High Country News,* June 27, 1994, p. 12.

168    *Rock Creek.*   Cherrill Crosby, "Utes Sue Government over Water Project," United Press International, June 2, 1988.

168    *never even broken ground.*   Daniel McCool, professor of political science, director of the American West Center, University of Utah, telephone interview with

# Notes

Andrew Huff, research assistant, Sept. 14, 1998. See also Daniel McCool, ed., *Waters of Zion: The Politics of Water in Utah* (Salt Lake City: University of Utah Press, 1995), p. 189; Lloyd Burton, *American Indian Water Rights and the Limits of Law* (Lawrence: University Press of Kansas, 1991).

168   *1992 Settlement.*   Central Utah Project Act, PL 102-575, 106 Stat. 4605, 43 U.S.C. §620(k) (1994); Daniel McCool, telephone interview; Tod Smith, partner, Whiteing & Smith law firm, interview with Andrew Huff, research assistant, Boulder, Colo., Nov. 4, 1998. The 1992 Settlement Act consists of two parts: a monetary settlement compensating the Ute for the failure of the federal government to implement the 1965 Deferral Agreement, and a water compact quantifying water rights for the Ute. The monetary compensation has been accepted by the tribe, but the water compact is still under review.

169   *attempts to establish Boyden's conflict of interest.*   See Indian Law Resource Center, "Report to the Hopi Kikmongwis and Other Traditional Hopi Leaders on Docket 196 and the Continuing Threat to Hopi Land and Sovereignty" (Washington, D.C.: Indian Law Resource Center, 1979); Tim Vollmann, acting associate solicitor, Division of Indian Affairs, letter to Steve M. Tullberg, Indian Law Resource Center (July 18, 1983); Jim Richardson and John A. Farrell, "Divided Opposition," in "The New Indian Wars," *Denver Post,* special reprint ed., Nov. 21, 1983, p. 19.

170   *"I think that you should know."*   Transcript, presentation on proposed thermal power plant (before the Utah Water and Power Board), p. 25, statement of John Boyden, counsel for Peabody Coal (Dec. 1964), in John S. Boyden Papers, Accession No. 823, Box Nos. 1–79, Manuscript Division, Special Collections, University of Utah Marriott Library, Salt Lake City, Utah.

170   *"If this development."*   Ibid., pp. 27–28.

170   *"60,000 acre-feet."*   Ibid., p. 29.

171   *Arizona v. California.*   *Arizona v. California* 373 U.S. 546 (1963).

171   *"We as a Board."*   Transcript, thermal power plant, p. 31.

### CHAPTER 9: PHOENIX

174   *Phoenix (generally).*   Bradford Luckingham, *Phoenix: The History of a Southwestern Metropolis* (Tucson: University of Arizona Press, 1989); G. Wesley Johnson Jr., *Phoenix: Valley of the Sun* (Tulsa, Okla: Continental Heritage Press, 1982); Jay J. Wagoner, *Arizona Territory, 1863–1912: A Political History* (Tucson: University of Arizona Press, 1970); Salt River Project, *The Taming of the Salt: A Collection of Biographies of Pioneers Who Contributed Significantly to Water Development in the Salt River Valley* (Phoenix: Salt River Project, 1979).

174   *population of Phoenix.*   U.S. Department of Commerce, Bureau of the Census, "Sixteenth Census of the United States: 1940," p. 89, table 2: "Population of Cities of 10,000 or More from Earliest Census to 1940" (Washington, D.C.: Government Printing Office, 1942).

174   *Hohokam (generally).*   Patricia L. Crown and W. James Judge, eds., *Chaco and Hohokam: Prehistoric Regional Systems in the American Southwest* (Santa Fe: School of American Research Press, 1991); Dr. Glen Rice, "Life in Hohokam

# Notes

Courtyards," *Arizona Highways* 60 (Feb. 1984): 12; Emil W. Haury, "Before History" in Thomas Weaver, ed., *Indians of Arizona: A Contemporary Perspective*, (Tucson: University of Arizona Press, 1974), pp. 7–25.

174   *Hohokam irrigation systems (generally).*   Rich Johnson, *The Central Arizona Project, 1918–1968* (Tucson: University of Arizona Press, 1977), pp. 18–22; W. Bruce Masse, "The Quest for Subsistence Sufficiency and Civilization in the Sonoran Desert," in Crown and Judge, *Chaco and Hohokam*, pp. 207–223.

174   *Phoenix railroads (generally).*   Luckingham, *Phoenix*, pp. 29–30.

175   *statehood battle.*   Lawrence Clark Powell, *Arizona: A Bicentennial History* (New York: Norton, 1976), pp. 59–71; Ellen Lloyd Trover and William F. Swindler, eds., *Chronology and Documentary Handbook of the State of Arizona* (Dobbs Ferry, N.Y.: Oceana, 1972), pp. 105–115.

175   *"Americanization" of Arizona.*   Luckingham, *Phoenix*, pp. 96–97.

175   *floods and drought (generally).*   Karen L. Smith, *The Magnificent Experiment: Building the Salt River Reclamation Project, 1890–1917* (Tucson: University of Arizona Press, 1986), pp. 7, 58–59; Johnson, *Central Arizona Project*, p. 47; Jay J. Wagoner, *Arizona Territory, 1863–1912: A Political History* (Tucson: University of Arizona Press, 1970), pp. 422–423.

175   *Reclamation Act.*   Reclamation Act of 1902, PL 57-161, 32 Stat. 388, 43 U.S.C. §§371–600(e) (1994). See generally, William E. Warne, *The Bureau of Reclamation* (New York: Praeger, 1973); Marc Reisner, *Cadillac Desert: The American West and Its Disappearing Water* (New York, Viking, 1986).

176   *Salt River Irrigation Project (generally).*   Smith, *Magnificent Experiment*; Salt River Project, *Taming of the Salt*.

176   *"of course."*   "Statehood Brought Nearer," *Arizona Republican*, Oct. 14, 1909, p. 1, reprinted in Howard I. Finberg, ed., *The Arizona Republic: Front Page, 100 Years of History* (Phoenix: Arizona Republic, 1990), p. x.

176   *"Statehood Brought Nearer."*   Ibid.

176   *Roosevelt Dam (generally).*   Smith, *Magnificent Experiment*, pp. 78–91 and 108.

177   *"Aggressive boosterism."*   Johnson, *Central Arizona Project*, p. 42.

178   *San Diego (generally).*   William Ellsworth Smythe, *History of San Diego, 1542–1907: An Account of the Rise and Progress of the Pioneer Settlement on the Pacific Coast of the United States* (San Diego: History Co., 1907).

178   *Santa Fe (generally).*   Oliver LaFarge, *Santa Fe: The Autobiography of a Southwestern Town* (Norman: University of Oklahoma Press, 1959).

178   *Los Angeles (generally).*   Lynn Bowman, *Los Angeles: Epic of a City* (Berkeley: Howell-North, 1974); Robert M. Fogelson, *The Fragmented Metropolis: Los Angeles, 1850–1930* (Cambridge, Mass.: Harvard University Press, 1967); Joseph S. O'Flaherty, *Those Powerful Years: The South Coast and Los Angeles, 1887–1917* (Hicksville, N.Y.: Exposition Press, 1978).

178   *Denver (generally).*   Stephen J. Leonard and Thomas J. Noel, *Denver: Mining Camp to Metropolis* (Niwot: University Press of Colorado, 1990).

178   *Salt Lake City (generally).*   Thomas G. Alexander and James B. Allen, *Mormons and Gentiles: A History of Salt Lake City,* vol. 5 of Western Urban History Series (Boulder: Pruett, 1984).

178   *Albuquerque (generally).*   Bradford Luckingham, *The Urban Southwest: A Profile*

# Notes

*History of Albuquerque– El Paso–Phoenix–Tucson* (El Paso: Texas Western Press, 1982); Marc Simmons, *Albuquerque: A Narrative History* (Albuquerque: University of New Mexico Press, 1982).

178   *El Paso (generally).*   Luckingham, *Urban Southwest,* pp. 7–11, 27–28, 57–58; W. H. Timmons, *El Paso: A Borderlands History* (El Paso: Texas Western Press, 1990).

178   *"intelligent white population."*   "Should Be Admitted," *Albuquerque Journal Democrat,* Dec. 16, 1899, p. 2.

179   *Salt Lake City population in 1900.*   Union Pacific Railroad Company, *Resources of the State of Utah* (Omaha: Union Pacific Railroad Co., 1911), pp. 5–6.

179   *paved roads figure.*   Richard White, *"It's Your Misfortune and None of My Own": A History of the American West* (Norman: University of Oklahoma Press, 1991), p. 417.

179   *Las Vegas (generally).*   Ed Reid, *Las Vegas, City without Clocks* (Englewood Cliffs, N.J.: Prentice-Hall, 1961).

180   *Postwar urban growth.*   Carl Abbott, *The Metropolitan Frontier: Cities in the Modern American West* (Tucson: University of Arizona Press, 1993), pp. 57–68; Gerald D. Nash, *The American West Transformed: The Impact of the Second World War* (Bloomington: Indiana University Press, 1985); White, *Your Misfortune,* pp. 542–573.

180   *population of the Southwest.*   U. S. Department of Commerce, Bureau of the Census, *Homepage* (visited Sept. 14, 1998) ‹http://www.census.gov/population/www/estimates/popest.html›.

181   *Walter Bimson and David Murdock.*   Harold H. Martin, "The New Millionaires of Phoenix," *Saturday Evening Post,* Sept. 30, 1961, pp. 25, and 27–30.

181   *"most of the reasons."*   "A Desert Blooms—and Booms," *Newsweek,* Feb. 13, 1956, p. 78.

181   *Air conditioning in Phoenix.*   Luckingham, *Phoenix,* pp. 106–107 and 159–160.

181   *military expenditures.*   "Arizona Sunburst," *Newsweek,* Jan. 26, 1953, p. 88.

181   *Sperry Rand.*   Joseph Stocker, "Arizona: America's New Mecca," *Coronet,* Nov. 1956, pp. 61 and 64–65.

182   *"industrial scouts."*   Luckingham, *Phoenix,* p. 159.

182   *Arizona fastest-growing state.*   "Desert Blooms," p. 78.

182   *Growth Committee.*   Bradford Luckingham, "The Promotion of Phoenix," in G. Wesley Johnson, ed., *Phoenix in the Twentieth Century: Essays in Community History* (Norman: University of Oklahoma Press, 1993), pp. 83–91.

182   *All-American City awards.*   Luckingham, *Urban Southwest,* p. 89.
"I don't think."   Stocker, "Arizona: America's New Mecca," p. 66.

182   *"capital" and "water."*   "Arizona Sunburst," p. 88.

184   *the Big Buildup (generally).*   Peter Wiley and Robert Gottlieb, *Empires in the Sun: The Rise of the New American West* (Tucson: University of Arizona Press, 1982); Allen V. Kneese and F. Lee Brown, *The Southwest Under Stress: National Resource Development Issues in a Regional Setting* (Baltimore: Johns Hopkins University Press, 1981); Philip L. Fradkin, *A River No More: The Colorado River and the West* (Tucson: University of Arizona Press, 1981); Alvin M. Josephy Jr., "The Murder of the Southwest," *Audubon* 73 (July 1971): 54–67; Russell Martin,

# Notes

*A Story That Stands Like a Dam: Glen Canyon and the Struggle for the Soul of the West* (New York: Holt, 1989); Reisner, *Cadillac Desert.*

184 *Freedom of Information Act.* Freedom of Information Act of 1996, PL 89-487, 80 Stat. 250, 5 U.S.C. §552 (1994). Although the original FOIA was passed in 1966 it did not become a forceful tool for the public until after the amendments of 1974. These amendments made definitions pertinent to the rule less ambiguous, and provided enforceable mechanisms for making requests for information. See Marie Veronica O'Connell, "A Control Test for Determining 'Agency Record' Status in the Freedom of Information Act," *Columbia Law Review* 85 (1985): 611–614.

185 *other industrial efforts.* Since World War II there have been other development efforts rivaling the Big Buildup of the Colorado Plateau. Both the Volga River system in the former Soviet Union and the Columbia River Basin in the Pacific Northwest, for instance, experienced intense energy development after World War II. In one mammoth enterprise, Brazil's Itaipu Dam nearly matched the total hydropower of the entire Colorado River Basin system. In addition, China's Three Gorges Dam project on the Yangtze River will, when completed, assume the title of world's largest hydropower project, capable of generating over 17,000 megawatts of electricity behind a lake nearly 400 miles long. But the diversity and scale of development on the Colorado Plateau during the Big Buildup are extraordinary in their own right: the coal mines and coal-fired power plants; the numerous dam and reservoir projects for hydroelectric, municipal, and agricultural purposes; the uranium mines, mills, and dumps; the oil and gas operations; and the transmission and road systems to support the development. For information on other development efforts see, for exmaple, Itaipu Binacional, *Itaipu Binacional: The World's Largest Hydroelectric Power Plant* (visited Sept. 18, 1998) ⟨http://www.itaipu.gov.br/homeing.htm⟩; Arthur Zich, "China's Three Gorges: Before the Flood," *National Geographic* 192 (Sept. 1997): 2–33; Report of the National Science Foundation, "Large Dams of the U.S.S.R.," 88th Cong., 1st sess., Senate Doc. no. 27 (1963); Northwest Power Planning Council, "The Existing Regional Electrical Power System," in *1991 Northwest Power Plan*, vol. 2, p. 57; *Power for Progress: Hydroelectricity in the Columbia River Basin* (Portland: Northwest Power Planning Council, 1992).

## CHAPTER 10: ROSA

187 *San Juan River (generally).* Stewart Aitchison, *A Naturalist's San Juan River Guide* (Boulder: Pruett, 1983); Philip L. Fradkin, *A River No More: The Colorado River and the West* (Tucson: University of Arizona Press, 1981), pp. 165–166.

188 *tailwater fisheries.* Steven J. Meyers, *Notes from the San Juans: Thoughts about Fly Fishing and Home* (New York: Lyons & Burford, 1992), pp. 55–59.

191 *Reies Tijerina and the Tierra Amarilla uprising.* Peter Nabokov, *Tijerina and the Courthouse Raid* (Albuquerque: University of New Mexico Press, 1969); John Nichols, *The Milagro Beanfield War* (New York: Ballantine Books, 1974).

191 *Pobladores.* Frances Leon Quintana, *Pobladores: Hispanic Americans of the Ute Frontier,* 2nd rev. ed. (Aztec, N.M.: Frances Leon Quintana, 1991; originally pub-

# Notes

lished under the title *Los Primeros Pobladores* by the University of Notre Dame Press).

191 *Frances Leon Quintana.* Frances Leon Quintana, interview with author, Aztec, N.M., Feb. 11, 1993.

192 *"I do think."* Quintana, *Pobladores,* p. 4.

192 *Spanish settlement of the Southwest (generally).* See, for example, John Francis Bannon, *The Spanish Borderlands Frontier, 1513–1821* (New York: Holt, 1970); Oakah L. Jones Jr., *Los Paisanos: Spanish Settlers on the Northern Frontier of New Spain* (Norman: University of Oklahoma Press, 1979); David J. Weber, *The Mexican Frontier, 1821–1846: The American Southwest under Mexico* (Albuquerque: University of New Mexico Press, 1982).

192 *The Brunot Agreement and Hispanic settlement of the Rio Chama and San Juan.* The Brunot Agreement is codified in the Act of April 29, 1874, chap. 136, 18 Stat. 36 (1874). See also Quintana, *Pobladores,* pp. 103–104.

193 *Hispanic–Ute relations.* Quintana, *Pobladores,* pp. 103–105.

193 *Early Rosa.* Ibid., pp. 127–130.

193 *Santiago fiesta.* Ibid., pp. 127–128.

193 *Martha Quintana.* Martha Quintana, interview with author, Aztec, N.M., Feb. 11, 1993.

193 *Miguel Quintana.* Miguel Quintana, interview with author, Aztec, N.M., Feb. 11, 1993. See also Richard S. Johnson, "Rooted in the Past: Colorado's Hispanic Heritage," *Empire Magazine* (*Denver Post* Sunday Magazine), Nov. 25, 1979, pp. 32–35.

195 *dispersal of Hispanic communities.* Frances Leon Quintana, interview; Miguel Quintana, interview.

196 *the reunion.* Johnson, "Rooted in the Past."

196 *Chaco Culture influence in San Juan Basin.* Frank W. Eddy, *Prehistory in the Navajo Reservoir District, Northwestern New Mexico,* Museum of New Mexico Papers in Anthropology, no. 15, 2 vols. (Santa Fe: Museum of New Mexico Press, 1966); W. James Judge, "Chaco Canyon–San Juan Basin," in Linda S. Cordell and George J. Gumerman, eds., *Dynamics of Southwest Prehistory* (Washington, D.C.: Smithsonian Institution Press, 1989), pp. 209–261.

196 *"imported over long-established trade routes."* Eddy, *Navajo Reservoir,* p. 498.

196 *number of cultural sites inundated by Navajo Reservoir.* Alfred E. Dittert Jr. and Frank W. Eddy, *Pueblo Period Sites in the Piedra River Section, Navajo Reservoir District,* Museum of New Mexico Papers in Anthropology, no. 10 (Santa Fe: Museum of New Mexico Press, 1963), p. 11; Alfred E. Dittert Jr., Jim J. Hester, and Frank W. Eddy, *Navajo Project Studies II: An Archaeological Survey of the Navajo Reservoir District Northwestern New Mexico,* Monographs of the School of American Research and the Museum of New Mexico, no. 23 (Santa Fe: School of American Research and the Museum of New Mexico, 1961), p. 211; James J. Hester and Joel L. Shiner, *Studies at Navajo Period Sites in the Navajo Reservoir District,* Museum of New Mexico Papers in Anthropology, no. 9 (Santa Fe: Museum of New Mexico Press, 1963), p. 3.

196 *rock art lost by Navajo Reservoir.* Polly Schaafsma, *Rock Art in the Navajo*

# Notes

*Reservoir District,* Museum of New Mexico Papers in Anthropology, no. 7 (Santa Fe: Museum of New Mexico Press, 1963), p. 5.

196    *Twin War Gods at confluence.* Polly Schaafsma, *Rock Art in New Mexico* (Albuquerque: University of New Mexico Press, 1975), pp. 34–38. See also, Maud Oakes and Joseph Campbell, *Where the Two Came to Their Father: A Navajo War Ceremonial Given by Jeff King* (Princeton: Princeton University Press, 1969).

197    *prior appropriation doctrine and western water law.* A. Dan Tarlock, James N. Corbridge Jr., and David H. Getches, *Water Resource Management: A Casebook in Law and Public Policy,* 4th ed. (Westbury, N.Y.: Foundation, 1993), pp. 149–155; Robert G. Dunbar, *Forging New Rights in Western Waters* (Lincoln: University of Nebraska Press, 1983), pp. 59–85; David H. Getches, *Water law in a Nutshell,* 3rd ed. (St. Paul: West, 1997), pp. 74–104.

197    *early Mormon irrigation.* Charles S. Peterson, *Take Up Your Mission: Mormon Colonizing along the Little Colorado River, 1870–1900* (Tucson: University of Arizona Press, 1973), pp. 181–185; Michael Scott Raber, "Religious Polity and Local Production: The Origins of a Mormon Town" (Ph.D. dissertation, Yale University, 1978), pp. 169–175.

198    *Hispanics.* See, for example, F. Lee Brown and Helen M. Ingram, *Water and Poverty in the Southwest* (Tucson: University of Arizona Press, 1987), p. 22; Oliver LaFarge, *The Mother Ditch* (Santa Fe: Sunstone Press, 1983).

198    *Powell on western water.* John Wesley Powell, *Report on the Lands of the Arid Region of the United States, with a More Detailed Account of the Lands of Utah* (Boston: Harvard Common Press, 1983); facsimile of the 1879 edition.

198    *John Wesley Powell.* Wallace Stegner, *Beyond the Hundredth Meridian: John Wesley Powell and the Second Opening of the West* (Lincoln: University of Nebraska Press, 1954).

198    *John Muir (generally).* Stephen Fox, *The American Conservation Movement: John Muir and His Legacy* (Madison: University of Wisconsin Press, 1981).

198    *Utah and prior appropriation.* *Munroe v. Ivie,* 2 Utah 535 (1880).

198    *Post–World War II water development.* Fradkin, *River No More;* Marc Reisner, *Cadillac Desert: The American West and Its Disappearing Water* (New York: Penguin, 1986); Daniel McCool, *Command of the Waters: Iron Triangles, Federal Water Development, and Indian Water* (Berkeley: University of California Press, 1987).

199    *"Water chauvinism."* Stewart Udall, interview with author, Boulder, Colo. April 2, 1993.

200    *"I have always believed."* Michael McCarthy, "He Fought for His West," *Colorado Heritage* 1 (1988): 33 and 38.

201    *"The river means."* Ibid., p. 44. On Wayne Aspinall, see Stephen Craig Sturgeon, "God's Dams: Wayne Aspinall and the Politics of Western Water" (Ph.D. dissertation, University of Colorado, 1998).

201    *Glen Canyon Dam and Lake Powell.* Russell Martin, *A Story That Stands Like a Dam: Glen Canyon and the Struggle for the Soul of the West* (New York: Holt, 1989); U.S. Bureau of Reclamation, *Reclamation Project Data* (Washington, D.C.: Government Printing Office, 1961), pp. 53 and 165.

# Notes

202    *San Juan–Chama Project.*   Charles F. Wilkinson, *Crossing the Next Meridian: Land, Water and the Future of the West* (Washington, D.C.: Island Press, 1992), pp. 219–231.

202    *Navajo Indian Irrigation Project.*   Fradkin, *River No More*, pp. 166–177; Peter Wiley and Robert Gottlieb, *Empires in the Sun: The Rise of the New American West* (Tucson: University of Arizona Press, 1982), pp. 234–236; Judith Jacobson, "A Promise Made: The Navajo Indian Irrigation Project and Water Politics in the American West" (NCAR Cooperative Thesis no 119, 1989); Judith Jacobson, "Sometimes the Feds Do Pinch Pennies," *High Country News*, Aug. 28, 1989, p. 6.

203    *squawfish.*   Buddy L. Jensen, "Colorado Squawfish Reintroduction Efforts in the Lower Colorado River Basin," *Endangered Species Update* 8 (Nov. 1990): 68.

### CHAPTER 11: CRETACEOUS

208    *Navajo Mine.*   BHP-Utah Minerals International, "Navajo Mine" Feb. 1990, pp. 5–6; interview and site inspection with company officials by author on March 27, 1990. See also Mark W. Sprouls, "Mining on the Mesa," *Coal*, Oct. 1994, pp. 50–51.

208    *Four Corners Power Plant.*   Salt River Project, "Fact Sheet—Four Corners Power Plant"; interview and site inspection with company officials by author on March 27, 1990.

209    *Plateau geology (generally).*   Donald L. Baars, *The Colorado Plateau: A Geologic History* (Albuquerque: University of New Mexico Press, 1983); F. A. Barnes, *Canyon Country Geology for the Layman and Rockhound* (Salt Lake City: Wasatch, 1978). The author also thanks Dr. Warren Hamilton, Dr. Jack Campbell, and Dr. Richard Reynolds for extensive explanations of Plateau geology.

210    *BTU and sulfur content.*   "Navajo Mine," p. 10; Senate Committee on Interior and Insular Affairs, "Problems of Electrical Power Production in the Southwest," 92nd Cong., 1st sess. (Washington, D.C.: Government Printing Office, 1972), p. 5.

210    *Salt River Project.*   Salt River Project, "Annual Report 1992–93"; Richard M. Hayslip, manager of environmental, land, and risk management, Salt River Project, interview with author, Phoenix, Ariz., July 29, 1994.

210    *"grow and build" campaign.*   WorldWatch Institute, *State of the World—1994* (New York: Norton, 1994), pp. 62–63.

210    *SRP today.*   Janet Perez, "Utilities Biggest Boosters of State Economic Growth," *Phoenix Gazette*, Feb. 16, 1993, p. B5.

212    *WEST and "the Grand Plan."*   See, for example, Peter Wiley and Robert Gottlieb, *Empires in the Sun: The Rise of the New American West* (Tucson: University of Arizona Press, 1982), pp. 42–47; Philip L. Fradkin, *A River No More: The Colorado River and the West* (New York: Knopf, 1981), pp. 174 and 176; "'West' Plans Largest Power Network," *Electrical West* 131(10) (1964): 32; William B. Loper, "Generation, Fuel Energy Flow Are Big Challenges to West Groups," *Electrical West* 133(9) (1966): 50–51, 55.

212    *"produce more than."*   "'West' Plans Largest Power Network."

212    *distribution of power.*   Salt River Project, "Balanced Strategy Report," Public and Communications Services Department, June 1992.

# Notes

212 *western power grid (generally).* U.S. Department of Energy, Economic Regulatory Administration, "The National Power Grid Study, Final Report," 2 vols. (Washington, D.C.: Dept. of Energy, Economic Regulatory Administration, Office of Utility Systems, 1980).

213 *western power issues.* "The Electric Revolution, Part 1: Conservation Comes of Age," *High Country News,* June 29, 1992, p. 6; "The Electric Revolution, Part 2: Dams and Coal Hit the Age of Limits," *High Country News,* July 13, 1992, p. 8.

213 *SRP trades.* Richard Hayslip, interview.

213 *"SRP has made life."* "A Thirsty World Visits Salt River Project," *Business Wire* (Phoenix: Press Release, Salt River Project, Aug. 12, 1992).

213 *oil and gas.* John D. Leshy, *The Future of the Colorado Plateau: Preserving Its Natural Wonders While Securing Economic Opportunity for Its Residents* (Flagstaff, Ariz: Grand Canyon Trust, 1990), pp. 14–17.

213 *oil shale (generally).* Andrew Guilliford, *Boomtown Blues: Colorado Oil Shale, 1885–1985* (Niwot: University Press of Colorado, 1989).

214 *uranium reserves on Plateau.* Jerome G. Morse, *Energy Resources in Colorado: Coal, Oil Shale, and Uranium* (Boulder: Westview, 1979), p. 236.

214 *uranium (generally).* Raye C. Ringholz, *Uranium Frenzy: Boom and Bust on the Colorado Plateau* (Albuquerque: University of New Mexico Press, 1989).

214 *Echo Park Dam.* Russell Martin, *A Story That Stands Like a Dam: Glen Canyon and the Struggle for the Soul of the West* (New York: Holt, 1989), pp. 50–74.

214 *David Brower (generally).* David R. Brower, *For Earth's Sake: The Life and Times of David Brower* (Salt Lake City: Peregrine Smith Books, 1990); John McPhee, *Encounters with the Archdruid* (New York: Farrar, Straus, 1971).

214 *Brower and House hearings.* Martin, *Stands Like a Dam,* pp. 60–62.

215 *Central Arizona Project (CAP).* Rich Johnson, *The Central Arizona Project, 1918–1968* (Tucson: University of Arizona Press, 1977); Charles Coate, "The Biggest Water Fight in American History: Stewart Udall and the Central Arizona Project," *Journal of the Southwest* 37 (Spring 1995): 79–101; Fradkin, *River No More,* pp. 250–262; Marc Reisner, *Cadillac Desert: The American West and Its Disappearing Water* (New York: Viking, 1986), pp. 281–316.

215 *Supreme Court decision.* *Arizona v. California,* 373 U.S. 546 (1963).

215 *CAP, Black Mesa, and 1968 act.* Coate, "Biggest Water Fight"; Martin, *Stands Like a Dam,* p. 251; Robert J. Glennon, "Coattails of the Past: Using and Financing the Central Arizona Project," *Arizona State Law Journal* 27 (Summer 1995): 677–756.

216 *Stewart Udall.* Stewart Udall, interview with author, Albuquerque, N.M., Oct. 22, 1994.

218 *Central Arizona Project (CAP).* Coate, "Biggest Water Fight"; Fradkin, *River No More,* pp. 250–262; Reisner, *Cadillac Desert,* pp. 281–316.

218 *Udall and Carson books.* Stewart Udall, *The Quiet Crisis* (New York: Holt, 1963); Stewart Udall, *The Quiet Crisis and the Next Generation* (Salt Lake City: Peregrine Smith Books, 1988); Rachel Carson, *Silent Spring* (Boston: Houghton Mifflin, 1962).

218 *Stewart Udall conservation achievements.* See, for example, Michael P. Cohen, *The History of the Sierra Club* (San Francisco: Sierra Club Books, 1998), pp. 268–273 (wilderness); Tim Palmer, *The Wild and Scenic Rivers of America* (Wash-

# Notes

ington, D.C.: Island Press, 1993), pp. 17–25 (wild and scenic rivers); Robert D. Arnold, *Alaska Native Land Claims* (Anchorage: Alaska Native Foundation, 1978), pp. 117–125 (Alaska land withdrawals); J. Douglas Wellman, *Wildland Recreation Policy* (New York: Wiley, 1987), pp. 205–206 (national parks); Charles Wilkinson, "Designating Paradise," *Plateau Journal* (Summer, 1997), pp. 35–38 (national parks).

218  *"my doubts about all the dams."*   Stewart Udall, interview.

219  *Sierra Club "battle ads."*   Cohen, *History of Sierra Club,* pp. 359–365; Brower, *Earth's Sake,* pp. 366–368.

219  *Udall's opposition to Grand Canyon dams.*   Stewart Udall, "Wilderness Rivers: Shooting the Wild Colorado," *Venture* 5 (Feb. 1968): 62–71.

219  *Bridge Canyon and Marble Canyon Dams.*   Martin, *Stands Like a Dam,* pp. 281–285.

220  *"that stupid."*   Stewart Udall, interview.

222  *"you have to realize."*   Stewart Udall, interview with author, Boulder, Colo. Jan. 24, 1989.

222  *1968 Colo. River Basin Project Act.*   Colorado River Basin Project Act, PL 90-537, 82 Stat. 885 (1968); Fradkin, *River No More,* pp. 233 and 252–254; Norris Hundley Jr., *Water and the West: The Colorado River Compact and the Politics of Water in the American West* (Berkeley: University of California Press, 1975), p. 325; Martin, *Stands Like a Dam,* pp. 282–284.

223  *Navajo Mine lease.*   Interview with John Grubb, general manager, Navajo Mine, March 27, 1990; Marjane Ambler, *Breaking the Iron Bonds: Indian Control of Energy Development* (Lawrence: University Press of Kansas, 1990).

223  *tribal taxation.*   See *Kerr-McGee Corp. v. Navajo Tribe,* 471 U.S. 195 (1985); *Southland Royalty Co. v. Navajo Tribe,* 715 F.2d 486 (10th Cir. 1983).

224  *renegotiation of leases.*   John Grubb, interview; Lynn A. Robbins, "Energy Developments and the Navajo Nation: An Update," in Joseph G. Jorgensen, ed., *Native Americans and Energy Development II* (Boston: Anthropology Resource Center and the Seventh Generation Fund, 1984), pp. 116–145; Lorraine Ruffing, "Fighting the Substandard Lease," *American Indian Journal* (June 1980): 2–8.

224  *Navajo Mine relocation.*   John Grubb, interview.

224  *"where they are mining."*   Stephen Trimble, *The People: Indians of the American Southwest* (Santa Fe: School of American Research Press, 1993), p. 166.

224  *"looking south."*   Tó'ahaní (Irene Nakai), "Sunrise Flight into Acid Rain Cancelled," in Larry Evers, ed., *The South Corner of Time: Hopi Navajo Papago Yaqui Tribal Literature* (Tucson: University of Arizona Press, 1980), p. 93.

224  *comparison to rape.*   Personal communication with author.

224  *air pollution.*   John C. Freemuth, *Islands under Siege: National Parks and the Politics of External Threats* (Lawrence: University Press of Kansas, 1991), pp. 85–130; Steve Hinchman, "The Blurring of the West," *High Country News,* June 28, 1993, pp. 10–13.

224  *air pollution on the Plateau.*   National Research Council, *Protecting Visibility in National Parks and Wilderness Areas* (Washington, D.C.: National Academy Press, 1993).

225  *climate change.*   Intergovernmental Panel on Climate Change, *Climate Change*

# Notes

*1995: The Science of Climate Change* (New York: Cambridge University Press, 1996), p. 5:

> Our ability to quantify the human influence is currently limited because the expected signal is still emerging from the noise of natural variability, and because there are uncertainties in key factors. These include the magnitude and patterns of long term natural variablity and the time-evolving pattern of forcing by, and response to, changes in concentrations of greenhouse gases and aerosols, and land surface changes. *Nevertheless, the balance of evidence suggests that there is a discernible human influence on global climate.* (emphasis added)

225   *greenhouse effect and acid rain (generally).* Jack M. Hollander, ed., *The Energy–Environment Connection* (Washington, D.C.: Island Press, 1992), pp. 6–7 and 50–72.

225   *acid rain in Flat Tops.* Dennis Haddow, wilderness and air program manager, Rocky Mountain Region, U.S. Forest Service, telephone interview with Nancy Nelson, research assistant, July 20, 1995; U.S. Department of Agriculture, Forest Service, Rocky Mountain Forest and Range Experiment Station, "Air Quality, Oil Shale, and Wilderness—a Workshop to Identify and Protect Air Quality Related Values of the Flat Tops," General Technical Report RM-91 (Jan. 1981); *Sierra Club v. Public Service Co.,* 894 F. Supp. 1455 (D.Colo. 1995); *appeal denied* 1995 U.S. App. Lexis 25612; Mark Obmascik, "Once in a While, Might Does Not Make Right," *Denver Post,* May 25, 1996, p. B1.

226   *"a little-known picture."* Elizabeth Sprang, *Good-Bye River* (Las Cruces, N.M.: Kiva Press, 1992), p. 32.

226   *"big deposits."* Ibid., p. 10.

226   *native and endemic fish.* Steven W. Carothers and Bryan T. Brown, *The Colorado River through Grand Canyon: Natural History and Human Change* (Tucson: University of Arizona Press, 1991), pp. 91–99.

226   *bald eagles.* George Hardeen, "Glen Canyon Dam's Unexpected Bonanza," *High Country News,* Feb. 11, 1991, p. 4.

226   *one hundred river runners.* Barry M. Goldwater, *Delightful Journey down the Green and Colorado Rivers* (Tempe: Arizona Historical Foundation, 1970), pp. 190–191.

227   *floodwaters blew out.* Philip H. Burgi, Bruce M. Moyes, Thomas W. Gamble, "Operation of Glen Canyon Spillways—Summer 1983," in David L. Schreiber, ed., *Water for Resource Development* (New York: American Society of Civil Engineers, 1984), p. 262; T. J. Wolf, "How Lake Powell Almost Broke Free of Glen Canyon Dam This Summer," *High Country News,* Dec. 12, 1983, pp. 10–14; Martin, *Stands Like a Dam,* pp. 315–318.

227   *decommissioning Glen Canyon Dam.* Daniel P. Beard, "Dams Aren't Forever, *New York Times,* Oct. 6, 1997, P. A19; Mark Muro, "Can the River Run Again? Draining Lake Powell Not Such a Crazy Idea," *Arizona Daily Star,* April 20, 1997, p. 1E; Tom Moody, "Glen Canyon Dam: Coming to an Informed Decision," *Colorado Plateau Advocate,* Fall 1997. See also Mission Statement: "The Glen Canyon Institute's mission is to provide leadership in re-establishing the free

flow of the Colorado River through a restored Glen Canyon," Glen Canyon Institute, *Homepage* (visited Jan. 12, 1999) ‹http://www/glencanyon.org/mission. htm›.

227   *uranium boom (generally).*   Ringholz, *Uranium Frenzy;* Arthur R. Gómez, *Quest for the Golden Circle: The Four Corners and the Metropolitan West, 1945–1970* (Albuquerque: University of New Mexico Press, 1994).

227   *testing and mining (generally).*   Philip L. Fradkin, *Fallout: An American Nuclear Tragedy* (Tucson: University of Arizona Press, 1989), pp. 1–26; Carole Gallagher, *American Ground Zero: The Secret Nuclear War* (New York: Random House, 1993); Stewart Udall, *The Myths of August: A Personal Exploration of Our Tragic Cold War Affair with the Atom* (New York: Pantheon, 1994), pp. 183–202.

228   *downwinder litigation.*   *Allen v. U.S.,* 527 F. Supp. 476 (D.Utah 1981); *Allen v. U.S.,* 588 F. Supp. 247 (D.Utah 1984); *rev'd* 816 F.2d 1417 (10th Cir. 1987); *cert. denied,* 484 U.S. 1004 (1988).

228   *Navajo miners' litigation.*   *Begay v. U.S.,* 591 F. Supp. 991 (D.Ariz. 1984); *aff'd* 768 F.2d 1059 (9th Cir. 1985).

228   *"and I was ashamed."*   Udall, *Myths,* p. 202.

229   *legislation.*   Radiation Exposure Compensation Act of 1990, PL 101-426, 42 U.S.C. §2210 (1994). See also Gay Jervey, "Stewart Udall's Newest Frontier," *American Lawyer* 13 (Jan./Feb. 1991): pp. 72–81.

229   *Central Arizona Project.*   Tony Davis, "High Water: Arizona Aqueduct Project Turns Out to Be All Too Wet," *Dallas Morning News,* Feb. 20, 1994, p. 41A.

CHAPTER 12: JUNCTION DAM

231   *proposed location of power plant near Capitol Reef.*   Michael D. Devine et al., *Energy from the West: A Technology Assessment of Western Energy Resource Development* (Norman: University of Oklahoma Press, 1981), pp. 129–130; Kevin Roderick, "Coal-Fired Generating Plant Power to the People," *Los Angeles Times,* June 12, 1987, p. 1; "Canyon Coalition Fights for Southwest," *High Country News,* March 14, 1975, p. 11.

231   *Capitol Reef (generally).*   Virgil J. Olson and Helen Olson, *Capitol Reef: The Story behind the Scenery* (Las Vegas: KC Publications, 1990).

232   *Intermountain Power Plant.*   Charles F. Wilkinson, "Toward an Ethic of Place," in Stewart Udall, Patricia Nelson Limerick, Charles F. Wilkinson, John M. Volkman, and William Kittredge, *Beyond the Mythic West* (Salt Lake City: Peregrine Smith Books, 1990), p. 92.

232   *Kaiparowits Coal Project (generally).*   Ronald Jepperson, Eric Hemel, and Robert Hauptman, *The Kaiparowits Coal Project and the Environment: A Case Study* (Palo Alto, Calif.: Ann Arbor Science Publishers/Electric Power Research Institute, 1981).

233   *Horse Bench nuclear power park.*   Utah Energy Office, for the U.S. Department of Energy, Final Summary Report (Draft), "Study of a Conceptual Nuclear Energy Center at Green River, Utah" (Salt Lake City: Utah Energy Office, Sept. 1982); Dames and Moore Consultants, Final Report for Western Interstate Energy Board/WINB, "Preliminary Assessment of Nuclear Energy Centers and

Energy Systems Complexes in the Western United States" (Denver: Western Interstate Energy Board, 1977).

234 *Project Plowshare.* David E. Engdahl, *Plowshare Technical Legal Papers* (Denver: Western Interstate Nuclear Board, 1973),vol. 3, pp. A3–A5.

234 *opposition to nuclear explosions.* Ron Wolf, "Colorado Fights to Control Blasts," *High Country News,* Dec. 21, 1973, p. 12; Hearings before a Subcommittee of the House Committee on Appropriations, "Public Works for Water and Power Development and Energy Research Appropriation Bill, 1978," 95th Cong., 1st sess. (Washington, D.C.: Government Printing Office, 1977).

234 *Junction Dam.* J. Rolla Mahoney, *Navigability of the Green River: Management of Its Waters for Resource Development* (Salt Lake City: University of Utah, 1964).

236 *western governors.* Federation of Rocky Mountain States, *Energy Development in the Rocky Mountain Region: Goals and Concerns* (Denver: Federation of Rocky Mountain States [Colorado, Montana, New Mexico, Utah, Wyoming], 1975).

236 *Edward Abbey.* James Bishop Jr., *Epitaph for a Desert Anarchist: The Life and Legacy of Edward Abbey* (New York: Atheneum, 1994).

236 *Desert Solitaire.* Edward Abbey, *Desert Solitaire: A Season in the Wilderness* (New York: Simon & Schuster, 1968).

236 *"industrial tourism."* Ibid., p. 49.

236 *"ragged"; "a sapless claw."* Ibid.

237 *"a degenerate juniper."* Edward Abbey, *The Brave Cowboy: An Old Tale in a New Time* (Albuquerque: University of New Mexico Press, 1977), p. 11.

237 *"the fire."* Abbey, *Desert Solitaire,* p. 12.

237 *slowing of Big Buildup (generally).* Marc Reisner, *Cadillac Desert: The American West and Its Disappearing Water* (New York: Viking, 1986), pp. 453–508; Peter Wiley and Robert Gottlieb, *Empires in the Sun: The Rise of the New American West* (Tucson: University of Arizona Press, 1982), pp. 286–310.

237 *regional haze.* National Research Council, *Protecting Visibility in National Parks and Wilderness Areas* (Washington, D.C.: National Academy Press, 1993); Steve Hinchman, "The Blurring of the West," *High Country News,* June 28, 1993, pp. 10–13.

238 *Navajo Generating Station settlement.* Keith Schneider, "Utilities to Take Steps to Cut Haze at Grand Canyon," *New York Times,* Aug. 9, 1991, p. A1; "The Bright Edges: Visions of the Future," *Colorado Plateau Advocate,* Summer 1992, p. 3.

238 *SRP opposition to installing scrubbers at Navajo Generating Station.* Central Arizona Water Conservation District v. United States Environmental Protection Agency, 990 F.2d 1531 (9th Cir. 1993), cert. denied., 510 U.S. 828 (1993).

238 *"it's irrefutable."* Richard M. Hayslip, manager of environmental, land, and risk management, Salt River Project, interview with author, Phoenix, Ariz., July 29, 1994.

239 *Grand Canyon Visibility Commission.* Mark S. Squillace and David R. Wooley, *Air Pollution,* 3rd ed. (Cincinnati: Anderson, 1999), pp. 237–245; Hinchman, "Blurring"; Jim Souby, executive director, Western Governors' Association, interview with Frank Wilson, research assistant, April 19, 1993.

240 *Grand Canyon Protection Act.* U.S. Department of Interior, Bureau of Reclamation, "Operation of Glen Canyon Dam: Colorado River Storage Project,

# Notes

Arizona, Final Environmental Impact Statement" (Denver: Bureau of Reclamation, 1995); Grand Canyon Protection Act of 1992, PL 102-575, tit. XVIII, 106 Stat. 4669 (1992); Florence Williams, "Government Tames Its Wild, Destructive Dam," *High Country News,* Aug. 26, 1991, pp. 1 and 10; Michael Conner, "Extracting the Monkey Wrench from Glen Canyon Dam: The Grand Canyon Protection Act— An Attempt at Balance," *Public Land Law Review* 15 (1994): 135–165.

241 *"I've seen grown Peruvenists."* Dr. Linda Cordell, interview with author, Boulder, Colo., Feb. 23, 1994.

241 *"when geologists."* Dr. Jack Campbell, interview with author, Denver, Colo., Jan. 18, 1994.

241 *50 million recreational visits a year.* In 1997 national parks on the Plateau received 14 million recreational visitor days. The National Park Service Website (visited on 3/5/99) (http://www.nature.nps.gov/stats/fiscal19397.htm). In the same year, the Plateau's national forests received more than 32 million recreational visitor days. Jim Upchurch, San Juan National Forest, telephone interview with Nancy Nelson, research assistant, Oct. 13, 1994; John Beckley, Grand Mesa/Uncompaghre/Gunnison National Forests, telephone interview, Oct. 21, 1994; Lori Long, Region 3, National Forest Service, telephone interview, Oct. 13, 1994; "State Summary of Total Recreation Use on National Forest System Lands by Activity," provided by Laura Conroy, Region 4, National Forest Service. A "visitor day" is counted as one person in the area for a twelve-hour period. The BLM sees about 10 million visitor days annually on the Colorado Plateau. "BLM Facts and Figures," provided by Renee Garsias, BLM, Utah State Office.

241 *Canyonlands.* Deborah Frazier, "Groups Clash over Curbs at Canyonlands," *Rocky Mountain News,* Jan. 20, 1994, p. 8A; "Canyonlands National Park and Orange Cliffs Unit of Glen Canyon National Recreation Area, Environmental Assessment for Backcountry Management Plan" (Dec. 1993).

241 *Canyon de Chelly.* Barry Meier, "Canyon de Chelly Journal: Putting Up an Exit Sign for Vehicles in Wonderland," *New York Times,* Oct. 18, 1991, p. A10.

241 *Grand Canyon (visitation).* Jennifer Sypherd, public relations, Grand Canyon National Park, data supplied by fax on Sept. 21, 1994.

241 *Grand Canyon and Zion (revision of management plan to exclude private vehicles).* U.S. Department of the Interior, National Park Service, Draft General Management Plan and Environmental Impact Statement, *Grand Canyon National Park, Coconino and Mohave Counties, Arizona,* p. 69 (March 1995); Roxane Naylor, National Park Service, Zion National Park, administrative technician, telephone interview with Kevin Geiger, research assistant, Nov. 3, 1998.

242 *Moab, Utah (history and sudden growth).* José Knighten, *Coyote's History of Moab* (Moab: Compost Press, 1994); Jim Carrier, "Mountain Bikers Leave Ruts in Moab's Psyche," *Denver Post,* Nov. 1, 1992, p. 1A; Bill Hedden, "Towns Angling for Tourism Should Beware of the Great White Shark," in Ed Marston, ed., "Grappling with Growth: An HCN Special Issue," *High Country News,* Sept. 5, 1994, pp. 20–21; Raye C. Ringholz, *Uranium Frenzy: Boom and Bust on the Colorado Plateau* (Albuquerque: University of New Mexico Press, 1989); Raymond Wheeler, "Whither the Colorado Plateau?" in Ed Marston, ed., *Reopening the Western Frontier* (Washington, D.C.: Island Press, 1989), pp. 248–258; Florence

379

# Notes

Williams, "A Passive Town in Utah Awaits Its Fate," *High Country News,* Nov. 18, 1991, p. 1.

242 *three hundred hotel rooms.*   Bill Hedden, member, Grand County Council, interview with author, April 6, 1994.

242 *cryptobiotic soil.*   Jayne Belnap, "Recovery Rates of Cryptobiotic Crusts: Inoculant Use and Assessment Methods," *Great Basin Naturalist* 53 (Mar. 1, 1993): 89–95; James R. Marble and Kimball T. Harper, "Effect of Timing of Grazing on Soil-Surface Cryptogamic Communities in a Great Basin Low-Shrub Desert: A Preliminary Report," *Great Basin Naturalist* 49 (Jan. 31, 1989): 104–107; Jim Dunne, "Cryptogamic Soil Crusts in Arid Ecosystems," *Rangelands* 11 (Aug. 1, 1989): 180. The terms "cryptobiotic," "cryptogamic," and "microbiotic" refer generally to the same type of soil.

243 *site-specific studies on Plateau.*   See, for example, David N. Cole, "Trampling Disturbance and Recovery of Cryptogamic Soil Crusts in Grand Canyon National Park," *Great Basin Naturalist* 50 (Dec. 1, 1990): 321–325; Apollo B. Orodho, M. J. Trlica, and C. D. Bonham, "Long-Term Heavy-Grazing Effects on Soil and Vegetation in the Four Corners Region," *Southwestern Naturalist* 35 (Mar. 1, 1990): 9–14.

243 *Comb Wash and BLM citizen challenge.*   Joseph M. Feller, "The Comb Wash Case: The Rule of Law Comes to the Public Rangelands," *Public Land and Resources Law Review* 17 (1996): 25–54.

245 *San Juan County archaeological sites.*   Dr. Dale Davidson, archaeologist, Bureau of Land Management, Monticello, Utah, telephone interview with Marlon Sherman, research assistant, March 1, 1994.

246 *New Mexico archaeological sites.*   Tim Seaman, Archaeological Resources Management Section, Museum of New Mexico, telephone interview with Marlon Sherman, research assistant, Feb. 25, 1994.

246 *percentage of sites on Plateau inventoried.*   Rick Moore et al., *Preserving Traces of the Past: Protecting the Colorado Plateau's Archaeological Heritage* (Flagstaff, Ariz: Grand Canyon Trust, 1994), pp. 1 and 7.

246 *recent Mesa Verde discovery.*   Julie Bell, National Park Service, Mesa Verde National Park, archaeologist, telephone interview with Kevin Geiger, research assistant, Nov. 3, 1998

246 *looting, vandalism, and ignorance.*   "Indian Ruins Ravaged at Night," *Arizona Republic,* Mar. 26, 1994, p. B5; Michael Murphy, "State's History Trampled," *Phoenix Gazette* May 9, 1994, p. A1; Moore, et al., *Preserving Traces* pp. 21–32; Society of American Archaeology, *Actions for the '90s: Final Report Taos Working Conference on Preventing Archaeological Looting and Vandalism* (Washington, D.C.: Society for American Archaeology, 1990).

## CHAPTER 13: CEDAR MESA CANYON

253 *Navajo origin of "Anasazi."*   Linda S. Cordell, *Ancient Pueblo Peoples* (Washington, D.C.: Smithsonian Books, 1994), p. 18; Gary Matlock, *Enemy Ancestors: The Anasazi World with a Guide to Sites* (Flagstaff, Ariz.: Northland, 1988); David Grant Noble, *Ancient Ruins of the Southwest: An Archaeological Guide,* rev. ed. (Flagstaff, Ariz.: Northland, 1991); F. A. Barnes and Michaelene Pendleton,

# Notes

*Canyon Country Prehistoric Indians: Their Culture, Ruins, Artifacts, and Rock Art* (Salt Lake City: Wasatsch, 1979), p. 46.

254 *rock art (generally).* See, for example, Sally J. Cole, *Legacy on Stone: Rock Art of the Colorado Plateau and Four Corners Region* (Boulder, Colo.: Johnson Books, 1990).

255 *Kokopelli.* Dennis Slifer and James Duffield, *Kokopelli: Fluteplayer Images in Rock Art* (Santa Fe: Ancient City Press, 1994).

256 *Ancestral Puebloan and Fremont cultures in Grand Gulch.* Cole, *Legacy*, pp. 109–200; Robert H. Lister and Florence C. Lister, *Those Who Came Before: Southwestern Archeology in the National Park System* (Globe, Ariz.: Southwest Parks and Monuments Association, 1983), pp. 72–73; Noble, *Ancient Ruins*, pp. 74–78; Fred M. Blackburn and Ray A. Williamson, *Cowboys and Cave Dwellers: Basketmaker Archaeology in Utah's Grand Gulch* (Santa Fe: School of American Research Press, 1997).

258 *Ancestral Puebloan and Fremont cultures (generally).* Linda S. Cordell and George J. Gumerman, eds., *Dynamics of Southwest Prehistory* (Washington, D.C.: Smithsonian Institution Press, 1989); Cordell, *Ancient Pueblo Peoples*; Reg Saner, *Reaching Keet Seel: Ruin's Echo and the Anasazi* (Salt Lake City: University of Utah Press, 1998); Barnes and Pendleton, *Canyon Country.*

258 *Ancestral Puebloan heritage of modern Pueblo peoples.* Claudia F. Berry and Michael S. Berry, "Chronological and Conceptual Models of the Southwestern Archaic," in Carol J. Condie and Don D. Fowler, eds., *Anthropology of the Desert West: Essays in Honor of Jesse D. Jennings* (Salt Lake City: University of Utah Press, 1986), pp. 253–327; Noble, *Ancient Ruins*, pp. 31–32.

258 *tree-ring dating (generally).* Marvin A. Stokes and Terah L. Smiley, *An Introduction to Tree-Ring Dating* (Chicago: University of Chicago Press, 1968).

258 *drought, A.D. 1276–1299.* Cordell and Gumerman, *Dynamics*, p. 167; Noble, *Ancient Ruins*, pp. 28 and 35; Barnes and Pendleton, *Canyon Country*, pp. 18–19.

258 *"these folks."* Dr. Dale Davidson, archaeologist, Bureau of Land Management, interview with author, Monticello, Utah, Feb. 28, 1994.

258 *cannibalism among Ancestral Puebloans.* Christy G. Turner and Jacqueline A. Turner, *Man Corn: Cannibalism and Violence in the Prehistoric American Southwest* (Salt Lake City: University of Utah Press, 1998); David Roberts, *In Search of the Old Ones: Exploring the Anasazi World of the Southwest* (New York: Simon & Schuster, 1996), pp. 157–164; Douglas Preston, "Cannibals of the Canyon," *New Yorker* (Nov. 30, 1998), p. 76. For criticism of Turner's work see, for example, Robert Gehrke, "Cannibalism among Anasazi Claimed," *Denver Post*, Dec. 26, 1998, p. 34A (quoting archaeologist Peter Bullock: "[Turner's] claims are somewhat preposterous. His methodology is somewhat questionable. His whole thing is constructed to prove a point. It's not unbiased research."

259 *Ancestral Puebloan planned gradual departure.* Ruth Underhill, *Life in the Pueblos* (Santa Fe: Ancient City Press, 1991), p. 17; Barnes and Pendleton, *Canyon Country*, pp. 17–19. Although recent studies suggest that violence may have played a part in the abandonment of certain Ancestral Puebloan villages, the extent of the violence and the parties involved are still matters of debate. See Cordell, *Ancient Pueblo Peoples*, p. 131. Jonathan Haas and Winifred Creamer,

# Notes

*Stress and Warfare among the Kayenta Anasazi of the Thirteenth Century* A.D. (Chicago: Field Museum of Natural History, 1993).

259   *Ancestral Puebloans and soil degradation.* Cordell and Gumerman, *Dynamics,* pp. 166–169; George J. Gumerman, ed., *The Anasazi in a Changing Environment* (Cambridge: Cambridge University Press, 1988).

259   *Hohokam and soil degradation.* Neal W. Ackerly, "False Causality in the Hohokam Collapse," *Kiva* 53(4) (1988): 305–319; Gary Huckleberry, "Soil Evidence of Hohokam Irrigation in the Salt River Valley, Arizona," *Kiva* 57(3) (1992): 237–249.

260   *Hopi tradition and the Badger clan.* Frank Waters, *Book of the Hopi* (New York: Ballantine, 1963), pp. 56–64.

260   *kivas (generally).* Watson Smith, *When Is a Kiva? And Other Questions about Southwestern Archaeology,* edited by Raymond H. Thompson (Tucson: University of Arizona Press, 1990).

262   *classification of ancient cultures.* Cole, *Legacy,* p. 13; Cordell and Gumerman, *Dynamics,* pp. 151–160; Noble, *Ancient Ruins,* p. 26.

262   *continuous habitation of villages.* Lister and Lister, *Those Who Came Before,* pp. 40–52; R. Gwinn Vivian, *The Chacoan Prehistory of the San Juan Basin* (San Diego: Academic Press, 1990), p. 2; Barnes and Pendleton, *Canyon Country,* pp. 14–16.

262   *archaic cultures.* Winifred Creamer and Jonathan Haas, "Pueblo: Search for the Ancient Ones," *National Geographic* 180 (Oct. 1991): 84–99; Lister and Lister, *Those Who Came Before,* pp. 16–17.

263   *linguistic analysis.* Joseph H. Greenberg, *Language in the Americas* (Stanford: Stanford University Press, 1987); Joseph H. Greenberg and Merritt Ruhlen, "Linguistic Origins of Native Americans," *Scientific American* 267 (Nov. 1992): 94. Joseph H. Greenberg, Christy G. Turner II, and Stephen L. Zegura, "The Settlement of the Americas: A Comparison of the Linguistic, Dental, and Genetic Evidence," *Current Anthropology* 27 (Dec. 1986): 477–497; Matt Crenson, "Tracking the First Americans," *Dallas Morning News,* Jan. 11, 1993, p. 6D.

263   *biological anthropologists.* Luigi Luca Cavalli-Sforza, "Genes, Peoples, and Languages," *Scientific American* 265 (Nov. 1991): 104–110.

263   *MacNeish.* Phil McCombs, "The Cave Bear Scotty MacNeish Is a Gruff, Cantankerous, Swaggering Scholar Who May Be Hip-Deep in the Americas' Greatest Archaeological Find," *Washington Post,* April 18, 1993, p. F1, F6, F7. See also, David L. Chandler, "Palm Print May Undo 'Clovis-First' Dogma: Could Prove Humans Have Been in Americas 38,000 Years," *Boston Globe,* Dec. 2, 1991, p. 25; Boyce Rensberger, "Placing Man in America 28,000 Years Ago: New Mexico Find Indicates Human Presence Far Earlier Than Believed," *Washington Post,* Feb. 10, 1992, p. A1; Linda Cordell, *Archaeology of the Southwest,* 2nd ed. (San Diego: Academic Press, 1997), pp. 78–79; See also John Noble Wilford, "Chilean Field Yields New Clues to Peopling of Americas," *New York Times,* Aug. 25, 1998, pp. B9 and B11.

264   *"my personal conclusion."* McCombs, "The Cave Bear," p. F7.

266   *Cedar Mesa formation.* Donald L. Baars, *Red Rock Country: The Geologic*

# Notes

*History of the Colorado Plateau* (Garden City: Doubleday, 1972), pp. 84–86.

268   *hematite (definition).*   Robert L. Bates and Julia A. Jackson, eds., *Dictionary of Geological Terms,* 3rd ed. (New York: Doubleday, 1984), p. 233.

268   *hematite in Cedar Mesa Formation.*   Baars, *Red Rock,* pp. 25–26.

268   *Permian Period.*   Ibid., pp. 78–93.

271   *protection of cultural resources.*   Native American Grave Protection and Repatriation Act. 25 U.S.C. §§3001–3013 (1994); Archaeological Resources Protection Act, 16 U.S.C. §§470aa–470ll (1994); Frank G. Houdek, ed., *Protection of Cultural Property and Archaeological Resources* (New York: Oceana, 1988); Walter E. Stern and Lynn H. Slade, "Effects of Historic and Cultural Resources and Indian Religious Freedom on Public Lands Development: A Practical Primer," paper presented at the Rocky Mountain Mineral Law Foundation Conference, Denver, Colo., Sept. 24–25, 1992, pp. 8–4 and 8–33.

271   *corn introduced to the Southwest from Mexico.*   Lister and Lister, *Those Who Came Before,* pp. 7 and 18; Underhill, *Life in the Pueblos,* p. 25; Cordell, *Ancient Pueblo Peoples,* p. 46.

272   *Cedar Mesa canyons.*   John Telford and Terry Tempest Williams, *Coyote's Canyon* (Salt Lake City: Peregrine Smith Books, 1989); Ann Zwinger, *Wind in the Rock: The Canyonlands of Southeastern Utah* (Tucson: University of Arizona Press, 1978).

272   *"Choovio built up."*   Mary Sojourner, *Sisters of the Dream* (Flagstaff, Ariz.: Northland, 1989), p. 7.

273   *"must have employed."*   Robert H. Lister and Florence C. Lister, *Chaco Canyon: Archaeology and Archaeologists* (Albuquerque: University of New Mexico Press, 1981), p. 14.

274   *painting of kivas.*   Bertha P. Dutton, *Sun Father's Way: The Kiva Murals of Kuaua* (Albuquerque: University of New Mexico Press, 1963).

### CHAPTER 14: BLACK MESA

278   *derivation of "Hotevilla."*   Harry C. James, *Pages from Hopi History* (Tucson: University of Arizona Press, 1974), p. 14.

279   *Hopi Home Dance (generally).*   Don C. Talayesva, *Sun Chief: The Autobiography of a Hopi Indian,* edited by Leo W. Simmons (New Haven: Yale University Press, 1974; originally published in 1942), pp. 137–140; Frank Waters, *Book of the Hopi* (New York: Ballantine, 1963), pp. 242–256.

280   *Black Mesa and spirituality.*   Appendix to Petition for a Writ of Certiorari to the U.S. Court of Appeals for the Ninth Circuit, Plaintiff's Brief, Statement of Hopi Religious Leaders, *Lomayaktewa v. Hathaway,* 520 F.2d 1324 (9th Cir. 1975) (No. 73–2132), *cert. denied,* 425 U.S. 903 (1976) (on file with the National Indian Law Library, Boulder, Colo.).

280   *mineral development.*   Burton A. Ladd, superintendent, Hopi Agency, letter to commissioner of Indian affairs (Feb. 15, 1944); James D. Crawford, superintendent, Hopi Agency, letter to commissioner of Indian affairs (April 30, 1948).

281   *Hopi views of government and difficulties of mineral leasing.*   John W. Ragsdale Jr., "Law and Environment in Modern America and among the Hopi Indians: A

# Notes

Comparison of Values," *Harvard Environmental Law Review* 10 (1986): 417–466; John W. Ragsdale Jr., "The Institutions, Laws, and Values of the Hopi Indians: A Stable State Society," *University of Missouri–Kansas City Law Review* 55 (1987): 335–391; Burton A. Ladd, superintendent, Hopi Agency, letter to commissioner of Indian affairs (July 9, 1947); D'Arcy McNickle, assistant to the commissioner of Indian affairs, letter to James D. Crawford, superintendent, Hopi Agency (Nov. 5, 1947).

281    *John Collier and the New Deal.*   Kenneth R. Philp, *John Collier's Crusade for Indian Reform, 1920–1954* (Tucson: University of Arizona Press, 1977); T. H. Watkins, *Righteous Pilgrim: The Life and Times of Harold L. Ickes, 1874–1952* (New York: Holt, 1990), pp. 530–548.

281    *Indian Reorganization Act.*   Indian Reorganization Act of 1934, PL 73-383, chap. 576, 48 Stat. 984 (1934) 25 U.S.C. §461–479 (1994).

281    *Collier and his campaign at Hopi.*   Philp, *John Collier's Crusade* pp. 166–167.

281    *"The Indians."*   James, *Hopi History,* p. 203.

281    *"[T]here are many examples."*   Audiocassette from Vernon Masayesva to the author (transcribed Sept. 16, 1998).

283    *1936 election (generally).*   Philp, *John Collier's Crusade,* pp. 166–167; Emily Benedek, *The Wind Won't Know Me: A History of the Navajo–Hopi Land Dispute* (New York: Alfred A. Knopf, 1992), pp. 126–131; Oliver LaFarge, "Notes for Hopi Administrators"(Feb. 1937, available from the U.S. Department of Interior Central Library), pp. 8 and 19; Indian Law Resource Center, "Report to the Hopi Kikmongwis and Other Traditional Hopi Leaders on Docket 196 and the Continuing Threat to Hopi Land and Sovereignty" (Washington, D.C.: Indian Law Resource Center, March 1979), pp. 47–54.

283    *"heavy opposition vote."*   Philp, *John Collier's Crusade,* pp. 166–167.

284    *John Boyden's application to Navajo in 1947.*   Benedek, *Wind Won't Know Me,* p. 134.

284    *John Boyden's application to Hopi in 1950.*   Orpha Sweeten Boyden, *John S. Boyden: Three Score and Ten in Retrospect* (Cedar City: Southern Utah State College Press, 1986), p. 175.

284    *Hopi Tribal Council.*   James, *Hopi History,* p. 205; D'Arcy McNickle, field representative, Office of Indian Affairs, notes of meeting with Hopi Indians (Sept. 23, 1944).

284    *BIA and energy companies.*   James D. Crawford, superintendent, Hopi Agency, letter sent to twenty oil companies and individuals "who have indicated an interest in the possibility of leasing Indian lands in the Executive Order Reservation" (March 21, 1950).

284    *Indian Claims Commission Act.*   Indian Claims Commission Act of 1946, PL 79-726, chap. 959 §12, 60 Stat. 1049.

285    *final extinguishment of land claim.*   See, for example, *United States v. Dann,* 470 U.S. 39 (1985).

285    *"I find it clear."*   Oliver LaFarge, letter to BIA Hopi Agency superintendent, cited in Indian Law Resource Center, "Hopi Kikmongwis," p. 88.

285    *criticism that John Boyden misled the Hopi.*   Benedek, *Wind Won't Know Me,* pp. 134–135; Vernon Masayesva, former Hopi tribal chairman, interview with

# Notes

author, Boulder, Colo., June 23, 1994; Indian Law Resource Center, "Hopi Kikmongwis," p. 91.

285    *five villages' refusal to approve Boyden's claims contract.*   Indian Law Resource Center, "Hopi Kikmongwis," pp. 91–92.

285    *official signing of contract.*   Boyden, *John S. Boyden,* p. 175.

285    *$500,000 fee in 1976.*   Indian Law Resource Center, "Hopi Kikmongwis," p. 188.

285    *"If I can do something."*   Transcript, meeting of John S. Boyden, Dow Carnal, superintendent, Bridget Whipple, secretary, Sam Shing, interpreter, and forty-five members of the Hopi Tribe, Kykotsmovi Village, Ariz., Sept. 4, 1951, p. 5.

285    *Boyden "pointed out."*   James S. Lindzey, memorandum to G. Warren Spaulding, March 27, 1952.

286    *Boyden's strategy.*   Allan G. Harper, area director, Window Rock Area Office, Office of Indian Affairs, letter to commissioner of Indian affairs (complete date unknown, 1952); Lindzey, memorandum to Spaulding, p.3.

286    *"the first step."*   Harper, letter to commissioner.

286    *"develop a representative tribal council."*   Lindzey, memorandum to Spaulding.

286    *"would effect recognition."*   Harper, letter to commissioner.

286    *"there will be a rebirth."*   Ibid.

286    *BIA approval of Boyden's contract in 1952.*   Lewis A. Sigler, acting chief counsel, memorandum recommending approval of contract to commissioner of Indian affairs (complete date unknown, 1952).

286    *BIA approval of the Hopi Tribal Council and its rationale.*   W. Barton Greenwood, acting commissioner of Indian affairs, letter to Allan G. Harper, area director, Window Rock Area Office, Office of Indian Affairs (July 17, 1953); Glenn L. Emmons, commissioner of Indian affairs, letter to Frederick M. Haverland, area director, Office of Indian Affairs, Phoenix, Ariz. (complete date unknown, 1955); Benedek, *Wind Won't Know Me,* pp. 135–136; Indian Law Resource Center, "Hopi Kikmongwis," pp. 109–120; Steven Trimble, *The People: Indians of the American Southwest* (Santa Fe: School of American Research Press, 1993), p. 35.

287    *Navajo–Hopi land dispute (generally).*   David M. Brugge, *The Navajo–Hopi Land Dispute: An American Tragedy* (Albuquerque: University of New Mexico Press, 1994); Jerry Kammer, *The Second Long Walk: The Navajo–Hopi Land Dispute* (Albuquerque: University of New Mexico Press, 1980); Benedek, *Wind Won't Know Me;* James M. Goodman and Gary L. Thompson, "The Hopi–Navaho Land Dispute," *American Indian Law Review* 3(2) (1975): 397–418; Kevin Tehan, "Of Indians, Land, and the Federal Government: The Navajo–Hopi Land Dispute," *Arizona State Law Journal* (1) (1976): 173–212.

287    *1868 U.S.–Navajo Treaty.*   Treaty between the United States of America and the Navajo Tribe of Indians, June 1, 1868, 15 Stat. 667 (1869).

287    *the Navajo Long Walk.*   Gerald Thompson, *The Army and the Navajo* (Tucson: University of Arizona Press, 1976), pp. 24–32; Ruth M. Underhill, *The Navajos* (Norman: University of Oklahoma Press, 1967), pp. 112–126; L. R. Bailey, *The Long Walk: A History of the Navajo Wars, 1846–68* (Los Angeles: Westernlore Press, 1964).

287    *Bosque Redondo.*   Underhill, *Navajos,* pp. 127–143; Trimble, *The People,* pp. 138–141; Thompson, *Army.*

# Notes

287 *1882 executive order.* Chester Arthur, president, Executive Order of December 16, 1882, Exec. Order No. 1882-33-9, *microformed* on Congressional Information Service. See also James, *Hopi History,* pp. 100–101; Kammer, *Second Long Walk,* pp. 27–28.

288 *legal effect of executive order on Indian reservations.* Felix S. Cohen, *Felix S. Cohen's Handbook of Federal Indian Law* (Charlottesville, Va.: Michie Bobbs-Merrill, 1982), pp. 127–128 and 493–499.

288 *"Moqui and such other Indians."* Arthur, Executive Order, p. 2.

288 *Navajo–Hopi land history (generally).* Goodman and Thompson, "Hopi–Navaho"; Tehan, "Of Indians."

289 *1937 creation of grazing districts.* Donald L. Parman, *The Navajos and the New Deal* (New Haven: Yale University Press, 1976), pp. 162–192.

289 *District 6.* Brugge, *Navajo–Hopi,* pp. 33–35.

289 *1958 statute.* Act of July 22, 1958, PL 85-547, 72 Stat. 403 (1958).

289 *Healing v. Jones.* Healing v. Jones, 210 F.Supp. 125 (D.Ariz. 1962), aff'd, 373 U.S. 758 (1963).

289 *$1 million attorney's fees.* Transcript, a special meeting of the Hopi Tribal Council, Oraibi, Ariz. (Dec. 3, 1964), p. v; "Indians Vote $1 Million Fee to Utahn," *Salt Lake Tribune,* Dec. 5, 1964, p. 35.

290 *Navajo–Hopi lawsuits and congressional action.* Writ of Assistance, No. Civil 579 (D.Ariz., Oct. 14, 1972), cited in Benedek, *Wind Won't Know Me,* pp. 147–148 and 405; *Hamilton v. MacDonald,* 503 F.2d 1138 (9th Cir. 1974); Navajo and Hopi Indian Relocation Act of 1974, PL 93-531, 88 Stat. 1712, 25 U.S.C. §640d (1994).

290 *division of Joint Use Area by federal judge.* Sekaquaptewa v. MacDonald, 575 F.2d 239 (9th Cir. 1978) and 626 F.2d 113 (9th Cir. 1980) (affirming unpublished 1977 partition order).

290 *effects of removal.* Thayer Scudder, *No Place to Go: Effects of Compulsory Relocation on Navajos* (Philadelphia: Institute for the Study of Human Issues, 1982).

290 *relocation and settlement efforts.* Benedek, *Wind Won't Know Me;* Kammer, *Second Long Walk;* Christopher McLeod, "Navajos Resist Relocation," *High Country News,* May 12, 1986, p. 6; Louis Sahagun, "Historic Pact Gives Hopis 500,000 Acres in Arizona Settlement," *Los Angeles Times,* Nov. 26, 1992, p. 1-A. In response to Hopi lawsuits against the federal government concerning the lack of enforcement of the 1974 relocation act, Congress passed the Navajo–Hopi Land Dispute Settlement Act on Oct. 11, 1996, amending the 1974 act; 25 U.S.C. §640d (Westlaw 1998). The act mandates the removal of Navajo from the Hopi Partition Lands if they refuse to sign an accommodations agreement contained in the act. The accommodations agreement allows Navajo families to stay on the land through a seventy-five-year renewable lease, provided the terms of the lease are respected. Many resisters have vowed never to sign the agreement. See Marley Shebala, "Navajo Protest Forced Relocation," *News from Indian Country,* Jan. 15, 1997 (1997 Westlaw 11694270); Bill Donovan, "Navajos Are Urged to Sign Land Pact: 'Final' Deadline Not Firm," *Arizona Republic,* March 31, 1997 (1997 Westlaw 8352474).

292 *"John Boyden set."* Benedek, *Wind Won't Know Me,* p. 151.

# Notes

292    *western power grid and "The Grand Plan."*  Peter Wiley and Robert Gottlieb, *Empires in the Sun: The Rise of the New American West* (Tucson: University of Arizona Press, 1982), p. 44–46; Philip L. Fradkin, *A River No More: The Colorado River and the West* (Tucson: University of Arizona Press, 1981), pp. 174–176.

292    *letters of opposition.*  See, for example, Benedek, *Wind Won't Know Me,* pp. 157–158.

292    *petition to President Truman.*  Letter from the "[H]ereditary Hopi Chieftains of the Hopi pueblos of Hotevilla, Shungopovy and Mushongnovi" to President Harry Truman (March 28, 1949).

293    *petition to Commissioner Emmons.*  Dan Katchongva, speaking on behalf of "Hopi Traditional Leaders and . . . the majority of the Hopi people," letter to Glenn L. Emmons, commissioner of Indian affairs (July 21, 1959).

293    *"you pass all kinds of laws."*  Thomas Banyacya, quoted in Benedek, *Wind Won't Know Me,* p. 161.

293    *1966 coal lease proposal.*  Transcript, a special meeting of the Hopi Tribal Council, Oraibi, Ariz. (May 16, 1966).

293    *Black Mesa lease.*  Mining lease between the Hopi Tribe, State of Arizona, and Sentry Royalty Company (June 6, 1966) (Sentry Royalty Company was a subsidiary of Peabody Coal Company).

293    *lack of public hearings.*  Richard O. Clemmer, "Black Mesa and the Hopi," in Joseph G. Jorgensen et al., *Native Americans and Energy Development* (Cambridge, Mass.: Anthropology Resource Center, 1978), pp. 17–34; Marjane Ambler, *Breaking the Iron Bonds: Indian Control of Energy Development* (Lawrence: University Press of Kansas, 1990), p. 59; Alvin M. Josephy Jr., "The Murder of the Southwest," *Audubon* 73 (July 1971): 55.

293    *Tribal Council minutes.*  Transcript, May 16, 1966.

293    *largest complex in the country.*  U.S. Federal Trade Commission, Bureau of Competition, "Staff Report on Mineral Leasing on Indian Lands" (1975), p. 5.

294    *"Benefit" of water lease.*  Transcript, May 16, 1966.

## CHAPTER 15: KACHINA

298    *"you may be sure."*  Indian Law Resource Center, "Report to the Hopi Kikmongwis and Other Traditional Hopi Leaders on Docket 196 and the Continuing Threat to Hopi Land and Sovereignty" (Washington, D.C.: Indian Law Resource Center, 1979), p. 154.

298    *accusations against Boyden.*  John Aloysius Farrell, "Hopi Fight for Resource Rights" in "The New Indian Wars," *Denver Post,* Nov. 21, 1983 (part of a special series published Nov. 20–27, 1983), p. 1B.

298    *"baseless, unfair and inaccurate."*  Ibid., p. 4B.

298    *"it is important."*  Marvin O. Young, counsel, Peabody Coal Company, letter to Robert T. Coulter, executive director, Indian Law Resource Center (March 13, 1979).

299    *"Mr. Phelps does not."*  Ibid. See also Patrick H. Bowen, assistant counsel, Kennecott Copper Corporation, letter to Steven M. Tullberg, attorney, Indian Law Resource Center (Jan. 22, 1979). Shortly after the Indian Law Resource

Center released its "Report to the Hopi Kikmongwis" in March 1979, which made public Boyden's representation of Kennecott with respect to its acquisition of Peabody Coal, Abbott Sekaquaptewa signed an affidavit stating that the tribe was aware of Boyden's representation of Kennecott in the Peabody–Kennecott transaction. Sekaquaptewa, who held the Hopi tribal chairmanship and other tribal offices between 1961 and 1981, stated: "The Hopi Tribe was advised of and consented to the handling of legal matters by Mr. Boyden involving Kennecott Copper and Peabody Coal Company during the 1960's. Said matters involved no issues which were adverse to the interests of the Hopi Tribe." Abbott Sekaquaptewa, Affidavit, paragraph 6, July 5, 1979. See also Abbott Sekaquaptewa, Affidavit, Jan. 26, 1983. Both affidavits are limited to the Peabody–Kennecott transaction. Neither affidavit refers to, or suggests, any disclosure by Byden to the tribe of his much broader representation, which in fact existed, of Peabody Coal Company.

300    *"Peabody Coal Company" file.*    John S. Boyden Papers, 1920s–1980s, Accession No. 823, Box 56, Folders 1–4, Special Collections, University of Utah Marriott Library, Salt Lake City.

300    *"recall any situations."*    Young, letter to Coulter.

300    *"Dear Ed" and "Dear Mr. Phelps."*    See, for example, John S. Boyden, letter to E. R. Phelps, vice-president, Peabody Coal Company (Aug. 13, 1963) ("Dear Mr. Phelps"); John S. Boyden, letter to E. R. Phelps, vice-president, Peabody Coal Company (Aug. 12, 1964) ("Dear Mr. Phelps"); John S. Boyden, letter to E. R. Phelps, vice-president, Peabody Coal Company (May 28, 1965) ("Dear Ed"); John S. Boyden, letter to E. R. Phelps, vice-president, Peabody Coal Company (Sept. 3, 1965) ("Dear Ed").

300    *meetings with state engineer and governor.*    Boyden, May 28, 1965, letter to Phelps; Boyden, July 1, 1965, letter to Phelps.

300    *Utah State Land Board.*    Clarence S. Barker, "Coal Firm Maps Giant S. Utah Power Facility," *Deseret News*, Dec. 18, 1964, p. B1.

301    *"possibility is to obtain."*    Transcript, presentation on proposed thermal power plant before the Utah Water and Power Board, John S. Boyden Papers (Dec. 1964), p. 27.

301    *royalty rates and lack of reopener in 1966 Hopi–Peabody coal lease.*    Reid Peyton Chambers, former associate solicitor for Indian affairs and attorney for the Hopi Tribe during lease renegotiation, telephone interview with author, July 15, 1994.

301    *"accurately reflect or compare."*    Farrell, "Hopi Fight for Resource Rights," p. 4B.

301    *"only a little more."*    Ibid.

301    *federal regulation on lease area.*    25 C.F.R. §211.9 (1995).

301    *value of water.*    See, for example, D. E. [LeCrue], acting assistant area director, Phoenix, Ariz., Bureau of Indian Affairs, letter to Clarence Hamilton, chairman, Hopi Tribal Council (Dec. 16, 1968).

301    *Peabody letter to Boyden.*    Richard P. Conerly, vice-president and general counsel, Peabody Coal Company, letter to John S. Boyden (Aug. 2, 1967).

301    *$100,000 payment to Navajo.*    W. Wade Head, area director, Phoenix, Ariz., letter

# Notes

to commissioner of Indian affairs, superintendent of Hopi Agency, and John S. Boyden (Feb. 14, 1968).

301   *"expedite" the matter.*   John S. Boyden, letter to Richard P. Conerly, vice-president and general counsel, Peabody Coal Company (Aug. 10, 1967).

301   *vague assurance to tribal council.*   Ibid.

301   *"the principle involved."*   John S. Boyden, letter to Jean Fredericks, chairman, Hopi Tribal Council (March 4, 1968).

303   *"The transportation of coal slurry."*   [LeCrue], letter to Hamilton.

303   *"defer action."*   Transcript, special meeting of the Hopi Tribal Council (Jan. 7, 1969), p. 3.

303   *request to increase lease area.*   E. R. Phelps, vice-president, Sentry Royalty Company, letter to Raymond Nakai, chairman, Navajo Tribe, and Dewey Healing, chairman, Hopi Tribe (July 26, 1967).

303   *"WEST Associates."*   Phelps, July 26, 1967, letter to Nakai and Healing.

303   *"there is a deficit."*   Ibid.

304   *council approval of expanded lease area.*   Transcript, meeting of the Peabody Coal Company and representatives of the Hopi Tribe, Aug. 19, 1969; "Drilling and Exploration Permit" between the Hopi Tribe and Peabody Coal Company, Nov. 28, 1969.

304   *letters of opposition.*   See, for example, letter from the "[H]ereditary Hopi Chieftains of the Hopi pueblos of Hotevilla, Shungopovy and Mushongnovi" to President Harry Truman (March 28, 1949); Dan Katchongva, speaking on behalf of "Hopi Traditional Leaders and . . . the majority of the Hopi people," letter to Glenn L. Emmons, commissioner of Indian affairs (July 21, 1959); Indian Law Resource Center, "Report to the Hopi Kikmongwis and Other Traditional Hopi Leaders on Docket 196 and the Continuing Threat to Hopi Land and Sovereignty" (Washington, D.C.: Indian Law Resource Center, 1979), pp. 144–145 (letter from Dan Katchongva to President Lyndon Johnson).

304   *"Hopi clans."*   Plaintiff's Brief, Statement of Hopi Religious Leaders, *Lomayaktewa v. Hathaway*, 520 F.2d 1324 (9th Cir. 1975) (No. 73-2132), *cert. denied*, 425 U.S. 903 (1976) (on file with the National Indian Law Library, Boulder, Colo.).

304   *lawsuit by Hopi traditionalists.*   *Lomayaktewa.*

304   *composition of Hopi Tribal Council.*   Richard O. Clemmer, "Black Mesa and the Hopi," in Joseph G. Jorgensen, ed., *Native Americans and Energy Development* (Cambridge, Mass.: Anthropology Resource Center, 1978), p. 27. See also Complaint, *Lomayaktewa.*

305   *"when lawyers were father figures."*   Vernon Masayesva, former Hopi tribal chairman, interview with the author, Boulder, Colo., June 23, 1994.

305   *renegotiated lease.*   Marjane Ambler, *Breaking the Iron Bonds: Indian Control of Energy Development* (Lawrence: University Press of Kansas, 1990), pp. 78-79; Reid Chambers, interview.

306   *Hopi Tribal Council (generally).*   Indian Law Resource Center, "Hopi Kikmongwis," pp. 24–47 and 98–120.

307   *Peabody Coal Company (generally).*   Peabody Western Coal Company, Information Sheet (1991); Sil Perla, general superintendent, Black Mesa and Kayenta

# Notes

Mines, interview with author, Black Mesa, Ariz., March 25, 1993; Reid Chambers, interview.

307 *"It's very simple."* Personal communication received by author (March 22, 1993).

307 *groundwater depletion problems.* Joanne Ditmer, "Running on Empty," *Denver Post,* March 20, 1994, p. 1A; Sil Perla and Fern Vest, Peabody Coal representatives, interview with author, Black Mesa, Arizona, Mar. 24, 1993.

307 *Vernon Masayesva.* Vernon Masayesva, interview.

307 *"All of our songs."* Ibid.

308 *"The Hopi want."* Sil Perla, interview.

310 *"a plea for a right."* Files of John Boyden, undated file memorandum.

310 *use of tribal land for church.* The courts have long held that the Constitution's free excercise of religion clause—which John Boyden used to support the Mormon Church's desire to use Hopi tribal land—is written in terms of what the government cannot do to the individual, not in terms of what the individual can exact from the government. See, for example, *Everson v. Board of Education,* 330 U.S. 1 (1947); *Sherbert v. Verner,* 374 U.S. 398 (1963); *Lyng v. Northwest Indian Cemetery Protective Ass'n,* 485 U.S. 439 (1988). The courts have applied this basic principle to conclude that governments are not required to allow religious use of government land under the "free excercise clause since such land-use decisions do not coerce or penalize religious activity. *Lyng,* 485 U.S. at 459. As the court stated in *Crow v. Gullet,* 541 F.Supp. 785, 791 (D.S.D. 1982), the free excercise clause places a duty upon a state to keep from prohibiting religious acts, not to provide the means or the environment for carrying them out." The free excercise clause, which applies to Indian tribes through the Indian Civil Rights Act of 1968, 25 U.S.C. §1302(1), would not create any rights in favor of a church wanting to lease tribal land; rather such a matter would be left to the discretion of the Hopi Tribal Council. See *Santa Clara Pueblo v. Martinez,* 436 U.S. 39 (1978).

310 *"The tremendous work."* Dale T. Tingey, president of the Southwest Indian Mission, Church of Jesus Christ of Latter-Day Saints (LDS), letter to John Boyden (March 28, 1971). Boyden replied: "I was perfectly justified in what I did, and I am perfectly satisfied to meet whatever problem may arise by reason of my activity." John Boyden letter to Dale T. Tingey (April 5, 1971).

310 *use of "Lamanites."* Orpha Sweeten Boyden, *John S. Boyden: Three Score and Ten in Retrospect* (Cedar City: Southern Utah State College Press, 1986), p. 245.

311 *"Look. To understand."* Vine Deloria Jr., author and professor, interview with author, Boulder, Colo, July 11, 1994.

CHAPTER 16: DRUID ARCH

315 *naming of Colorado River.* Hearings before the Committee on Interstate and Foreign Commerce, "Renaming the Grand River," 66th Cong., 3rd sess. (Feb. 18, 1921) cited in David Lavender, *Colorado River Country* (New York: Dutton, 1982), p. 184.

317 *"wonderland."* Ibid., p. 112.

317 *"I believe it."* Ibid.

318 *proposed Escalante National Monument.* Elmo R. Richardson, "Federal Park

# Notes

Policy in Utah: The Escalante National Monument Controversy of 1935–1940," *Utah Historical Quarterly* 33 (Spring 1965): 109–133.

318 *Bates Wilson.* David W. Johnson, *Canyonlands: The Story behind the Scenery* (Las Vegas: KC Publications, 1990), pp. 47–48; Dave May, "The Trouble with Bates," *Canyon Legacy* 1 (Winter 1989): 18–21.

318 *"I saw the Needles."* Stewart Udall, interview with author, Albuquerque, N.M., Oct. 22, 1994.

319 *"I can hear."* Dr. Jack Campbell, interview with author, Denver, Colo., Jan. 18, 1994.

320 *Canyonlands land classifications.* Canyonlands National Park and Orange Cliffs Unit of Glen Canyon National Recreation Area, *Environmental Assessment for Backcountry Management Plan* (Moab, Utah: National Park Service, 1993).

322 *BLM wilderness (generally).* John D. Leshy, "Wilderness and Its Discontents: Wilderness Review Comes to the Public Lands," *Arizona State Law Journal* (2) (1981): 361–446.

323 *Negro Bill Canyon.* Bill Hedden and Jose Knighton, interview and site visit with author, Negro Bill Canyon, Utah, May 18, 1994.

323 *Bulldozer Wars.* Raymond Wheeler, "Boom! Boom! Boom! War on the Colorado Plateau," in Ed Marston, ed., *Reopening the Western Frontier* (Washington D.C.: Island Press, 1989), pp. 16–26.

323 *Wilderness at the Edge.* Utah Wilderness Coalition, *Wilderness at the Edge: A Citizen Proposal to Protect Utah's Canyons and Deserts* (Salt Lake City: Peregrine Smith Books for the Foundation for the Utah Wilderness Coalition, 1990).

324 *1995 Utah wilderness bills.* Margaret Kriz, "The Wild Card," *National Journal,* Jan. 13, 1996, pp. 65–68; Timothy Egan, "In Utah, a Pitched Battle over Public Lands," *New York Times,* Nov. 13, 1995, pp. A1 and A14.

325 *Ute's name for Powell.* John Wesley Powell, *Report on the Lands of the Arid Region of the United States, with a More Detailed Account of the Lands of Utah* (Boston: Harvard Common Press, 1983; facsimile of the 1879 edition), p. 323.

325 *Kaiparowits Plateau (generally).* M. Lee Allison, "The Geography and Geology," in Robert B. Keiter, Sarah B. George, and Joro Walker, eds., *Visions of the Grand Staircase–Escalante: Examining Utah's Newest National Monument* (Salt Lake City: Utah Museum of Natural History/Wallace Stegner Center, 1998), pp. 3–12.

325 *"wilderness right down."* Utah Wilderness Coalition, *Wilderness at the Edge,* p. 146.

326 *1960s Kaiparowits proposal.* Ronald Jepperson, Eric Hemel, and Robert Hauptman, *The Kaiparowits Coal Project and the Environment: A Case Study* (Palo Alto, Calif.: Ann Arbor Science Publishers/Electric Power Research Institute, 1981).

326 *current Kaiparowits proposal.* Martha Hahn, "Andalex: Just When You Thought the Kaiparowits Plateau Was Safe," *Colorado Plateau Advocate* (Grand Canyon Trust) 2 (Spring 1991), p. 2; "Big Wilderness versus Big Coal: Slicing Open the Kaiparowits Plateau," *Southern Utah Wilderness Alliance Newsletter* 8 (Summer 1991): 3–5; Mike Noel and Verlin Smith, interview and site visit with author, Kanab, Utah, May 20, 1994.

327 *disturbance in communities. Andalex: The Facts,* published by Taxpayers for

# Notes

Safe Utah Roads, PO Box 314, Cedar City, UT 84721; Hahn, "Just When You Thought"; "Big Wilderness."

327    *"in thirty years."*    Mike Noel, interview.

329    *Antiquities Act of 1906.*    Antiquities Act of 1906, 34 Stat. 225, 16 U.S.C. §§431–433 (1994); *Cameron v. United States,* 252 U.S. 450 (1920); *State of Wyoming v. Franke,* 58 F.Supp. 890 (D.Wyo. 1945). See also, Robert W. Righter, "National Monuments to National Parks: The Use of the Antiquities Act of 1906," *Western Historical Quarterly* 20 (Aug. 1989): 281–301.

329    *broke the story.*    Frank Clifford, "Mine Plan for Lonely Plateau Sparks Fight," *Los Angeles Times,* Sept. 3, 1996, pp. A1 and A12.

329    *Grand Staircase–Escalante National Monument and Proclamation (generally).* William J. Clinton, president, Presidential Proclamation No. 6920, *Establishment of Grand Staircase–Escalante National Monument,* Sept. 18, 1996; Keiter, George, and Walker, *Visions of the Grand Staircase–Escalante.*

329    *public opinion.*    James Brooke, "Utah Is Warming Up to Newest Monument," *New York Times,* Oct. 13, 1997, p. A12.

334    *Merlin (generally).*    Nikolai Tolstoy, *The Quest for Merlin* (Boston: Little, Brown, 1985); Charlotte Spivack, *Merlin: A Thousand Heroes with One Face* (Lewiston, N.Y.: Edwin Mellen, 1994).

### CHAPTER 17: MOUNT BLANCA

340    *"all of those things."*    Personal communication received by author (July 30, 1994).

348    *Window Rock–Monument Valley basketball game.*    In cross-checking facts for this book, I learned that this game did not involve, as I had thought, the Monument Valley High School in San Juan County, Utah, that had been built as a result of the school litigation in the 1970s. Instead, the game was played by another Indian high school on the Navajo Reservation—also named Monument Valley High School—in nearby Kayenta, Arizona. Thus, on my drive home, I was mistaken about the identity of the school in the game on the radio. But since the anecdote is fundamentally about life on today's Navajo Reservation and my reaction to it, I have left the passage as I originally wrote it because it accurately reflects what I heard and experienced at that time.

# Acknowledgments

This book has been more than seven years in the making and many people have been generous with their time, knowledge, and friendship.

I would like to begin by thanking those who have been with me all the way. My family, Ann and Seth, Philip, Dave, and Ben, made many trips with me to the canyon country and my love for them flows through all of these pages. Carl Brandt, my agent and deeply admired friend, helped me conceive the shape of this book and, in those several times when I ran up against roadblocks, guided me around them. Cynthia Carter, my assistant, helped organize this complex project and became a main adviser. Terry Tempest Williams and Don Snow offered advice that could come only from their separate brands of genius. Vernon Masayesva patiently walked me through both the intricacies of Hopi culture and the way in which Black Mesa became the linchpin for the Big Buildup.

Diane Sylvain, mapmaker for *High Country News,* took the time to get inside the text and accentuate the works with her illustrations. Thank you, creative lady, thank you always.

"My kids." My research assistants are not blood relations, but then again they are. They have been colleagues in the fullest sense, keeping the details in order, tracking down obscure sources, working through new ideas, expanding others. They have been, over the course of these years, Ellen Kohler, Brian Kuehl, Frank Wilson, Cherche Prezeau, Marlon Sherman, Nancy Nelson, Kristin Howse, Scott Miller, Kevin Geiger, Andy Huff, and Julia Miller. Have I told each of you how much I value you, how much affection I hold for you? I hope so.

I have been blessed by the many people who have been kind enough to read and react to the manuscript. Ed Marston, Bill Smart, Fran Joseph, Roger Clark, Linda Spiegler, Kay Wilkie, David Getches, Patricia Nelson Limerick, Don Snow, and Terry Tempest Williams read various incarnations of the whole manuscript. Vernon Masayesva, Clifford Duncan, Herb Yazzie, Robert Anderson, Joanna Endter-Wada, Lloyd Burton, Dan McCool, Rick Williams, Dick Trudell, Deanna Martinez, Harris Sherman, Reid Chambers, John Leshy, Floyd O'Neil, Eric Swenson, Richard Hayslip, Sandy Hansen, Anne Guthrie, Fran Korten, Sarah van de Wettering, Mary Sojourner, and John Echohawk all commented on one or more chapters.

Several specialists in particular fields offered me their expertise. Richard Reynolds spent a great deal of time explaining the geology of the Plateau. He also arranged lengthy and instructive sessions with other geologists, Warren Hamilton and Jack Campbell. Linda Cordell, director of the University of Colorado Museum and leading

393

# Acknowledgments

authority on the Ancestral Puebloans, gave all manner of perspectives on the archaeology of the Colorado Plateau. Dale Davidson, archaeologist with the Bureau of Land Management, took me out into the Cedar Mesa and Comb Ridge country he knows so well. Joelle Clark, Rebecca French, and Cathy Cameron also gave me valuable perspectives on archaeological issues. Roger Clark, a naturalist who has an extraordinary grasp of the Colorado Plateau, spent an enormous amount of time briefing me on the region. Jayne Belnap, a biologist with the Bureau of Land Management and National Park Service, explained the distinctive ecological characteristics of the Kaiparowits Plateau and the importance of cryptobiotic soil. John Cook, John Reynolds, Patricia Parker, Walt Dabney, and Dick Martin deepened my understanding of national park policy. Richard Hayslip of the Salt River Project, Don Wharton of the Native American Rights Fund, and Bruce Driver of the Land and Water Fund of the Rockies all walked me through the intricacies of energy production in the Southwest.

Field interviews and site visits were critical to my understanding of the Colorado Plateau. Several people arranged invaluable tours of specific places: Mort Meyerson and Walt Dabney (the Maze District of Canyonlands National Park); Bill Hedden and Jose Knighton (Negro Bill Canyon); Bob Heyder (Mesa Verde National Park); Fern Best and Sil Perla (Black Mesa Mine); Mike Outlaw and L. D. Shakespear (Navajo Generating Station); John Grubb (Navajo Mine); Ken Beck (Animas–La Plata Project); Sarah van de Wettering and Mike Noel (Andalex Mine site); Roger Clark (Hopi clan symbol site); Paul Curtis and Nick Sandberg (Cedar Mesa); Janet Lever and Ann Harrison (Comb Ridge); Jamie Williams, Brian Richter, and Holly Richter (the Morgan Bottoms stretch of the Yampa River); and Dave Edwards, Lorna Corson, Matt Kaplinski, B. J. Boyle, and Ed Norton (the Grand Canyon).

In addition, I benefited from these individual interviews: Darrell Knuffke; Vine Deloria Jr.; Miguel, Frances, and Martha Quintana; Robert Urias; Frank Maynes, Tom Shipps, Janice Sheftel, and Pat Hall; Sally Wisely and Sandy Thompson; Hardy Redd; Liz Thomas and Scott Groene; Stanley Pollack, Peterson Joe, Britt Clapham, Robert Allen, and Amy Alderman; Robert Yazzie, Raymond Austin, and James Zion; Claudeen Arthur and Tamsen Holm; David Wilson Sr. and David Wilson Jr.; Robinson Honani and Nat Natongla; Gary La Rance; Eugene Kaye; Tom Jensen and Jim Ruch; Danny Michaud; Stewart Udall; J. Clifton Fleming; Brooke Williams; Bruce Babbitt; Jim Souby; Betsy Neely and Mark Burget; Howard Arnett; Ken Rait and Susan Tixier; C. B. Copley; D. Michael Quinn; Parker Nielsen; and John Echohawk.

I thank the several libraries that have been so helpful. The University of Colorado School of Law Library, the Norlin Library at the University of Colorado, the University of Utah Library, the National Indian Law Library at the Native American Rights Fund, and the Brigham Young University Library all gave their cooperation. Special thanks to Greg Thompson at the University of Utah and Barbara Bintliff and Jane Thompson at the University of Colorado.

This book would not have been possible without the financial support that allowed me extensive periods of time for travel and writing. The Ford Foundation provided a grant, administered by the Grand Canyon Trust, that, along with my sabbatical from the University of Colorado and support from the Natural Resources Law Center, allowed me to work nearly exclusively on this book during the years 1993 and 1994. I

394

# Acknowledgments

give deep thanks to Fran Korten at Ford, who understood this project and provided valuable advice. At the Grand Canyon Trust, I send my best spirits to Tom Jensen, Geoff Barnard, and Fran Joseph.

My debts are many to the University of Colorado, a place where the interdisciplinary study of the American West is flourishing. My deans at the Law School supported me in every way: I give my lifelong appreciation to Gene Nichol, Mimi Wesson, and Hal Bruff for their friendship and encouragement. The central administration at the University of Colorado also believed in my work: I am grateful to chancellors Jim Corbridge and Dick Byyny and vice chancellors for academic affairs Phil DiStefano, Wallace Loh, and the late Bruce Ekstrand. I thank for their help, direct and indirect, my colleagues across the campus: Patty Limerick, Bill Riebsame, Jim Roab, Jim Wescoat, Vine Deloria Jr., Gilbert White, Lynn Ross-Bryant, Larry McDonnell, Chuck Howe, Deward Walker, Linda Cordell, Cathy Cameron, David Getches, Rebecca French, Jim Corbridge, Emily Calhoun, Dale Oesterle, Kathryn Mutz, Doug Kenney, Reg Saner, Spence Havlick, Chuck Forsman, William Wei, Phil Deloria, Tom Precourt, Brad Johnson, Roni Ires, Jane Bock, Carl Bock, Pat Long, Bob Sievers, Susan Avery, Len Ackland, Sam Fitch, Bill Lewis, Dave Armstrong, Ken Iwamasa, Jim Nickel, Dale Jamieson, Ron Brunner, Linda Hogan, Lee Krauth, Ed Dorn, Peter Michelson, and Marilyn Krysl.

I give my gratitude to Island Press. Chuck Savitt, the president and publisher, has long believed in my work. Barbara Dean, my editor, gave me easily the single best edit I've ever received (better even than her work on our earlier collaboration, *Crossing the Next Meridian*). Barbara Youngblood also performed spectacularly—and with relentless patience and cheerfulness—during the editorial process. I also thank production editorial supervisor Christine McGowan, copy editor Don Yoder, and David Bullen, who did the cover and text design.

Finally, I would like to thank my students. You enriched my understanding of the Plateau during class and seminar discussions, work on masters and Ph.D. dissertations, and on memorable field trips. I crossed one of my life's best watersheds when I realized how much learning I could gain from you.

# About the Author

Charles Wilkinson, the Moses Lasky Professor of Law and Distinguished Professor at the University of Colorado, has written widely on law, land, history, and society in the American West. His ten books include *Crossing the Next Meridian, The Eagle Bird,* and *American Indians, Time, and the Law.* A former attorney with the Native American Rights Fund and a member of The Governing Council of The Wilderness Society, he is a recipient of the National Wildlife Federation's National Conservation Award. He has four boys, Ben, Dave, Phil, and Seth, and lives in Boulder with his wife, Ann.

# Index

# Index

# Index

# Index

# Index

# Index

THE FOUR CORNERS STATES

Salt Lake City
Denver
COLORADO
UTAH
ARIZONA
NEW MEXICO
Phoenix
Albuquerque

0   25
miles

UINTA BASIN

Price

GREEN R.

UTAH

CANYONLANDS

GRAND STAIRCASE-ESCALANTE

SAN JU

ZION

St. George

LAKE POWELL

BLACK MESA

GRAND CANYON

RIVER
HAVASUPAI

HOPI

HUALAPAI

NAVAJO

COLORADO

Flagstaff

ARIZONA

MOGOLLON RI